The PRAIRIE POPULIST

Dear Shaun & Len

Maybe we can
learn something
about what needs
to be done —
love John
December, 2018

The PRAIRIE POPULIST

George Hara Williams and
the Untold Story of the CCF

An Essay on Radical Leadership in a
Time of Crisis and the Victory of
Socialist Agrarian Populism, 1921–1944

J.F. CONWAY

University of Regina Press

Printed and bound in Canada at Marquis. The text of this book is printed on 100% post-consumer recycled paper with earth-friendly vegetable-based inks.

Cover design: Duncan Campbell, University of Regina Press
Text design: John van der Woude, JVDW Designs
Copy editor: Alison Jacques
Proofreader: Kristine Douaud
Indexer: Patricia Furdek
Cover art: "Vintage Farmer Person 1930's Old Man Smoking Hat." Licensed under CC0 1.0 Universal (CC0 1.0), public domain.

Library and Archives Canada Cataloguing in Publication
Conway, John Frederick, author
 The prairie populist : George Hara Williams and the untold story of the CCF : an essay on radical leadership in a time of crisis and the victory of socialist agrarian populism, 1921-1944 / J.F. Conway.

Includes bibliographical references and index. Issued in print and electronic formats.
ISBN 978-0-88977-545-9 (softcover).—ISBN 978-0-88977-546-6 (PDF).—ISBN 978-0-88977-547-3 (HTML)

1. Williams, G. H. (George Hara), 1894-1945. 2. Politicians—Saskatchewan—Biography. 3. Co-operative Commonwealth Federation. 4. Populism—Saskatchewan—History—20th century. 5. Socialism—Saskatchewan—History—20th century. 6. Saskatchewan—Politics and government—1905-1929. 7. Saskatchewan—Politics and government—1934-1944. 8. Biographies. I. Title.

FC3522.1.W546C66 2018   971.24'02   C2018-900968-3   C2018-900969-1

10 9 8 7 6 5 4 3 2 1

University of Regina Press, University of Regina
Regina, Saskatchewan, Canada, S4S 0A2
TEL: (306) 585-4758 FAX: (306) 585-4699
WEB: www.uofrpress.ca

We acknowledge the support of the Canada Council for the Arts for our publishing program. We acknowledge the financial support of the Government of Canada. / Nous reconnaissons l'appui financier du gouvernement du Canada. This publication was made possible with support from Creative Saskatchewan's Creative Industries Production Grant Program, and with the help of a grant from the Federation for the Humanities and Social Sciences, through the Awards to Scholarly Publications Program, using funds provided by the Social Sciences and Humanities Research Council of Canada.

Dedicated to Muriel Wiens and Friedrich Steininger,
who kept the story of George Hara Williams alive.

A great man is great, not in his personal features lending an individual complexion to historic events, but in his possession of traits which make him the most capable of serving his time's great social needs, which have arisen under the influence of general and particular causes....A great man is precisely great because he sees *farther* than others do and his desires are *stronger* than in others.... [H]e indicates the new social needs created by the previous development of social relations; he assumes the initiative in meeting those needs....Therein lie all his significance, all his power. But it is a vast significance, and an awesome power.
— G. V. Plekhanov, *On the Question of the Individual's Role in History* (1898)

Social science deals with problems of biography, of history, and of their intersections within social structures.
— C. Wright Mills, *The Sociological Imagination* (1959)

TABLE OF CONTENTS

List of Photographs **xi**
Author's Note   **xiii**
Preface   **xv**
Acknowledgments   **xix**

Prologue   George Hara Williams: A Word Portrait   **xxi**

Part I. Introduction

Chapter 1 George Hara Williams: Roots to 1921   **3**
Chapter 2 The Political and Economic Context:
          The Rise of the United Farmers of Canada
          (Saskatchewan Section), 1922 to 1926   **17**

Part II. The Drive for Power

Chapter 3 Leading the Farmers into Politics: 1926 to 1931   **51**
Chapter 4 Building the CCF:
          Leadership Lost and Regained, 1931 to 1936   **91**
Chapter 5 Building the CCF:
          Defeating Social Credit, 1936 to 1938   **139**

Part III. The Fall of Williams

Chapter 6 Fighting the War in the CCF and in Europe:
                1937 to 1944   **169**
Chapter 7 Endgame: The 1944 Election   **201**

Part IV. Williams in Canadian History

Chapter 8 The Shame of the Intellectuals   **217**
Chapter 9 Conclusion: Williams in Canadian History   **245**

          Afterword   **259**

          Chronology   **261**
          Abbreviations   **269**
          Notes   **271**
          Bibliographic Notes   **295**
          Bibliography   **313**
          Index   **325**

LIST OF PHOTOGRAPHS

George Hara Williams, 1929, official portrait upon election as President of the United Farmers of Canada (Saskatchewan Section).   **160**

Margery and George Williams on their farm, 1924.   **161**

George Hara Williams speaking from the back of a truck, Saskatchewan Wheat Pool Picnic, St. Walburg, 1930.   **161**

The Douglas Cabinet of 1944.   **162**

CCF Members of the Official Opposition after the 1934 election.   **162**

The Williams farm home, Semans, 1938.   **163**

CCF Members of the Official Opposition after the 1938 election.   **164**

The Land of the Soviets, Williams's controversial booklet about his 1931 tour of the Soviet Union, was published by the United Farmers of Canada (Saskatchewan Section) in 1931.   **165**

AUTHOR'S NOTE

In an effort to capture the essence of George Hara Williams's ideology as it developed and matured, I adopted the phrase "socialist agrarian populism." Though an admittedly clumsy construct, it captures Williams's foundational political beliefs and their priority. His "socialism" cannot be easily separated from his "agrarian populism." He wove a complex tapestry of the two in his speeches, pamphlets, and radio broadcasts. Most importantly Williams was a socialist, in the sense of Naylor's "labour socialism."[1] This was the filter through which he engaged agrarian populism. Socialism was the ultimate goal, and by socialism Williams meant class struggle—to wrest state power from capitalist control by "those who toil on farms, or in the mines, or on the railways, and in the offices, shops, mills and factories—and the unemployed."[2] Upon winning power through democratic means, the new socialist government would take the commanding heights of the economy, natural resources, and all transportation systems and utilities into public ownership. He was also a left agrarian populist. He was convinced that middle-level farmers could be won over to socialism. He admired the political, economic, and organizational successes of the farmers' self-organization from the turn of the century to the 1920s. He cleaved to the minority opinion in the agrarian populist movement of advocating an alliance with labour in order to build a people's party to achieve socialism.

Williams was a working farmer in a province where farmers were the majority. Saskatchewan farmers dominated politics through their organizations, first the Saskatchewan Grain Growers' Association, and then the United Farmers of Canada (Saskatchewan Section). When Williams became politically active he combined his socialism with agrarian populism, devoting his efforts to winning the major organization of farmers to socialist political action in alliance with the working class. This was his political project. His success was unprecedented.

PREFACE

The idea for this book first came to me in the early 1970s while immersed in the archives, working on my PhD dissertation on Prairie populism in Canada. I kept encountering the name of George Hara Williams. It was obvious he had played a significant role in the radicalization of Saskatchewan's organized farmers during the Depression and in founding and building the Saskatchewan Farmer-Labour Party, which became the CCF. Yet his contributions were typically mentioned only rarely and fleetingly in the published scholarship. Often they were not even mentioned. The more I examined his role, based on the archival evidence, the more I realized there was an important untold story here. But since it was not vital to a "big picture" study of populism on the Canadian Prairies, I set the idea aside.

The story was fascinating because the most successful founding leader of the Saskatchewan CCF was unceremoniously ousted from office while serving overseas in World War II. The basic facts of the rise of the Saskatchewan CCF to power on the heels of the Great Depression have been well researched and widely published in scholarly and popular versions. Most Canadians are familiar with the basic historical facts. I therefore concluded that a traditional academic approach—either a political biography or another study on the rise of the CCF—would not be particularly engaging. The most significant role of Williams was the complex and effective leadership he provided in achieving an unprecedented and remarkable feat in Canadian history: leading farmers into politics on a socialist platform and driving to the threshold of power. Therefore, an interpretive essay on radical leadership in a time of crisis seemed the most useful and interesting approach.

The gap on Williams was filled by an excellent MA thesis in history written by Friedrich Steininger in 1976, "George Hara Williams: Agrarian Socialist," based on the archival materials available at the time. But recognition of Williams in the published scholarship remained elusive. In the official party history he fared no better. I contacted Mr. Steininger, a Regina high school teacher, and discussed the idea of a book, but the discussion went nowhere, as both of us were diverted by other, more pressing work. Many years later I contacted Muriel Wiens, one of Williams's daughters; I told her I was interested in writing a book on her father and requested access to family papers to supplement existing archival sources. Ms. Wiens was not interested in collaboration at the time, since she was already working on a book on her father. She had pretty harsh words about the official party line on her father and the short shrift her father's role had received at the hands of academics. I offered to work with her, but she declined.

Muriel Wiens wrote her book, *Finding George Williams: A Tale of the Grass Roots*, but it failed to interest a publisher. She deposited her manuscript with the Williams papers in the archives. A few years later she contacted me, offering the unconditional and full use of her manuscript and the family's papers. I agreed. Due to other writing projects, work on the book was delayed until 2014. I contacted Mr. Steininger and requested permission to use his thesis, which he verbally provided. Ms. Wiens's manuscript and Mr. Steininger's thesis were immensely important in guiding me through the material and providing portraits of Williams, one highly personal and loving, the other, the objective observations of the historian. This present work enjoyed particular advantages over that of Mr. Steininger: new material had been added to the archives and old material was better organized; a series of biographies and recollections of other leading figures in the Saskatchewan CCF were published since 1976; and I had access to the private papers of the Williams family.

This essay is an argument, a point of view, based on the evidence available. When the evidence was unclear, I present a reasonable version of events consistent with the context as well as with preceding events and those that followed. It is not a political biography in the traditional, academic sense, nor is it a hagiography of the man. Rather, it is a critical essay on radical leadership in a time of crisis. It provides George Hara Williams long-deserved recognition for his pivotal role in Canadian political history. It also provides lessons on the interaction between social forces and the leaders who understand and guide them in battles for social and economic change.

It is a timely set of lessons for us in the Canada of 2018. Four of ten eligible voters routinely decline to vote in federal elections. In some provincial elections the rate of abstention on occasion has reached five or six out of ten. Canadians appear to have given up on struggling to change history's trajectory, surrendering to the neoliberal mantra that it is the market that shapes history, not the popular democratic will of the people.

George Hara Williams would not have agreed. What he accomplished explains why.

ACKNOWLEDGMENTS

The author gratefully acknowledges the permission of Muriel Wiens to use her unpublished manuscript, *George Hara Williams: A Tale of the Grass Roots*, and of Friedrich Steininger to use his MA thesis, "George Hara Williams: Agrarian Socialist," for guidance in writing this narrative. James Lorimer also provided permission to use selected material previously published in my book *The Rise of the New West: A History of a Region in Confederation* (2014).

A special thanks to Valerie Zink, who searched through the archives and old newspapers for photographs and then enhanced them for use.

Finally, I acknowledge the patience of my family, friends, and colleagues who endured many conversations about George Hara Williams while I was writing this essay.

GEORGE HARA WILLIAMS

A Word Portrait

I t is not possible to get a true sense of Williams as a personality
from archives, books, letters, and texts of speeches. Such documents record the evolution of his political thinking and his tactical
and strategic moves. They provide documentary evidence of his
popular support and of his effectiveness as a political leader and organizer. But reading Williams's speeches gives us no indication of why they
were self-evidently so effective, whether before a crowd of a thousand or
in the board meetings of the United Farmers of Canada (Saskatchewan
Section) (UFC[SS]) or the executive, council, and convention meetings
of the Farmer-Labour Party/Co-operative Commonwealth Federation
(Saskatchewan Section). That he usually got his way tells us something
of his dynamism and persuasiveness. But one fails to get a full sense
of the electricity that seemed to emanate from him to move crowds
to ovations or to convince smaller meetings of the personal sacrifice
required for the hard work necessary for success. Some might call it
charisma, but that begs the question, telling us nothing of what actually
transpired. This portrait is based on gleanings from the documents. As
I read through the sources, each time someone who had encountered

him made a comment about Williams as a personality or as a physical presence, I jotted it down. The family life of historical figures is often absent from chronicles of their political engagements and contributions. Therefore, I noted comments from Williams's wife and daughters about the impact of his political work on family life.

Williams was a striking physical presence in 1930, at the age of thirty-six. He had slightly sandy hair, a broad and wide forehead, clear and brilliantly blue eyes that protruded slightly. He was 5 feet, 7½ inches tall, "stockily built, well-muscled, and easy motioned." It was noted he had a "handsome aspect." His eyes were frequently noticed, not only because of their arresting colour, but because he looked directly into the eyes of those to whom he talked. While speaking he sought out members of the audience for eye contact, which, for some, was memorable in its effect.

In confrontations he was never flustered, but relentless, looking his opponent in the eye as he reasoned with him. He was intellectually courageous and confident in debates, "fluent and forceful." His biting wit was used freely against opponents. "His sarcasm" was "rapier-like and Voltarian," and some who endured public ridicule and humiliation at his hands never forgave him, especially those in his own party. His wife, Margery ("Madge"), recalled "his wit cut too close to the bone and he was too quick with his smart remarks, making fools of his opponents." (She once threw a pound of butter at Williams in response to his smart remarks.) His wit also had a gentle side. His daughter Ruth recalled his "puckish sense of humour" and his love of puns. He also "loved all types of sports, bridge, music and reading."

One national newspaper correspondent, who observed Williams's performance at a key UFC(SS) convention, noted that "he reasons about everything, the results of his logic arise from a smouldering deliberate calculation fanned by some unseen bellows…forged from the white-heat of intellectual temper." Then, "out of the sparks come brilliant if hasty assertions and decisions." Williams was obviously good on his feet in the heat of controversy at conventions. Others noted that, when he was campaigning for political office, hecklers were grist for his mill as he pilloried them mercilessly with wit and sarcasm to the delight of audiences. When he got angry or annoyed in debates, the only sign was that he got "red just in front of his ears." In 1938 a leading CCFer from Alberta, after observing Williams at a national convention, described him as follows:

"capable, astute and fully self-possessed," "the best organizer in the CCF movement," and "an idealist who is a complete realist—a combination that is as rare as it is useful."

Williams had an enormous capacity for hard work, resting on what seemed a limitless fountain of intellectual and physical energy. Organizers who travelled with him complained good naturedly about the endless hours at meetings large and small each day while on the road: a poll meeting in the morning around a farm family's kitchen table, to name a poll captain and assign duties; the afternoon spent going from farm to farm; a modest Depression-era supper meeting of poll captains from across the constituency; and to end the day, an evening public meeting at a hall or a church to convey a message of hope and political struggle to farm families haunted by the Depression. During these tours Williams would note down the details of individual problems—need eyeglasses, but no money; inadequate relief, the family goes many days without food; cut off relief at the whim of some local Liberal-appointed bureaucrat; a new baby, but no money for baby supplies and baby food; a local tax problem; a threat of foreclosure, and so on. He kept a list of names and the problems, stroking them off only when they had been dealt with, often using his own legislative indemnity to buy the needed items. After he became an MLA and leader of the opposition, his interventions on problems like access to relief and local tax problems were often successful. The party advocated universal, publicly funded health care. To make the case in the legislature, Williams and his staff collected legal affidavits documenting the individual tragedies resulting from a lack of access to timely medical care. He would table these in the legislature, denouncing the government for its callous disregard of such tragic, preventable events.

Those who worked with him reported that his expectations were high. He demanded a lot, but personally always worked the hardest. One noted that Williams was "a great stickler for finishing a job" and "excuses were no use." After Williams had brought in the harvest, he would be on the road until Christmas and back on the road after New Year's. The same pattern was followed in the spring: after seeding he was on the road, returning to the farm only to tend the crops and animals as needed, and then back on the road. In 1938 he put ten thousand miles on his car, and he went through car after car between 1931 and 1941. Family and friends worried about his health due to the demands he put on himself.

Williams never let a political attack on him or the party go without a head-on counterattack. When he or the party were smeared as communists, as frequently happened in the news columns and letters to the editor of daily papers in the cities and rural weeklies, he would demand an apology and a retraction, sending a detailed reply explaining the differences between communism and socialism. A Tory MP in the House of Commons once attacked Williams as a communist and an agent of Moscow. Williams demanded he repeat the charge outside the House, where he was not protected from libel laws. He demanded an apology. Williams wrote Prime Minister Bennett, daring him to arrest him under Section 98, so he could prove the scurrilous nature of the smear.[1] The member did not apologize, nor did he repeat the charge outside the House. Williams made a public issue of it, receiving much sympathetic national attention.

The Liberals once charged that Williams had bought a plow from a farmer, providing the farmer's name, and never paid for it. Williams tracked down the farmer at his farm in a remote rural area, told him of the false allegation, and returned with a letter signed by the farmer and witnessed, stating Williams had never bought a plow from him and owed him no money. Williams got an apology. He was even more thorough when correcting distortions and misrepresentations of his public speeches or the party's policy positions. He would send in a detailed explanation of the distortion and demand it be printed. The newspapers often complied.

Williams married Margery Cass in 1922. They had five daughters: Betty, Ruth, Shirley-Anne, Muriel, and Rosemary. A second pregnancy, a son, was a stillbirth; Margery and George attributed this loss to the tough times they endured on the farm in the first few years. In 1933, at eighteen months, Shirley-Anne died of meningitis. Williams nursed his grief partly by writing a long open letter addressed to "the People of Saskatchewan," laying out an impassioned and detailed argument against capitalism and in favour of socialism. He seemed to find solace in reminding himself why he had to rise above his grief and carry on: "You will see in this mad struggle for existence, in competition for the necessities of life, millions of unemployed, facing starvation in the midst of a world bountifully provided by God and Science with everything that goes toward human well-being, and you will see, in the midst of all this, while the cries of hungry children are still ringing in your ears, riotous, luxurious, wasteful, heartless people, bent on furthering their own interests, regardless of the general welfare of their fellow man." The document was never shared publicly, nor does it appear to have been finished, but was saved by his friend Barney Johnson and rests with Johnson's papers in the Williams family's private collection.

Williams's family life can be divided into two eras: before and after the UFC(SS) went into politics. His daughters' memories of the first era are fond and warm: being read to; Williams's love of reading and quoting poetry; his remarkable ability to make up children's stories that went on night after night; learning to fish and shoot; riding horseback; building a playhouse and a pony-drawn sled; the arrival of the Shetland pony. Williams enjoyed riding, often accompanied by one of his daughters. He had acquired a love of horses in his childhood, and this no doubt lay behind his decision to enlist in the cavalry in World War I. He would often ride to think through political and organizational problems. It was the same with routine farm work—plowing, seeding, and harvesting were times for hard physical labour and intellectual reflection.

After the founding of the Farmer-Labour Party in 1932, Williams was absent from family life for long stretches. Muriel recounts an early memory of standing on the sofa peering out into the wintry darkness: "Daddy was coming home, and the whole family was breathless with anticipation." She listened avidly to his radio broadcasts, lying on the floor staring at the radio: "I listened raptly to his voice, it was proof he was around somewhere." He became "less a parent than a deity." Clearly a woman of great strength and intelligence, Margery held things together at home. She managed the farm operation and dealt stoically with loneliness and the stresses of single parenthood: "We always had to have a hired man when George was away working for the farmers. Later on I had to have a girl for company and this of course meant there were no profits whatever." Margery recalled, "I didn't enjoy [the long absences], this is true, but I felt that there didn't seem to be anyone else who could do the kind of work George was doing. He had the ability and he had the confidence of the people.... That I had to stay home and look after the farm was just one of the things that had to be done, that's all." When George became an MLA, his indemnity didn't help much: "Most of it had to be used by George in his work"—room and board, office expenses, and "all the many demands from people who were in despair [and] came to the office for help."

Seriously ill, Williams returned from overseas, now a major, just in time to participate in the election of the CCF in June 1944. Upon his return, and despite his illness, he immediately made a province-wide radio broadcast and embarked on a campaign tour of his constituency, winning it with the highest popular vote in the province. He was named minister of agriculture. Shortly thereafter he resigned because of his deteriorating health, having suffered strokes and a heart condition. He moved to the West Coast to convalesce. Muriel, who was twelve at the time, recalls, "I was unaware he had come home from hospital to die, and I pestered him.... Towards the last, he used to ask me to come and sit beside him, and I wondered then at the intensity of his feelings as he held my hand or hugged me. Perhaps he knew that some day I'd be bitter about the time he spent for other people instead of with me. I've gone through that, and know now he did what he had to do, and that he's given me the best legacy a daughter could have—a father I can respect for his integrity, energy and humour."

On September 12, 1945, Williams died, two months short of his fifty-first birthday.

Part I

INTRODUCTION

Chapter 1

GEORGE HARA WILLIAMS

Roots to 1921

There is little in Williams's family history suggesting that a socialist agrarian leader was being prepared for a future role of historical significance in Canadian politics. He was born on November 17, 1894, into a small-c conservative petit-bourgeois family. His father was a hardware merchant and tinsmith in Binscarth, Manitoba, and his mother a dressmaker of considerable skill. The family decamped briefly to Sintaluta, Saskatchewan, in 1900 to set up a hardware store, but it did not go well. George was the youngest of seven children, and the family suffered its share of tragedy and hardship: the eldest son died of kidney disease; the father suffered a serious head injury from a fall while repairing a roof. As a result of problems stemming from the father's head injury, the family moved to Winnipeg, where George's mother struggled to provide for the family as a dressmaker. There is no information as to what kind of political influence his father may have had on Williams, nor on whether Williams and his older brothers had any lively political discussions. What information does exist suggests these were tough times for the injured father, who was moody and suffered severe headaches; the mother, who tried to keep everything together; and the surviving children.

We do know the Williams family had a deeply rooted counter-revolutionary legacy.

Williams's male ancestors on his father's side were United Empire Loyalists, fighting against the American Revolution in Jessup's Rangers. In 1786 the family fled from Massachusetts to the Niagara Peninsula. Subsequently, father and son each received land grants of one hundred acres as rewards for their loyalty to the Crown. Williams was proud of these British roots and was greatly influenced by them. In 1933 he joined the United Empire Loyalist Association after the organization confirmed his loyalist genealogical credentials. He was an enthusiastic monarchist and saw military service in World War I as a duty to Britain. Williams was also proud of his Irish ancestry. His middle name, Hara, honoured his grandmother from Bantry, County Cork, Ireland; her family had dropped the O' upon conversion to Methodism. There was certainly scant political influence on Williams by either the Irish struggle for independence or the colonial resistance by American revolutionaries. His wife, Margery, claimed he had no real interest in politics until his experience as a Saskatchewan farmer in the early 1920s.

Williams's high school education was interrupted by a bout of rheumatic fever, which required a lengthy confinement to bed and a gradual convalescence. Perhaps it was during this time that Williams developed his love of reading, laying the foundation for his later fluent command of the written and spoken word. Upon recovery, rather than returning to high school, he attended a bookkeeping course at a business college to acquire some useful employment skills. He gained his high school credential at night school, achieving matriculation with two months of intensive work.

Prior to and during the early years of World War I, Williams had to earn a living. He spent a year teaching in a one-room school at Fielding, Saskatchewan. Though he did not pursue a teaching career, his sympathy for the working conditions and low salaries facing teachers became a common theme in his speeches when he went into politics. He worked as a bookkeeper for the Eaton's department store in Winnipeg.[1] He was determined to enlist in Lord Strathcona's Horse, a cavalry regiment in which his older brother Sam became a captain and George's commanding officer. Sam Williams went overseas in 1915. Upon witnessing the realities of this modern industrial war, Sam wrote George to extract a promise: not to enlist until he was over twenty-one.

George had been just shy of his twentieth birthday when the war began and was determined to enlist. He honoured his brother's wish, delaying his enlistment until February 10, 1917, becoming a trooper and light machine-gunner in the regiment at the age of twenty-two. In August 1917, Williams was posted overseas to join the trench war, seeing action in France and Belgium. Now three Williams brothers were overseas: the oldest, Harry; Sam; and now George, the youngest.

When Britain declared war on Germany and her allies on August 4, 1914, Canada, as a British Dominion, was automatically at war.[2] The Canadian government asserted its autonomy by declaring war on August 5. There was enthusiastic popular support for the war in Canada, particularly among British immigrants and descendants of British immigrants. There was no shortage of young men in their late teens and early twenties eager for the adventure of going off to war—to defend Britain, to safeguard democracy, and to fight the war to end all wars. Secure and confident in assurances that the war would be short and that the boys would be home by Christmas, recruitment was brisk and the hope was that Canada's army would be one made up entirely of volunteers. Canada, with a standing army of just over 3,000, proceeded to build an expeditionary force that numbered 620,000 by the end of the war. These early days were exciting, almost festive: bands, marches, cheering crowds, and recruiting booths festooned as if it were a day at the local fair.

No one anticipated the carnage to come. By the time the war ended, six million young men from the Allied countries had died, and twelve million had been wounded. (Germany and her allies suffered four million dead and eight million wounded.) Nor did anyone expect the price Allied civilians would pay: four to five million dead due to military actions, war crimes, and famine. A generation of young men was fed into a military industrial meat grinder on the fields of Europe.

By the time Williams enlisted the mood had darkened, both at home and among Canadian troops in the trenches on the Western Front. Sam's letters to George no doubt conveyed that mood carefully, with an eye to the censor. In Canada, opposition to the war was growing louder and more insistent, though still a small minority opinion drowned by loud patriotism and jingoism. The casualty figures were ghastly on both sides. Canadian casualties had been horrendous in the early battles.[3] The public was shocked. Williams doubtless knew of the casualties in 1915 and

1916 when he enlisted in 1917. As the debate raged in Canada, he could not have helped being aware of the growing criticism in Canada of the ineptitude resulting in such militarily useless slaughter.

From the beginning there was strong minority opposition to the war, which grew more vocal as the war went on, especially in the ethnically diverse West and in Quebec. The Québécois were firmly opposed to entering what was seen as a "British war." Many among those of non-British origin saw the war as an imperialist war in defence of the British Empire. Canadians of American and Irish Catholic extraction remained resistant to the war bandwagon. Religious groups with strong pacifist convictions who had been enticed as settlers by the government's group settlement policy—Mennonites, Hutterites, Doukhobors—were not prepared to join the war effort, for reasons of religious conscience. Those with roots in the enemy nations—Ukrainians, Germans, Austrians, Hungarians—were not enthusiastic and resisted calls to join and fight. The War Measures Act, 1914 categorized those born in such countries "enemy aliens," forcing them to register. Over eight thousand "enemy aliens" were interned in forced labour camps, losing their jobs, farms, businesses, and homes. Those among the estimated eighty thousand registered "enemy aliens" not confined in camps were required to report regularly to local police authorities. These Canadians were subjected to abuse and indignity by their fellow citizens. A measure of the hysteria generated against them was reflected in the campaign to change the name of Berlin, Ontario, to Kitchener, to honour Field Marshal Kitchener, Britain's secretary of state for war, who died in 1916 when the ship carrying him to meetings in Russia hit a German mine and sank. Expressions of public opposition to the name change were not tolerated, nor did the referendum ballot include the option to retain the existing name.

In addition to nationalist opposition in Quebec and ethnic and religious resistance across the country, there was significant class opposition to the war. All elements of the capitalist class were united in wanting a firm, full, and patriotic prosecution of the war. The organized farmers, though small capitalists who stood to profit from the demand for foodstuffs, were nevertheless critical and suspicious.[4] They were at the height of their power and influence, with 143,000 organized farmers in Ontario and across the West. Mistrustful of both Tory and Liberal parties, denounced loudly as the willing captives of the "Special Interests," the organized farmers were deeply ambivalent. On the one hand, the farmers were by and large eager to do their duty to Britain. On the other hand, they were convinced that a government dominated by "partyism" and patronage would engage in war profiteering as both parties sought private economic gain from the war. Hence, the organized farmers demanded policies to prevent and punish war profiteering and a disinterested national agency to plan for supplying the war effort.

The organized working class—those in trade unions and various labour and socialist political parties—were polarized between adamant opposition to the war and patriotic calls to duty. The polarization had ethnic, regional, and ideological dimensions. Unions in the West embraced socialism, syndicalism, industrial unionism (organizing all workers in an industry into one big union), and militant tactics. The national labour central, the Trades and Labour Congress (TLC), was deeply split between militant and socialist western trade unions, rooted in mining, the fishery, forestry, construction, and unskilled general labour, and the more moderate traditional unions representing the skilled trades and tariff-protected industries in Central Canada. Largely unskilled, and working in dangerous jobs characterized by low pay, long hours, back-breaking work, and harsh bosses, out of necessity western trade unions pioneered more confrontational industrial tactics (sympathetic and general strikes; occupations and sit-ins; fighting scabs). Clashes between militants and moderates became annual events at TLC conventions. Western unions represented a more ethnically diverse membership, with a large and growing bloc of immigrants of non-British origin who did not farm, or had failed to prove on a homestead, filling the ranks of unskilled labour in the West. The class radicalism of western trade unions found political expression in a variety of socialist and labour parties that began to succeed in electing a handful of MLAs across the West, and even the odd MP.

Opposition to the war among the western working class was strong from the outset. Many opposed the war on the ideological grounds of international solidarity among workers. Others argued the war was cynically engineered by the capitalist class for imperialist and economic goals. Some feared that the war would be used as a patriotic pretext to crush the labour movement, robbing it of the meagre gains won at great cost. Others embraced secular pacifism as a political and moral principle. Moreover, the war-induced industrial boom brought few benefits to the western working class, compared to the good jobs and high wages it brought workers in the industries of Central Canada. Understandably, many elements of the western working class, especially among the key leadership, feared that western workers were seen as just so much cannon fodder. This sentiment was very strong in British Columbia, where unemployment remained high throughout the war—many BC workers who received layoff or termination notices in their pay packets also found a cryptic note: "Your King and Country need you—we can spare you."

During the early war years, the resistance expressed itself at public rallies, meetings, and demonstrations, often involving clashes with counter-demonstrators. Of deeper concern to the government was its reflection in declining rates of enlistment. As casualties escalated beyond all expectations, the government, fearing an inevitable political storm, reluctantly determined that conscription was necessary to fulfill Canada's manpower commitments to the war effort. Many western workers, especially those in militant trade unions and left-leaning political parties, deeply opposed conscription—an opposition they shared with the people of Quebec. The organized farmers in the West were gravely concerned about conscription but were not as hostile toward it as working-class organizations. Labour and farm organizations had participated in a public campaign criticizing war profiteering, incompetence in organizing the war effort to get quality supplies and weapons to the troops, and the evils of patronage that became rampant as groups of capitalists with political connections scrambled shamelessly to profit from the war. Both groups demanded that conscription be imposed on wealth before it was imposed on men.

The government feared this anti-conscription sentiment might find reflection in independent farm and labour candidates, or in support for Laurier's Liberals. In such a situation, the final outcome of an election on conscription was uncertain. Tory prime minister Robert Borden moved to form a Union government. Liberal leader Wilfrid Laurier had already rejected a coalition government and made clear his intention to continue as leader of an anti-conscription opposition, even if he lost everywhere but in Quebec. Nevertheless, Borden formally invited Laurier to join a wartime coalition government based on the government's conscription policy. Laurier again refused, despite Borden's promise not to proceed with conscription until a clear mandate was won in a general election.

Borden's Union government united the Tories with English Canadian elements of the Liberal Party. An election was inevitable, given Laurier's position as leader of His Majesty's Loyal Opposition. The required election of 1916 had been postponed in an effort to form a wartime coalition government. When this failed, an election became politically and constitutionally necessary. Most importantly, the air had to be cleared on the issue of conscription. Borden needed a clear democratic mandate to proceed. Leaving little to chance, Borden's government passed the Wartime Elections Act, 1917, denying the vote to all war objectors and to those of "enemy alien" birth naturalized after March 1902 (unless they had a son, grandson, or brother in the military), while granting the vote to wives, mothers, and sisters of soldiers and to women on active military duty. This was supplemented by the Military Voters Act, 1917, which permitted soldiers at the front to vote in their previous constituency of residence or to leave it to officials of the two parties to decide where their votes would be counted. This allowed party officials to steer the military vote to local races where the votes were most needed. The soldier's ballot was a simple choice between "Government" and "Opposition." The military vote was assigned after the civilian vote was counted. This was decisive for Borden in fourteen seats. In a final touch to win the farm vote, Borden's cabinet approved a last-minute order-in-council exempting farmers' sons from conscription. As it turned out, Borden did not need to engage in such skulduggery, given the victory the government enjoyed. But the fact that he had felt such tactics necessary reflects the government's own lack of conviction that conscription could win an honest popular mandate.

The Union government won the December 17, 1917, election with 153 of 235 seats and 57 per cent of the vote. Most anti-conscription adherents opted for Laurier's Liberals rather than running anti-conscription independents. (A smattering of independent and labour candidates pulled just under one hundred thousand votes.) But Borden's victory was hollow in a broader political sense, since it resolved nothing and in fact fanned the flames of the polarization over conscription. Laurier's anti-conscription Liberals won 82 seats with 39 per cent of the vote. In addition to sweeping Quebec (62 of 65 seats with 73 per cent), Laurier won 8 seats in Ontario, 10 in the Maritimes, and 2 in the West. After the election the nation was even more deeply split—the civilian vote had given Borden a mere hundred-thousand-vote margin of victory, which was topped up with two hundred thousand military votes, representing over 90 per cent of the military votes cast.

The opponents of conscription, especially in Quebec and among left-leaning working-class organizations in the West, were determined to continue the resistance by defying the law. In the West there were demonstrations and riots. Many draft resisters were summarily fired by their bosses. Some went to jail for resisting the draft, while many hundreds more found willing aid in draft-resistance networks across the West. It became a cat-and-mouse game between the Dominion Police and those evading draft notices. Ginger (Albert) Goodwin, a secular pacifist and one of British Columbia's most successful and militant union leaders, argued that workers should not kill each other to enrich their bosses. Upon registering for the draft, as required by law, he was found unfit for duty for health reasons ("black lung," from his years in the coal mines). While leading a 1917 strike at a smelter in Trail, BC, Goodwin was suddenly reclassified as fit for duty and ordered to report for enlistment. He fled, hiding out in the bush with the help of fellow workers. He was hunted down and shot to death by Dominion Police on July 27, 1918. His death provoked a general strike in Vancouver on August 2. His funeral drew mourning crowds in numbers that rivalled those for a head of state. Working-class resistance to the war now had a martyr. In the final year of the war, working-class resistance became epidemic as 169 strikes occurred—more than in the previous three years combined. The biggest and most bitter strikes occurred in the West. The Borden government invoked the War Measures Act, banning strikes and a list of left-wing working-class organizations. Western trade unions repeatedly brought unsuccessful resolutions to TLC conventions calling for united working-class resistance to the draft, up to and including a general strike on the issue.

Resistance was deeper and more successful in Quebec because nearly the entire Québécois population joined in defying the draft. Demonstrations were held across the province and serious riots occurred in Montreal. The pro-conscription Montreal *Star* was bombed. The National Assembly briefly debated a motion to separate from Canada. Local draft boards granted wholesale exemptions. Draft dodging and aiding draft dodgers became nearly universal. Deserters fled to the United States. Even prosecutors and judges within Quebec's legal system could not be counted on to enforce the law. Under pressure from English Canada, the Borden government redoubled efforts to enforce the law in Quebec, despite the fact that the vast majority of the province's population was prepared to continue in defiance.

The crisis came to a head in Quebec City on Easter weekend 1918. On March 29 the public arrest by Dominion Police of a man who could not produce his draft exemption papers sparked rioting which continued until April 2. Rioters burned a police station, vandalized a newspaper building, and stormed and burned the registry office of the Military Service Act. The government imposed martial law. A battalion of English Canadian troops from Toronto was brought in to restore order. Bayonet charges and mounted attacks using clubs served only to further enrage the crowds. On April 1, military authorities claimed the troops were fired on by snipers. The troops responded with rifle and machine-gun fire into the crowd. Five civilians were killed, many wounded, and scores were placed under military arrest. At a later inquest, a local jury placed the entire blame for the incident on the military authorities, exonerating the crowd.

In the aftermath of the Easter confrontation the Union government wisely refrained from enforcing the law in Quebec too zealously, and the Québécois continued their open resistance. Later in April, all special exemptions from the draft were withdrawn across Canada, resulting in riots and increased draft resistance in English Canada. As a result, the government backed off vigorous enforcement all across the Dominion. The situation in Europe was less urgent. The tide in the war was turning in favour of the Allies. The end was in sight. Enforcing conscription harshly as the war was ebbing toward victory would only widen the political chasm between English Canada and Quebec and more deeply offend anti-conscription adherents from coast to coast.

There is no record of Williams's views on these political events. He witnessed the growing opposition to the war and the heated debate over conscription. He enlisted in February 1917 and by August of that year he was overseas, joining other Allied soldiers in the trenches on the Western Front. If he voted in the December 17, 1917 conscription election, it would have been to cast a soldier's ballot. Given his eagerness to enlist, he probably marked his x for the "Government" side. The intensification of the conflict in Quebec and in the West would have been distant news on the battlefield, and troops in action were unlikely to sympathize with opponents of conscription back home.

Williams's war was a short war: he saw action in France and Belgium for eight months, from August 1917 to March 1918. No detailed record exists of Williams's memories of his personal war experience. Like most veterans, he preferred not to talk about the horrors he had witnessed and participated in directly. But the last battle he fought was well documented by historians. His brother Sam wrote a book that contained details of the battle. Williams rode in the last cavalry charge of the war, and this experience was doubtless the one that affected him most.

The use of cavalry in the war was uncommon. Cavalry charges, while an effective shock tactic in commencing general offences in earlier wars, constituted wholesale slaughter when mounted troops charged enemy forces with repeating rifles and machine guns, backed up by mortar and artillery fire. In the trench warfare of the Western Front, cavalry charges had proved largely useless given the small stretches of land separating opposing sides. No Man's Land was littered with barbed wire, steel, and cement defensive emplacements and riddled with craters from mortar and artillery ordnance. Most cavalry regiments on both sides were gradually reborn as mobile armoured divisions. The Lord Strathcona's Horse was initially deployed as infantry in France in 1915. The regiment's soldiers were not returned to their mounts until 1916 and were used with little effect and many casualties at the Somme. They served in the trenches for most of the war, their mounted activities limited to small localized actions from time to time. But cavalry was again used significantly in resisting the German 1918 spring offensive, the failure of which marked the beginning of the end for Germany and her allies. This offensive was a final act of desperation to break the three-year stalemate on the Western Front. The Germans were hopeful. The war on the Eastern Front had ended when the Russian revolutionary government signed a peace accord, freeing up large numbers of fresh German troops to join the offensive.

The German offensive was all along the front. The Canadian Cavalry Brigade, including the Lord Strathcona's Horse and the Royal Canadian Dragoons, was dispatched to the Moreuil Wood to block and roll back the German advance in that sector. The advance had penetrated the Allied lines deeply, threatening to split concentrations of British and French forces. The Germans had occupied the wood, which was located near the Arve River and provided control of the rail line between

Paris and Amiens. Williams's squadron of one hundred men, led by Lieutenant Gordon Flowerdew, charged an advancing force of three hundred Germans supported by machine guns, mortars, and a six-inch Howitzer. Upon Flowerdew's order to charge, the bugler and his horse were felled by fire before he could sound a note. By the end of the battle, an estimated fifty of Williams's comrades had been killed and another twenty-five wounded. Williams was among the wounded. Charging with his sabre drawn, his horse was shot from under him, falling on his leg and pinning Williams to the ground, unconscious. After regaining consciousness, the charge over but general fighting continuing around him, Williams shot his wounded horse, extricated himself, and ran for cover in the woods. His left ankle was shattered by machine-gun fire. The battle ended in an Allied victory, with the Germans driven from the woods. Lieutenant Flowerdew died of his wounds and was posthumously awarded the Victoria Cross. For Williams the war was over. He had sustained what the British called a "Blighty wound"—neither fatal nor seriously crippling, but sufficient to end his fighting days.

Williams was evacuated to the Canadian General Hospital at Basingstoke, Hants, England. There he successfully persuaded the doctors not to amputate his lower leg, and the surgery to save his leg was successful. Williams suffered episodes of pain over the next few years and a slight limp, which became less and less pronounced but never disappeared. During his lengthy stay in hospital, Williams took courses through the Khaki University, set up by military authorities to encourage educational improvement among the convalescing wounded. Williams took a course in accounting and read widely in economics, history, and socialism.[5] He also enrolled in a correspondence course with the Pelman Institute of London. Pelmanism was a mental discipline and memory system teaching concentration, speed-reading for retention, and detailed writing exercises. It claimed to be a scientific system of mental training inspired by the Victorian doctrine that the mind, like the body, needed regular hard exercise to improve. It was the fashion of the day among many in the British ruling elite, as well as among the middle classes. The course clearly impressed Williams; upon his death, detailed exercises and lessons were found carefully saved in his personal files.

Williams returned to Winnipeg and was discharged on December 6, 1918, with a pension of $15.75 a month. He was twenty-four years old, with experience as a teacher, a bookkeeper, and a soldier. What impact did the war have on him? Did it change his values, ideology, or understanding of power? We know he entered the war willingly to do his duty to Britain. We do not know if he believed all the war propaganda claiming that victory by "the Hun" would lead to tyranny and the end of democracy; an Allied victory in this war would end all war; the enemy was bestial and brutal. What did he believe upon his return home? Again, no specific answers to these questions are to be found in his papers. His daughter, Muriel Wiens, provides some insight, perhaps reflecting views she learned from her father:

> The Canadian young men who had joined the army in fervent support of the British Empire were appalled to discover that their fallen comrades had not given their lives in a noble cause, but in a dispute among greedy merchant princes, pulling the strings of national governments. Many, George among them, returned to Canada prepared to train a more sophisticated and sceptical eye on the economic adventures of government.[6]

She recalls the following:

> Years later, he was to mention in a speech discussing the grave effects of war, how he would forever remember an old woman, somewhere in France, pushing a wheelbarrow through the mud with a small child sitting atop their few possessions, and with nowhere to go.[7]

Perhaps the most objective way to assess the effects of the war on Williams is to examine the life choices he made upon returning to Winnipeg. He did not return to Eaton's as a bookkeeper. (His brother Sam enjoyed a long and successful career serving the Eaton family.) He enrolled in a year's short course at the Manitoba Agricultural College. There he excelled and was selected for the college team in a national competition judging livestock at the Brandon fair. After the course, having won the livestock judging contest, in 1919 Williams was awarded a position with the Soldier Settlement Board in Regina, Saskatchewan, as manager of livestock and equipment acquisitions. The Soldier Settlement Act, 1917 granted homesteading veterans quarter sections of land and $2,500 interest-free loans. This choice indicates Williams's desire to work in the public sector, in this case assisting veterans to take up farming. Yet he very quickly decided to leave the board, in 1921, and go into farming himself. There is no indication whether this decision was partly a result of the controversies surrounding the government's selection of very poor land for the veteran-settlers (lands on which many homesteaders had already failed) and the illegal expropriation of First Nations reserve lands for distribution to veterans. Many farmers had also complained that some of the land had formerly been available as community pastures. Williams's first venture failed. He and a partner briefly went into the cattle business at Preeceville; a severe winter wiped out virtually the entire herd. He then went into wheat farming, acquiring a half-section soldier settlement farm near Semans. Many local farmers were annoyed because part of Williams's land had served as a community pasture. His neighbours were initially quite unfriendly for this reason—and because he was from the city and, though well educated, knew little of the practical side of farming. He proved to be a quick learner.

Williams's farm was virgin prairie. He cleared the bush and broke the land with a single-disc plow and a team of Belgian horses. Williams had become a homesteader and a farmer. In 1921 he broke and seeded fifteen acres and harvested 270 bushels of wheat. Though initially a very good crop, the grade and hence the price were reduced dramatically due to heavy rain during harvest. The income was not enough to pay on his debt or to cover the costs of seeding and harvesting. The next year he had eighty acres to seed and harvest. The crop was reasonable, but prices had fallen from $2.31 a bushel to 77 cents. Williams, like all farmers, was weighed down with debt and faced a pricing system that robbed him of a fair return on his labour.

He decided to become active in the farm movement. There were two competing farm organizations: the moderate, long-established Saskatchewan Grain Growers' Association (SGGA) and the new breakaway, left-wing, and militant Farmers' Union of Canada (FUC)—the preamble to its constitution, inspired by the One Big Union, championed a "class struggle" to advance the interests of "the Great Agricultural Class."

In 1922 Williams married Margery Cass, his former secretary at the board. After bringing in that year's harvest, he joined the FUC. In November he turned twenty-eight. He was a very different Williams from the one swept up in the holocaust of World War I.

Chapter 2

THE POLITICAL AND ECONOMIC CONTEXT

*The Rise of the United Farmers
of Canada (Saskatchewan
Section), 1922 to 1926*

Georg Williams arrived on the political stage at a key historical
moment. The agrarian populist crusade had reached its apo-
theosis in the Progressive Party's decision to contest the 1921
federal election. Having won victory after victory, many supporters of
the crusade expected great changes to benefit the common people. But
abruptly the agrarian movement faltered, slipping quickly into crisis and
decline, leaving its popular base confused and rudderless. The struggle
of the western working class evolved into an aggressive, confrontational
campaign with considerable popular support. The battle over conscription, and the growing strike movement of the war's final years, met the
full force of repressive state power. During the postwar depression the
western working class went on a coherent offensive to win union recognition and collective bargaining rights. Some dreamed of a socialist
revolution. The offensive was defeated decisively in the 1919 Winnipeg

General Strike, followed by a nationwide wave of state repression of militant trade unions, the Communist Party, and various socialist parties and
organizations.[1] The lessons Williams drew both from his war experience
and from the collapse of the two popular class offensives became clear in
the leadership role he played from the moment he joined the FUC.

Williams remained an agrarian populist, but the failure of the
Canadian movement convinced him that socialism had to be the ultimate objective of agrarian populism. Otherwise, the movement would
continue in ideological confusion and organizational incoherence. He
was also persuaded from the outset that the movement must seek and
win political power in order to effect desired changes. Williams concluded that the agrarian movement had to form an effective political
alliance with the other popular class engaging in struggle: the working
class. There is no evidence Williams had a master plan when he joined
the FUC. But incrementally, as he struggled to win and to guide the organization, both his own thinking and his strategic understanding of what
had to be done flowered and matured. In that process he learned to be a
superb tactician and an effective organizer; he also became an outstanding orator. Certainly in 1922 what was to come wasn't clear, but what had
happened to the farmers' movement was.

The organized farmers dominated political debates in Canada during
the first two decades of the twentieth century, yet their domination was
ephemeral. Although they won some concessions, the organized farmers
proved unable to change the course of development of Canadian capitalism in ways congenial to them. They failed to maintain the momentum
of their surging, combative class. Efforts to forge alliances with the working class and the urban middle classes were wrecked on the reef of a
self-interested view of what the world ought to be like.

The agrarian upsurge awaited the successful settlement of the Prairies
during the "wheat boom," between 1896 and 1913, when the export
of wheat dominated the Canadian economy. The pieces of the economic design of Confederation finally fell into place. From the outset,
Confederation's economic strategy depended on the West, especially the
Prairies. The so-called National Policy included the following elements:
the construction of an all-Canada transcontinental railway; the erection
of a tariff wall to force domestic industrialization; the settlement of the
Prairies with farmers to produce grains, mainly wheat, for export and

to serve as a vast captive market for Canadian industrial capitalists; and the establishment of a new investment frontier for foreign and domestic capital. After years of failure, prosperity arrived in 1896 as the national economy took off, powered by the production and export of wheat. Over one million people moved into the Prairies, the area of occupied lands jumped from ten to seventy million acres, and annual wheat production went from twenty to over two hundred million bushels. By 1913 the value of wheat and flour exports was greater than the combined value of all exports in 1896.

The production and export of wheat, and the resulting east–west railway traffic, was one cornerstone of the original design, enriching railway investors and land speculators, the private grain trade, banks and trust companies, and commercial wholesalers and retailers who trafficked in farm production inputs and consumer goods. The other cornerstone was those industrial capitalists who enjoyed a sudden expansion of their captive market. The farmers and the essential, if small in number, wage-earners who settled the Prairies were a capitalist's dream come true—they were forced to buy dear and sell cheap (in 1913 the Prairies were home to two hundred thousand farmers; forty-nine thousand farm labourers; and fifty thousand non-agricultural workers).[2] The protected manufactured goods needed for production, consumption, and amusement cost up to 50 per cent more than if there had been free trade. At the same time, the commodities they produced for a cash income—grains, especially wheat; livestock; and livestock products—had to be forwarded though middlemen, each of whom took a share of the final price gained on national or world markets, as well as transported great distances by rail and sea. From the farmers' point of view, given their share of the final price, they sold cheap indeed. Add to this the cost of credit needed to buy land, to purchase machinery, to construct buildings, and for the annual purchase of production inputs, and even the ability to produce was subject to a tariff in the form of interest.

The farmer-settlers were small capitalists who embraced private enterprise, individualism, hard work, and entrepreneurial ability. They were a key element in the nation-building capitalist project embodied in the National Policy. Immediately there was a clash of interests. Much of the best land in the region had been granted to the Hudson's Bay Company (5 per cent of "the fertile belt"), the Canadian Pacific Railway

(25 million acres, and more as work progressed, of choice land bordering the main line and the branches—the best land for a farmer), as well as land colonization companies and many political friends of the government. Farmers found that in order to expand their holdings beyond the initial quarter-section homestead, they must buy land at boom-time prices. The capital they needed to begin and expand their farm operation, and to borrow for inputs during planting, led to debt at high interest rates. They were at the mercy of a railway monopoly charging excessive freight rates. They were forced to buy all their manufactured necessities and conveniences at prices inflated by the tariff. In general, they were involved in a highly sophisticated capitalist agriculture dedicated to the industrial cultivation of specialized grain crops for a distant market. In effect, they were trapped in an economic situation that, for them, had all the vices of a free market (insecurity, price fluctuations, high production costs, price speculation, uncertain harvests due to weather) and none of the virtues (windfall profits, large rewards for sound entrepreneurial decisions, good returns on invested capital)—at least none in so far as the vast majority of farmers were concerned.

In this economic context, farmers in Canada organized a populist assault on the National Policy. Agrarian populism in this era (similar phenomena occurred in the United States, Russia, and a number of European countries) was a characteristic response of farmers, as independent commodity producers, to the threat posed by capitalist industrial modernization. Industrialization was a threat due to the unavoidable consequences of unfettered capitalist industrial development for all small producers: either they enlarged themselves at the expense of others and invested in production technology, or they went out of business, joining the ranks of wage labour. This dynamic applied as much to agriculture as it did to handicraft and workshop production. Inevitably, industrial techniques had to be applied to the production of agricultural commodities, particularly the purchase of modern machinery. The individual producer was forced to apply the modern techniques and acquire more land in order to produce more as the new competition lowered prices received on the market. As the logic of capitalist modernization began to negatively affect farmers to the point where they organized to demand redress of their grievances, that class, more or less politically united, began to attack aspects of capitalism while retaining a commitment to its essence for the farmer—private property and small commodity production.

As a result, the farmers were simultaneously hostile to and supportive of elements of the capitalist economy that ensnared them. Their interests were neither completely those of labour nor completely those of capital. Consequently, their politics were confused as they vacillated between the left and right of the political spectrum. The instability of the farmers' position in the capitalist economy, exaggerated during times of crisis and rapid modernization, was reflected in unstable politics. Populist farmers, therefore, tended to idealize small commodity production for its own sake (i.e., as "a way of life") while criticizing commodity production on a large scale. Failing to fully understand their real location in the larger economy, agrarian populists did not recognize themselves as a class from the past that stood between the working class and the capitalist class and whose interests lay completely with neither. They were unable to recognize that their historical fate was to join one or the other class as the logic of capitalist competition threatened the ability of growing numbers of farmers to survive. This explained the two faces of agrarian populism. On the one hand, the movement mounted a widely supported general assault on the particular form of Canadian capitalist modernization that transformed the small property of the many into the big property of the few, as well as imposing—as industrialization must—heavy costs on the agricultural sector to provide the capital, labour, and cheap food so essential to industrial modernization. On the other hand, the movement exhibited a profound reluctance to reject the fundamental principles of capitalist production—private property, commodity production, competitive self-enrichment—which resulted in the adoption of policies tending to oppose development and modernization. Socialism was rejected out of hand by the vast majority.

Background: The Agrarian Populist Agitation in Canada, 1900 to 1922

Prior to the wheat boom, agrarian organizations flourished in the more settled regions of Central Canada and the Maritimes but had only marginal political influence. The settlement of the Prairies made the farmers of Canada a national power not only because of their increased share of the population, and not only because of the importance of wheat to the national economy, but also because the Prairie farmers pioneered new forms of organization and acted with a new militancy. Armed with a well-developed ideological perspective from earlier agrarian organizations, Prairie farm organizations popularized that perspective more aggressively. They elevated the farmer and the vocation of agriculture to the primary moral status in the hierarchy of occupations, while expressing disdain for nonproductive occupations; they assailed the businessman, the professional, the entrepreneur, and, most odious, those in trusts and monopolies. They contrasted the manipulations of such groups with the productive primacy of the vocation of farmer, the sneaky methods of business enterprise and city ways with their own innocent but crucial knowledge. Urban classes—with the exception of a cool respect granted the industrial working class and the crafts—were seen as little more than parasites sucking value out of the honest labour and enterprise of farmers. Farmer organizations saved their deepest contempt and strongest attacks for the corporations, the trusts, the banks, and the railways—especially the railways. As for politicians, there was nothing but cynicism. The party system was a fraud. Both Liberal and Conservative parties were bought and paid for by the capitalists. Both parties sought power on behalf of capitalists to fill their pockets through patronage.

Agrarian populism's respect for the industrial working class was heavily qualified. The urban working class did not benefit from the exhilarating benefits of rural life, huddling instead in the slums of the cities. Skilled craft workers enjoyed the most respect. Factory workers were looked at with some resentment, since many of their jobs with what were seen as inflated wages were created by the protective tariff. Farm labour was becoming more costly and harder to get, to the annoyance of farmers, due largely, they argued, to the inflated wages paid in tariff-protected industries. Nevertheless, the working class was theoretically the farmers' natural ally in the struggle for economic and social justice. Agrarian populists embraced their own version of the labour theory of value, retaining the belief that agriculture would always precede industrial activity in its wealth-producing importance.

Early efforts to achieve farmer/labour unity failed. Despite this, the active and militant sections of the organized farmers developed a complete ideology reflecting their place in the system of capitalist production and a clear articulation of the interests of farmers as a class. The vision of the ideal, just society was painted in bold strokes. All parts of the society would work together in harmony to produce wealth. The grossly uneven distribution of wealth had to be remedied, since unjust inequality provoked strife and instability. Each among the producers of wealth should enjoy a fair share of the fruits of his labour and enterprise, and each citizen had a right to an appropriate share of the wealth produced collectively by the efforts of all classes. They did not advocate an interventionist state to achieve these goals. Rather, each group should organize on the basis of class and elect representatives, based on their numbers and roles in wealth production, as the foundation for a truly democratic group government embracing cooperative principles. The ultimate objective was a harmonious, cooperative community founded on an economy that served the needs of the people rather than providing profits for capitalists. Only the democratic self-organization of class groups, most importantly farmers and workers, could control the organized, concentrated power of the capitalists.

With the turn of the century, Prairie farmer organizations quickly won a mass following. Earlier agrarian organizations had emphasized small-scale cooperative enterprises, education, and government lobbying, only occasionally running farmer candidates in elections. The Prairie organizations were more ambitious, demanding immediate and practical measures to improve the economic position of farmers. They targeted the price-fixing, under-weighing, and under-grading practices of private grain elevators at shipping points along the rail line, successfully demanding legislation to regulate the grain trade. They studied the Winnipeg Grain Exchange, exposing its price-fixing and speculative manipulations that deprived farmers of a fair share of the final price gained on the market. They documented the gouging freight rates of the Canadian Pacific Railway and its deliberate practice of delaying access to shipping until prices fell. They concluded that farmers' organizations must take the grain trade away from the capitalist grain merchants and establish a farmer-controlled cooperative marketing system to ensure that the farmer gained the final price won on the market less fair charges for marketing, shipping, and storage. All this they proceeded to do with great success. In response, and in an effort to defend itself, the private grain trade organized the North West Grain Dealers' Association, to engage in more systematic price-fixing and to warn governments and the public about these dangerous radical farmers. The political class struggle between farmers and the private grain trade was now out in the open. By 1910 the farmers' first cooperative marketing company, the Grain Growers' Grain Company, had signed up nine thousand farmers. This campaign ended in the great cooperative wheat pools of the Prairies, which came to dominate the grain trade.

The successes of the organized farmers in these areas led to self-confidence and a sense of class strength, as farmers flocked to join the struggle. In turn, this set the stage for an agrarian populist political intervention to transform the very structure of Canadian capitalism and win political reforms that would deepen democracy. The centrepieces of the political agitation were the protective tariff and rural depopulation. The organized farmers saw the tariff not as simply a systematic extraction of unfair shares of the wealth they produced to enrich industrial capitalists, made possible by a corrupt party system using government powers for selfish purposes. The protective tariff had broader, more insidious purposes. Protection was in fact the key element of a national policy of forced capitalist industrial modernization, threatening the viability of the rural social structure. The spectre of rural depopulation had haunted earlier agrarian organizations in Ontario and the Maritimes, where it was an accelerating demographic trend from the 1870s onward. Prairie farmers saw a dark future awaiting them if nothing changed. The agrarian populists argued that rural depopulation was a consequence of the tariff, which created and sustained "unnatural" industries with legally guaranteed profits. Such industries served as a magnet to the cities since they could pay higher wages than would have been possible under free trade, luring the sons and daughters of farmers to city life.

From 1900 to 1922 the nation witnessed a last great agrarian populist agitation—to slow, to stop, and hopefully to reverse the trend leading to the decimation of rural Canada. It was the last hurrah for the passing, pre-industrial rural way of life. The fear of rural decimation and depopulation was central to the assault on the National Policy launched by the more conscious elements of Canadian farmers. Never before (and never since) were Canada's farmers so united and strong. Their local organizations became hubs of social and political life in most farm communities, organizing picnics, dances, banquets, book clubs, educational

2. The Political and Economic Context: 1922 to 1926   25

programs, and political rallies, thus building and consolidating their popular support.

In 1909, when Prairie farm organizations joined the Canadian Council of Agriculture (CCA), uniting with the Ontario Grange (later the United Farmers of Ontario), Canada's organized farmers had over thirty thousand members. In the summer of 1910, Laurier, impressed by the growing influence of the agrarian movement and eager to mend political fences, became the first prime minister to tour the Prairies. Large cheering crowds greeted him at his many stops, but after the greetings and the speeches, delegations of farmers presented petitions containing their demands. Laurier was reminded of his many unfulfilled free-trade promises. In 1896, he had championed free trade; upon winning power, he had embraced the National Policy and tariff-forced industrialization with the same dedication as the Tories, forbidding further consideration of free-trade policy within the Liberal Party. That had not stopped individual Liberal candidates, especially those in rural areas, from promising to fight for free trade within the party upon election, hence keeping the issue alive. The meetings, with a now apparently sympathetic Laurier in front of crowds of skeptical farmers, galvanized the organized farmers to send more than eight hundred representatives to what they billed as a "Siege on Ottawa" to put further pressure on Laurier. It was the very opposite of the old cap-in-hand pleadings at the seat of power. The organized farmers presented an uncompromising and coherent distillation of their demands in *The Farmers' Platform of 1910*. Lurking beneath the demands was the very public discussion among farm organizations about the need to form a farmers' political party.

The 1910 platform's central demand was for a speedy move to free trade, beginning with reciprocal free trade with the United States in agricultural products and key manufactured items important to farming (farm machinery, trucks and cars, and parts). The farmers were content to keep the imperial preferential system, as long as it was phased out in ten years leading up to free trade with Great Britain. It was proposed that the lost revenue be recovered through direct taxation on all citizens. Next on the agenda was rural depopulation, because "the greatest misfortune which can befall any country is to have its people huddled together in great centres of population." Tariff-induced industrialization was to blame, as it led to "the constant movement of our people away from the farms" and resulted in "the greatest problem…[of] the Canadian people,…the problem of retaining our people on the soil."[3] The farmers also called for a number of government interventions of direct benefit to farmers: a public railway to Hudson Bay; public owner-ship of terminal elevators; and a publicly owned chilled-meat industry. The document was silent on reforms of concern to the working class or the general public.

Laurier dismissed the demands as "too radical…to be adopted in the east."[4] The private grain trade's attacks on the organized farmers were joined by those of a Toronto meatpacker. In an open letter pub-lished widely in the press, J. A. Flavelle lamented that farmers had been "diverted from enterprise" and instead were looking "for returns through agitation." He considered their claim that "they were deprived by the greed of others of a legitimate share of the returns of their labour" to be erroneous.[5] With one eye on the election due in 1912 (hoping to forestall the farmers from fielding free-trade farmer candidates) and the other eye on the views of industrial capitalists, the prime minister granted some minor concessions to the farmers in preparation for the election. It was the biggest miscalculation of his career, resulting in one of the most polarized and defining elections in Canadian history.

The Laurier government adopted a policy of limited reciprocity and quickly concluded a new trade agreement with the United States, intro-ducing the measure in the House of Commons in January 1911. The complex agreement involved a limited list of reciprocally free items, as well as lower reciprocal tariffs on many others. Compared with the demands of the farmers, it was a very modest step into free-trade waters. Free trade was granted in natural products, especially agricul-tural products; certain semi-finished industrial products were free, mainly construction materials; and very few fully finished manufac-tured goods were on the free list, but many, including farm machinery, were on a list with lower fixed reciprocal tariffs. Sensing that the prime minister had stumbled, and hungry for power after fifteen years in opposition, the Tories embarked on a filibuster, accusing the govern-ment of selling out Canada to the Americans. The Tory filibuster was so effective that passage of the bill became impossible, denying Laurier the opportunity to pass the law, implement it, and go to the people in 1912 or 1913. Given the opposition in the House, and growing opposition among prominent and powerful Canadians, Laurier called an election for September 21, 1911.

An aroused and united capitalist class turned on Laurier with unexpected political ferocity, denouncing him for adopting a measure that would destroy the carefully crafted, east–west national economy and set the stage for Canada's economic and political integration into the United States. The Canadian Manufacturers' Association, alleging that Laurier had opened the Pandora's box of free trade, said these limited measures could only lead to a further expansion of free trade, ultimately dismantling Canada's industrial foundation. The farmers happily agreed: though the agreement was but a small step, it was nevertheless an important breakthrough toward their ultimate goal. According to the farmers' *Weekly Sun*, the capitalist class saw that "the promised success of the agitation by farmers…may be but a prelude to an assault on the whole citadel of Special Privilege."[6] Elements of the capitalist class that previously supported Laurier turned against him, withdrawing political and financial support. Key Liberals in the cabinet defected. The public debate became hysterical. Advocates of reciprocity were accused of disloyalty and near treason. The dark scenario drawn suggested the entire edifice of Canada's modern industrial economy would collapse, with Canadians serving as hewers of wood and drawers of water for the U.S. industrial monolith. As Governor General Earl Grey put it, "the feeling in Montreal and Toronto against the Agreement could hardly be stronger if the United States' troops had already invaded our territory."[7]

In 1911 Canada again voted for the National Policy and against limited free trade. The capitalist class, spearheaded by the industrialists, and the industrial working class voted against Laurier's modest proposals. Even the farmers were split: in Manitoba, eight Tories were elected and only two Liberals. The argument that free trade in agricultural products would result in U.S. domination of the grain trade and lower prices split the farm vote. The working class was also divided: the greater numbers in Central Canadian tariff-protected industries voted against free trade, while those in western trade unions, dominated by miners, forest workers, farm labour, and railway workers, tended to support it. The election was a divisive and close one. Just over 40,000 of 1.3 million votes separated the two parties—but in terms of seats the Tory victory was overwhelming: 134 to 87.

The 1911 defeat did not discourage the organized farmers' movement. In fact, the farmers embarked on a new political offensive in 1913, organizing a "Second Siege on Ottawa" on the third anniversary of the 1910 siege. The farmers gave up on the Liberal Party. Laurier had betrayed them in 1896, and then he had failed to campaign aggressively for his own policy (about which, quite frankly, he had deep doubts) in 1911. The small concessions won were stolen in an election poisoned by a fear campaign orchestrated and funded by "Special Interests."

After 1911 the organized farmers matured politically. They clearly understood the reasons for their defeat. The class forces ranged against them were powerful and formidable. The Canadian Manufacturers' Association, the banks and other institutions making up "the money power," the railways, and the large national commercial wholesale and retail conglomerates united to speak with one voice. The fear campaign included not only predictions of economic disaster, but charges of disloyalty to Britain and Canadian nationhood by selling out to the Americans. A clear presentation of the issues became impossible. The weak, lacklustre campaign by the Liberals again confirmed that both parties were owned by the "Special Interests," a constant populist refrain. Some argued the farmers' political agitation must reach out to other popular classes—workers, teachers, professionals, small business—to build a people's coalition. There was little doubt among many in the leadership that a new people's party, led by the organized farmers, must be formed in time for the 1915 election.

Nineteen eleven was a census year. The numbers confirmed the worst fears of the organized farmers. The decimation of rural Canada and the triumph of urban, industrial capitalism were indeed occurring. Since 1901 the country's rural population had declined from 62 per cent to 54 per cent of the total. Fully two in three employed Canadians were now in non-agricultural occupations. Though continuing settlement on the Prairies kept national occupied-farm figures up, significant declines had occurred in the Maritimes and Central Canada. Even the rural population of the Prairies had declined, from 75 per cent to 65 per cent.

The populist agitation therefore intensified between 1911 and 1914, becoming more sharp and vigorous. The critique of the political and economic forces oppressing farmers was generalized beyond one of the hopelessly corrupt political parties and vaguely defined "Special Interests" to one of capitalism and parliamentary democracy in Canada. Now the farmers spoke of the excessive concentration of wealth and power in the hands of a "capitalist plutocracy." They denounced "the money power," the "New Feudalism" of debt enslavement, and the tentacles of capitalist "Special Interests" subverting democracy through "partyism" and patronage. They predicted "a pitched fight between capitalistic groups and the people at large, led by the farmers." If unity was achieved, victory was certain, since "what chance will Special Privilege have against the public desire for Equal Rights?"[8] They advocated new forms of direct democracy (the initiative, the referendum, and recall), proportional representation, and the fielding of a people's party. Though free trade was still front and centre in their economic program, to this they added proposals for anti-monopoly laws, progressive taxation reform, and the construction of a social democracy including pensions and general social welfare. The growing reform list included liquor prohibition, policies to build world peace, the vote for women, and higher standards of morality in politics and business. They called for nothing short of a revolution by ballot in order to radically change Canada's entire political and economic system.

In 1913 the wheat boom began to falter, though that did not reduce the flow of settlers into the region. Wheat prices dropped to 89 cents/ bushel, the lowest price since 1906. Wheat production slowed and began to fall as increased competition caused international markets to shrink; this squeezed farmers, as the costs of production, especially the tariff-protected industrial inputs, continued to increase. Fears of a general depression spread, as the prices for all Canada's exports fell in 1913, interest rates increased, and unemployment spread across the Prairies and into British Columbia as construction slowed down. Industrial unemployment in the large cities across Canada climbed higher as layoffs increased. To make matters worse, the 1914 harvest was poor due to drought. The farmers' agitations intensified as they dealt with the usual boom-and-bust cycle of the wheat economy.

The arrival of World War I saved Canada from economic calamity, but the price for that salvation was high in Canadian blood spilled on the battlefields of France and Belgium. The war forced the organized farmers to temporarily mute their agitations and shelve their plans for a new party. The deepening depression was reversed overnight. Prices for wheat climbed astronomically, from 89 cents in 1913 to $2.24 in

1918. During the war, Ottawa set up the Board of Grain Supervisors (commonly called the Wheat Board) to control prices and prevent speculation and market manipulation by the grain trade, eventually closing down the Winnipeg Grain Exchange to loud applause from farmers. The board ensured that farmers received their fair share of the final price less costs of freight, storage, and marketing. Though farmers felt that the administered price was kept too low, they enthusiastically supported the board. Settlement was spurred on as the Prairie population rose dramatically and the number and size of farms grew. Agriculture retained first place in value of Canada's exports, but manufactured goods, including munitions, had begun to close the gap by 1918. Nevertheless, the Prairie success in settlement and increased production pushed Canada from third place among world wheat exporters to second by war's end (Canada took first place in 1923). Acreage in crops increased 84 per cent, and the Prairie population by 19 per cent, as a result of the war boom. Farmers, however, complained that their fragile prosperity depended on fluctuating wheat prices, while debts, interest rates, and production costs grew dramatically.

While the Prairies did well out of the war, Central Canada, the focus of capitalist industrialization, did better as industrial and financial capital grew to maturity. The demographic consequences were exactly as the organized farmers had feared: the combined population of Montreal and Toronto grew by 38 per cent between 1911 and 1921. While Prairie prosperity was uncertain, haunted by the boom-and-bust cycle, capitalist industrialization and resulting urbanization had forged ahead. Central Canada emerged from the war as the industrial heartland of Canada with a more secure and resilient base to its economic prosperity.

Inevitably, the war created an aggravated sense of grievance among the organized farmers. Facing loud demands for national unity during the early years of the war, the farmers largely complied, doing their part to support the war effort. But as the war dragged on, they renewed agitations out of anger about the unequal sacrifices demanded for the war and brought their long list of earlier grievances back into sharp relief. The war boom was not shared equally. Though it pulled agriculture out of its slump, the organized farmers pointed the finger at the manufacturers and banks for engaging in war profiteering while farmers found the price of wheat strictly controlled in the national interest. The organized farmers accused the government of complicity in systematic war profiteering. With the war boom came inflation, threatening the agricultural boom and denying security and prosperity to the farmer. Credit, so vital in the expansion of the wheat economy, became hard to get and expensive. If wheat prices could be strictly controlled in the national interest, why couldn't inflation, interest rates, and prices for war supplies be similarly controlled? If the farmers' main output, wheat and other grains, faced price controls, why couldn't price controls also be imposed on industrial inputs to farm production?

The organized farmers went on the offensive, publicly criticizing the government, and the two parties, of incompetence and corruption in prosecuting the war. When the conscription debate began, farmers demanded the conscription of wealth before the conscription of men. A series of scandals around corruption in war production contracts—for instance, inferior goods at inflated prices, even munitions and weapons, sent to soldiers in the trenches—provoked cries of outrage. The wartime demands for unity and sacrifice from the government and its capitalist friends were seen as hypocritical. The political agitation therefore erupted with a new vigour, and now it included a determination to go into politics.

During 1915–16 three options were debated in the farm organizations and on the pages of the *Grain Growers' Guide*. First, farmer candidates could seek nominations in one or the other of the two established parties. This option had the least support. Second, the organized farmers could found a third party. This option had both strong support and strong opposition: those opposed worried that forming a party and plunging into politics would divide and destroy the movement, and that the disease of "partyism" would inevitably corrupt the party. Third, independent farmer candidates could run in selected ridings on a free-trade platform, thus forming a core of MPs around whom to build a new party at a future, more opportune time. At first, this option had the most support. But as the debate continued, support grew for the third-party option. In December 1916 the CCA issued an expanded and harder-hitting version of the 1910 farmers' platform in preparation for political action, but the roar of the debate over conscription and the 1917 election on the issue forced the farmers to put their plans aside. The farmers' political project was again trumped by the politics of war. In the end, these events

conspired to win the day for the third-party option and thereby effectively end Canada's two-party system in national politics.

The war's end brought economic depression and, with it, deep popular disaffection and heightened class conflict. The dream of peace and
prosperity, clung to during the dark years of war, was abruptly snatched
away. Inflation, high interest rates, plant closures as industry adjusted
to the end of war production, high unemployment, a steep fall in wheat
prices, and a large war debt led to economic frustration and political
anger. This was particularly true among farmers and workers, the classes
burdened with the heaviest sacrifices for the war effort both at home
and in Europe. Going into politics as a third party became a foregone
conclusion for the organized farmers. The rise of increasingly aggressive
working-class struggles deeply disturbed the farmers, who saw them as
symptoms of a capitalist system bent on self-destruction. The growth in
militant working-class organizations, particularly the Industrial Workers
of the World (iww) and the One Big Union (obu), frightened the organized farmers, especially when the workers' battle crystallized in the
1919 Winnipeg General Strike. The *Grain Growers' Guide* denounced
the strike while blaming the current corrupt capitalist system, a system
incapable of fairness and justice and hence unable to bring harmony and
class peace to the nation.

The lingering postwar depression in agriculture and the general
downturn in other economic sectors—resulting in polarized class conflict between capital and labour—pushed the organized farmers into
political action. The third-party option was embraced with confidence.
The widely held view was the farmer had to "go into politics, or go out
of farming."⁹ Furthermore, the salvation of the nation lay in embracing
the leadership of "the Man behind the Plow," replacing the "deep furrows
of dissension" with "the level seed-bed of greater unity among men."¹⁰ In
1918 the cca issued a new version of the farmers' platform, submitting
it in 1919 to member organizations for discussion and approval. Revised
for the coming election in 1921, it was dubbed the *New National Policy*.
It was more detailed, far-reaching, and complete than earlier versions.

The protective tariff still occupied centre stage, but the indictment
was more brutally harsh, providing a back door for nothing less than a
general, if self-interested, condemnation of capitalism.¹¹ The new platform attributed to the tariff all of Canada's political and economic ills: the

existence of trusts, combines, and monopolies; exploitation of the whole population through the elimination of competition, the destruction of small industry, and the inflation of prices for manufactured goods; the creation of "a privileged class at the expense of the masses thus making the rich richer and the poor poorer"; rural depopulation resulting from driving farmers out of business; the undermining of the whole economy by bleeding agriculture, "the basic industry upon which the success of others depends." The tariff system encouraged capitalists to purchase political parties in order to ensure high levels of protection and thus secure higher profits. Indeed, it was "the chief corrupting influence in our national life,...lowering the standard of public morality." The list of tariff demands, if implemented, amounted to a virtually complete move to free trade, requiring a fundamental restructuring of the Canadian economy to the greatest advantage of farmers and consumers.

In addition, the platform presented a long list of fundamental reforms. It proposed a reform of the entire tax system: taxes on undeveloped lands and natural resources held for speculative purposes, and progressive graduated taxes on personal income, large inheritances, and corporate profits. It advocated the public ownership of the following economic sectors and industries: all natural resources (rights to develop by short lease through public auction); all transportation systems (rail, water, and air); telephone and telegraph systems; express shipping; all power development; and coal mines. It proposed a series of miscellaneous democratic reforms: Senate reform; an end to routine governing by order-in-council; disclosure of campaign donations and expenditures; publication of details on newspaper ownership; proportional representation; direct legislation (initiative, referendum, recall); full political equality for women; and the prohibition of alcohol.

The manifesto's labour program was a big disappointment for those arguing for effective farmer-labour unity. Discussions between labour and socialist parties and left-leaning elements of the farmers' movement went nowhere. The entire labour program was a call for relief for the unemployed and "the adoption of the principle of co-operation...in future relations between employer and employee—between capital and labour." The trade union movement and the various workers' parties were not particularly inspired by the platform. Labour candidates were not allowed to run under the Progressive banner. In line with the residue of group-government notions of agrarian populism, labour was expected to run candidates in the cities under its own banner.

Between 1919 and 1922 the organized farmers won some notable provincial victories and made a stunning federal showing. The strongest weapon in their arsenal, which included the *New National Policy* and a large and aroused organizational base, was the postwar depression. With the end of the war, Ottawa had cancelled the orderly marketing of the Board of Grain Supervisors. Under pressure from farmers, the government created the Canadian Wheat Board for the 1919 crop only and cancelled the board in 1920. Wheat prices on the open market collapsed, falling 67 per cent between October 1920 and December 1923. It was not just an agricultural depression, though that sector took the hardest hit. Given the centrality of the wheat economy, the depression very quickly became general. National real income, the total volume of business activity, and exports fell precipitously due to a 30 per cent drop in agricultural productivity. Working-class unemployment tripled.

In 1919 the United Farmers of Ontario (UFO) won 44 of 111 seats in Ontario and formed a coalition government with the support of eleven Labour Party members and three successful independent farmer candidates. In July 1921 the United Farmers of Alberta (UFA) swept to majority power in Alberta, while the Dominion Labour Party won four seats. (In July 1922 the United Farmers of Manitoba would win a narrow majority in Manitoba, forming a government with the support of six Independent Labour members.) Most attention, however, was riveted on the coming 1921 federal election. The organized farmers were elated by the results in Ontario and Alberta. Some among them even contemplated victory.

In the December 1921 federal election, the Progressive Party won fifty-eight seats, Independent Labour won three, and independent farm/ Progressive candidates picked up four. With sixty-five seats, the Progressive Party and its allies held the second-largest bloc of seats in the House and hence were eligible to form the official opposition. The organized farmers delivered in spades: eleven of twelve seats in Alberta; fifteen of sixteen in Saskatchewan; twelve of fifteen in Manitoba; and twenty-four of eighty-two in Ontario. It was an astonishing achievement and wholly unexpected by all but the organized farmers, who expected to do much better.

Clearly, on the face of it, the Progressive Party's strong showing and the successes at the provincial level suggested the party had a national electoral base with the capacity to deliver power in the future. But the party declined to become the official opposition, given its opposition to "partyism" and the lingering populist fantasy of "group government." These convictions made it impossible to build and consolidate a national party. The federal and provincial results simultaneously marked the organized farmers' greatest political success and the eve of the party's implosion and collapse.

It was a sad public spectacle, given the preceding years of hope and hard work. There was no ideological or programmatic coherence. Progressive MPs spent as much time attacking one another as they did the Liberal government or the Tory opposition. There was simply no agreement among Progressives on the policies essential for the organized farmers to win confidence in their leadership from other classes, especially the industrial working class and the urban middle classes. The Progressives expressed markedly ambivalent, ambiguous, and contradictory attitudes about the working class, failing to develop a coherent policy on wages, union recognition, and the right to strike. No agreement existed on the economic role of the state. The Progressives had no alternative credible plan for industrial modernization to replace the abolition of tariffs and the introduction of free trade. There was a bloody-minded resistance to the establishment of a coherent federal political party separate from the founding farmer organizations and open to inviting non-farmers to join the crusade. As Progressive MPs in the House became a ridiculous spectacle of disunity and discord, public support declined quickly. In the elections of 1925 and 1926 the Progressive Party effectively collapsed. In the 1930 election the party held only twelve seats, nine of which were delivered by the UFA in Alberta.

The farmer governments in Ontario and Manitoba did not fare well. In 1923 the UFO government was defeated, broken apart by a debate between those who wanted to keep it farmer-only and those who advocated "broadening out" to win a wider base of support. The UFO's membership of sixty thousand had collapsed to thirty thousand in 1922, largely due to political divisions. In Manitoba the UFM government gradually edged back into the Liberal fold, uncertain of exactly what a farmers' government should be doing that was different from what Liberals advocated. Only the UFA government in Alberta survived, but it governed conservatively, constantly rejecting the demands of the UFA's membership for more progressive and innovative legislation.

The crisis of the Progressive Party reflected a crisis at its base. In the early 1920s, membership in farmers' organizations fell precipitously. It was ironic that at what appeared to be the moment of its greatest success, the organized farmers' movement began to disintegrate. Organizations bled members after 1921: the UFO fell from 60,000 to 30,000; the UFM from 38,000 to 15,000; the SGGA from 29,000 to 21,000; and the UFA from 16,000 to 11,000. In 1923 the UFO withdrew from politics. Ridiculed as "Liberals in a hurry," the UFM established an arm's-length relationship with its political offspring, a provincial Progressive Party, and then amalgamation with the Liberals in the Liberal-Progressive Party.[12] In 1923 the CCA withdrew its support for national political action, leaving politics to provincial organizations and thus ending the national organizational focus for farmer political action. For the organized farmers, events seemed to confirm the worst fears of those who had warned against political action from the start: that it would divide and destroy farmers' organizations.

The collapse of the Progressive Party in the House of Commons was hurried by the political astuteness of William Lyon Mackenzie King, Laurier's successor as Liberal leader. As a result of the Progressive upsurge, King found himself prime minister of a government with a razor-thin majority. To govern for the full term, King needed support from enough Progressive MPs to sustain the government on key votes, and to secure this he made significant concessions to farmers. In 1922, King reimposed the Crow rate of lower freight rates on grain and flour moving east and agricultural inputs moving west. Laurier had granted this concession to farmers in 1897; the Tory government had cancelled it under the War Measures Act in 1919. There followed a series of multi-year tariff reductions on farm machinery, trucks, and cars. Federal agricultural credit assistance was established. The Wheat Board was re-established, to the delight of farmers, having been approved quickly by the House of Commons and the legislatures of Alberta and Saskatchewan. Aggressive lobbying by the private grain trade through the Winnipeg Grain Exchange persuaded the Manitoba legislature to refuse to pass the necessary enabling legislation, thus torpedoing the board's resurrection. At a key moment King secured the support of a bloc of Progressive MPs by promising federal old-age pensions. King won a majority victory in 1926 with the help of eight Liberal-Progressive MPs (seven from Manitoba;

one from Saskatchewan) and he fulfilled the promise in 1927 with the Old Age Pensions Act, the first brick in the welfare state. The Progressive Party was truly a meteoric political phenomenon, entering and exiting the effective political stage within five years.

The Rise of the United Farmers of Canada (Saskatchewan Section)

Williams entered farming at the height of the postwar depression, just a year before wheat prices steeply declined and a year after the Wheat Board was cancelled. In 1921 he witnessed the rise of the Progressive Party and the spectacle that quickly followed as it began to disintegrate. That year, Williams's first wheat crop was damaged by rain during harvest, resulting in a low grade and a poor price. In 1922, like all farmers, he faced the collapse in wheat prices and a growing debt. He and his new family faced hard times. Yet Williams was more fortunate than many— his $15.75 monthly war pension kept food on the table.

Williams's choice of the FUC over the SGGA was not unusual in the early 1920s, especially among younger farmers and those on the left in the provincial association. The SGGA, increasingly discredited among much of its popular base, continued to lose members: its membership fell to fifteen thousand in 1922. Since the beginning it was a close friend of the Liberal Party in the province, so close that leaders of the SGGA often served as sitting MLAs and cabinet ministers. The Liberals proudly referred to themselves as the farmers' party. The SGGA was a loose organization; unlike the UFO and UFA, which both strictly limited membership to farmers, SGGA membership was open to anyone willing to pay the fee. Aspiring politicians, as well as entrepreneurs and professionals seeking profitable networks among farmers, joined to work the delegates at conventions. During the push to go into provincial politics, a foot-dragging cabal of top SGGA leaders in league with the Liberal Party effectively killed resolutions passed by convention directing the SGGA to do so. As a result, the association never went into politics at the provincial level, assuring the continuing hegemony of the Liberal Party. The SGGA did play a significant role in the 1921 federal election, but through an arm's-length New National Policy Association, winning fifteen of sixteen seats. Due to continuing divisive clashes over whether to actively enter provincial politics, and the alliance between the top SGGA leadership and the Liberal Party, the 1924 convention officially withdrew the SGGA from politics. The provincial Liberal Party was saved from the agrarian upsurge, but the battle over farmer political action had fractured the close relationship between the SGGA and the Liberals, particularly after the association supported the Progressive Party in the 1921 election.

In December 1921 in Ituna, a town hall meeting of disillusioned farmers agreed to work to establish the Farmers' Union of Canada. The meeting approved a few basic principles: "the farmers of Canada had to unite to I. protect themselves, II. to obtain complete control of their produce, III. to market their produce themselves."[13] There would be no pleading with governments to help farmers. There would be no forays into electoral politics to distract and divide them. Rather, one big union of farmers must be organized to take control over the marketing of all agricultural products. Class power in the marketplace was the goal.

The FUC held its founding convention in Saskatoon in July 1922, declaring a clear intention to focus on the marketing issue and resist the temptation of electoral politics. The estimated few hundred members (the FUC was secretive about its membership, its finances, and internal debates) were determined to avoid the fate of the SGGA. A strict membership criterion was imposed: only a "bona fide farmer" could join.[14] No elected officer could hold a position for more than two consecutive one-year terms. No elected MLA or MP of a party in government was welcome. No one in a "paid political office"—that is, members of opposition parties—could serve as a convention delegate. A "bona fide farmer" was strictly defined as "a man or woman in actual residence on his or her own farm, or a retired farmer, man or woman, or a farm wife or widow, living on the proceeds of his or her farm and not engaged in other business." The FUC was to be "non-party political and non-sectarian." What was meant by this became clear as the organization began to act—it was very much involved in a political class struggle, but not in electoral party politics. The FUC did not hold its conventions in public. Attention from what was seen as a hostile capitalist press was not welcome. Looking back on the wreckage of the farmers' movements in Saskatchewan and Canada, the FUC was determined to construct a militant, activist farmers' organization for working farmers, undiluted by an influx of non-farm members or infiltration by aspiring or existing partisan politicians.

Ideologically the FUC was agrarian populist, but it adopted the Marxist notion of class struggle as the engine of historical development and was inspired by the OBU, the main expression of militant working-class syndicalism. The preamble of the FUC constitution was a version of the OBU's, revised from a farmer's perspective; it was really more a manifesto than a preamble. According to the manifesto, a continuous struggle occurs between two antagonistic classes: "those who possess and do not produce and those who produce[;] alongside this main division, all other classifications fade into insignificance." This struggle leads to a concentration of the ownership of industry and wealth in the hands of "finance," compelling farmers to organize. The "Great Agricultural Class" must unite to speak with one voice and exert its true political and economic power. Two other main classes—"Organized Labor Unions and Organized Capitalists"—are "paid by the Unorganized Tillers of the Soil, lengthening their hours of labor, reducing the profits accruing to them, increasing their responsibilities and lowering their standard of living." The farmers "as a class have the power in number, if thoroughly united in a Common Brotherhood,...to fix their own price above the cost of production, a price reasonable towards producer and consumer."[15]

Clearly such a hard-edged orientation to class struggle did not sit well with the more staid SGGA or prominent western politicians. In 1923 Clifford Sifton attacked the FUC as "an out and out radical deadbeat organization, appealing directly to the impecunious and those so loaded with debt that they do not expect to get out of debt."[16] Relations with the SGGA became openly hostile, especially when the FUC began to draw members away from the old organization, which viewed itself as the farmer's only legitimate voice. In its pamphlets the FUC attacked capitalism, especially finance capitalism, in terms of the Douglas system of social credit, declaring that the "system of finance" was "the basic cause of our ever-increasing economic troubles." The "great pyramid of debt" imposed on farmers required a national, publicly owned bank lending at cost. The cause of "poverty in the midst of plenty" was not "over-production but under-consumption due to the lack of purchasing power." The root cause of all economic troubles was the private ownership of the means of production and the banks, which prevented the construction of a truly just and cooperative society.

Upon joining the FUC, Williams had found his political home, and he committed himself to the work of the organization with energy and determination. He quickly rose to prominence, becoming a member of the executive under the mentorship of the president, L. P. McNamee. Williams and McNamee drafted the FUC's constitution, establishing its strict membership criteria and rules governing meetings open only to members. In order to join, a new member required the approval of members of the local and swore an oath of loyalty. A member could be expelled by the members of the local for failing to adhere to FUC rules and policies.

Williams proved to be a clear thinker, a persuasive speaker, and a compelling writer. Hired as an organizer to recruit members and establish locals, he proved to be an effective grassroots organizer. He rarely left a rural community without leaving an FUC local behind. More importantly, his name became widely known both within the organization and across rural Saskatchewan for the debt adjustment plan he drafted (and with which his name was forever associated).

The war boom in agriculture led to a large increase in the number and size of farms in the province and a large investment in farm mechanization in response to the growing demand for wheat and a dramatic rise in wages for farm labour. The demand for recruits for the army and the attraction of high wages in industrial war production made farm workers increasingly hard to find. Farmers borrowed heavily to expand and improve their farms and to buy the latest farm machinery. The boom led to high interest rates, making borrowing increasingly expensive as the war went on and putting pressure on farmers in servicing their debt, which often grew with each spring planting and each fall harvest. With boom-time prices for wheat, the situation was manageable. When the 1920–23 depression hit and wheat prices collapsed, farmers faced difficulties in meeting debt obligations. Many faced bankruptcy and foreclosure. The FUC noted that complaints about an impossible debt load due to falling prices and high wartime interest rates were the most common among aroused and angry farmers. As a working farmer, Williams faced the same situation. In 1923 he was named secretary of the FUC's Debt Adjustment Committee, charged with developing a plan for dealing with the farm debt crisis.[17] Williams's *Debt Adjustment Plan*—an instant hit among farmers—was so popular that the SGGA endorsed it and it became the template for farm organizations across Canada. The plan was anathema to finance capitalists, who accordingly denounced it as too radical and impractical. No Prairie provincial government adopted the plan, including the UFA government in Alberta, despite its popularity among farmers. The official position was that, despite its many merits, the plan was beyond the constitutional power of a province without the consent of Ottawa, and Ottawa was unlikely to consent. But to the working farmer, the plan seemed eminently fair and reasonable.

The plan proposed provincial arbitration boards composed of a representative of the farmer-debtor, a representative of the creditor, and a third person mutually acceptable to the other two. No debt proceeding could begin against the farmer-debtor until the case was first heard by the board. The board would become trustees of the debtor's assets until final disposition. The decision of the board would be final and legally binding on all parties. But the plan went further, providing protection of the farmer-debtor even after a finding in the creditor's favour (an inevitable outcome, since farmers appealing to the board would be either bankrupt or on the verge of bankruptcy, a short step from foreclosure and seizure of assets). A series of clauses outlined what would be exempted from seizure for debt: sufficient cash or crops must remain with the farmer for covering living and operating expenses; cash or crops sufficient for seed, feed, taxes, and land payments were exempt. Debt repayment could occur over thirty-four years, at a fixed interest rate of 6 per cent. In the case of crop failure, the farmer-debtor was entitled to a provincial loan, which would be rolled into his existing debt on the same terms. The farmer retained full control of his operation, including making marketing decisions. Clearly the plan sought to establish a quasi-judicial means of reconciling the interests of the farmer-debtor and the creditor on terms of unprecedented advantage to the farmer-debtor. The exemptions protected from seizure for debt left little for the creditor to proceed against in seeking a legal remedy, especially at a time of depression or catastrophic crop failure. Above all, it kept the working farmer on the land in full control of his farm and his business decisions. The foreclosure and seizure of farms for debt would become extremely rare—and that was the whole point of the plan.

The FUC did not just issue pamphlets and write policy documents. It carried out an ambitious program of internal education to equip its members with a full understanding of the system they were fighting. It engaged in militant direct action on occasion, and held well-attended public meetings to arouse the farmers against the capitalist system. Locals had considerable freedom of action and discussion. Some FUC locals organized and enforced boycotts of sheriff sales of land seized from bank-rupted farmers. They held public meetings to denounce the government for not adopting an effective debt adjustment plan and sought support for a plan to defy the government and the banks by unilaterally declaring a moratorium through refusing to make debt payments. Some locals held meetings calling for "mass resistance" against property seizures for debt if the government failed to deal with the debt crisis. One local proposed that the FUC affiliate with the International Council of Peasants, a radical organization strongly influenced by the Communist Party. (The same local denounced the Boy Scouts and army cadets as "agencies of the present ruling class.") The FUC took its non-sectarian political position seriously. All shades of political radicalism were welcome and locals were free to debate any policies they wished. Such proposals typically failed on the floor of the provincial convention, but they reflected a growing shift to the left in the organization and among farmers.

By the summer of 1923, Ottawa had made it clear that the compulsory, universal marketing model of the wartime wheat board was dead. This temporarily ended the debate among organized farmers, who had polarized those who favoured a compulsory, universal model and those who preferred a voluntary approach. The Alberta and Saskatchewan legislatures favoured a voluntary cooperative marketing approach, urging action by organized farmers. Each year, SGGA conventions expressed virtually unanimous support for cooperative marketing and demanded a plan from the leadership. But the leaders continued to equivocate on the issue, failing to come up with a plan of action. The contract cooperative wheat pool idea, in which farmers signed contracts to market their wheat through the pool, was already well established in the U.S. Midwest. Aaron Sapiro, a populist lawyer from New York, played a central role in assisting farmers in organizing and establishing pools in the United States. He was invited to Alberta in 1923 by the UFA, with the blessing of the UFA government to help organize a pool in Alberta. The campaign took off, and in short order twenty-six thousand farmers in that province enjoyed a cooperative pool marketing option. Pointing to the instant success of the

Alberta pool movement, Saskatchewan farmers grew angry at the SGGA's failure to act decisively. Rumours spread that a small clique of former SGGA leaders, working with business interests, planned to establish a private cooperative marketing organization and then issue an invitation to farmers to join, with an expectation of handsome personal financial returns. This was the final straw for the FUC leadership.

The FUC decided to organize a pool on its own, ignoring the SGGA. The FUC proposed that farmers sign a five-year contract to market their wheat through the pool. The pool would be a democratic, member-owned cooperative. Following the advice Sapiro had given in Alberta, the pool would pay the farmer an initial price upon delivery; it would then market the wheat, seeking the best price in national and international markets. If there was a cash surplus after paying all costs, as there typically was, it was distributed to the farmers based on the amount of wheat each had delivered to the pool. Thus, the pool was nonprofit. Every member received the same initial and final price for each bushel of wheat delivered. Sapiro agreed to help in the Saskatchewan campaign. Williams was selected as the FUC's lead organizer and advocate of the plan. The two men travelled the province, speaking to overflow audiences and exhorting farmers to sign up and free themselves of the shackles of the private grain trade. The plan proved wildly popular, and farmers flocked to sign up. A chastened SGGA petitioned to join the FUC in a joint campaign. The FUC agreed, and the board of the wheat pool was jointly composed of FUC and SGGA representatives. By the end of the campaign, forty-five thousand farmers had signed contracts. In 1926, over 73 per cent of seeded acreage in Saskatchewan was under contract to the pool. In the minds of farmers, the credit for pulling this off so quickly and successfully went to Williams and the FUC. Williams's debt adjustment plan had made him a household name in rural Saskatchewan, and the wheat pool campaign elevated his reputation to that of one of the most effective farm leaders in the province.

In ordinary times the FUC's organizational toughness and left-leaning ideology would have doomed it to remain a rather small, militant pressure group on the left of the larger farm movement. But events had intervened, catapulting the FUC to the undisputed leadership of Saskatchewan's farmers in the campaign to organize the pool. Its militancy, its uncompromising approach, and its organizational discipline were just what Saskatchewan farmers needed at the time to take wheat marketing away from the private grain trade. And Williams proved he had the organizational and oratorical skills to win and move farmers forward to united, collective action. By 1924 the FUC's few hundred members at the founding convention had grown to ten thousand. And at the end of the victorious campaign, Williams was a figure revered around the kitchen tables of farm homes, feared among the business community, and loathed by the private grain trade.

Williams, however, did not rest on his laurels. He believed the voluntary wheat pool was merely a half measure. For him, and for the FUC, only a fully "socialized" cooperative marketing system, democratically controlled by farmers, was acceptable. Such a system had to be a compulsory 100 per cent cooperative operation. If a majority of farmers voted in favour of a 100 per cent compulsory pool, then all farmers had to be compelled by law to join. Controlling the marketing of 73 per cent of seeded acreage, as in 1926, was a step forward, but the other 27 per cent remained controlled by the private trade. Farmers selling to the private market benefited from the pool, since the private grain trade had to be competitive with the pool's price, yet those farmers paid none of the pool's costs—for administration, shipping, handling, storage, and marketing. Furthermore, Williams recognized that the private grain trade would spare neither effort nor expense to win farmers from the wheat pool, given the huge losses they suffered. The private trade would do everything it could to break the pool. Since the pool was voluntary, there was a danger that individual farmers could be enticed one by one to shift back to the private market if the price was right. As far as Williams was concerned, the job remained unfinished until a 100 per cent compulsory pool was in place and the door had been permanently slammed on the private grain trade.

Williams believed that winning political power was crucial to making the fundamental changes necessary to build a better world. He pushed arguments in favour of the necessity for political action at every opportunity, despite strong resistance from most of the FUC leadership. Frustrated by the FUC's uncompromising resistance to electoral political action, Williams, and those who agreed with him, decided to organize a political vehicle independent of the FUC. As far as they were concerned, the provincial Progressive Party was unacceptable. It had already failed miserably, desperately clinging to a few seats in the legislature for no good reason. Besides, the Progressives were not a true farmers' party. In a letter to the *Western Producer*, Williams declared, "Their leader is not a farmer, nor does he have the farmer viewpoint; also the Progressives contest urban seats which no farmer group has the right to do. Such seats should be left to the industrial and labour groups to contest."[18]

In December 1924, the Farmers' Political Association (FPA) was founded, with Williams as *de facto* leader. The FPA held a founding convention at Bulyea, Saskatchewan, on December 17, 1924. It approved a platform, widely distributed in the province over Williams's name as secretary-treasurer and provincial secretary. Williams was the public spokesperson for the organization. Undoubtedly, he had drafted the platform, had organized the convention, and proceeded to seek support through many submissions to the *Western Producer*, thanks to a sympathetic editor. The FPA platform—which provides a clear distillation of Williams's political thinking at the time—was a political restatement of the many principles and policies of the FUC, presented as a "distinctly farmers' platform, designed primarily to benefit the basic industry." The FPA would only organize in rural school districts and was "to be regarded as the farmers' political organ of this Province, and [would] confine its candidates to Farmers and its activities to agricultural seats." The FPA advocated group economic action and group government. In a letter to the *Western Producer*, Williams outlined the FPA's core position:

> (1) That normal production must be guaranteed and the maximum of production must be steadily sought after; (2) That the equitable distribution of wealth produced must be effected; (3) That no economic group must be allowed to dominate the other economic groups of the social structure.[19]

Williams still endorsed agrarian populism, tied to certain fundamental socialist ideas: class struggle was the key to seeking fundamental change, wealth should be more fairly distributed, domination and control of government had to be taken from the hands of the capitalists, and the basic purpose of production should be to provide for the general welfare of humanity, not to profit capitalists. Thus articulating key principles of the FUC, Williams and the FPA clearly hoped the success of the wheat pool campaign and the growth in prominence of the FUC would spill over into the political arena, winning farmers to the new political option.

The FUC leadership was annoyed with Williams's violation of their organization's fundamental opposition to electoral political action. They invoked the constitutional rules Williams had helped draft. His punishment was not expulsion, but he was censured by the FUC board and fired as an organizer. Meanwhile, farmers, happy and busy with the successful drive to establish a wheat pool, failed to flock to the FPA. Prosperity returned in 1925–26 as wheat prices rose. For the first time since the days of the wartime wheat board, farmers who joined the pool got a fair final price for their wheat. Williams and his group, having been rebuked sternly by the FUC and largely ignored by rank-and-file farmers, ran no candidates in the June 1925 provincial election. They quietly buried the FPA, and Williams again turned his full attention to the work of the FUC, to the delight of the leadership. Williams, somewhat disillusioned, complained privately, "I am persuaded that the average man does not want equalization of opportunity or just distribution of reward for service rendered. Rather do they want personal advantage or at the best group advantage, and the greatest amount of reward possible."[20] The experience convinced him that any organization hoping to make progressive change had to make a serious commitment to the political education of its rank-and-file members. Williams did not surrender his conviction as to the necessity of political action. He realized, however, that the conditions for success, both within the FUC and among farmers, did not yet exist.

In the wake of the successful joint FUC/SGGA wheat pool campaign, the SGGA petitioned the FUC to amalgamate into one united organization. The reason was clear: the SGGA's membership was in steep decline. The FUC emerged as the larger farmer organization. Both sides agreed it made sense to unite; rather than two competing organizations that fought each other for members and influence, a united organization would be more influential by allowing the organized farmers of the province to speak with one voice. The combined membership of the new organization would fluctuate annually between twenty and thirty thousand members. But the FUC leadership and many among its members were leery about the proposal, fearing the SGGA influx would water down the organization and divert it from its fundamental principles and goals. Hence, the FUC entered into the July 1926 negotiations with reservations.

The FUC board directed President John Stoneman to take a hard line in negotiations with the SGGA's George Edwards. If the negotiations fell through on principled grounds, the FUC was confident that it could continue to displace the SGGA among farmers. Stoneman was determined that the new organization must closely resemble the FUC in all important respects.

Expecting tough bargaining, Stoneman was surprised when he won all fundamental arguments, as Edwards made concession after concession. The SGGA demanded two things as absolute conditions for amalgamation: the word "union" would not appear in the name of the organization and the class-struggle preamble of the constitution had to go. On every other issue Edwards eventually yielded, but for minor housekeeping issues of little significance. The new organization adopted the FUC constitution—absent the preamble—which would limit the terms of office of the president and directors to two years in succession. This upset the SGGA leadership the most, since they had enjoyed routine re-election year after year. For some, holding high office in the SGGA had become largely an indefinite term; their former well-paid sinecures were now at risk. But they agreed, no doubt expecting they would emerge as the dominant leaders of the new organization, given their years of experience in the SGGA. The new organization was anointed the United Farmers of Canada (Saskatchewan Section) (UFC[SS]) and held a one-day founding convention on July 15, 1926. The interim executive was dominated by SGGA officers. The only FUC member was Stoneman, who was selected as president, while Edwards became vice-president. The first vice-president and the president of the women's section were SGGA stalwarts. All but Stoneman were in the top leadership of the provincial Progressive Party.

The first annual convention was set for February 1927.

Part II

THE DRIVE FOR POWER

Chapter 3

LEADING THE FARMERS INTO POLITICS

1926 to 1931

L ed by Williams and former FUC president McNamee, the left of
the FUC immediately organized within the new organization. The
Farmers' Educational League (FEL) began meeting in July 1926,
in parallel with the amalgamation negotiations and the founding convention. The FEL was determined that the UFC(SS) would not be diluted
by the excessive caution and conservatism of the old SGGA. Confident
of their base among former FUC members, and certain they could sway
left-leaning elements of the SGGA membership, the FEL became a very
public caucus within the UFC(SS), while denying that was what it was.
McNamee was named FEL president, with Williams serving as secretary
in 1926 and 1927. Under Williams's name, the FEL manifesto was circulated widely in the run up to the UFC(SS)'s February 1927 convention.

The manifesto very publicly challenged the right wing of the established agrarian movement and mobilized FUC members to attend
the convention. Williams and the left wing suspected the right wing
confidently assumed it would emerge as the leadership of the new organization. From this point on, the terms "right wing" and "left wing" were

used widely and openly to characterize the inevitable polarization. The "right wing" was the old guard from the conservative leadership of the SGGA and the increasingly irrelevant provincial Progressive Party. The rising "left wing" faction, rooted in the FUC, believed and didn't hesitate to imply that this group's time was past.

The manifesto asserted that the FEL was not "a competitor of the United Farmers of Canada," but rather intended to "work inside of every existing farmer organization with the object of welding them into a powerful mass movement." The FEL was "merely a means of co-ordinating radical thinking," leading to "less friction and more action." Its bluntly stated purpose was "to prevent a recurrence of splits in the ranks of the organized farmers through overconservatism on the part of the recognized leadership." The FEL was "a prodding machine" and "a vigilance committee":

> The Farmers' Educational League is an educational and agitational organization which bases its activities on the realities of the class struggle and endeavours to educate and organize the farmers to change the existing system of exploitation into one that will produce for use and not for profit...with the ultimate objective of a co-operative commonwealth in the full meaning of the term.[1]

The manifesto closed with a call for farmer-labour unity and for the development of a legislative program in preparation for the eventual establishment of a cooperative commonwealth government.

The manifesto was clear in its ideological orientation, but it avoided the word "socialism." It reflected the class-struggle position of the former FUC, focusing on the necessity of agrarian class unity. References to the previous failures of farm leadership reminded the membership of who had acted decisively to achieve the wheat pool and taken aggressive action to defend farmers from the burden of debt by agitating for effective debt adjustment. But its primary purpose was to wave the flag to get FUC delegates out to the first annual convention of the UFC(ss).

The UFC(ss) conventions in 1927 and 1928 constituted a preliminary struggle between right and left for control of the organization. The stakes were high. The prize was possession of what could be irresistible political power in the province. As the single organized voice of farmers in the province, the UFC(SS)—like its predecessor, the SGGA—had tremendous popular influence. In a province dominated by farmers, its political clout was enormous, if it decided to use it aggressively. The SGGA had kept the Liberals in power. Had the SGGA gone into provincial politics in the 1921 election, they doubtless would have defeated the Liberal government easily, just as the UFA had in Alberta. Even though the SGGA had not gone directly into politics, the organization had provided funding, influence, and organizational assistance in support of provincial and federal Progressive candidates. The federal Progressives had humiliated the Liberal Party, winning fifteen of Saskatchewan's sixteen seats with 61 per cent of the vote. (The SGGA, still cozy with the Liberal government, had provided provincial Progressives only *pro forma* support, but got fully behind the federal effort.)

Led by Edwards, the former SGGA president and the interim UFC(SS) vice-president, the right's political agenda was to steer the organization onto a moderate policy course while continuing to support the provincial Progressives (or whatever future form the party might take) to field candidates in future elections. Led by Williams, the left's political agenda was to steer the organization down the radical path pioneered by the FUC. The left, though strongly committed to political action in principle, was determined to block any move to support reformist-capitalist political action. When the UFC(SS) went into politics it would be on a clear socialist platform advocating deep structural changes in the economy.

The key organizational issue tested between right and left was the highly decentralized, democratic structure the UFC(SS) had inherited from the FUC. The structure had been carefully designed to ensure popular control of the organization and prevent the top-down elitism that characterized the SGGA. Nevertheless, like the FUC, the UFC(SS) conferred strong powers between conventions upon the board of directors and its executive committee, ensuring that the organization could act quickly on behalf of organized farmers between conventions. To prevent an entrenched leadership, members of the board and executive were limited to two consecutive one-year terms. Only bona fide working farmers could join, and each member had to be voted into membership at a local meeting. Only resolutions originating in the locals could come to the convention floor. Major changes in policy, or to the constitution, approved by convention had to be ratified by two-thirds of the locals after the convention. All delegates had to be elected by locals. The left was convinced that such a structure would ensure that the popular will of farmers, as a class, would be faithfully reflected in the UFC(SS)'s policies and leadership.

The proxy for the organizational battle was the limit of two consecutive one-year terms imposed on the top leadership. The right wanted this limit deleted, but hesitated to push for it prematurely; instead, they campaigned informally for the change among the membership, hoping to persuade a future convention. The left, however, went further in 1928 by adopting a democratic district council system of decision-making developed and presented by Williams: locals would feed resolutions into a district council for discussion and approval; the councils would send these to the board of directors; and the board would put them together into a coherent form and send them back to all locals for discussion prior to the convention. As a result, every delegate would arrive at the convention fully informed of the issues at stake and the thinking of all locals. In addition, each delegate would arrive with informed direction from the local she or he represented. The proposal passed handily. The view of the left was that not only would the democratic structure and limits on terms of office ensure popular control, but with this improvement the membership was fully informed of all policy proposals under consideration, and delegates would arrive with clear democratic direction from the locals.

The proxy for the policy battle became the 100 per cent compulsory pool. Though debated at the 1927 convention, no clear position was taken. It was a contentious issue. Farmers across the province were divided, and this was reflected at the convention. The left opted not to push the issue to decision in 1927, preferring the more prudent course of continuing discussion. Delegates were not yet ready to decide the issue. This debate sharply demarcated the "right wing" and the "left wing" in the minds of farmers and the public. The compulsory pool previously proposed by the FUC was seen as a necessary step in winning full class power in the market. It was repeatedly labelled as "socialistic" and "dictatorial" by opponents in the farm movement and among the business community. The SGGA leadership was committed to the voluntary approach, insisting this was a founding principle of the cooperative movement. The leaders of the newly founded Wheat Pool were firmly opposed to compulsory pooling. Feelings were high on the issue and neither side was prepared to compromise, since there was no compromise to be had—either you supported a compulsory pool or you did not. After a year of further discussion, a resolution favouring compulsory pooling was narrowly approved at the 1928 convention. The left wing believed that the narrow margin meant they needed only to educate farmers further to win them over to the idea. The key was to persuade the membership of the Wheat Pool to break with their leaders and support compulsory pooling.

The "left wing" came out of the 1927 and 1928 conventions stronger than they had expected when the FEL manifesto was issued. Williams was nominated for president at both conventions, based on his stature that derived from his work on debt adjustment and the pool campaign. He declined both times. In 1927 he won a seat on the board of directors, which in turn named him to the executive; in 1928 he ran for vice-president, defeating two opponents with strong SGGA credentials. Many members were not ready to clearly identify with either right or left, hence the boards elected in 1927 and 1928 contained SGGA and FUC stalwarts. Most importantly, in 1928 former FUC president Stoneman continued as president, now joined by Williams as vice-president. Which side would finally dominate the organization remained unclear, but the "left wing" was in the stronger position. Edwards was worried but still sanguine in his opinion that the right would prevail, as he noted in a letter to a friend:

> I am sorry to say that Geo. Williams of Semans was elected to that position [vice-president]. If I had known that there was any likelihood of his being elected, I would have stood for the position, and would have had no difficulty in again being elected. We had a very good Convention, and the only two things I am somewhat concerned over was passing a resolution in favour of Compulsory Pooling, although by a small majority, and electing an unreliable man for the Vice-President....But I rather fancy he will never go any higher.[2]

The final confrontation between right and left occurred at the 1929 convention, as key issues came to a head. The debate on compulsory pooling had to be resolved one way or the other. The Wheat Pool controlled about 50 per cent of each annual harvest, despite having contracts with 60 per cent of farmers. The private grain trade was still strong and was actively winning individual farmers away from the pool by offering better prices. The only solution was compulsory pooling by law. Given the effectiveness of the FEL and the rise of Williams to vice-president, an alternative right-wing leadership had to act quickly if the organization was to be won. The political issue had to be resolved. Both right and left were agreed on the necessity of political action, but had very different views on how this political intervention ought to proceed. Both faced the constitutional barrier in Section 2: the UFC(SS) "shall not, as an Association, ally itself with any political party or contribute any funds thereto."[3] Williams, in consultation with FEL and other activists, decided it was time for him to run for president.

Both sides worked hard to get their supporters to the 1929 convention, and over a thousand delegates attended. The atmosphere was tense, the debates hard-hitting on both sides. Aggressive lobbying during breaks, at meals, on the sidewalks, and in the hotels and billets never stopped. The left prevailed on each issue on which Williams had staked his candidacy for president. In the end Williams won, defeating five opponents including Edwards. The elections to the board of directors were less clear, since many members were still undecided between left and right. As it turned out, when the new board began meeting, left and right held ten seats each, with Williams as president and chair holding the deciding vote on the twenty-one-member board.

Efforts by the right to delete the constitutional clause outlawing political action failed, thus forestalling the plan to throw the weight of the UFC(SS) behind the Progressive Party in the coming June 1929 election. This left the matter of political action exactly where Williams wanted it. The field was clear for him to propose political action on a socialist program at a future time.

On the issue of compulsory pooling, Williams prudently decided not to polarize the convention on the issue, but to propose a careful approach in pushing it forward. He knew the opposition of the leaders of the Wheat Pool, dominated by Progressive Party adherents, would have to be countered by education and agitation among the membership at large. The price for wheat in 1929 was good, reducing the sense of urgency. Williams's carefully crafted resolution instructed the board to "formulate an education program, for the purpose of securing support of the farmers and the public generally, favouring legislation that will cause all grain produced in this province to be marketed through" the Wheat Pool. Edwards vehemently objected to the resolution, since it was one-sided; he proposed an amendment directing the board "to disseminate information in connection with any advantages or disadvantages and legal questions involved."[4] During the debate, delegates were reminded the UFC(SS) had supported compulsory pooling in principle in 1928 and therefore it made no sense to circulate information contrary to the organization's existing policy. The amendment was defeated. The original resolution passed overwhelmingly.

At the age of thirty-five, Williams had won the leadership of the most powerful political force in the province, defeating opponents of greater experience and long-established reputations in the organized farm movement. The FEL and Williams, clearly with strong support from members of the old FUC and the left of the SGGA, had out-organized and defeated the right. The right was shocked, having never expected that Williams could so quickly win the presidency. In truth, the FEL, with only a few dozen members, merely reflected and guided the rising left-wing sentiments of rank-and-file farmers. Williams was aware that the fight for control of the organization was far from over; therefore, his victory speech was carefully prepared to avoid sounding overly adventurous and to hold out the hand of reconciliation. Given that the convention had overwhelmingly passed a resolution calling for "the abolition of the present system of capitalist robbery," Williams's words sounded moderate.[5] At the same time, his words unmistakably heralded a new direction for the organized farmers of Saskatchewan—involving a commitment not just to battle for the best interests of farmers as a class, but also to use the class power of farmers to build a better world:

> I believe that as long as there is a single farm home in Saskatchewan where poverty looks in at the door, that just as long as there is a single piece of legislation not in the best interests of the people of Saskatchewan and as long as there is a single industry that is not operated and controlled co-operatively, just that long has this organization a duty to perform and a task undone.[6]

His speech was greeted with thunderous applause and a sustained standing ovation.

Upon Williams's unexpected victory, the right wing immediately embarked on a coordinated effort to drive him from office. Besides being uncomfortable with his left-leaning ideology, they disliked his populist openness with the membership and his efforts to put paid staffers under the direct political control of the elected leadership. Prior to the 1929 convention, Williams, while vice-president, had examined the books and discovered the UFC(SS) had inherited a large debt from the SGGA's trading company. This fact had not been revealed by the SGGA during amalgamation negotiations. The deception and the debt were then revealed at the 1929 convention, damaging the reputations of the old SGGA leadership. Williams, speaking as the newly elected president, assured angry delegates that the new administration would take all necessary austerity measures to eliminate the debt quickly. The right wing and the top bureaucracy were not happy with the austerity measures Williams was contemplating or with the fact that the debt and its origins had been aired openly at the convention. Williams issued a directive stating that paid staffers could no longer participate in debates at board meetings, unless invited to speak by elected members; staffers could also be asked to leave a meeting during debates on key controversial issues until a decision was made. The top bureaucracy had enjoyed a pivotal role in shaping and directing board decisions, often essentially running the organization. This had been the case in the SGGA. As far as the right wing and the bureaucratic elite were concerned, Williams's election had resulted from a coup by the left, and neither he nor the left-wing policies he proposed truly represented the general membership. If allowed to continue in office, he would wreck the organization. Convinced they could succeed in ousting Williams and win broad support from the membership, the right wing acted quickly.

The confrontation occurred at the board meeting of March 5 to 13, 1929, less than a month after the convention. An item of some contention was the cost-cutting measures proposed by Williams that were made necessary by the debt inherited from the SGGA. To set an example, Williams announced he would forego his $4,000 annual salary as president until the debt was retired, thus putting pressure on others drawing a salary and receiving per diems to embrace austerity sacrifices.

The women's president quickly followed suit. The next battle was the surprise resignation of the secretary-treasurer, W. M Thrasher. Thrasher declared a lack of confidence in Williams's leadership. He insisted the convention had made a mistake in supporting 100 per cent compulsory pooling, a measure that clearly contravened the basic principles of cooperatives. Hoping this might bring Williams to heel, the right was shocked when a motion to accept Thrasher's resignation was met with a tie vote, 10 to 10. Williams broke the tie, accepting the resignation. Suggesting a carefully laid ambush, four other staffers resigned immediately: head of the research department (George Edwards), head of the organization department, and the two lawyers heading up the legal department. They all echoed Thrasher's reasons. Again, Williams broke the tie to accept the resignations. Having thus decapitated the top bureaucracy, the right wing sought some conciliation and compromise, but efforts at conciliation failed. Williams's position was clear: it was the elected leadership who ran the affairs of the organization and decided policy, not the top bureaucracy, which served at the pleasure of the membership and their elected representatives.

The disgruntled staff went public, issuing a press release on March 12, 1929, that made front-page news in the Saskatoon *Star-Phoenix*, increasing tensions and making the battle a public issue.[7] The press statement expressed a lack of confidence in Williams, opposition to the 100 per cent compulsory pool, and allegations of a left-wing conspiracy led by FEL to capture the organization. It was alleged that Williams and the compulsory pool did not represent the views of a majority of members of the organization. Defending Williams, the UFC(SS) executive issued a release noting that "at the outset of the first session of the Board it was quite evident that a determined effort was being made to connect the President to the Educational League and force his resignation."[8] Although a founder and supporter of the FEL, Williams had severed his formal relationship with the organization in 1928. Nevertheless, it was clear that Williams and the FEL shared similar views on ideological and policy matters. The FEL remained a champion of Williams and the direction he set for the UFC(SS), continuing to act as a very public caucus within the organization.

In the ensuing uproar, a supporter of Williams introduced a motion of confidence in the president. Williams left the meeting while it was discussed. When the vice-president called the vote, it was a 10–10 tie. Rather than the vice-president (a Williams supporter) casting the deciding vote, a board member opposed to Williams suggested the chairman convey the discussion and the tied vote to Williams. Evidently it was hoped Williams would decide to resign voluntarily given the impasse. The following day Williams informed the board that he intended to continue as president until the next convention. It was his duty, since the convention had elected him, not the board. The vice-president announced that had he voted, he would have voted confidence in Williams. Some of the right-wing directors announced their intention to return to their districts to seek support for their lack of confidence in Williams—and if not sustained by the members, they would resign.

The final battle at the meeting was anti-climactic. The implementation of the 100 per cent compulsory pool convention resolution was discussed. The right wing wanted the board to ignore the instruction that only arguments and educational materials favouring the measure be included in the education campaign. Williams ruled that the board must follow the resolution as passed. His ruling was challenged, but again the vote tied and again Williams broke the tie. The last item on the agenda was the election of the executive. Only Williams's supporters agreed to stand and were elected by acclamation. Williams had prevailed. He had survived as president and now had a solidly supportive executive. But he knew the fight wasn't over. It would now occur in skirmishes in every local across the province as directors returned to their districts to report on the meeting.

When Williams's opponents returned to their locals, they learned that the rank and file overwhelmingly supported Williams and the education campaign about compulsory pooling. The farmers told them to follow the convention resolution and support the president or resign. Four did so and were replaced by supporters of Williams. A new administrative staff was hired. George Edwards and his supporters tried to persuade members to support a special summer convention to oust Williams and clean up "the mess." In a letter to a supporter, Edwards stated:

> I have become convinced that a summer convention would
> be about the best way of cleaning up the mess, and giving the
> sick patient, the UFC, a chance for life. If this is not done, I am

afraid that there will be such a number of withdrawals that
the whole life of the organization will be endangered.[9]

The effort failed. There was little support for a special convention.
Contrary to the gloomy predictions of the organization's collapse under
Williams, the UFC(SS) grew to thirty-one thousand members by 1930.

The UFC(SS) campaign for 100 per cent compulsory pooling went
from victory to victory. Williams personally assembled the educational materials, as well as writing pamphlets marshalling arguments.
His reputation as an expert on the national and world grain-marketing
systems grew, as he educated himself on the details of a complex and
often opaque system. Though the leadership of the Wheat Pool and the
Progressive Party remained firmly opposed, as early as 1927 delegates at
the Wheat Pool convention passed a motion requesting a thorough discussion of the issue through the UFC(SS). Farmers, having experienced
the booms and busts in the cycle of wheat prices, were eager to consider
anything that might stabilize prices and ensure they got a fair share of the
final price gained in the market. The 1930 UFC(SS) convention passed a
resolution to continue the aggressive campaign in favour of compulsory
pooling, with only three dissenting votes.

It is unclear whether the campaign would have succeeded as well as
it did had the October 1929 crash on Wall Street not occurred. Though
unaware that the decade-long Great Depression had just begun, farmers
instantly saw the merits of compulsory pooling when the average wheat
price went into a free fall, from $1.03 a bushel in 1929 to 47 cents in 1930.
Further persuasion was provided when the Wheat Pool made a serious
overpayment on the 1929 crop. When the dust had settled, the Wheat
Pool faced a debt of over $15 million and required a government bailout.
The price instability threatened the farmers' most cherished institution.
Accordingly, the June 1930 Wheat Pool convention overwhelmingly
passed a resolution to hold a referendum among members on whether
the compulsory pool should be enforced by law if two-thirds of farmers agreed, as long as it remained member-controlled. The ballots were
mailed in July. The UFC(SS) paid for a province-wide radio broadcast
by Williams to plead the case; after a brief tutorial on developments in
the world marketing system and farmer-driven efforts around the world
to achieve orderly and fair marketing, he declared, "The day is almost

here when we can link up" with "a world's wheat marketing arrangement which can set wheats at their relative prices, and do away with both the dumping and the speculation....Let the farmers of Saskatchewan obtain a 100 per cent pool, and I have every confidence that the farmers of Manitoba and Alberta will have the good sense to follow suit."[10] A total of 48,466 pool members voted, with 34,621 in favour—a victory of over 70 per cent. Williams and the UFC(ss) were completely vindicated. It was clear who spoke for the farmers of Saskatchewan.

The Wheat Pool petitioned the government to enact the necessary legislation. A coalition of the right wing of the farmers' movement joined the business lobby to organize the Association Opposing a Compulsory Pool, attempting to persuade the government to refuse to do so. In response, the UFC(ss) organized a February 19, 1931, demonstration on the legislative grounds, calling on farmers in favour of compulsory pooling to make their position clear. More than fifteen thousand farmers showed up. The convention of the Saskatchewan Association of Rural Municipalities unanimously endorsed the compulsory pool. The newly elected government of Premier J. T. M. Anderson passed the requested laws that spring: the Grain Marketing Act, 1931 and the Referendum Act, 1931. The Grain Marketing Act was later ruled *ultra vires* by the Saskatchewan Court of Appeal. The UFC(ss) did not bother to appeal, but instead confronted more serious problems as the downward economic spiral continued. The average price for wheat fell to 38 cents in 1931 and 35 cents in 1932.

Though still acting as the organized voice of farmers in the class struggle, the UFC(ss) under Williams's leadership also presented itself as the voice of broad political and economic reforms in the interests of the wider public. It made a serious effort to recruit non-Anglo-Saxon farmers. Thanks to Ottawa's policy of relatively unrestricted immigration, the ethnic composition of Saskatchewan's farmers was changing dramatically; in particular, immigration from Eastern Europe increased rapidly. Many such immigrants, often escaping persecution by autocratic governments, were on the broad ideological left. While the SGGA had largely ignored this expanding demographic, the UFC(ss) under Williams welcomed them. Its central focus remained on issues of direct interest to farmers, and agriculture was still presented as the first industry on which all others depended; but a concerted effort was made to broaden its appeal beyond a narrow agrarian class focus. Even on the tariff issue, which still occupied centre stage, the UFC(SS) presented the issue as one of general justice and fairness for all:

> We desire to build up in Canada, a well-rounded Dominion, where the best of feeling prevails between class and class, province and province, and believe that this can only be done by treating fairly all classes and parts of the country, and eliminating all special privileges to any class or section.[11]

In the 1929 version of its tariff demands, the UFC(SS) widened its appeal by detailing the advantages to consumers and to all classes, except the industrial capitalist class, of tariff reductions and ultimate abolition. What it proposed, therefore, was not a reform in the narrow interest of farmers, but one leading to a more just and rational economic order. As he studied world markets for agricultural commodities, Williams began to recognize that tariffs also hurt Canada's farmers in other ways; for instance, he found that protective tariffs blocked many markets from Saskatchewan's farmers. His position on tariffs became more nuanced, but retained its ever-present class edge:

> At the present time [Canada] is a country torn between two policies, that of free trade for agriculturalists and the present tariff for the industrial magnates. The present tariff, to my mind, tends to make more millionaires, but does not make for a united Canada.[12]

In addition to comprehensive policy proposals on key agricultural issues, the UFC(SS) adopted and disseminated policies on such matters as life insurance, affordable funerals, immigration reform, the cessation of cadet training, plans for world peace, welfare measures to protect women and children, publicly funded health care, educational reform, and the need to develop cooperatives in all spheres of economic life. Many of these ideas had been current in the old SGGA, but the UFC(SS) made them a central focus of public education and agitation. Behind all such proposals for reform were arguments that the political economy as a whole had to be transformed into a cooperative commonwealth. The UFC(SS), given the increasingly comprehensive set of policies presented to the public, became a political party in all but name.

The left of the farm movement had grown increasingly frustrated with the deterioration of politics in the province throughout the 1920s. Williams, like many young activists, was eager to see a left-wing party emerge to carry the ideological message of left-wing agrarian populism linked to socialism. The FUC and the apathy of farmers had blocked his efforts in 1924–25. In 1927, now a member of the new UFC(SS), Williams proposed a motion at a meeting of the Semans local—his own—that the organization work toward an alliance with labour to form a socialist political party. The local, no doubt persuaded by Williams's passion and eloquence, passed the motion; however, the local rescinded the motion at its next meeting, in Williams's absence. It would not go to the first annual UFC(SS) convention, but the local sent Williams as a delegate.

The provincial Progressive Party occupied what was publicly seen as the left of the electoral spectrum. Left agrarian activists viewed the party as hopelessly conservative and organizationally moribund, and therefore a roadblock to a relevant left-wing party. This was the reasoning behind Williams's successful move to block the right-wing effort to change the constitution at the 1928 convention in order to throw the UFC(SS)'s resources and influence behind the provincial Progressives in the June 1929 provincial election. He made very clear the UFC(SS) did not support the provincial Progressives, and he did the same in the July 1930 federal election, refusing to endorse the new incarnation of the federal Progressives, the Saskatchewan Farmers' Political Association (SFPA). The SFPA decided not to present a detailed program to which all candidates were committed, leaving it up to constituencies to choose the issues on which to campaign. Writing in the *Western Producer*, Williams declared, "[It is] political chicanery for any political party to be able to have one of their candidates stand on one platform in one constituency and be elected and for another to stand on the opposite side of the question in another constituency and get elected."[13] The UFC(SS) provided its members with a list of central policy issues and suggested they refuse to support any candidate who failed to embrace the farmers' cause. Recalling the mess in Ottawa when the Progressives elected sixty-five members with no coherent program, Williams was determined that the next serious political intervention by the organized farmers would be on a clear socialist program. (The Progressives in Saskatchewan did very poorly in 1929 and 1930: five provincial seats with less than 7 per cent of the vote; two federal seats with 8 per cent.)

In the early 1920s the provincial Progressives presented cautious programs and failed to capture the political leadership of Saskatchewan's increasingly radicalizing farmers. In the absence of support from the SGGA, which remained closely allied with the Liberals, and unwilling to break to the left of the SGGA, the Progressives remained on the political sidelines. A detailed study concluded the Progressives were "a thoroughly conservative force." The crucial middle leadership was mainly middle-class urban professionals and prosperous farmers—well educated, entirely Protestant, overwhelmingly Anglo-Saxon—actively involved as directors and officers in the SGGA and/or successful cooperative institutions and cautiously moderate in political outlook. The few workers in the party were largely skilled tradesmen, often small construction contractors. Progressive views on the working class and its struggles were deeply divided, ranging from unapologetically anti-labour to sympathetic to labour's cause. The party was unable to make the shift to the increasingly popular idea of the cooperative commonwealth until late in the game. Such basic disagreements and lack of political vision reflected the "untenable and ephemeral nature of Saskatchewan progressivism."[14]

The political situation in the province therefore became a morass of confusion and remained so throughout the 1920s. Though the Liberals remained easily in power (they had ruled the province since its founding in 1905), the government became a "beleaguered machine."[15] The Opposition in the legislature, composed of Tories, Progressives, and Independents, was united only by a single-minded passion to oust the Liberals. The Liberals, as relations soured with the SGGA, opted for all-out partisanship, dropping all pretense of being a farmers' party. In reality, all parties claimed to represent the farmers' best interests, including the many Independents elected in rural seats on "anti-partyism" platforms. The overwhelming majority of MLAs of all parties were farmers, rising in the legislature to speak on behalf of farmers. Each year, the big demands by farmers for federal agricultural policies were passed unanimously by the legislature and forwarded to Ottawa for action. But with the legitimacy of friendliness of the SGGA gone, and sustained attacks on the corruption of "partyism" by the FUC and then the new UFC(SS), the Liberals depended more and more on the evocation of partisan loyalty and the judicious application of blatant patronage to stay in power.

From 1921 to 1929 the opposition parties united to expose Liberal corruption and patronage with relentless dedication, arguing that the Liberal "machine" was unfit to govern.[16] Little else united the opposition. The effect was a deepening of the growing public cynicism about party politics and an undermining of Liberal hegemony. Because the left of the farmers' movement had opted out of political action, there was little debate about larger issues. The Tories were rooted in the provincial rights movement, having contested the 1905 election under that banner. They had established their political reputation by opposing the terms imposed on the creation of Saskatchewan, fighting separate schools, denouncing unrestricted immigration that opened the gates to waves of non-Anglo-Saxon immigrants, and engaging in a great deal of anti-French and anti-Catholic posturing. The provincial Tories bore some of the burden of blame laid at the feet of Ottawa Tories for the hated tariff law, pandering to the "Special Interests," and cancelling the Crow rate and the Wheat Board. The Progressives rode the tide of the populist upsurge in 1921, but had no clear idea of what to propose as an alternative governing program. Certainly, they didn't like Liberal patronage and corruption, which they saw as the inevitable disease of "partyism," but beyond that they had little to propose as to how they would govern the province that was significantly distinctive from what Liberal governments had done. The Liberal Party still had strong rural roots and was seen by Catholics and ethnic immigrants as their champions. The Liberals had brought in the compromise that allowed separate schools in the West, thus giving Catholics their own school system, and it was the Liberal government in Ottawa that had welcomed ethnically diverse immigration. Quite frankly, the Liberals continued to be seen by many as the most sympathetic of the "old parties" to the interests and concerns of the "little man." Increasingly, as the economy improved and prospered in the 1920s, the issues dominating public debate were religious and racial—particularly, unrestricted immigration and separate schools for Catholics.

The Tory-led opposition was helped immeasurably in its campaign to defeat the Liberals by a new extraparliamentary force. The Ku Klux

Klan began organizing in the province in the 1920s and attracted a large membership: estimates range from ten to fifty thousand, but the most reliable figure is twenty-five thousand.[17] The Klan escapade certainly had its relatively comic aspects, not the least of which was grown men in ridiculous costumes surrounding burning crosses and making silly oaths in obscure language. The first organizers were a couple of American con artists who absconded in the mid-1920s with an estimated hundred thousand dollars in membership fees (the thirteen-dollar fee was high for the era, and those selling memberships were allowed to keep half, ensuring an aggressive sales effort all over the province).

But many in the movement were deadly serious, and the con artists left behind a large local membership who reorganized the Klan and turned it into a formidable, if short-lived, organization. The Klan launched a frontal attack on Catholics, Eastern European immigrants, Jews, Asians, separate Catholic schools, and the French language outside Quebec. (The fact that the targeted groups made up over one-third of the province's population may help to explain the Klan's quick demise.) The Klan denounced those who would erode morality, patriotism, British institutions, the Anglo-Saxon "race," and law and order. Organizations like the Orange Lodge—with its slogan "one school, one language, one flag"—and the Tories were staid and careful in expressing such concerns, but the Klan was unfettered by reserve, bitterly attacking these groups in abusive, potentially dangerous language. They burned crosses, threatened individuals and groups, and even physically assaulted a few individual targets of hate.

The movement, pandering to deeply held pre-existing prejudices, united largely lower-middle-class and working-class urban members with farmers on a platform of twisted, bigoted unity that briefly enjoyed a disturbing, widespread public acceptance. The Klan attracted many prominent community members: the Grand Wizard was a prominent Tory; Tory leader Anderson helped the Klan organize Saskatoon by providing party membership lists; a young John Diefenbaker shared public platforms with the Klan; many prominent Protestant clergymen joined. Members of all political parties joined, but the Tories led the field followed closely by the Progressives; many Liberals and UFC(SS) members signed up. Obviously the Klan appealed to the darker sentiments of a wide swath of the population, attracting people who ordinarily had no other reason to meet in the same organization for common objectives.

The Klan had a brief but significant impact on politics. The organization was decisive in electing aldermen and mayors in the cities. Most significantly, by publicly attacking Liberal premier Jimmy Gardiner as a "puppet of the Pope," the Klan helped defeat the Liberal government in 1929. Though the Tories and Progressives denied any direct cooperation with the Klan in the election, the fact remains that both parties included planks in their platforms pandering to the hate stirred up by the Klan. A Tory plank promised a "thorough revision of the educational system of the province"; this was code, of course, for getting rid of separate Catholic schools. The Progressives went further, with a plank promising "An Immigration Policy which will insure the permanency of British Institutions and Ideals." Tory and Progressive candidates tended to win in those areas where the Klan was well organized with large memberships. Though collaboration between the Klan and the opposition parties may not have been well orchestrated, that between the Tory and Progressive parties certainly was. The platforms of the two parties were uncannily similar, and of the battles for the province's sixty-three seats, only twelve were three-way races. The Tories won twenty-four seats, the Progressives five, and Independents six, while the Liberals won twenty-eight. The Tories, Progressives, and Independents formed a coalition government, presented to the public as "the Co-operative Government." As far as Williams and the UFC(SS) were concerned, a Tory government by any other name was still a Tory government. Nevertheless, it was a historic moment. The Liberal "machine," humbled after twenty-four years in power, was replaced by an unstable coalition government.

The Klan interlude, which ended with a whimper as the organization quickly collapsed and disappeared, brought into sharp relief the political bankruptcy of the Progressives. Incapable of gaining the blessing of left-leaning farmers, confused about what alternative they should offer, and constantly dithering about what issues to push, the Progressive Party degenerated, submerging itself in a parliamentary alliance with the Tories. The party suffered irreparable damage by benefiting from the Klan agitation and appearing to pander to it. The Progressives were a spent and discredited political force. In retrospect, Williams and the UFC(SS) were wise to have washed their hands of the party in 1928.

The Klan was quickly forgotten as the wider implications of the sharp fall in wheat prices on the heels of the Wall Street crash became increasingly ominous. When the Co-operative Government, with Tory leader J. T. M. Anderson as premier, took office on September 9, 1929, the boom of the 1920s was expected to continue. Optimism was high, as the 1920–23 depression receded in memory. When wheat prices fell, the initial expectation was that this was just another brief downturn, to be followed quickly by an upswing. It was hardly novel to see swings in wheat prices from year to year. But wheat prices continued to fall with good harvests around the world creating a glut of unsold wheat into 1929, 1930, and 1931. Very quickly the reality began to sink in: this was not just a blip in the world wheat market, but a national and global general economic collapse. Between 1929 and 1932 the prices for Canada's seventeen major exports fell an average of 53 per cent, while agricultural export prices, with wheat as the principal export, fell 70 per cent.[18] This led to a general economic collapse: industrial production fell 48 per cent as exports fell 33 per cent. Canada's national income was cut almost in half. Saskatchewan, dependent almost exclusively on the wheat economy, was hit fast and hard. Per capita income in Saskatchewan fell 72 per cent. Prairie agriculture as a whole experienced a net money income decline of 94 per cent. The Prairie region bore the brunt of the collapse, with Saskatchewan at the bottom due to its excessive dependence on the monoculture of wheat. For example, in 1925, 93 per cent of the net value of all production in the province was agricultural, most of that from wheat (70 per cent of the province's field crop was in wheat in 1926). Between 1920 and 1943 an astonishing 70 per cent of the total income earned in Saskatchewan was directly and indirectly related to planting, harvesting, and selling wheat.

Farmers were heavily in debt and had just begun to see possible prosperity as the 1920s boom turned wheat into what was called "the new gold." The debt was partly inherited from the war boom to finance the growth in farm size and a heavy investment in mechanization in response to labour shortages. The 1920–23 depression in wheat prices added more debt. Then the new boom resulted in further borrowing, for investment in land and accelerated mechanization to capture the benefits of high wheat prices. The province, school boards, cities, and rural municipalities went into deeper debt to finance the needed infrastructure. The boom witnessed a dramatic increase in population as settlement was virtually completed. In 1931, farm mortgage debt equalled 18 per cent of the total value of all farms. Unsecured public debt grew 107 per cent between 1921 and 1931. By 1937, interest on the provincial debt consumed 52 per cent of all provincial revenues. To pay the interest on the mortgage debt owed by farmers took half the value of the entire 1935 crop. Given the sudden and steep collapse in wheat prices, thousands of farmers immediately confronted the real possibility of bankruptcy and foreclosure. In 1930–31 the situation was bad. Few in Saskatchewan knew the worst was yet to come.

The 1930 and 1931 UFC(SS) conventions were pivotal in Williams's tactical manoeuvres to lead the farmers into politics on a socialist platform. Strategically, by 1930, the move into politics had become inevitable given the 1929 election result and the sudden onset of the economic collapse. Both left and right factions felt a sense of political urgency. The calls for a progressive, left-leaning electoral alternative were insistent across the country. J. S. Woodsworth worried about the lack of preparation and action in Saskatchewan.[19] He considered the province—the third most populous in the Dominion—of key importance for the national movement, given the strong showing of the Progressive Party in 1921. But Williams opposed rushing into action prematurely, especially on a reformist-capitalist program. Though it was possible to push the UFC(SS) into political action quickly, Williams was concerned about two things. First, the UFC(SS) had yet to develop a comprehensive socialist program on which to stand. And second, Williams was convinced farmers were not yet ready to support socialist remedies to their troubles.

By the time of the February 1930 convention, the right wing had abandoned any hope of removing Williams from office. The issues on which they attempted the coup—opposition to compulsory pooling and allegations of a left-wing conspiracy—failed to mobilize the membership. The conspiracy charge was largely dismissed by members. The convention had been open and democratic; all delegates on the convention floor were selected by their locals. The FEL was known for what it openly proclaimed to be, and it enjoyed general respect, though that respect often failed to materialize as support for many of its proposals. The FEL's ranks boasted a number of highly regarded, committed activists. Compulsory pooling now had close to unanimous support among UFC(SS) members. Moreover, members of the Wheat Pool were moving quickly to support the idea. The convention met in the midst of the successful public campaign for compulsory pooling. In the president's report to the convention, and obviously referring to the effort to drive him from office, Williams said, "I have followed your dictates without fear or favour. If I have failed it has not been because of lack of desire to serve, or lack of sincerity of purpose."[20] His speech was greeted with loud, sustained applause. During the elections, five members were nominated for president, and four of those nominees withdrew in favour of Williams, making his re-election unanimous. The message to the right was clear. Williams enjoyed strong support among the rank-and-file membership.

The issue dominating the convention was the timing of going into politics. There was little disagreement that the UFC(SS) had to do it, given the unfolding economic crisis and the ineptitude of the Co-operative Government. During a long and bitter debate, three factions emerged among delegates. The "right wing"—the conservative element of the SGGA and adherents of the Progressive Party—was eager to commit the organization to immediate political action supporting the reincarnated Progressives, the SFPA, in the coming July 1930 federal election. Then there was a new voice, a "far left," led by members and supporters of the Communist Party (CP) with some support in the old FUC and the FEL.[21] (McNamee, the founding president of both the FUC and the FEL, and Williams's mentor in the FUC, had joined the CP.) The far left also supported immediate and urgent political action. Finally, the "left wing," led by Williams, was committed to political action on a socialist platform and united most of the old FUC, the left of the old SGGA, and the activist leadership core that, with Williams, had founded the FPA in 1924. The largest factions were the "right wing" and the "left wing." The far left generally supported Williams, but had a falling-out over his reluctance to take the organization into politics immediately. The debate between the Williams faction and supporters of the SFPA was particularly hostile and nasty. When the question was finally put on the constitutional amendment to allow direct political action, it failed to achieve the required two-thirds majority by nine votes. The alliance between the right and the far left almost succeeded. In a gesture of unity, the convention then unanimously adopted a resolution committing the UFC(SS) to support the formation of "an organization outside the UFC for the purpose of

more directly selecting and electing representatives to the Legislature
and the House of Commons, pledged to support the demands of organized agriculture."[22]

Following the convention's direction, the executive went through
the motions, drafting a proposal for a new farmers' party outside the
UFC(SS), the New Saskatchewan Farmers' Party. Its founding principles
were simple: "1. That the farmers set up an Organization. 2. That such an
organization be set up outside of the UFC. 3. That only such candidates are
elected that will support the demands of Organized Agriculture."[23] At the
insistence of supporters of the Progressives, it was agreed that the organization would fuse with the remnants of the Progressive Party in the SFPA.
The fate of the fusion was sealed when the founding meeting deleted the
clause that obliged candidates to support the demands of "Organized
Agriculture," despite protests from Williams and the UFC(SS) executive.
UFC(SS) members were thereafter advised to support only those candidates declaring support for the demands of the UFC(SS). That was the
extent of the organization's involvement in the 1930 federal election.

The UFC(SS)'s moves to set up a farmers' party and fuse with the SFPA
were merely gestures, designed to heal the wounds from a bitter and divisive debate. The essential fact remained that the SFPA was denied the
considerable political influence, organizational strength on the ground,
and financial resources of the UFC(SS). The SFPA delivered a dismal
showing in the July 1930 election and died a quiet death. In October,
Williams reassured the province that the UFC(SS) would be going into
politics in the very near future:

> Some future convention of the UFC shall take the necessary
> time and trouble to lay down a political policy for agricul-
> ture in Saskatchewan. I hold this opinion so strongly that it
> has become a conviction. If that is done, it will then remain
> for the convention to say whether they wish that an outside
> political organization be created.[24]

Williams was attacked from the right and the far left as a result of the
convention decision on political action and for the key role he played in
steering the convention to the result he desired. Supporters of the SFPA
never forgave Williams, and their animus followed him for the rest of his

career. According to them, Williams bore the blame for the poor showing of SFPA candidates in the election. He had blocked the UFC(SS) from
entering the fray behind their candidates. He and the executive had sent
clear messages to the membership that the UFC(SS) did not consider
SFPA candidates reliable representatives of the class interests of farmers. The party's supporters accused him of failing to assert his leadership
at a key historical moment when progressive politics were on the electoral agenda. Criticism of Williams was not confined to Saskatchewan,
but was repeated across Canada in the moderate circles of the emerging social democratic movement. In the *Canadian Forum*, the unofficial
national organ of moderate social democracy, H. M. Rayner complained,
"Mr. George H. Williams, who is president of the United Farmers, waits
for the membership to give him the lead, and gets behind anything as
soon as he feels it will be popular." A defender of Williams replied in the
Forum's pages that the role of the president was indeed to act as directed
by a democratic convention:

> Your Mr. Rayner is apparently misinformed. If he would
> take the trouble to ascertain the opinion which is held by the
> 30,000 members of this organization, at this time, he would
> find that Mr. Williams is regarded as the most efficient,
> clear-thinking leader that has ever headed a farm organiza-
> tion in Saskatchewan.[25]

Williams had expected attacks from the right, given the battle at the
convention and the dashed hopes of SFPA leaders and supporters. He
shrugged them off while declaring that political action by the UFC(SS)
was on the immediate agenda.

Williams viewed the attacks from the far left much more seriously
since they threatened a split in the ranks of the broad socialist left. The
far left criticized Williams for leaving uncontested political terrain on
the left to the SFPA in the 1930 election. They pointed at the failure of
the moderate SFPA to win popular support, arguing that farmers and
the working class were more than ready for a militant, socialist choice
in elections. As a result, the FEL dissolved itself and joined in founding
the Farmers' Unity League (FUL), a front for the illegal CP. In December
1930, founding conventions of the FUL were held in five Western

Canadian cities to formally launch the organization. (The CP also formed a front to organize militant workers in response to the depression: the Workers' Unity League.) The FUL's aims were radical and reminiscent of the FUC. Williams intellectually supported much of what they declared, but politically he was disappointed that the split was now irreconcilable, hence causing division on the socialist left. The FUL's manifesto mirrored Williams's core views:

> [The FUL's] policy is one of militant struggle for the needs of farmers, leading up to the replacement of the capitalist system by a socialist society in which the workers and farmers will own the machinery of production and distribution and will use them to satisfy their needs. For this purpose it will strive to establish a firm alliance between the toiling farmers and the industrial workers of the cities whose interests will compel them to strive for socialism. We shall expect to have the utmost opposition of the present owner class and shall prepare to meet the opposition of the preponderance of wealth with the united strength of the toiling people.[26]

Personally, for Williams, the split meant permanent alienation from some of his closest comrades in the old FUC and FEL, who had been successfully recruited by the CP.

The FUL identified Williams as the major roadblock to their strategy of deflecting radicalizing farmers from democratic socialism. *The Furrow*, the league's newspaper, assaulted Williams not only politically but personally. An open letter to Williams stated nastily:

> Your self-importance is out of all proportion to your understanding of social questions. You seem entirely incapable of debating a matter of policy without making yourself the central pivot around which the whole question revolves. Do you think that you are an uncrowned king and the farmers are staging a show for Your Highness to pass judgement on?[27]

Williams did not bother responding to the personal slights. However, the *Furrow's* accusation that he and other leaders of the UFC(SS) were guilty of "collusion with capitalist exploiters" by dampening the membership's radicalism provoked this blunt and pragmatic response from Williams:

> The reason the policy of the U.F.C. is as radical as it is, is because the average director and official is just a little more radical than the bulk of the membership, and the reason it is not even more radical is because the membership will not go any faster.[28]

The political problem among the unorganized farmers was even greater. As Williams noted in an August 1930 memorandum to the UFC(SS) executive,

> We have no guarantee of the time that will elapse before the people will discard this outworn system of private ownership and profit. I feel that at the present time no more than twenty per cent of the agrarian population are willing to discard the system; that ten per cent do not know what to think and seventy per cent still cling to it.[29]

Williams did not believe the time was yet ripe to lead the farmers into politics on a socialist platform.

Williams refused to shut the door on those who fell under the influence of the CP and joined the FUL. This accommodating position would be used against him later, when he was accused of being a communist and a communist sympathizer. Williams frankly admired the ideological commitment and organizational abilities of many who embraced the CP or the FUL. He had worked closely with some of the best of them in the early days. He never gave up hope he could win them back by the force of argument or, failing that, by the unfolding of political reality. When some among the UFC(SS) leadership proposed that those holding official positions in the UFC(SS) should be barred from serving as officials or organizers in the FUL, Williams rejected the idea instantly. He would not countenance such a measure, nor would he consider proposals for expulsion for holding FUL or CP memberships. Williams's position was firm. All bona fide farmers were free to join the UFC(SS) as full members as long as they took the oath of membership and were accepted as a member by a democratic vote at a local meeting.

Williams ignored the 1930 election, opting instead to spend the months from March to spring seeding on an ambitious speaking tour of locals across rural Saskatchewan. For him, there were more important political problems to be dealt with than continued squabbling with the Progressive ghost. Due to the economic downturn, cash-strapped farmers were lagging in renewing their UFC(SS) memberships. Williams knew this was mainly due to the dramatic fall in farm income, but he also recognized it could be the beginning of a crisis of confidence in the organization's response to the economic collapse. Membership was falling from its 1930 high of thirty-one thousand. The downward trajectory had to be staunched. Williams was concerned about the growing challenge from the far left, as the FUL began to organize well-attended protest meetings and rallies. He revived and massaged the debt adjustment plan he had prepared for the FUC. To this he added a demand that the Anderson government declare a moratorium on debt repayment until the crisis passed. He carried messages of anger and hope, backed up by aggressive emergency measures to respond to the immediate realities of the crisis faced on the farm: the spectre of bankruptcy and foreclosure. It was politically essential that the UFC(SS) not lose its reputation as the angry voice of farmers facing hard times. Speaking to small kitchen meetings and packed halls across the province, Williams was successful. The membership drop slowed (in 1932, membership was twenty-seven thousand). The UFC(SS) remained the hegemonic voice of the farmers of Saskatchewan, having successfully met challenges from the right and the far left.

Williams and key members of the UFC(SS) leadership spent the summers of 1929 and 1930 drafting a political platform for the 1931 convention. The draft was circulated among the membership during the autumn. In October 1930, Williams issued a public call to action in the *Western Producer*:

> Things must change! Our present method of human and business relationships inevitably means that more of the world's goods is concentrated in a few hands, through the control of wealth. You need not expect to give birth to a new and better organization in which the good things of life will be available to more and more of humanity, without travail. Everything

has its price. Perhaps we have not realized we were trying to change things; perhaps the revolt from the old system has been unconscious, but it has been very real. Now we are rapidly approaching the time when it will become conscious and definite.[30]

In December he demanded action from the prime minister in his "Memorandum to Mr. Bennett," outlining the federal policies in the draft program that required immediate implementation. This received wide publicity in the press.

The district conventions of the UFC(SS) were rapidly moving left, demanding more militancy from the leadership. The FUL's influence was spreading. A large district convention at Wilkie, Saskatchewan, adopted a program considerably to the left of the draft of Williams's proposed platform. The program became known as the "Wilkie Charter." Though most of it reiterated the draft platform, it proposed stronger socialist remedies. This did not overly concern Williams. But the charter also threatened secession in the form of "a co-operative commonwealth within the British Empire," a fatal political error from Williams's perspective. Even more disturbing was that key local leaders of the UFC(SS) were being swept away in the dizzying rhetoric provoked by the deepening depression. A supporter of the secessionist plank argued,

> This "Charter of Liberty" is an ultimatum to the federal government, and failing the assurance of immediate and sufficient action, we shall organize at once for the political conquest of this province, along with other such provinces as will join us, for the purpose of forming a co-operative commonwealth within the British Empire, trading directly with Great Britain and other countries on a free trade and barter basis.[31]

Rural Saskatchewan was aroused and in turmoil. Williams was concerned the political leadership of this spreading mood for fundamental change might be captured by the FUL, or by secessionists, risking a loss of mass popular support among farmers. The looming convention of the UFC(SS) had to win over and channel this emerging political energy by seizing the historical moment. In the president's call to the

Saskatoon convention, Williams declared that participation was crucial, because "decisions will be made which will re-echo all over Canada." He stressed its historical significance, stating that "this is one Convention which every delegate who attends will in future say, 'Yes, I attended that Convention.'" He added, "[You] can be one of the voices that shaped the destiny of Western Canada."[32]

When the 1931 convention opened, the hall was packed and electric with anticipation. Representatives of labour—the Trades and Labour Congress, the All-Canadian Labour Congress, and the National Unemployment Association—were given places of honour in the front row of the hall. Williams opened the convention with a presidential address carefully crafted to rally the left to stay the course, persuade the far left to pull back from extremism, reassure the uncertain, and silence the right. It was a careful tightrope walk that concluded with a call for unity. Williams was concerned the clashing ideological tendencies could fracture the organization in its transition to political action:

> There has been a barrage of advice to the farmers of Saskatchewan during the past few weeks. So much, "Be careful! Be careful!" But no sensible suggestion as to how to keep your home and feed your children. "Be careful of the radical." Yes, I agree you can be extremist. Yet, I will tell you frankly, I have less fear of the radical than I have of the conservative. The visionary may get you into trouble, but the ultra conservative will get you into the graveyard. Today it is more dangerous to drift than it is to try new paths. What would my advice be to you in these times of trial?
>
> Do not be lulled into false security by promises of prosperity just around the corner. Do not be frightened into submission and silence by dread warnings of Bolshevism, the surest way to bring disaster is to do nothing. Do not be stampeded into foolish actions by conditions. To the group who keeps their head today comes the victory of tomorrow.
>
> Pick out some practical things that will give you security in the possession of your homes, and the wherewithal to live, even if it be only temporary security. Demand them and if they are not given, elect men and women pledged to get them

for you. Get them and then, after you have these things go to your objective, a new and better economic system, which ultimate objective you must always have before you.

My friends, you have the right to the possession and enjoyment of the homes you have built. You have a right to a living from the fruit of your labour. You have a right to give your children the kind of future you planned for them when you brought them into the world.

Stand shoulder to shoulder as men and women. Have nothing to do with the people with a personal grouch who would drive you apart; forget your paltry partyisms. Stand shoulder to shoulder in demanding and getting those things to which you and your children are entitled.[33]

The mood of the convention was militant far beyond Williams's fondest hopes. The delegates were determined to go into politics on a socialist platform. The motion to amend the constitution to allow direct political action passed without discussion. The show of hands in favour was so overwhelming that the chair asked, and the assembly agreed, that it be recorded as unanimous. The delegates moved quickly to animated debates on important policy matters.

Anticipating a significant bloc of right-wing delegates, Williams and the executive had drafted an ideologically cautious set of proposals, hoping thereby to cement unity. They had misread the quickly changing mood in the countryside. The right had either been won over or had stayed home. The rhetoric of the leadership's proposal was radical in its denunciation of capitalism, but most of the economic demands were decidedly reformist: price guarantees, low freight rates, debt adjustment, foreclosure protection, cheap credit. The most left-leaning economic policy proposed a cautious but significant move to public ownership of land and resources: that "no more Provincial lands or resources be alienated, that no more homesteads be granted or farm lands sold, but that 'Use Lease' be instituted by the Province and all titles to land and resources now owned be permanently retained by the Province." The delegates promptly amended this as follows: that "all land and resources now privately owned be nationalized as opportunity will permit."

The convention devoted almost an entire day to debating the complex "use lease" land nationalization program before approving it enthusiastically.[34] Although the UFC(SS) continued to proudly promote it as a "Land Nationalization Programme," it was really no such thing. The program was designed to ensure "security of tenure" to the working farmer in perpetuity, protecting farms from "confiscation" by finance capitalism. The policy divided the province's lands into four classifications. Crown lands already under the control of the province and open for settlement would be distributed only on a use lease basis (Class A). Lands seized by rural municipalities for tax arrears would revert to provincial control upon the province's payment of the taxes owed; these lands would then be open for acquisition through use lease, though the evicted farmer would enjoy first claim on his farm (Class B). Lands under a debt load so large that the farmers could no longer continue to meet obligations, support families, and purchase inputs to continue production would be referred to arbitration boards under the new debt adjustment plan. The fair settlement determined for the creditor would be paid out of a rental fund; the farmer-debtor would pay into this fund out of the proceeds of the farm. The amount to be paid to the creditor would be amortized over an agreed term of years established by the board (Class C). The final category included those farms owned outright by a farmer and unencumbered by an impossible debt load. These lands "can only be nationalized upon the owner making application to the government" (Class D). All other natural resource developments would be publicly owned and developed. The wealth produced would be devoted to the public good. Those resource developments currently under private control would be gradually taken into public ownership with compensation based on a fair assessment of their real value, including the consideration of depreciation of capital assets, past windfall profits, and any previously excessively low resource rents paid to the province.

The section in Williams's proposal presenting the "ultimate objective" of socialism decried "the inherent unsoundness of the capitalist system," declaring that "social ownership and co-operative production for use is the only sound economic system." The delegates systematically applied that standard as they amended proposal after proposal and added new ones, to adequately reflect the ultimate objective. From the beginning, political power must begin building the foundation of the new socialist system. In the end, the final policy document reflected the more radical Wilkie Charter more than it did the moderate proposals presented by the leadership.

To emphasize the importance of adopting a clear socialist platform prior to political action, Williams's closest collaborator among the leadership, Tom Johnston, reminded delegates of the failure in Alberta, where the UFA had ruled with a comfortable majority since 1921: "Alberta has a farmer controlled legislature, and they have brought into being no socialistic legislation that matters. They are carrying on a capitalist method and have not made any real effective effort. Whether they are afraid, I don't know. If Saskatchewan goes it will give the lead." Like the Progressive failure in 1921 at the federal level, the sorry, conservative record of farmer power in Alberta had been at the motivational core of the strategy of Williams and his supporters since the founding of the FUC and the failure of the FPA in 1924. It made no sense for farmers to go into politics without a clear socialist platform to win a mandate to implement meaningful progressive change. Winning power without a plan for what to do with that power can only lead to disunity, confusion and collapse. Or, as in the case of Alberta, it results in co-optation by the powerful capitalist system.

Williams became embroiled in heated exchanges with secessionists, the far left, and militant members of the women's section as the policy debates neared completion. Late in the convention a resolution proposing a form of secession came up for debate. Many delegates appeared swayed by the argument that such a threat would result in the move into politics having a greater and more positive impact. It would convey the depth of the desperation and alienation of the farmers. Williams intervened, arguing that such a plank would be suicidal as it would inevitably become the entire public focus in the move to political action: "You cannot at this time elect a Government on a platform of Secession." He stated, "You have come here in an attempt to get the farmers of Saskatchewan the things they should have through the power of the ballot." Delegates on the far left, who favoured the secessionist plank, heckled Williams, accusing him of "favouring a capitalistic government." Williams responded angrily, "Why do you have the idea that you have to rise up in revolution and start all over again from the bottom?...Why don't you believe the people have enough intelligence" to use the power of the ballot "instead of destroying everything and starting afresh?" The idea of proposing secession was promptly dropped. The exchange deepened the chasm between Williams and those influenced by the far left. Joe Phelps, a district leader and a protégé of Williams, denounced him for using "the weight of his office to kill a rank-and-file movement."[35] The fact was, of course, that Williams's intervention had saved the move to political action from disaster.

The issue of advocating the legalization of birth control once again came to the floor of the convention. In 1931, birth control was a controversial issue. Like abortion, it was forbidden under the Criminal Code. The powerful Catholic lobby used its influence to oppose any move toward its legalization. A successful effort by the more progressive women in the UFC(ss), led largely by United Church members, had convinced the 1930 convention to adopt a policy in favour of birth control. The women's president moved to rescind that policy. Apparently, during the interceding year, meetings of farm women across the province had revealed widespread opposition to the policy, largely spearheaded by members of the Catholic faith. It had proven to be a deeply divisive issue best left to the personal conscience of individual women. The motion to rescind passed. In response, a committed feminist successfully persuaded delegates to adopt a more limited proposal: that doctors educate needy women on matters of birth control as a public health measure. Under pressure from the board, and no doubt from Williams, a motion to rescind that policy was later introduced. Williams intervened in the debate. He reported on meetings with Catholic members of the organization and leaders of the Catholic Church. Williams was convinced it was possible to persuade Catholics to support socialism, but impossible to persuade them to support birth control as a public policy. He argued that including such a policy in the political platform would result in the loss of Catholic members and supporters. He begged the convention to leave birth control as a matter of conscience. Birth control, he declared, "isn't a principle that is worth while dividing the farmers of Canada on right now."

It was not Williams's finest hour. But Williams had already proven he could be brutally tactical when necessary. The Catholic Church was a powerful political force in Saskatchewan. The church had become heavily politicized in the battle for separate schools and in their continuing defence. The church had loyally supported the Liberals against the feared Tories for obvious reasons. The KKK episode had further politicized the church, making them nervous about popular mass movements. The bishops routinely directed priests to give clear political direction from the pulpit to congregations during election campaigns. Williams anticipated an uphill battle to overcome the bishops' inevitable opposition to the new party. He would rather fight them on the principles of socialism without at the same time having to defend public health policies favouring birth control.

When nominations for president opened, delegates tried to persuade Williams to continue in office despite the constitution's provision limiting officers to two consecutive one-year terms. Thunderous applause greeted an offer to amend the constitution or, failing that, all nominees could decline, forcing Williams to stay in office. According to the constitution, an officer remained in office until a successor was elected. Williams refused, saying:

> When any man who is at the head of this organization thinks that the organization depends on his ability and efficiency he is misled. It depends on the faith in his sincerity to a great extent. You are going to hurt that faith back in the country, and that must not be allowed.

After delegates elected his successor, Williams said, "Now Mr. Macauley, in turning this over to you, I came with one idea in mind. I tried to keep the faith. I have tried to." Greeted by an ovation and shouts of "You have!," Williams declared, "All I ask of the man who takes my position is this, that he will keep the faith, that he will keep the faith with the farmers of this province and that his watchword will always be—the farmers first and the individual last."

The motion taking the UFC(SS) into politics was passed unanimously. Earlier resolutions at this and previous conventions had approved in principle seeking the cooperation of labour in any move to political action. The convention did not clearly decide whether the organization itself would become a political party or would proceed to found a party independent of the organization. From the discussions noted in the minutes, delegates tended toward the latter option, and this was certainly implied in the wording of the resolution and the commitment to work with labour. That decision was left in the hands of Williams, who was elected leader of the United Farmers' Political Association (UFPA), a creation of the convention within the UFC(SS). Details of the move into politics were therefore in the hands of Williams, his successor as president, and the board of directors. But the details, and any action, had to wait. The constitution required that two-thirds of the locals approve both the constitutional amendment and the operative motion to go into politics. That process would take two or three months, but there was little doubt that support at the local meetings would be overwhelming.

Williams had succeeded in leading the organized farmers of Saskatchewan into politics on a socialist platform. He was widely seen as the soon-to-be anointed leader of the new party. A headline in the *Western Producer* announced, "Williams Likely to Marshall New Party."[36] In another article, the paper had celebrated "the spirit of unity of the delegates' intense desire to fight for their rights":

> The policy adopted is truly a national policy, and if the conventions of the past had seen fit to adopt a similar policy, and had been able to find a way to put such a policy into practice, the farmers of the West would not now be facing starvation and bankruptcy.[37]

The Canadian Press reported:

> Canada's newest political party appears likely to be marshalled under the command of one of the country's youngest leaders. Thirty-six-year-old George H. Williams looms as probable chieftain of the farm-party formed by the entry of United Farmers of Canada (Saskatchewan Section) into the political field.[38]

Williams was absent from Saskatchewan in March and April 1931, attending an international wheat conference in Rome from March 26 to April 3, followed by a three-week tour of the Soviet Union. The wheat conference, jointly sponsored by the League of Nations and the International Institute of Agriculture, sought solutions to the problem of the European wheat glut, which was largely responsible for driving down world prices. The agenda included a proposal to form a coalition of European nations to create a trade zone with high tariffs that would protect European wheat from competitors; this would replace the individual tariffs already imposed by each producer nation in Europe, thus granting preferential trade access among those nations while protecting the European market from outside competition. The UFC(SS) was invited to send a representative and chose Williams. Although not a member of Canada's official delegation, Williams—given his knowledge of the world wheat-marketing system—very quickly became a member of the conference's "committee of experts" and was frequently called upon for advice. He persuaded the Canadian delegation to oppose the tariff proposal and instead to propose a system of international cooperative marketing based on pooling principles. Other delegations were favourably influenced. The conference agreed this proposal was worth considering further and recommended another conference in London a month hence. The idea of a tariff-protected European common market was shelved, at least temporarily.

The UFC(SS) leadership planned that Williams would request permission from the Soviet delegation at Rome to tour the Soviet Union, focusing on agricultural policies and conditions. The Soviet Union's socialist system was a topic of intense debate in Canada, especially as the Depression worsened and the CP, together with its front groups, grew in influence. Desperate farmers were most interested in the revolutionary changes in Soviet agriculture, including the centralized state-planning process and the collectivization of agriculture. Williams sought the answer to a key question: Was Soviet socialism "a menace to the farmers of the west," or did it contain "the germ of a plan which will lead us out of the slough of depression?"[39] Unprejudiced accounts of conditions in the Soviet Union were impossible to get. Typically, those who visited already had their minds made up at the outset. Accounts were polarized between enthusiastic support and total condemnation. Hence, as Williams noted, "everything is tinged by the wish which is the father of the opinion." Furthermore, those in Canada fighting for change and reform found themselves frequently smeared as communists; their ideas were dismissed out of hand "while western conditions [become] worse." Williams wanted to see for himself and, if successful in going to the Soviet Union, he was charged with the task of fully reporting what he saw there upon his return. Doubtless impressed by this Prairie agrarian socialist, and his keen interest in the changes in Soviet agriculture since the revolution, the Soviet delegation invited Williams to tour the Soviet Union. Williams stipulated he must be free to travel wherever he wished. He did not want a stage-managed tour. The Soviet delegation consented.

We have a full account of Williams's observations and commentary on what he saw in the Soviet Union. Upon his return he wrote an eighty-six-page booklet, *The Land of the Soviets*, that was published and sold widely by the UFC(SS). It was attractively printed and featured a dramatic cover design—a large Russian bear rising from the land mass of the USSR. The UFC(SS) sponsored Williams on a sixty-six-community lecture tour, complete with slides, across rural Saskatchewan and in the key cities. The halls were packed, the sales of the booklet brisk, and the donations to support the organization generous. (The funds raised were badly needed to replenish the organization's depleted coffers due to cuts in membership fees in response to the collapse of farm income.) Public interest was high, and the tour was a great success. Whenever possible, Williams and his entourage took the opportunity to organize constituency associations for the new farmers' party. The visit to the Soviet Union and the heavily publicized speaking tour were very quickly used against Williams by his opponents, both within and outside the new party. He was smeared as a communist sympathizer by some, as an out-and-out communist by others. An editorial comment in Estevan's *Mercury* was typical of the editorial response of the capitalist press:

> An apostle of Communism [Williams] is billed to speak in Estevan, to tempt his hearers with the promise of betterment through the overthrow of government, confiscation of property, suppression of religion, dissolution of the marriage tie and family life and enslavery of labor as exemplified in Russia. Must the movement be allowed to drift and gain momentum until guns are again forced into action?[40]

No doubt in response to Williams's angry complaints about the editorial, the *Mercury*'s reporter later provided a somewhat more balanced and quite detailed front-page news report on Williams's lecture.[41] The *Western Producer*, on the other hand, provided extensive and favourable coverage throughout his trip to Rome and the Soviet Union, as well as a thorough report on his lecture during the fall 1931 tour. Only much later did Williams become aware of the anti-communist whispering campaign against him among his detractors in the new party.

Williams's account of what he saw cannot reasonably be characterized as "pro-communist." If there was sympathy in his account, it was contained in an effort to enumerate honestly the facts of what he saw and learned during visits to agricultural districts and extensive interviews with prominent bureaucrats involved in economic planning for agriculture. And what he saw and learned impressed him greatly. With perhaps more prescience than he was aware of at the time, Williams predicted that "in the success or failure of the Russian experiment lies the future history of the world." Just over a decade later, the USSR would defeat Hitler's apparently invincible military juggernaut and rise from the ashes of World War II as a world superpower, facing off against the United States in a world-defining confrontation lasting until the USSR's collapse in 1991. By any standard, what the regime had accomplished was miraculous when Williams visited in 1931. Emerging from three years of war with Germany (1914–17), a five-year civil war (1917–22), and battles against hostile interventions by some hundred thousand Allied troops (including over five thousand Canadians), the Bolshevik regime had inherited an infrastructure in shambles and an economy in a state of collapse. In the decade since victory, great strides had been made rebuilding, modernizing, and industrializing the society. Only the most ideologically blind failed to recognize that reality.

Williams returned from the Soviet Union more deeply committed to his socialist convictions. The Soviet Union was demonstrating that socialism was no longer just an untested theory or an impossible dream. It was being realized in the real world. A social economy was under construction based on production and distribution to fill human needs as a first priority. The profit motive, private capital, and irrationality and instability of the competitive free market were not necessary to build a successful economic system. Economic planning at the local, regional, and national levels could steer the economy toward clearly stated goals, achieving the rational and just fulfillment of human needs.

For Williams, Canada, as a mature democracy and a modern economy, could construct socialism peacefully through the election of a socialist government. The ultimate objective of socialism—social and economic justice and security for all—could be achieved with greater ease and certainly less pain than in the Soviet Union. "The all-important question with us is whether we can make the necessary corrections in our economic life without the bloodshed and destruction that usually accompanies economic change." The key is to have "wisdom, tolerance, sincerity and courage." Our "greatest enemies" are "prejudice, hatred, self-seeking, and fear." The problem is, simply stated, "how to obtain reconstruction, justice and efficiency." Williams's trip to the Soviet Union had firmed up his opposition to those who spoke irresponsibly and easily of rising up in revolution without carefully considering the enormity of what they were proposing.

While impressed by the efforts to socialize agriculture in the Soviet Union through state, collective, and cooperative farms, Williams remained committed to the family farm as a cornerstone of a socialist Canada. Though the Soviet socialized agricultural system was still in its formative stages, Williams recognized that if it were carefully planned and managed, it could become enormously efficient and productive. He noted the rapid advances in science-based agricultural practices and mechanization on state farms, which were given priority in economic planning. But he saw this as resulting from the backwardness of the semi-feudal agricultural economy prior to the 1917 revolution. Canadian agriculture was already scientific, efficient, highly mechanized, and very productive. Therefore, his agrarian populism remained intact, unchallenged by what he had observed. The wide distribution of land among family farmers in Canada was a form of social economy, and it remained a bulwark of Canadian democracy. In a sense, Williams remained, like most North American populists, a Jeffersonian democrat. Canadian farmers were threatened by a form of capitalist collectivization as banks, trusts, and mortgage companies foreclosed on bankrupt farmers and leased the land back to be worked by the former owner. This inspired his "use lease" land policy. According to Williams, a socialist government must defend and support the family farm as the foundation of both the agricultural economy and our democratic system.

Based on Williams's writing and speeches, it is difficult to believe that he may not have admitted, if perhaps only to himself, that a future, mature socialist Canada might well abandon the traditional family farm in favour of a fully socialized and modernized agricultural economy. He was aware of the growing stratification among farmers from rich to poor, from very large to very small. In his era, middle-level farmers constituted the overwhelming majority and provided the backbone of the organized farmer movement. Indeed, this stratum would provide the primary popular base of the new socialist party in Saskatchewan. Williams was certainly willing to face controversy by rejecting an unthinking defence of private ownership in the usual sense and embracing the "use lease" system for farm tenure. Granted, "use lease" kept the farmer, and his or her heir, on the land as an independent commodity producer. But its impact would dull the sharp edges of unfettered capitalism. "Use lease" would slow down the concentration of farmland into fewer and fewer, larger and larger farms, dampening the emergence of a class of very rich farmers with large land holdings. "Use lease" would also block capitalist speculation in farmland. Far fewer farmers would be driven from the land by market forces leading to bankruptcy. Williams was very much advocating what can only be characterized as a populist, anti-finance-capitalism policy that represented the immediate class interests of the majority of family farmers in the Great Depression.

If Williams harboured any thoughts about a fully socialized agriculture in a well-developed future socialist economy, he kept them to himself. As a pragmatist he knew that to even speculate publicly about such matters would be political suicide in Saskatchewan in 1931.

Chapter 4

BUILDING THE CCF

*Leadership Lost and
Regained, 1931 to 1936*

U pon returning from the Soviet Union, Williams led building the
new party. Over 90 per cent of the locals had approved the constitutional change allowing political action and the decision to
go into politics. In April 1931 Williams attended a series of UFC(SS) district conventions, urging practical support for the move into politics and
emphasizing the importance of quickly organizing constituency associations. Williams and M. J. Coldwell, the leader of the Independent Labour
Party in Regina, worked together coordinating political education sessions throughout the province for members of both organizations.[1]
Williams urged Coldwell to move quickly to a formal founding of a provincial ILP, which was at the time a series of small, independent local
organizations in the major urban centres. In June 1931, Williams and
Coldwell co-chaired a public meeting in Regina, where delegates from
both organizations presented their joint demands to the provincial
government. Upon receiving an unsatisfactory response from the government, the meeting unanimously supported a resolution to build a
new political party in order to achieve a cooperative commonwealth.

Throughout 1931 Williams argued that the formal fusion of the UFC(SS)'s political arm and the ILP was needed urgently to prepare for the imminent election. On October 24, 1931, the ILP locals formally founded a provincial ILP, with Coldwell as leader and a program nearly identical to that of the UFC(SS). The stage was set for founding the new socialist party uniting farmers and workers. There was no doubt the UFC(SS), with twenty-seven thousand members, would be the dominant partner. The ILP had never had more than five hundred members. Furthermore, the UFC(SS)'s interim political arm, the UFPA, had already established viable constituency associations in many rural seats. In the urban centres, the small pockets of ILP members faced the daunting task of establishing constituency associations largely from scratch. The widely shared public consensus was that Williams would lead the new party. Indeed, in letters to the editor of the *Western Producer*, farmers wondered about the kind of socialism Williams planned to establish in Saskatchewan.

The February 1932 UFC(SS) convention took the final steps in preparing for formal fusion. Independent Labour Party representatives were given delegate status. The final platform contained a revised iteration of the previously adopted economic policy as the basis for political action. Resolutions from the 1931 convention were consolidated into a five-point provincial platform and a seven-point federal platform. Williams was asked to be president, since he was now eligible again under the constitution. He declined, whereupon he was made honorary president in recognition of having brought the UFC(SS) "to the pitch of excellence it had attained."[2] Of more importance, Williams was named to the new joint political directive board, composed of three UFC(SS) and three ILP representatives, as well as the UFC(SS) executive. The board was directed to prepare a final draft of the platform for the new party's founding convention in July 1932.

Significant developments took place behind the scenes, suggesting Williams's widespread popularity in the movement provoked considerable anxiety among elements of the leadership groups both in Saskatchewan and in Ottawa. Williams began pushing for a national conference of radical organizations to found a nationwide socialist party. He corresponded with leaders of radical labour, socialist, and farm organizations across Canada about such a project. He proposed a meeting in Saskatoon on June 6, 1932, and invited Woodsworth, who was initially enthusiastic and agreed to attend, as did some other MPs in the Ginger Group.[3] In mid-February, Williams toured Alberta and British Columbia, giving his Soviet lecture to finance the trip, in order to meet with radical organizations. Eagerness for the meeting among left-wing circles spread across Canada. Then, suddenly, everything changed. Woodsworth and the other MPs withdrew their promises to attend, pleading other commitments. Williams was informed his plan conflicted with a proposed western conference of labour political parties, tentatively scheduled for August in Calgary. Williams was asked to cease his efforts and instead support the Calgary meeting to which the UFC(SS) and the ILP would be invited. Disappointed, Williams reluctantly agreed and sent his file of correspondence and contact list to the organizers of the Calgary meeting.

What Williams did not know was that Woodsworth, his group of MPs, and the League for Social Reconstruction (LSR), a group of left-leaning academics, had been discussing forming a national party and were well advanced in their planning.[4] Williams's proposed meeting in Saskatoon would divert energy and resources from their project. It would also be out of their control. In May 1932 the Ottawa group of MPs and the LSR met in a House of Commons office and agreed to found a preliminary party, the Commonwealth Party, with Woodsworth as interim leader. The Calgary meeting of labour political parties would be broadened by invitations to unions, farm organizations, and the various small socialist parties. It would become the founding convention of the new party. Unions and labour or socialist parties under communist control or influence would not be invited. Without Williams realizing it, his successful initiative threatened to undermine, or perhaps replace, the plan devised in private by the Ottawa Ginger Group/LSR. This was just the first of many clashes Williams would have over the years with the Ottawa-based "central office."

The next blow Williams suffered was delivered at a hastily convened informal meeting of the political directive board. He was blindsided by a request he not accept the leadership of the new party. Members present, including his colleagues from the UFC(SS), begged him to forego the leadership in favour of Coldwell. Williams, the membership of the UFC(SS), and farmers across the province all assumed Williams would be anointed leader. His colleagues on the board argued that his visit to the Soviet Union, his widely distributed booklet, and his well-publicized lecture tour would only increase the effectiveness of the inevitable communist smears against the party. This could fatally wound the party's chances of winning the election.

In what he later realized was the biggest political miscalculation of his career, Williams agreed. On the face of it, this decision was wholly uncharacteristic of the Williams of the recent past. He agreed to step aside in favour of Coldwell, a person long associated with the right wing of the UFC(SS), the irrelevant Progressive Party, and the leaders of the Wheat Pool who had fought compulsory pooling to the end. Coldwell was close friends with some of Williams's strongest opponents in the recent battles in the UFC(SS). He was not a farmer and Williams knew the party's agrarian base expected a farmer as leader. Though Williams was deeply personally wounded by the request, he was persuaded—because the UFC(SS) members on the board agreed, and given the vicious red-baiting he had endured during his lecture tour, he was initially convinced of the wisdom of the decision. In the final analysis, he was persuaded this was the right thing to do for the good of the movement, given the consensus that Coldwell would have greater electoral appeal. That Williams would sacrifice his personal ambition for the greater good was entirely consistent with his character. On retiring from the UFC(SS) presidency he had told the delegates his credo was "the farmers first, the individual last." He lived up to that credo with this decision. On the other hand, he had allowed himself to make a hasty, momentous decision in a secret elitist meeting without consulting the rank and file, which very much conflicted with his populist principles. Nevertheless, the die was cast. Coldwell would lead the new party.

In the months following the February convention, prominent members of the leadership of both organizations fanned out over the province to present the economic policy and the detailed political platform of the new party. The meetings were well attended and enthusiastic, especially in the rural areas, but urban meetings drew large crowds as well. Given the growing desperation due to the Depression, people were looking for hope. Optimism grew that the party was on a trajectory to success in the coming election. A leading UFC(SS) official, upon prodding by the press regarding the leadership of the new party, said, "Mr. Williams has been acclaimed by a great number of people throughout the province as the leader of this new political organization and, of course, is the individual upon whom the attacks of opponents is [sic] mostly concentrated."[5]

Despite the large public meetings and growing optimism, Williams grew concerned about the problems being encountered by those organizing constituency associations in urban centres. The rural organizing was going very well, and constituency associations, especially in those seats containing concentrations of UFC(SS) members, were established quickly and began preparing for the coming election. By contrast, in the cities, clashes among competing left-wing groups, a variety of small labour parties, the CP, and important trade unions made it difficult to organize constituency associations. Near unanimity existed among left-leaning farmers in support of the new party, with the exception of the FUL. In the cities, the many competing working-class organizations were uncertain about this alliance with farmers, particularly when the farm wing would be in charge.

Farmers, as a class, did not have a good reputation in supporting labour's cause, especially during strikes. Nor were many farmers among the best of employers—for farm labour, working conditions and wages were poor and daily hours of work long. Many workers in urban centres had personal experience working for farmers during harvest. Packing houses, flour mills, the railways, and construction sites would typically lay off part of their workforce during harvest, freeing them to help take off the crop. Many workers had arrived in the province on the annual harvest trains that brought temporary workers from across Canada to help in the harvest and decided to stay; many of these workers, however, took better-paying and more secure jobs in the towns and cities at the first opportunity. Some militant union leaders and activists had worked with the IWW to organize farm labour in the province prior to World War I. The union organizers were not warmly received by the farmers who employed the workers the IWW tried to organize. While farmer-labour unity made good theoretical and political sense, the reality of achieving it in one political organization was proving vexatious. Nevertheless, the urban public meetings were large, providing a strong sense of a rising tide of support.

At the founding convention, held from July 25 to 27, Williams was given primacy of place as the keynote speaker, followed by Coldwell and Woodsworth. Responding to the relentless smears of communism by opponents of the new party, which had been given extensive coverage in the press, Williams carefully presented a moderate and reassuring vision of the socialism to be built in Saskatchewan and Canada:

> Socialism does not intend that anyone shall be asked to work
> without reward, nor does it intend that anyone shall receive a
> reward unless they earn it in service to the state. The greater
> the service, the greater the reward. I know that is not Marxian
> socialism, but you cannot reach that state at once, and until
> you reach that day you must travel as your steps take you:
> what you want and what you must have is a Canadian social-
> ism that will work.[6]

Throughout his speech he mixed a yearning for the ultimate objective
of a fully realized socialism with pragmatic advice on the difficult incre-
mental steps that must be taken to achieve it. The future was secure as
long as the ultimate objective remained the goal. In the meantime, it was
time to begin taking steps to improve the conditions of the people in the
march toward the new dawn of a just and socialist society. He reminded
the audience that "use lease" did not mean the collectivization of agriculture, as opponents alleged, but security of tenure for family farmers. The
family farm, secure from seizure by financial interests, was a foundation
of Canadian socialism.

   Williams was followed by Coldwell and Woodsworth, who presented
inspirational visions of socialism. Revealing how important this new
party was seen to be by the Ottawa leadership, Woodsworth reminded
the delegates of their historic task in building Canadian socialism, proclaiming, "I have the firm conviction that as far as politics is concerned
in Canada today, Saskatchewan is the key province." The speeches were
greeted with ovations. This ended the portion of the proceedings devoted
to the official UFC(SS) convention. The delegates had been inspired, and
the next day, July 27, the meeting convened as the founding convention
of the new party.

   For Williams the founding convention was an uneasy mixture of people, yet one that attested to his ability to unite moderate and radical in
one organization supporting a socialist platform. The convention was
clearly his. In attendance were 194 UFC(SS) delegates and 23 ILP delegates. Williams's arrival in the hall, even the mention of his name, was
greeted with cheers. Yet the convention also included many of his old
opponents from the bitter wars over control of the UFC(SS), his battles
with the Progressive Party, and the confrontations with the cooperative

leadership over compulsory pooling. He had won all of those battles with incontestable grassroots support, but many among those who had fought him never forgave him. This group continued to be uneasy about Williams's populism and left-leaning socialism. Some among them were convinced that if he was not a communist, then he was a communist sympathizer. The vigorous whispering campaign they had carried out against him lay at the roots of the secret meeting to persuade Williams not to seek the leadership. But Williams was proud of what he had accomplished. It was a bittersweet day for Williams: sweet because he had taken the farmers into politics on a socialist platform and persuaded them to unite with labour; bitter because he had surrendered his dream of leading the party to victory.

The adoption of the political program was not controversial. The foundational economic policy was adopted, as delegates voted on it clause by clause, as were the provincial and federal platforms. A successful amendment from the floor included a plank committed to "the socialization of all health services." There was much more heat over the selection of a name for the new party. Williams proposed the Socialist Party of Saskatchewan. He argued, "You have adopted a socialist platform and whether or not you call yourself a socialist party, your opponents will do so. Those countries that have come out four-square for socialism are closer to the realization of their ideals than those that have side-stepped the issue." He reminded delegates that the ultimate objective must be contained in the name, to remind the public, and the party itself, of the final goal. He also noted that continuing education on socialism, and on the nature of the capitalist economy, was essential to win the support necessary to implement it. Hence, explaining the differences between socialism and communism were vital educational and political tasks. Williams failed. The majority was persuaded by the argument that the public could not easily understand the difference between communism and socialism. This name would make the party a more vulnerable target of anti-communist smears. Other serious names were proposed: the Social Reform Party, the Co-operative Commonwealth Political Association, and the Farmer-Labour Party. The last of these was adopted on the grounds that it was neither too evasively moderate nor too radical, but conveyed a clear message of the social and class forces behind the party.

The next task was the selection of a leader. There were five nominees: Williams, Coldwell, Louise Lucas, Andrew Macauley, and John Evans.[7] As arranged, Williams nominated Coldwell. Williams was nominated by a chorus of voices. Coldwell, with considerable disingenuousness, declared that the leader should be a farmer—and accepted the nomination. Lucas, Macauley, and Evans declined their nominations. Williams rose at the microphone. As he prepared to address the convention, waves of applause and cheers erupted. He hesitated, growing emotional. The delegates responded with increased applause. Williams stunned the convention when he declined the nomination. He explained his reasons carefully. He had made many powerful enemies over the years as the movement marched to this day. He had played a major role in helping to steer the movement through controversial battles. The socialist platform just adopted was the culmination of that process; it will be widely feared and stridently denounced by the powerful and the press. If he accepted the leadership it would injure the party's electoral chances. The attacks would be focused on him and his trip to the Soviet Union, and this would detract from the party's message. Delegates, clearly disappointed, shouted that he had made a lot of friends too. When it became clear that Williams could not be convinced to become leader, the delegates applauded the acclamation of Coldwell as leader. Williams, however, was elected president of the party and chairman of the twenty-one-member political directive board. It was in reality a dual leadership, with Coldwell designated as political leader. The Farmer-Labour Party had a platform and a leader.

On July 31, two car loads of UFC(SS) delegates, including Williams, left for the Calgary western labour conference, which had been selected as the founding convention of the new socialist party to contest federal power. Coldwell and the ILP delegates were already there to attend the conference as a labour political party. The plan was for the western labour conference to end on July 31, with the founding convention convening on August 1. The UFC(SS) delegates had been instructed to push for the Socialist Party of Canada as the name of the new party. Williams was hoping to win in Calgary what he had lost in founding the Farmer-Labour Party. He was slated to present the joint economic policy to the convention as a proposed founding policy document. The Ottawa group had decided that the party should be founded with labour organizations in the lead, not farmers' organizations. Farmers' organizations were invited to attend the founding meeting and join the new party. The reason behind the opposition of Woodsworth and others to Williams's proposed June national conference of radical organizations was now obvious. Labour political parties, the Ginger Group, and the LSR would go down in history as the founders of the new party.

Just outside Calgary the car carrying Williams was hit by a farmer's car entering the highway from a side road. Williams suffered three broken ribs and extensive facial cuts from glass shards. He and the others arrived at the meeting a day late, bruised and battered. The joint economic policy had already gone through the convention and been reduced to an eight-point provisional program. The use-lease policy had been reduced to a promise of "security of tenure." Nevertheless, the program still contained the core planks. As reported in the *Canadian Forum*, "the eight-point programme proved to be a condensed version of the United Farmers of Canada and Independent Labour Party's joint Economic Policy."[8] Finally, the new party's name had already been approved: the Co-operative Commonwealth Federation of Canada (Farmer, Labour, Socialist).

Williams was a commanding presence at the convention, and not just due to his oratorical skills and the sympathy elicited by his heavily bandaged face. His earlier speaking tour of Alberta and British Columbia had favourably exposed him to most groups on the left. His correspondence with groups across Canada had provided him additional exposure. He was a leading political figure among farmers all across Canada, most importantly in Saskatchewan and Alberta. During his tour of British Columbia, Williams and Ernest Winch—the left-wing leader of the Socialist Party of BC, with roots in militant trade union organizing and an avowed commitment to Marxism—had established a warm political relationship, which continued throughout the 1930s.[9] Given Williams's stature, some among the right wing in his own party privately feared he might go for the leadership of the new party. He could count on strong support among farm delegates in general and the large left-wing BC delegation. In fact, the Saskatchewan farm delegation and the BC delegation formed a large bloc at the convention, second only to Ontario. Williams was indeed nominated for the leadership, but declined and nominated Woodsworth. Williams was elected to the seven-member provisional national council and named chair of a committee assigned to draft a constitution for the new party. As a result, he played an important role in organizing the first national CCF convention in Regina on July 19, 1933. The provisional council spent the three preceding days, July 16, 17, and 18, massaging the LSR's draft of the *Regina Manifesto* clause by clause.

The famous concluding sentence of the manifesto was a bit jarring given the largely moderate tone of the document, and doubt and controversy still prevail regarding its origins: "No CCF government will rest content until it has eradicated capitalism and put into operation the full programme of socialized planning which will lead to the establishment in Canada of the Co-operative Commonwealth." In fact, after becoming leader of the national CCF a decade later, Coldwell complained bitterly that the phrase was "a millstone around the neck of the party." LSR intellectuals worked with the provisional council in the drafting; those involved most closely in the final drafting just before the convention, Frank Underhill and Eugene Forsey, denied any recollection of where the sentence came from, especially the "eradicated capitalism" phrase.[10] Speculation remains strong that Williams, who worked with Forsey in drafting the final paragraph, inserted the phrase if not the entire sentence.[11] This seems possible. There is no record of an amendment from the floor to insert the phrase or the sentence, suggesting the sentence and the phrase were indeed contained in the document presented to the convention for approval. The manifesto was presented to the convention by Norman Priestly. He and Williams, as convention chair, guided it through to acceptance. The sentence certainly reflects Williams's often-expressed view that the ultimate objective of the movement must be clearly stated and always kept in the forefront in the hurly-burly of the fight for socialism. The response of the convention to the final phrase was electric—it led to a sustained standing ovation. There was no going back to the drafting table. Williams carefully led delegates through the now more moderate agricultural policy. He also shepherded the draft constitution through the meeting, carefully safeguarding provincial autonomy. He was elected to the eighteen-member national council and thus continued to play a prominent role in shaping the national party.

Upon returning from the national CCF's founding convention in Calgary, Williams began to work in earnest for the inevitable 1934 provincial election. Anticipating certain defeat, Anderson's Co-operative/Tory government clung to power as long as possible, but having been elected in 1929 the government had to call an election in 1934. Many saw the Farmer-Labour Party (FLP) as a major contender for power. But the powerful Liberal Party fully intended to regain office. A brutal three-way fight was inevitable, and the Liberal Party and the FLP were increasingly seen as the major contenders. The FLP's fifteen-point platform was distributed province-wide. It was an uneasy mixture of hard-nosed socialism and reformist agrarian populism. Yet in order to appeal to the working class in the cities and towns, it failed to include a comprehensive labour program—a major strategic error. The "ultimate objective" remained unchanged: "the present economic crisis is due to inherent unsoundness of the capitalistic system.... We recognize that social ownership and co-operative production for use is the only sound economic system."[12] The first three points, which would become the focus of attention in the election, proposed "a planned system of social economy"; "socialization of the...financial system of the country together with the social ownership, development, operation and control of utilities and natural resources"; and "security of tenure...by perpetual 'use-hold'" backed up by "the prevention of foreclosures."

The central elements of the FLP's economic policy were planning, public credit, publicly owned natural resources and utilities, and the protection of farm and home from foreclosure; it also proposed "social legislation to secure to the worker and farmer an adequate income." There followed a series of specific reforms: social security, electoral reform, debt relief, support for cooperatives, socialized health services, and educational reform. The program gave prominence to significant socialist planks constituting the first steps toward the ultimate objective of a fully socialized cooperative commonwealth. But taken as a whole, the program was crafted most importantly to defend the people of the province from the immediate ravages of the Depression. Upon implementation the program would take major economic activities out of the private sphere, massively expand public ownership in the economy, and generate large public revenues for social programs. But from an immediate political point of view, it would most significantly keep farmers on their land and protect their right to independent commodity production. The program's promises to save workers' homes, provide work with wages, and guarantee adequate incomes for all, though of great significance in the Depression context, do not lessen the greater benefits promised to farmers.

For the FLP the 1934 election began with the founding convention and the adoption of the platform. The new party was immediately attacked by the existing political parties and the press. The Tory minister of public works denounced the FLP as a "union of socialists, communists, and men of all shades of radicalism."[13] The press embarked on a sustained campaign against socialism, communism, and radicalism in all its guises, with the primary target being the FLP. The efforts of the Liberal and Tory parties, the daily press, and the Catholic Church to label the FLP as tainted by communism were unrelenting. Simultaneously, the Communist Party, through the FUL's publication *The Furrow*, denounced the FLP from the left, accusing it of deceiving people into believing it was possible to reform capitalism, thus deflecting the population from the struggle for real change. The FLP was on the defensive from the outset, defending itself against hysterical attacks and smears of communism. Inevitably, the most savagely attacked policy was the proposed nationalization of the land through the "use-lease" system. The simple defence that the program was purely voluntary did not appease critics who charged that farmers in difficult straits would have no real choice but to go along with the system. The FLP responded that "use-lease" was preferable to having the farm confiscated by the bank and leased back to the farmer to work as a serf. Williams's repeated statements that "the basis of the CCF land policy was a recognition of the family farm as the fundamental unit" did not satisfy those who insisted the policy was tantamount to forced collectivization.[14]

In 1932, Williams was invited by the FLP in Wadena constituency to accept the nomination for the coming election. The area included Williams's UFC(SS) district, one of the largest in the organization. He was well known throughout the area and he, in turn, knew most farm families. On November 19 he was acclaimed in a packed hall of cheering supporters. As Williams worked to organize Wadena for the coming election, and as he travelled to other rural areas to help organizing efforts, he began to realize he may have acted hastily in agreeing to decline the leadership. His decision, which in his mind had been made for the good of the movement, may have in fact been a monumental error. It appeared to have hurt the movement more than it had helped. His decision had not put to rest the communist smear campaign, which continued with intensity even with Coldwell as leader.

Williams found that his detractors were arguing that his decision not to become leader indicated he may well be a communist: otherwise he would have taken the job. Therefore, as he canvassed and attended meetings, Williams found himself again explaining that he was not a communist. Many farmers were deeply disappointed that he had not become leader, seeing it as an abandonment of the farmers' cause at its most important stage. Williams also discovered that Coldwell was not warmly accepted as leader among farmers. Many were skeptical that a schoolteacher from Regina could truly understand farm issues, while UFC(SS) activists and militants did not trust Coldwell's political credentials, recalling his political association with their old enemies on the right of the organization and in the Progressive Party. Williams began to fear his decision had been a major strategic error. It might have been better for the movement had he accepted the leadership, fought the communist bogeyman head-on rather than running from it, and provided the radical agrarian socialist leadership the UFC(SS)'s rural base expected. He began to doubt that the party, led by Coldwell, would do as well in the rural areas as anticipated. But the task now was to fight the election as best he could in Wadena and do everything he could to help the party win in 1934.

Premier Anderson delivered a speech in Yorkton early in the Depression, promising "no one will starve."[15] This was hardly a grand promise, but as the Depression deepened and continued, evidence was produced that indeed some had starved. Anderson never lived down his failure to keep his vow. Governments all across Canada were simply not equipped, either ideologically or economically, to deal with a disaster of this magnitude. And in Ottawa, the Tory government under Prime Minister R. B. Bennett refused to take the necessary action promptly, for ideological reasons. As a result, there was general political disaffection as governments fell all across Canada during the first years of the Depression: in 1933, Tory governments in British Columbia and Nova Scotia; in 1934, the Tory government in Ontario; in 1935, Tory governments in Prince Edward Island, New Brunswick, and Ottawa, joined by Alberta's UFA; and in 1936, the Quebec Liberal government. Only Premier John Bracken's uneasy Manitoba coalition of Liberals and

Progressives survived the Depression. In Saskatchewan, the Anderson government was doomed the moment the election was called.

As Saskatchewan entered the fourth year of depression, the situation had become catastrophic—each year more catastrophic than the last.[16] In 1929–30, the province's expenditures on relief were just under $800,000. In 1934–35, they topped $21 million. The value of farm property plummeted. Farm ownership had fallen to 61 per cent, while 19 per cent were part owner/part tenant, and 20 per cent were tenants. Much of this trend resulted from foreclosure agreements; such agreements on some or all of a farmer's land converted the farmer from owner to tenant. The price of wheat fell to 35 cents a bushel in 1932, and rose to 61 cents in 1934. The rise made little difference in meeting costs of production and living expenses.

The collapse in wheat prices was not mirrored in the costs of farm production. In 1934 a farmer's purchasing power was 59 per cent of what it had been twenty years earlier. Farmers staggered under a collective debt load of half a billion dollars. The market crisis was worsened by widespread drought, as average wheat yields fell to eight bushels an acre. The topsoil of whole farms—indeed, of whole crop districts in areas that never should have been put to the plow—simply blew away. In the mythology of the Depression in Saskatchewan, often too much is made of the drought. Had the price structure remained normal, the drought would have meant a few bad years for the areas affected. Throughout the Depression, the prices paid for wheat could not pay the costs of production even for those farmers who continued to harvest decent crops. Their crops could not find a price to make their planting and harvesting worthwhile.

In 1931 the Anderson government established the Saskatchewan Relief Commission, to ensure survival through the provision of the necessities of life and, in rural areas, to ensure continued agricultural production. In urban areas the provision of direct relief was tied to working on public works projects. Farmers applying for relief funding for inputs to maintain production signed agreements to repay the advances in the future. The per capita relief burden on the Saskatchewan government was the highest in Canada, almost four times the national provincial average. Add to this the existing provincial debt that had to be serviced and the expenditures for keeping the machinery of government running, and Saskatchewan faced bankruptcy without help from Ottawa. This support was granted with a heavy political price tag. The province was required to impose harsh austerity measures. The Farm Loan Board was granted no funds. Taxes were increased and new ones added, including a provincial income tax. All government expenditures were cut again and again. Civil service salaries were cut in 1932 and again in 1933. Highway construction was cancelled. However, these measures did not help; in fact, they made matters worse as cuts in services, incomes, and public sector jobs led to even greater unemployment and dependence on relief. As relief costs shot up each year, the province's deficit grew out of control. The increased and new taxes provided little extra revenue. The measures angered the population, who blamed the Anderson government and the Tories in Ottawa.

The Anderson government tried to salvage its reputation with a series of measures. Local tax arrears were a serious problem that resulted in many foreclosures and tax sales. In 1933 and 1934 the government adopted legislation to consolidate tax arrears on land, while allowing a temporary, penalty-free deferral of payment. This provided protection from immediate foreclosures and tax sales, but it only postponed the day of reckoning. Furthermore, the policy eroded the ability of rural municipalities to provide public services. On the matter of contracted private debt to banks, mortgage companies, and individuals, from 1931 to 1934 the government equivocated; it enacted a series of laws, beginning with a conciliatory debt-mediation plan and finally ending with a regulated, compulsory debt-adjustment program. In the final iteration, the law gave the provincial debt-adjustment board extensive powers to intervene directly in dealings between debtor and creditor. No creditor could sue for any debt without the board's permission, and permission was granted only if the debt was judged reasonable and the debtor was actually able to pay. This prevented foreclosures, but interest piled up as the debtor and creditor awaited the return to prosperity. As a result, the Anderson government pleased no one and angered many. The equivocations and delays in a plan with real teeth annoyed farmers. The final plan did not go far enough for the UFC(SS) because there was no downward adjustment of actual debt: debt just grew and grew. Nor were there measures to impose lower interest rates and longer amortization periods. The business lobby, especially private financial institutions, denounced the plan for going too far down the road of intervention and regulation.

The government won some strong points with farmers by helping to save the Wheat Pool and the Co-operative Creamery from threatened bankruptcy. And, as noted earlier, the government passed the laws requested by the UFC(ss) and the Wheat Pool to enable the establishment of 100 per cent compulsory pooling. On February 15, 1934, the Tory-led Co-operative Government presented its last Speech from the Throne:

> During the past year our people have again experienced unusual difficulties occasioned by abnormal economic conditions which have been world-wide in their scope and which have brought distress and difficulties to the peoples of all nations. Our Province, in addition, has had to face more than its fair share of adversity owing to another disastrous crop failure…with the result that today approximately 180,000 men, women and children on our farms have been and are being provided with assistance.[17]

But prosperity was just around the corner, and thus "our country may again soon be well on the road to definite progress and enduring prosperity." In the meantime, the Depression was beyond the government's control. It was worldwide. The government in Saskatchewan was doing everything it could and must: relief, retrenchment, austerity, tax and debt adjustment, salvage operations to protect important cooperative institutions, and agricultural production assistance. No more could be done within the constitutional limits of the powers of a province. On May 25, 1934, the government dropped the writ for the election: it would be held on June 19.

The Liberal Party came out swinging in a cynical campaign that combined nasty red-baiting attacks against the FLP with a dramatic rebirth of the Liberals as a left-wing party of the people. Liberal propaganda did not waste much time on the Anderson government, which was widely expected to crash. The Liberals went through the obligatory motions, accusing the Anderson government of "playing politics with relief," humiliating those who sought relief, and political patronage not only in distributing the jobs generated in the relief commission but also in deciding who got relief and how much they got. Liberal attacks on the FLP, on the other hand, were nothing short of vicious. The Liberals accused the party of planning to take away the titles to homes and farms. One pamphlet levelled the following charge:

> Coldwell proposes to drive you down deeper still.... He would rob you of the privilege to possess in your own right the proverbial six feet of earth—a plot of ground sufficiently large to allow your coffin to rest in peace. If he were at the head of the government he wouldn't give consideration to your debt difficulties until you handed over the... title to your farm and with it of course, your individual liberty to enjoy the right of ownership—a freedom for which your forefathers fought for centuries.[18]

Attacks of this sort were unrelenting throughout the campaign.

On the positive side, the Liberal Party was reborn as a left-leaning party of the people. The Liberals promised every "needy family" "food, shelter and clothing;" every farmer "feed for his stock and seed for his land;" and everyone "the titles to their own homes." The inadequate Tory debt adjustment plan would be toughened. New debt adjustment tribunals would be given sweeping powers to protect "all resident debtors." After a full investigation of the debtor's circumstances, the tribunal was empowered "to bring about, as between debtor and creditor, a fair and equitable adjustment or reduction of such debts, both as to principal and interest." Longer periods would be provided for repayment, and above all, any settlement must "secure to the debtor and his family the title and tenure of his lands and production and living expenses during the whole period of twelve months between successive crops." The tribunal could also "order an individual moratorium with respect to any debtor." Any other necessary measures would be taken "to protect the debtor and his family." The goal of the policy was "the reduction of debt to the point" to guarantee "the re-establishment in Saskatchewan of our farmers and workers in contented and comfortable homes of their own with freedom from the worries of an impossible debt, carrying on their calling under conditions which will ensure them security in their old age, and induce their children to remain with them and succeed them." The policy also promised "state medicine and health insurance." These were heady promises in the Depression—promises the Liberal government was never to fulfill. Obviously the Liberals borrowed heavily from the FLP platform, demanding also that Ottawa "take such steps as may be necessary to regulate industry and relieve unemployment," establish a publicly owned national central bank, and provide grants to provinces to re-establish a viable agriculture.

The FLP heaped scorn on both Liberals and Tories, who represented the hopelessly corrupt and patronage-ridden "old party system of government." Despite the daily hysteria conveyed by the press, and the harsh anti-communist attacks by both Liberal and Tory parties, the FLP did not back off its proposed remedies. Its declaration of policy for the election, with the slogan "Humanity First," was blunt in its commitment to socialism, although it now directed its attacks on the economic system more against "the financial interests" than against capitalism in general. The FLP promised a series of sensible reforms to deal with the crisis: a system of relief unblemished by patronage and corruption, a guarantee of adequate and fairly distributed relief, work and wages for the unemployed, socialized health care, pensions for the infirm, mothers' allowances, educational reform, and so on. But, of necessity, the main manifesto focused on the big economic questions on everyone's mind:

> What do you need at this time? First, to retain your home and land for your use, and prevent its confiscation by the financial interests. The Farmer-Labour Group (CCF) pledges itself to enact...all the legislation necessary to secure to you the use and possession of your home and land....The Farmer-Labour Group pledges itself to prevent your dispossession by financial corporations....The safety of your home depends on the election of a Farmer-Labour Government....Now is the time to strike a blow for economic freedom. The Province has the power of moratorium and we propose to use this power...to give our people a measure of justice....The Farmer-Labour Group is prepared to challenge the power of the money barons.[19]

Much of the FLP's propaganda was defensive: the party was not anti-Christian, would not engage in forced state expropriation, and stood firmly in defence of the family farm. The FLP felt it necessary to answer all charges against it. It was evident that the campaign of smear and red-baiting was quite effective in undermining trust in the FLP, and this forced the party to spend funds and time answering charges and reassuring the public, rather than engaging in a positive presentation of its program. In fact, as the election came to an end it became clear that it had been a disaster for the FLP, not only because of the effectiveness of the negative propaganda campaign, but also because of the party's pre-election overconfidence and poor organization at the constituency level. The FLP was no match for the Liberal machine. Except in the few seats won in rural areas, the FLP had no electoral organization to speak of, especially on the day of the vote, when getting supporters to the polls was essential.

Throughout 1933, and during the 1934 election, Williams criticized the electoral strategy devised by Coldwell and his leadership circle, who in turn were advised by key figures from the CCF office in Ottawa. Rather than responding to his criticism and suggestions, Coldwell and those around him tried to persuade Williams to run in the October 1933 federal by-election in Mackenzie, a rural constituency where the new CCF had a good chance of victory. Evidently, one way to get Williams out of the provincial scene was to convince him to go to Ottawa, where, he was told, his skills were sorely needed in the House of Commons. Williams, already committed to running in Wadena in the provincial election, declined the offer. Nevertheless, he shared the view that the Mackenzie seat was eminently winnable and worked hard in the by-election. On October 23 the CCF candidate lost to the Liberal by over 1,600 votes. Although CCF canvassing had indicated a solid chance of winning—and large public meetings featuring Coldwell and other leadership figures seemed to have confirmed that the momentum was in the CCF's favour—the result wasn't even close. Williams investigated the situation (Wadena was part of the federal riding) and concluded that victory had been snatched from the CCF because the party was out-organized by the Liberals on election day. The Liberals put in place an extensive carpool, picking up voters and taking them to the polls. He learned the Liberal drivers picked up anyone who wanted a ride and proceeded to harangue them on the evils of the CCF. Five days after the by-election, in a letter to a colleague, Williams expressed a view he shared with the party leadership:

> If we are going to win elections, it is absolutely necessary
> that we have more live Committees, that we will have more
> house-to-house canvassing and have an Intelligence Service
> that will report by long distance telephone to each constit-
> uency headquarters on the activities of the Opposition and
> then headquarters immediately dispatch someone to that
> section to counteract what has been done....In my recent let-
> ter to Candidates, I pointed out that the Justice of our Cause
> was not sufficient to insure us success.[20]

At the 1933 party convention, Williams had proposed a motion that
the proceeds from fundraising at public meetings and rallies be shared
fifty-fifty with local constituency organizations. The motion was defeated
and all funds collected went into the central coffers. He warned that
this deprived local associations of the funds needed to prepare for the
election. When campaigning for the 1934 election began, Williams complained that too much focus was put on mass public rallies, and as a
result, money that should be spent on building local organizations was
wasted on speakers touring the province. These large public rallies, he
noted, were simply preaching to the saved. The provincial organizer
agreed with Williams, complaining that "speakers are touring the country wasting the hard-earned nickels and dimes of our supporters and
not attending to the only thing that can keep our fellows in power once
we snatch victory at the polls."[21] He, like Williams, insisted that the
first priority had to be building strong, well-organized constituency
associations. The advice went unheeded. Meanwhile, Coldwell kept an
exhausting schedule, speaking at over two hundred public rallies during
the election campaign, with a total estimated audience of between fifty
and sixty thousand. It was not surprising that Coldwell and his election
team were confidently optimistic.

Williams was concerned the CCF leadership in Ottawa was overly
influential in shaping Coldwell's election strategy. Williams had already
clashed with the Ottawa group over making the building of strong provincial parties a first priority in the national strategy, rather than pursuing the
illusion of a quick victory at the federal level. At the founding convention,
Williams had successfully defended provincial autonomy in the national
CCF constitution, against the wishes of the Ottawa group. Pointing to the

old parties, each of which had strong provincial organizations with which to fight federal elections, Williams unsuccessfully insisted the CCF must do likewise. Williams's lack of organizational and tactical confidence in the national leadership increased dramatically when, on June 11, 1934, just eight days before the provincial vote, the national party inserted a centrepiece in its newspaper dismissing the significance of fighting elections at the provincial level, calling instead for a focus on the coming 1935 federal election. The centrepiece featured prominent photos of Woodsworth and Ontario CCF MP Agnes Macphail.[22] Woodsworth was quoted: "The Provincial field is not our natural element. We must aim higher—Ottawa our goal!" Under Macphail's photo appeared the following: "Miss Macphail knows…the Federal field is where the CCF should concentrate. Organize, therefore, for the approaching Federal election. Don't waste your ammunition on the Provincial 'sprat' to lose the Federal 'mackerel.'" Williams was incensed at the tactical stupidity this exhibited, and it confirmed his conviction that the national leaders, obsessed with Ottawa, were cavalier and thoughtless in their approach to provincial parties. His constant refrain about the need to focus on the grassroots organization of constituency associations and provincial parties, which he presented at meetings of the provincial party and of the CCF national council, continued to go unheeded.

Not only did Coldwell ignore Williams's advice, but he froze Williams out of the central campaign. Williams was not on the roster of speakers funded to tour the province, doubtless due to fears of communist-baiting. A survey of the two major daily newspapers in the province, the Saskatoon *Star-Phoenix* and the Regina *Leader-Post*, reveals not a single mention of Williams, nor of any of his comments during the election. Williams was notable by his absence on the platform at the biggest FLP rally of the campaign, in Regina on June 15. Only the *Western Producer* commented on Williams's campaign in Wadena, listing twenty meetings across the constituency at which he spoke during June.

Williams took his own advice. At his nomination, forty-two of forty-three polls in Wadena had representatives at the convention. By the time the election was called, Williams had over three hundred men and women organized into election committees: guides, canvassers, car drivers, plants to pose questions at meetings of opposing candidates, poll secretaries, poll managers, and a committee to take care of visiting speakers. Every poll was war-ready on election day. Every voter had been canvassed, and the committed and the undecided were canvassed a second and a third time. As the campaign entered the final days, Coldwell's chief organizer, sensing problems in rural areas the party had counted on, asked Williams to do a tour of rural seats. Williams pointed out he was broke and would need a car and expenses to do so. That support was not forthcoming, and the tour never happened. On his own, at the request of local candidates, Williams spoke in a limited number of rural constituencies. Like most farmers in the Depression, Williams faced tough times. He did not have the hundred-dollar deposit required of candidates. The deposit was raised from supporters during his many tours of the constituency. No blame can be laid at the feet of Williams for the FLP's 1934 electoral debacle. He had no hand in developing the election strategy, nor any significant role in organizing the provincial campaign. He was certainly free with his blunt advice, but it went unheeded. He was simply not wanted on the voyage by Coldwell and his group.

The results were devastating for the FLP, doubly so since the large successful rallies around the province had led many to expect a very strong showing. Some had even dreamed of victory. The FLP won five rural seats with 24 per cent of the vote, outpolled by the Tories, who won 27 per cent of the vote yet failed to elect a single candidate. The Liberals won fifty of fifty-five seats, with 48 per cent. The fact that the FLP vote was concentrated in certain rural areas resulted in its five seats and the title of official opposition. The distribution of the FLP's vote was significant, indicating it rested firmly on the popular base of the UFC(SS). The party did best in the richest and second-richest rural areas, with 30 per cent of the vote in the sixteen richest areas and 28 per cent in the seventeen next richest rural areas; support dropped to 23 per cent of the vote in the nineteen poorest areas.[23] In urban areas of all sizes the FLP was humbled, failing to win a single seat and trailing both Liberals and Tories in the popular vote. The 1934 results reflected the political and economic reality of the FLP's class basis at that point in its development. The party emerged as the challenger to Liberal political hegemony among the more economically advanced sectors of Saskatchewan's farmers. Among the more decimated sectors, it ran a poor third behind Liberals and Tories. In 1934 the FLP was the political expression of the organized farmers, the UFC(SS), which encompassed the "middle sort" of farmer, the better off though not the rich: those with a viable stake, those with something to defend and extend, those with sufficient class consciousness and self-confidence to organize and fight to improve their economic situation. In Saskatchewan this base was composed of those farmers who would embrace the uniting of agrarian populism with socialism under the leadership of Williams.

The postmortem at the FLP convention in July 1934, and among the inner circle during discussions before and after the convention, revealed general agreement as to what had gone wrong.[24] It was something that had been foreshadowed in the warnings and criticisms of both Williams and the provincial organizer before and during the election campaign: Coldwell and his leadership circle had been overcome with irrational optimism. In 1932, Louise Lucas, an open opponent of Williams, had predicted that "six months to a year of education" would bring the party to power. In the same year, Coldwell's provincial campaign manager predicted that with an election fund of ten thousand dollars the FLP could easily elect thirty to thirty-five members in the 1934 election.[25] After the election, everyone, including Coldwell, agreed that organization had been lacking, even "slip-shod," in the words of the provincial organizer. Coldwell reluctantly admitted that "Williams was a very good organizer" and conceded, "You cannot put the idea over unless you have organization and we had not the organization."

The significance of the results could not be evaded. The victorious candidates in the five rural seats were all prominent activists in the UFC(SS). They had heeded Williams's early advice and organized strong constituency organizations, modelled on Wadena (which in fact was based on the FUC's approach to grassroots organizing). They were all among the first candidates nominated (Williams was the first) and had begun to fight the election before it was called. Williams won Wadena with 51 per cent of the vote; Andrew Macauley, Williams's immediate successor as UFC(SS) president and a central member in Williams's inner leadership circle from the beginning, won Cut Knife with 46 per cent; Louis Hantelman, a leader in his UFC(SS) local and district council, won Kindersley with 39 per cent; Herman Kempler, a member of the UFC(SS) board of directors, won Gull Lake with 38 per cent; and Clarence Stork, an active member of his UFC(SS) local, won Shaunavon with 38 per cent. (Of the five, all kept the faith but Stork, who, after losing in the 1938 election, denounced socialism in 1939 and became an organizer for the Liberal Party.)

The FLP ran second in eighteen other rural constituencies: in six of these, the party lost by five hundred votes or less, and in three by two hundred votes or less. It can be reasonably argued that if Williams had accepted the leadership and ran a campaign his way, focusing on grassroots and detailed election-day organizing, the FLP would have done much better. The whole dynamic of the campaign would have been markedly different, with a primary focus on rural areas, where elections were won or lost in Saskatchewan. With the province's most popular farm leader leading the party, the FLP might well have swept rural Saskatchewan. But leaving aside the socialist agrarian populist campaign Williams might have led, a simple improvement in organization could have netted the party an additional nine to eighteen victories. Rural Saskatchewan was the birthplace of the party and remained its popular foundation. Ironically, Coldwell had been correct when he suggested, upon accepting Williams's nomination as leader, that the leader should be a farmer. Getting Williams to step aside had not avoided the communist smear, and Williams, seen as an albatross around the party's neck by Coldwell and his group, had done better than any FLP candidate. Apparently, Williams enjoyed greater electoral appeal than Coldwell after all.

The FLP had a great deal of work to do in the urban areas, large and small. In Moose Jaw, Prince Albert, Saskatoon, and Regina, FLP candidates distantly trailed the Liberals and Tories. In Regina, a two-member riding, Coldwell was humbled, placing fifth in a field of seven. In Weyburn, Tommy Douglas—destined to lead the CCF to victory in 1944—ran third in a field of four.[26] The wisdom of selecting as leader an urban schoolteacher with credentials as a moderate, and of focusing on a high-profile, leader-centred campaign characterized mainly by large public rallies, had failed as an electoral tactic. The results of the 1934 election confirmed that the FLP remained a militant farmers' party, though one committed to socialism and determined to realize an effective electoral alliance with the working class. In this the party had failed miserably. Williams and the UFC(SS) had at least delivered five seats and the status of official opposition. Coldwell and the ILP had delivered nothing.

Applying the same standard to his own leadership as he and his supporters had earlier imposed on Williams should logically have led

Coldwell to resign. Given the results of the election, and Coldwell's self-evident failure as leader, it was in the best interests of the movement for him to step down, convene a leadership convention, and graciously embrace Williams as the new leader. After all, Williams, despite his personal disappointment, had been gracious when he stepped aside from the leadership that had been his for the taking, nominated Coldwell, and declined his own nomination. Such a transition would publicly convey a clear sense of unity and undermine the widespread rumours of deep differences between Coldwell and Williams. The Liberals had made much of the alleged divisions between the two men during the election campaign, ridiculing the FLP as a house divided. There was enough truth in this to disrupt the party's work. The political facts of the case were incontestable. Williams was by far the most popular choice for leader among the delegates at the founding convention, and he continued to be the most popular figure among the party's membership. Williams had outperformed all FLP candidates at the polls—the acid test in any electoral strategy for winning power. The UFC(SS)'s popular base, with Williams's leadership, had delivered five seats and the status of official opposition to the party. The obvious next step was to move speedily and smoothly to crowning Williams as leader at the earliest opportunity and begin preparing for the next election. Coldwell, however, was determined to remain leader. Williams was just as determined to take the leadership from him.

Immediately following the election, Coldwell behaved not only with (perhaps understandable) personal disappointment and petulance, but also with indefensible irresponsibility as party leader. His behaviour was most consistent with a deliberate effort to sabotage the effectiveness of the five elected MLAs and to do whatever was necessary to deny Williams the leadership. On the day after the election, Williams telegraphed Coldwell urging that the elected members meet quickly to prepare for the coming legislative session. A House leader had to be selected, and preparations made on strategy and tactics in the assembly. Premier Anderson, upon conceding defeat, announced he would turn over power to Premier-elect Jimmy Gardiner in mid-July. Gardiner stated he would immediately convene an emergency session of the legislature (this never happened, however; the first session was convened in the fall). Williams emphasized the urgency to meet and plan for the session, given its importance to the FLP's political credibility. He received no response from Coldwell.

Williams then made a series of phone calls in a futile effort to reach Coldwell. During these calls he learned that Coldwell planned to leave for a vacation in Alberta on June 25, but would be at the FLP office in Saskatoon on June 23. Increasingly angry at Coldwell's failure to convene a meeting of the elected members, Williams drove from his farm to Saskatoon to confront Coldwell. He arrived in the street outside the office just as Coldwell was leaving. The confrontation between the two men in the street was unpleasant. Williams strongly emphasized the importance of the coming emergency session and the necessity to prepare for it. He told Coldwell he did not support any of the five elected members resigning to make way for Coldwell in a by-election. Coldwell would not win, given the Liberal sweep and the lack of support for Coldwell among farmers. Williams said he had made a mistake in stepping aside from the leadership in Coldwell's favour, a mistake he had no intention of repeating. Coldwell left and went on vacation.

Acting as president of the party, Williams convened a meeting of the five elected members in Regina on June 28. Members of the political directive board were not invited. By not including the board, Williams clearly intended to present the party, convening in convention on July 27, a *fait accompli*, politically impossible to rescind. The MLAS selected Williams as House leader and therefore leader of the official opposition. The group discussed plans for the coming session of the legislature. A press release issued by the group made it clear that Williams had been named House leader. Coldwell remained party leader. Williams had crossed his Rubicon, and there was no going back. Either he or Coldwell would prevail in the inevitable confrontation. If necessary, the choice would be made by the party's delegates assembled in the convention.

Upon returning from vacation, Coldwell struck back. Acting as party leader, he called a conference of the five elected members, defeated candidates, campaign managers, and the political directive board for July 26, the day before the convention. Reading from a prepared statement, Coldwell launched an attack on Williams.[27] His version of the Saskatoon confrontation was quite different from that of Williams. He made no mention of his failure as leader to quickly convene a meeting of the legislative caucus, nor did he mention the telegraph and phone messages he had ignored. He made no concession that Williams was concerned about the urgency of preparing for the session and the importance of the FLP's performance in the legislature. Instead, Coldwell's focus was on the issue of House leader and his own reluctance to support Williams, even though he allowed that, in the end, Williams probably would have been selected. But Coldwell had reservations about Williams's leadership. Coldwell did not agree with many of Williams's political views, nor did he appreciate his abrasiveness and outspoken approach in debates. Coldwell stated he had no confidence in Williams and was perhaps hoping an alternative House leader could be found. He saw no problem with postponing the decision for further reflection.

In other words, Coldwell conveyed the impression that the Saskatoon confrontation had focused on the House leadership and Williams's desire for the position. Coldwell criticized Williams for convening a meeting of the MLAs to choose a House leader without consulting either him as party leader or members of the board. Coldwell laid out the alternatives from his perspective: he could resign and Williams become provincial leader; he could seek a federal seat; he could stay on as leader, with Williams acting as House leader and Coldwell leading from the public gallery, and in the meantime seek a provincial seat, or alternatively, run in the 1935 federal election. Coldwell was arguing from a weak position, given the electoral disaster he had presided over. Nevertheless, he could not bring himself to graciously embrace Williams as the obvious choice for leader, an action that was obviously in the best interests of the party at that moment. Instead, he chose to justify himself personally and to launch an attack on Williams, thus deepening rather than healing divisions within the party.

Williams had not expected to be attacked at the conference. It became immediately clear to him that this had been the main intention of Coldwell and his supporters. Williams presented his case off the cuff. He carefully went over his version of the Saskatoon confrontation. Coldwell had made it clear as party leader that he saw no need for calling a speedy meeting of the elected members to select a House leader and plan for the emergency session. As president, Williams argued, he had had no choice but to act decisively to convene a meeting, select a House leader, and begin planning for the session. He noted that at the meeting the five elected members had agreed none among them should resign to clear the way for Coldwell to run in a by-election. He repeated his analysis of why Coldwell's defeat was inevitable. He reminded the conference he was selected as House leader, not as party leader. Williams forcefully rejected the argument that he was not an acceptable leader, reminding the conference that he had stepped away from certain election as party leader to give the position to Coldwell. Williams bluntly stated that he saw this conference as nothing less than an effort to prevent him from becoming leader. He rejected the notion that only Coldwell was capable of leading the party, given the recent election disaster.

The other elected members, and the provincial campaign manager, generally supported Williams's arguments and version of events, despite aggressive and persistent cross-examination by Coldwell's supporters. At one point Williams noted he had been unfairly put on trial, but he would concede one thing:

> I may have erred in political tactics, but I did what I did with the best of intentions, with honest intentions. I had no hope that Mr. Coldwell intended to make plans in time for the session. Every indication supported that belief. I do not think it entirely my fault, not by a long shot.[28]

At the same time, he stated that he had lost confidence in Coldwell's leadership and would not again step aside in his favour. "Two years ago I was of the opinion that it was in the best interests of the movement. Now I do not think it is the right thing for me to do." Coldwell did not respond to Williams's comments. Clearly if the conference did not find some mutually acceptable compromise, the leadership controversy would, of necessity, have to be resolved by delegates the next day on the convention floor. If that occurred, Williams would publicly humiliate Coldwell by defeating him in an open and democratic contest.

The meeting appointed a committee, made up of Coldwell, Williams, and three others, to find a mutually acceptable way out of the impasse. The committee quickly returned with a solution. A general procedure was established for selecting a premier, cabinet members, and a leader of the opposition: these decisions would be made within twenty-one days following an election at a meeting of the political directive board, elected MLAs, and defeated candidates. The decision of June 28 naming Williams as House leader was rescinded. Coldwell would continue as party leader with a salary of $4,000 per annum to replace his lost income. (When

Coldwell became leader, the Regina Board of Education had ordered him to either get out of politics or resign from his teaching position. Coldwell took an unpaid leave of absence, expecting he would have a legislative indemnity to live on. After his defeat, the party set up a fund to replace his lost income.) The conference accepted the solution. Prior to the convening of the convention the next morning, the political directive board, elected MLAS, and defeated candidates met to name Williams House leader. The recommendations and the appointment of Williams were ratified by the convention. Later, Williams and Coldwell drafted a memorandum of understanding outlining the relationship among the House leader, the elected members, and the party leader.

Williams and the caucus had complete freedom to act as they thought best in the legislature, determining all policies and tactics. On the other hand, Coldwell was obliged to consult with the caucus before issuing public statements. Coldwell rarely attended caucus meetings and was notable by his absence from the public gallery. With his income assured, he engaged in the full-time pursuit of a winnable seat to contest the coming 1935 federal election. Williams was the *de facto* leader of the party.

As 1935 began, Williams was in uneasy control of the party, in both the legislature and the party organization. The UFC(SS) and the FLP had officially separated, with the UFC(SS) continuing as a farm organization and the FLP adopting the name Co-operative Commonwealth Federation (Saskatchewan Section), or CCF(SS). In addition to appointing Williams House leader and hence leader of the opposition, the convention elected Williams to the executive of the political directive board while replacing him as chair. The convention, siding with Williams, re-affirmed the "use-lease" land policy, despite determined efforts from the right to replace the policy with something more moderate. The head office was moved from Saskatoon to Regina. Coldwell recommended that Williams run the central office, serve as party secretary, chair the committee to draft a constitution for the CCF(SS), and become provincial organizer. Williams was therefore in complete control of the party apparatus—as office manager, party secretary, provincial organizer, and House leader. Despite the fact that Coldwell had made these recommendations as party leader, some within the party began to criticize Williams for "running a one-man show," as Tommy Douglas put it later.[29]

In the aftermath of the 1934 election, the party was in organizational and financial disarray. Williams began to reorganize the party, get its finances in order, and devise a continuous membership drive. The Depression was worsening with each passing year, and the party's popular constituencies—farmers and workers—were increasingly destitute, yet Williams gradually turned the party around into a fighting machine. Persuaded by the effectiveness of his province-wide radio broadcast calling for farmer support for compulsory pooling, Williams made extensive use of education and propaganda through more paid province-wide radio broadcasts. The text of each broadcast was printed as a pamphlet and widely distributed. Though limited by a shortage of funds, Williams made radio broadcasts a high priority.

Based on the Wadena model, Williams drafted a detailed election campaign handbook and a curriculum for election schools for candidates, campaign managers, and party activists. These became templates for the national CCF and all provincial sections of the party. The electoral tactics that made the CCF famous—the focus on grassroots organizing, repetitive door-to-door canvassing, and a well-oiled election-day machine—were pioneered by Williams in his 1934 Wadena campaign. He argued that such tactics were necessary in order to win elections in a milieu where the party was under constant attack by the capitalist press and faced well-funded capitalist political parties.

Although Williams and Coldwell had worked out an uneasy *modus vivendi*, heated clashes between Williams and Coldwell supporters continued. The main issues were ideological and tactical. Coldwell and his wing of the party experienced deep discomfort at Williams's continuing principled and unapologetic advocacy of socialism as the party's chief *raison d'être*. Williams rejected any form of electoral opportunism that compromised the party's organizational and policy integrity. He insisted that the party must win power on a clear socialist program if it hoped to have the continuing popular support necessary to implement socialism successfully. He noted that the toughest battles with capitalism would occur after winning power, as the party moved to implement its program. Coldwell and his supporters were overly eager to give priority to winning elections first, and implementing socialism afterwards. Williams ridiculed such an idea as a convenient illusion fostered by office-seeking opportunists. He repeatedly warned party members of the danger of nominating candidates of questionable ideological commitment to socialism, declaring that "elections are won at the polls, but countries are lost at the nominating conventions."[30] Privately, Williams began to see men like Coldwell and Douglas as careerists whose first priority was to get elected and who were willing to engage in unacceptable political compromises to do so.

Williams was in his element in the legislature. He was an outstanding orator and debater in the assembly, easily the equal of the legendary Jimmy Gardiner, unsparing in his ridicule and sarcasm directed at the Liberal premier and government. Gardiner went to Ottawa in November 1935, appointed minister of agriculture in King's new Liberal government, a post he would hold for twenty-two years. His replacement as premier, the plodding William Patterson, was no match for Williams. Backbench Liberal attacks on Williams were personal, without substance, and typically peppered with communist smears. In his first reply as leader of the opposition to a Speech from the Throne, on November 19, 1934, Williams established the recurring themes for his speeches throughout his years as CCF leader in the legislature. He pilloried the phony "inward radicalism of the Liberal party," whose "lip service to radicalism" was a dishonest, cynical manipulation of a desperate population to gain election.[31] Yet here they were, now a government with an overwhelming mandate, ignoring "the economic needs of the day" they had promised to address. On the top of the Liberal priority list was the dismantling of the independent civil service commission in charge of hiring and firing put in place by the Anderson government. This was one of the few decent things that government had done, and it had done so under pressure from its coalition partners, the Progressives and the Independents. Obviously the Liberal government's most urgent priority was to bring back the Liberal machine of patronage and corruption, which was already resulting in "a Reign of Terror" within the professional civil service. This Liberal intention slipped out in a chance remark to a reporter by a newly elected Liberal MLA: "to the victor belong the spoils." Williams, in dismantling the government's entire legislative program outlined in the speech, established a reputation as a critic who did his homework and knew the details of the government's actions and failures to act. Williams's attention to detail, even the smallest, became legendary—the terror of cabinet ministers who often knew less about what was happening on the ground than he did.

More important were the political and ideological themes Williams enumerated as the foundation on which the CCF stood. Williams noted that this was a historic day: "For the first time in history," there existed "a fundamental dividing line between the Government and the Opposition." In all previous assemblies the difference had been "merely one of administration." The Liberals realized that the reason they cannot deliver their radical election promises was self-evident; that is, it was "impossible to keep both capitalism and the Liberal promises." Today the government and the opposition "disagree on a fundamental question of economics." The Liberals were "elected to make capitalism work." Therefore, on the Speaker's right were "the supporters of capitalism" and on his left were those who believed "the solution can only be found in socialism." The Depression was "the direct result of capitalism, and can never be permanently rectified." The basic issue was the control of "capital," the consolidated wealth produced by all who work and labour. Under socialism, capital was controlled for the common good. But under capitalism, capital was controlled privately to enrich those who possess it. This government was a capitalist government, charged with passing and enforcing "laws to protect the ownership of capital," "to protect invested capital," and "to guarantee the earnings of capital." All around the world capitalism was failing "and about to be superseded by socialism." Later, Williams detailed his critique of capitalism and vision of a socialist Canada in a booklet, *Social Democracy in Canada*, concluding with "a plea for social justice." The booklet, full of passion and anger, provided a record of Williams's ideological core. It became a political handbook of the early CCF, read widely by members and supporters and quoted frequently by candidates on the hustings. It was a cry from the heart of a political leader in the province hardest hit by the Depression:

> The system of profit-making means hunger, thirst, naked-
> ness, eviction, broken homes. It means children crying for
> bread and dying for lack of medical attention....The cruelty
> of this system is all the more cruel because it is impersonal.
> Would I could take all well-fed, satisfied men and women
> and show them the other three-fourths of Canada, homes
> of fear, men who have lost their courage, women who have
> lost their hope, and children who have lost their birthright

to happiness.... [W]ill you make one more attempt to lend your aid earnestly and honestly in making a better world, and thus fulfill your duty to the coming generations? Think not to do it without suffering and sacrifice. You will find, as others have, that you will be vilified, lied about and despised by people with power and prestige. It will be necessary for you to remember, times without number, that they who would not suffer, will never be great enough to serve.[32]

Party members in Coldwell's wing were genuinely convinced that Williams's firm socialist convictions, militant speeches on dismantling capitalism and building socialism, and strongly worded radio broadcasts and pamphlets would render the CCF unelectable. They were convinced that moderation was the road to power, whereupon they could build a better world.

Williams was annoyed that some refused to give priority to building the party organization and recruiting members. A group of prominent moderates, led by Douglas, founded the province-wide Saskatchewan Home Protective Association, advocating that farmers' home quarter sections and workers' homes be exempt from seizure for debt through amendments to the Debt Adjustment Act. These were already part of the CCF's program of immediate emergency reforms and had been one small part of the agricultural policy of the FUC and then the UFC(SS) from the beginning. Such an effort served to divert members, finances, and the energy of activists into a single-issue reformist movement.

From the beginning of his political journey, Williams had disagreed with the moderate and reformist approach. He argued that the only purpose for seeking power must be to build socialism, and in order to do so the public must support the project. Only with popular support could the party, once in power, begin to implement socialism. It was difficult to reconcile the two positions, though Williams was not opposed to tactical zigs and zags on the road to power.

Coldwell's very public attack on Williams had split the party badly, and the chasm deepened between the majority supporting Williams and the minority on the right. In a letter to fellow MLA Andrew Macauley, Williams—very much aware of the opposition against him—commented that some of it stemmed from political fear due to the communist smear campaign and some from personal jealousy at his ascension to the leadership, but most of it was due to their "reactionary" ideology. But he also noted that this opposition was not supported "by the great bulk of the rank and file, but only by a small group with ulterior motives."[33] The group's primary motive was to oust Williams from the leadership and replace him with a moderate. Yet Williams was confident. It was the same scenario he had faced when he won the leadership of the UFC(SS). He had prevailed then because the rank and file supported him, and he was confident he would prevail again.

The right of the party was particularly critical of Williams's approach to problems posed by the activities of the Communist Party. The CP was active in organizing and working in a variety of front groups, most importantly the FUL and the Workers' Unity League. The CP gave priority to organizing among those hardest hit by the Depression and hence was a growing organization, largely due to its militant and courageous political work. Party activists provided leadership in organizing groups to battle on behalf of evicted farmers, striking workers, relief recipients, and the unemployed, many of whom worked for relief on public works projects. These extraparliamentary actions involved sit-ins, hunger marches, aggressive picket lines at relief offices, strikes of the unemployed working for relief on public projects, and militant strike support. At the same time, CCF activists, especially members of the Co-operative Commonwealth Youth Movement (CCYM), were strongly committed to working in "the day-to-day struggle" and, therefore, inevitably worked side by side with CP members.

Williams's approach to the "political problem" posed for the CCF by the CP was sophisticated and nuanced, informed by his earlier battles with the FUL. In his ongoing correspondence with Ernest Winch, the left-wing leader of the CCF in British Columbia, both men discussed the CP problem. One part of the problem was how to handle political competition with the CP for popular support; another part was how to handle the right wing in their own party, which advocated public denunciation of the CP and refused to work with CP members in all situations. Winch faced the bigger problem, since the CP was much stronger in BC, having won the leadership of some of the biggest and most militant unions. Both men were aware the CP had two main objectives in its political work in relationships with the CCF: first, the CP worked to convince activists and the general population that the CCF was hopelessly right wing and therefore not a vehicle for fundamental progressive change; second, the CP sought to recruit activist and left-leaning members of the CCF and the CCYM, as well as activists generated spontaneously in the day-to-day struggle. Both Williams and Winch believed the CCF had no choice but to play an active and public role in all day-to-day struggles. As a principled socialist movement, it was vital that the CCF stand shoulder to shoulder with the victims of capitalism. More pragmatically, it was essential to prevent the CP from gaining recognition as the main public voice for socialist change and to win over to the CCF activists generated in the daily struggle.

Inevitably, controversies arose from the day-to-day struggle. Moderate members in some constituencies sent letters complaining about the activities of those they suspected of being CP members—most importantly, their domination of party meetings and proposal of radical motions. There were complaints from rural areas about CCF members working with FUL members to picket and disrupt auctions of foreclosed farms. In Regina, Moose Jaw, and Yorkton, CCYM members participated in relief protest groups and unions of the unemployed, working with CP members. In Yorkton, a strike of relief workers on public works projects clashed with police, and a number of CCF, CCYM, and CP members were arrested. In Regina, CCYM members were involved in a protest organization battling Regina's city council over relief policy. The group included known CP members. Regina CCYM members, working with CP members, held a public meeting in Moose Jaw protesting relief. The group stepped over the line by publicly proposing a joint CCF-CP candidate in Moose Jaw for the 1935 election. The Moose Jaw CCF was understandably angry.

Such events generated a lot of press coverage, especially the fact that CCF and CP members were working together.[34] It was grist for the communist smear mill of the Liberals, the Tories, and the press, and it led to a major confrontation between the right of the party and Williams. The right demanded that the members involved be censured and disciplined. In what became a coordinated campaign, complaints poured into central office about Williams's failure to publicly criticize those CCF members working with CP members, or to denounce the CP's tactics. Williams agreed the proposal for a joint CCF-CP candidate was unacceptable and sternly reprimanded those responsible. They apologized and promised it would never happen again. The right brought their complaints to the executive. It was proposed that the CCF become an exclusively parliamentary party and abandon the day-to-day struggle; that Williams take a hard public line denouncing the CP and its tactics; and that those who worked with CP members, or appeared on public platforms with a CP member, be expelled from the party. Even Woodsworth weighed in, advising Williams by letter that CCF members should never, under any circumstances, associate with, or work with, members of the CP. Williams disagreed and stood firm. If the advice of Woodsworth and other members on the right were followed, it would mean the CCF would be entirely absent from the day-to-day struggle. The reality was, as Williams pointed out to Woodsworth, the CP was a large and "fluid" organization, its members moving quickly and easily from group to group. It was impossible to work for the unemployed, the hungry, the relief recipient, the dispossessed farmer, or the striking worker—indeed on behalf of any of the victims of capitalism—without working beside members of the CP. To entirely abandon that political terrain to the Communist Party would be a serious mistake.

Williams prevailed at meetings of the party's executive. The executive declared support for members working in the day-to-day struggle. Given the continuing public controversy, and continuing opposition within the party, Williams sent a circular to all constituency associations, federal CCF candidates, and their campaign managers. The letter focused on the Yorkton situation, which was the subject of extensive press coverage:

> The CCF is the "Peoples' Party." When the people are in trouble the CCF is their champion. Once more the CCF is in the Front Line Trench. Relief schedules at Yorkton have proven inadequate. Not only is this the case, but in addition, the town of Yorkton has adopted a "Work Before You Eat" Policy. We do better than that for our work horses. No respectable farmer thinks of making his horses work before he feeds them. Grave doubts exist as to the right of Canadians to undertake Mass Demonstrations, peaceful picketing and collective bargaining.[35]

The circular explained why the executive believed the CCF had to take a stand on these issues whenever they arose.

However, this did not settle the matter. Opposition continued, fuelled by fears of a negative impact on CCF candidates in the 1935 federal election. Williams answered the letters of complaint in great detail, particularly those that argued Williams and the executive had violated existing party policy by allowing these events to go on. The Yorkton relief strike and the arrests were often the focus, given the headlines generated. Williams noted that the party platform stood for a living income for all and the rights to freedom of speech, public assembly, and collective bargaining. Rejecting the charge that such events hurt the party's chances in elections, Williams replied, in this case, to the secretary of Saskatoon's federal constituency association. He pointed out the political importance of the CCF's involvement in direct action:

> I hardly think any large number of people believe our program is anything to be talked about and not acted upon. If there are any large number of people who hold this opinion the future of the CCF is doomed. In the past we have always allowed the Communists to take direct and effective action, while we stand on the side lines and then are placed in the position of the Communists coming along and asking if we were going to help them fight for the workers. Thus they become the people who get the credit for taking the initiative and we become the fifth wheel on the buggy.[36]

The pressure from the right continued. As a result, the chair of the political directive board, a Coldwell ally, threatened to resign over the issue. The executive had not consulted the board in formulating the party's position. Another member of the board was criticized for appearing frequently on public platforms with Tim Buck, the national CP leader. Some demanded Williams be censured for his position on working with the CP and that members of the board appearing on public platforms with CP members be removed from office. A June board meeting was convened to resolve the matter. The board supported Williams and the executive, stating that "local organizations of the CCF have taken and will continue to take part in the daily struggles of the people against the efforts of the Capitalist system to restrict their standard of living."[37] Members of the CCF could therefore work with other groups, as long as it was clear this was not a political arrangement. As for appearances on public platforms with CP members, the board refused to single out the Communist Party and instead further limited the ban: appearing on the public platform of any opposing political party would lead to a member's suspension from the CCF. However, appearances on public platforms sponsored by groups fighting to defend victims of capitalism, even if a CP member was on the same platform, were permitted.

The day-to-day struggle was a growing political reality, especially that of unemployed workers.[38] If you were a socialist in a political party claiming to represent workers, their struggle was impossible to ignore. Even in Saskatchewan, a province dominated by farmers, the struggles became desperate and confrontational. Given the results of the 1934 election, the CCF had yet to gain significant support among the working class. To stand with workers in these struggles would begin to turn this around. The year of the FLP's founding, 1932, had been a tumultuous one. In Regina, a May Day parade of ten thousand workers and supporters ended in violence and arrests when police attempted to disperse the crowd. In October a strike by relief workers was suppressed by the police. In November, in Saskatoon, a large rally supporting the unemployed was attacked and dispersed by police; a riot ensued, with dozens on both sides injured and hundreds arrested. As a result, in 1933 May Day parades were forbidden in Regina, Saskatoon, and Moose Jaw. Police raids on union halls and the offices of organizations designated by police as "radical" became commonplace. On May 8, 1933, outside a relief camp near Saskatoon, a demonstration of the unemployed and their supporters was broken up by police. Many were injured, an RCMP officer was dragged to death by his horse after being unseated in the scuffle, and many were arrested. Twenty-two were convicted of various charges, including unlawful assembly, rioting, and assaults on police. To march, picket, rally, or strike invited instant declaration as an unlawful assembly followed by police attacks to break up the event. Such struggles, though on a smaller scale, continued throughout the 1930s in defiance of police repression.

Williams was next criticized within the party for his role in supporting the 1935 On to Ottawa Trek. In 1932, faced with 30 per cent unemployment and growing political unrest across Canada, the Bennett government's Department of National Defence established a national network of unemployment relief camps for single unemployed men. As a group, these men were feared as a fruitful field for political radicalization and dangerous unrest; hence, the camps were located in remote and rural areas. Single unemployed men were denied relief and arrested for vagrancy, thus forcing thousands to "voluntarily" enroll in the camps. The alternative was stark: hunger, homelessness, and police harassment. Over 170,000 young men spent time in the camps. In exchange for a bunk bed, three meals and 20 cents a day, work clothes, and minimal medical care, the men provided forty-four hours a week of hard physical labour. Ironically, rather than curtailing unrest, the camps became hotbeds of radicalism and protest, training camps for budding militants. The CP and other militants organized the camps, leading strikes and sit-downs to protest conditions. Militants organized the Relief Camp Workers' Union, with locals in virtually every camp. In April 1935, BC relief camp workers went on strike and decided to converge on Vancouver to protest the conditions in what they called "slave camps." Over fifteen hundred strikers made the journey. The Vancouver May Day parade to Stanley Park, featuring the strikers, attracted twenty thousand. After weeks of rallies, picket lines, and sit-ins in Vancouver, which enjoyed general popular support, strikers voted to go "on to Ottawa" to submit their case to the Bennett government. In early June, hundreds of strikers climbed onto and into boxcars, with the tacit complicity of the Canadian Pacific Railway (CPR), and headed for Ottawa. Stopping for a few days at every major centre en route, the trekkers found gratifying popular support in the form of food, beds, funds, and willing local participants in marches and rallies.

The Trek arrived in Regina on June 14. Preparations had been made by a local emergency committee, which Williams joined. Bennett ordered the RCMP to stop the Trek in Regina, insisting that no striker be allowed beyond that point and that police assist the CPR in denying strikers access to boxcars moving east. The trekkers camped out on the exhibition grounds, making the stadium their home. Local supporters mobilized to fill their needs. Some restaurants declared they would not charge trekkers for meals. Williams made a radio appeal to farmers to provide trucks to transport strikers. Some moderates, and even members of his own caucus, expressed concern about Williams's prominent public exposure as an active Trek supporter, given the widely known role of the CP and indications that the whole situation could end very badly.

Williams defended his position: "Behind it all is a principle, the principle being these boys have no chance to become citizens in the true sense of the word. They cannot get jobs, build up a home and have a wife and family as each citizen is entitled to have."[39] The large RCMP presence around the exhibition grounds and at the CPR yard indicated the trekkers would be stopped by all necessary means. As a compromise, eight Trek leaders were invited as a delegation to travel to Ottawa to present their case to the prime minister. In return, it was agreed that after the delegation reported back on the Ottawa meeting, the Trek would disband. It appeared the Trek would end peacefully.

The June 22 meeting in Ottawa turned ugly, however, deteriorating into a shouting match. The delegation was unceremoniously escorted from the building with nothing accomplished and arrived back in Regina on June 26. Police presence around the exhibition grounds and the stadium was increased. Trekkers trying to leave the city by car or truck were turned back by police. A July 1 public meeting was called in Market Square, in the centre of the city. The purpose of the meeting was to report on the Ottawa confrontation with Bennett, declare the Trek disbanded, and appeal for funds to assist the trekkers in their return to homes or camps. Estimates of the evening crowd vary from fifteen hundred to two thousand. Having already been informed about the Ottawa meeting and the plan to disband, only three hundred trekkers attended what was assumed would be a low-key rally. Most remained at the stadium preparing for departure. But the rally turned out to be a police ambush. What neither the crowd nor the Trek leaders knew was that Bennett had ordered the RCMP to arrest the leaders. Large ice cream trucks near the rally contained the RCMP's riot squad; Regina city police hid in a garage in the vicinity; and some distance away, mounted RCMP officers awaited instructions to advance. Upon a signal, the police attacked the crowd, as the opening salvo in a four-hour moving riot throughout the city centre.

Williams was viewing a movie at a downtown theatre when the riot began. Entering the lobby, he found a number of young men seeking sanctuary, some injured by club blows and all suffering the effects of tear gas. He led them out the back exit to safety, where they could wait until the violence subsided. The police, mounted and on foot, attacked with clubs and tear gas. Some fired their pistols over the crowd's heads, and some witnesses claimed shots were also fired into the crowd. The crowd broke in all directions and began to fight back. Over 120 strikers and locals were arrested. Hundreds, both police and demonstrators, were injured. A police officer and a trekker died of their injuries. Those taken to hospital were arrested, whereupon those helping the injured began to hide and treat them in private homes. The police force around the exhibition grounds was increased, now armed with machine guns. Barbed wire was erected around the grounds. The next day, armed with a pass from the trekkers, Williams gained access to the grounds. Finding the men there in desperate need of food, he issued an appeal to farmers around Regina to truck in food. Food and financial donations poured in. The police blockade was moderated, allowing access to food, medical supplies, and volunteers. Bennett ordered the arrest of those aiding the trekkers. Wisely, the order was never carried out. Williams issued a press release from his office informing Bennett that he had been, was, and would continue helping the trekkers as much as possible. If the prime minister wished to order his arrest, Williams could be found in the office of the leader of the opposition at the legislative building.[40]

Public opinion across Canada, already sympathetic to the trekkers' cause, turned massively in their favour and against the Bennett government. The government's reputation was shredded, despite Bennett's insistence that his government had stopped a revolutionary uprising. Williams's reputation was enhanced. No damage was done to the CCF's credibility; indeed, the event provided a boost in support. Williams, however, had to share accolades with Premier Gardiner. Gardiner accused the police, acting on Bennett's orders, of provoking the riot just as his government was in the midst of negotiating an orderly end to the Trek. The Gardiner government helped end the Trek peacefully by rejecting Ottawa's plan to forcibly assemble the trekkers in Lumsden for orderly processing. The provincial government paid the rail fare for trekkers to any destination in the West. Most returned to Vancouver.

With the end of the Trek, Williams was confident the CCF had a good chance of winning power in the 1938 election. Party membership and popular support were growing. The party was getting its finances in order. Constituency associations were under construction in the urban centres. The obstacle to victory was Coldwell. He had to go. In private correspondence with Macauley, Williams was blunt: "As a propagandist Coldwell ranks 100% but as a Leader? Coldwell has not a dog's chance of either being elected next election, or succeeding as an Organizational Leader. He does not understand farmer reactions well enough and is not practical."[41] Coldwell secured the nomination for the 1935 federal election in Rosetown-Biggar, a winnable seat. If Coldwell won and went to Ottawa, he would resign from the leadership, providing an orderly succession. Williams would then have the opportunity to realize his ambition of leading the party to victory. Then events in Alberta intervened, changing everything.

———

In 1932, schoolteacher and part-time radio evangelist William Aberhart had no idea of the political prairie fire he was igniting when he began to introduce social credit ideas into his radio broadcasts.[42] The ground in Alberta was fertile. Proposals for monetary and credit reform, the Douglas system of social credit most prominent among them, were widely popular in the province.[43] Indeed, the core ideas had been ideological centrepieces of the agrarian populist crusade from the beginning. The UFA organization supported much of the doctrine. In Ottawa, UFA MPS were among social credit's most passionate advocates. Simplified versions of social credit ideas were therefore deeply embedded in agrarian populist political culture. The overwhelmingly positive popular response Aberhart received convinced him to focus his broadcasts more on social credit and less on religious themes. His broadcasts became tutorials on his reinterpretation of social credit, one repudiated by orthodox social crediters. In 1933, Aberhart began to carry his message across the province in person, speaking to large public meetings. He proved an electrifying speaker. He trained a cadre of public speakers to meet demand for lectures. Printed propaganda was sent out in response to many requests from listeners. Donations poured in. Aberhart's Calgary Prophetic Bible Institute became the headquarters of the new movement, and a network of study groups was established throughout the province.

By 1934, thanks to Aberhart's agitation, social credit dominated the province's political debates, on the streets and in the legislature. Alberta Federation of Labour and UFA conventions demanded the UFA government investigate social credit and its application to Alberta's economic problems. The pressure on the UFA government from the membership of the UFA organization was enormous. In 1933, the UFA organization officially affiliated with the national CCF. The UFA government ignored this, however, and refused to implement a CCF program. The search for Depression remedies—social credit or cooperative commonwealth—resulted in a surge in the UFA's membership, from eight thousand in 1933 to thirteen thousand in 1934. The new arrivals wanted action, and action now.

At the January 1934 convention it was evident the rank and file of the UFA organization was slipping from the grasp of the UFA government. Proponents of social credit and CCF Depression remedies dominated the convention. Many argued that the two sets of ideas could be reconciled and supply the basis for a plan of action for the government. Those favouring social credit far outnumbered those favouring the cooperative commonwealth. The same was true in the legislature, as UFA backbenchers pushed social credit while the small group of Labour-CCF MLAs pushed the cooperative commonwealth. Both factions united in denouncing the government for failing to adopt either set of remedies, thus allowing conditions to worsen with each passing year. Under irresistible pressure, the government agreed to allow the legislature's Agricultural Committee to hold public hearings to inquire into the application of social credit to the crisis in agriculture. Both Douglas and Aberhart were invited to testify. As the UFA government had hoped, the two men contradicted each other on whether the province had the constitutional powers to proceed with social credit. The government had expected this would discredit Aberhart, but this plan backfired. Instead, Aberhart's appearance before the committee received front-page news and greatly enhanced his stature as a public figure. The committee's report concluded that, though "controlled Social Credit" might be beneficial and even necessary, it "did not offer any practicable plan for adoption in Alberta under the existing constitutional conditions."[44] In response, Aberhart quickly published a pamphlet, *The B.N.A. Act and Social Credit*, in which he insisted it was possible to implement social credit in Alberta with existing constitutional powers and lambasted those who would hide behind the constitution to avoid action. The committee endorsed social credit while insisting that legalistically it could not be done; Aberhart's highly political response to the committee discredited the government. The population urgently wanted solutions, not a debate about the constitution.

During the summer and fall of 1934 the UFA government was alienated from the membership of its own organization, and hence from its rural political base (the UFA never contested urban seats). The organization was split between a minority of CCF and a majority of social credit supporters, all united by anger with their own government. Things deteriorated further. Premier Brownlee resigned when found guilty in a seduction case brought by a young secretary in the Attorney General's office and her parents, family friends of the Brownlees. The minister of public works made headlines in a divorce scandal. Evidence of irregularities in awarding highway construction contracts emerged in the legislature. Such events further wounded the government, which was increasingly under attack by Aberhart. Mass defections of UFA members to the newly founded Social Credit League took place. Many UFA locals simply voted themselves out of the organization and became Social Credit League study groups. Long before the 1935 convention, the UFA government had become a government without a popular mandate and without a viable mass organization. The final humiliation occurred at the convention when UFA political and organizational leaders were forced to debate Aberhart about whether the UFA should campaign in the next election on a social credit platform. Though the resolution to do so was defeated by delegates, Aberhart had scored another political victory. In a radio broadcast two days before the convention, Aberhart announced a "straw vote," asking voters if they would support a "100% Social Credit candidate."[45]

During the 1935 session of the legislature, Aberhart announced he had 90 per cent support in his straw poll. He put out a call for one hundred honest men to help him. His attacks on the government became harsh; he accused them of "graft, fornication, and hypocrisy" and denounced them as "reprobates who denied the truth."[46] In March he released the Social Credit platform, describing it as a plan for Alberta to solve the problems of debt and unemployment and to rescue agriculture. In June he released a more detailed personally authored booklet, *Social Credit Manual: Social Credit as Applied to the Province of Alberta; Puzzling Questions and Their Answers*. He described his "wondrously simple plan," based on one premise: "It is the duty of the State…to organize its economic structure in such a way that no bona fide citizen…shall be allowed to suffer for lack of the basic necessities of food, clothing, and shelter, in the midst of abundance." Economic control of Alberta's natural resources must be taken from the "Fifty Big Shots of Canada," since the resources were "the property of the…bona fide citizens of our province."[47] On August 22, 1935, the Social Credit party swept the province, winning fifty-six of sixty-three seats with 54 per cent of the vote. Voter turnout reached a record 83 per cent. The UFA failed to win a seat, while the Tories won two and the Liberals five. Labour-CCF and Independent Labour were decimated.

The Social Credit victory in Alberta confronted Williams and the CCF with a deepening political crisis, particularly when the party's organizers entered Saskatchewan in large numbers to organize for the October 14, 1935, federal election. CCF candidates and their campaign managers, especially in seats identified as winnable, became frantic. The party was already in serious difficulty, given the FLP's poor showing in 1934. Enthusiasm for the CCF had waned. The UFC(SS), now under more moderate leadership, was less inclined to participate actively in the party. Like Alberta, Saskatchewan was fertile ground for social credit ideas. The UFC(SS) had supported many of its tenets since its founding. The rank and file, and therefore the rural public, were confused; many believed the two sets of doctrines were similar and could be readily reconciled. Many among the CCF leadership, including Coldwell, had earlier expressed support for social credit analyses of the banking system. Williams's denunciations of finance capitalism echoed with rhetoric freely borrowed from social credit, while he insisted social credit doctrine was fundamentally opposed to socialism and supported capitalism. There were calls for fusion of the two parties, joint candidates, and "saw-offs." The prospect of splitting the progressive reform vote in 1935 worried many. Social Credit's phenomenal success in Alberta gave the party incontestable credibility. The anticipated success of CCF candidates in a number of seats was at risk if Social Credit candidates ran, and if Social Credit swept many seats, the very existence of the CCF in the province was in jeopardy.

On September 3, a joint memorandum from Coldwell and Williams to federal candidates instructed them to argue that "Social Credit cannot be made to operate in a capitalistic economy," though Ottawa should not block Aberhart's efforts in Alberta.[48] Within the month, Williams's position hardened in response to efforts by Social Credit organizers to convince CCF candidates to stand down or agree to become joint candidates. A September 28 memorandum from Williams declared the only way to stop Social Credit was "to get out and fight it." Now he directed candidates to inform the public that Social Credit and CCF ideas were contradictory—Social Credit was capitalist; the CCF was socialist. As events unfolded, Williams heard rumours that Coldwell's campaign organizer was negotiating to convince Social Credit not to run in Rosetown-Biggar. Coldwell denied any knowledge of this. Yorkton CCF candidate Jacob Benson, already nominated by the CCF, sought and received Social Credit endorsement, signing a Social Credit recall pledge.[49] Williams, Coldwell, and the provincial executive acted quickly, stripping Benson of the CCF nomination. Concerned about the damage a political alliance between Social Credit and the CCF in Saskatchewan would cause the federal party, Woodsworth agreed with taking a hard line—a CCF candidate must be only a CCF candidate.

Having stripped Benson of his CCF candidacy, the executive then faced the problem of Tommy Douglas, nominated as the CCF candidate in Weyburn. The local Social Credit party had publicly pledged support for Douglas; in turn, he had publicly accepted that support and expressed general support for Social Credit principles. Social Credit's provincial organizer viewed Douglas as a joint CCF–Social Credit candidate, and posters and handbills to that effect were widely distributed in the constituency. Douglas was summoned to a meeting with the provincial CCF executive. Their interrogation of Douglas led them to conclude that he should be stripped of his CCF candidacy. Williams was particularly unrelenting and effective in his cross-examination of Douglas. Coldwell, though willing to repudiate Benson, defended Douglas completely, opposing the majority. Coldwell threatened public resignation as party leader if Douglas were repudiated. In the end, Douglas was saved because of four contributing factors: one, he had not signed the recall pledge; and two, the election was just days away. A third factor was Coldwell's threat to resign. But Williams's tactical instincts were the fourth, and most important, factor. The executive stood firm against Coldwell's threat; they insisted that Douglas be stripped of the CCF candidacy and that the decision be immediately released to the press. Williams then chose not to act on the decision. He concluded, given Coldwell's threat, that doing so would hurt the party on the eve of the election. He did this even though, prior to the decision, Woodsworth had written a letter supporting repudiation, in which he said, "Much as I should like to see Douglas elected I feel that…he should make his choice now."[50] A month later, fully informed of the Douglas case, the CCF national council upheld Williams's position, establishing a policy that no provincial or local organization of the CCF could enter into a political alliance with any other political party or group. In December the political directive board of the provincial CCF approved a motion of censure against Douglas, accompanied by a press release. The release contained the reasons for the censure and included a declaration by Douglas of his loyalty to the CCF and its program. The board did not have much choice in imposing this rather mild penalty—Douglas was now the CCF MP for Weyburn. Nevertheless, Williams was vindicated in his hard line against cooperating with Social Credit: Douglas was publicly called to account and embarrassed.

The 1935 federal election results were ominous for the CCF. After just two months of organizing, the Social Credit party ran in twenty of the province's twenty-one seats, winning two rural seats and 18 per cent of the province-wide vote. The CCF also won two rural seats, with 21 per cent. The combined vote of those voting for radical change was 39 per cent, confirming the solid foundation of the CCF's pre–Social Credit optimism. The two seats won by the CCF had been won with Social Credit cooperation. In Weyburn, as far as the voting public was concerned, the victorious Douglas was a joint CCF–Social Credit candidate. No official Social Credit candidate opposed him, and he won by fewer than 300 votes. A self-advertised Social Credit candidate stood, and was widely rumoured to be financed by the Liberal Party, but the official party repudiated him; he received 362 votes. In Rosetown-Biggar, Coldwell was widely known to have received the blessing of the provincial Social Credit party. Though a local maverick Social Credit candidate opposed him, the provincial party had put out the word to support Coldwell (the Social Credit maverick received 836 votes; Coldwell received over 6,800). In the overall vote, the CCF came close to losing the political leadership of radicalizing farmers. Of the seventeen rural seats, each party won two; but in the other thirteen seats the CCF was outpolled by Social Credit in eight, some quite heavily. Clearly, politically advanced farmers were deeply split between the Depression remedies of the Social Credit party and those of the CCF. In the four urban seats—Saskatoon, Regina, Prince Albert, and Moose Jaw—the CCF was deeply disappointed. Social Credit outpolled the CCF in Saskatoon 18 to 10 per cent, and in Prince Albert 19 to 9 per cent; the CCF beat Social Credit in Regina 19 to 8 per cent; and the two parties tied in Moose Jaw at 14 per cent. Williams immediately surrendered his expectation of victory in 1938. The prospect of a Social Credit victory was real. The CCF's major political foe was no longer the Liberals, but Social Credit.

On December 13, 1935, Coldwell resigned as CCF leader and decamped to Ottawa. The next day, the political directive board appointed Williams acting leader and replaced him as chair of the board with a loyalist. At the 1936 convention, Williams was elected political leader and president, now combined in one office, with a free hand to hire provincial organizers as he deemed necessary. He was now securely in charge of what could be a dying political party.

Chapter 5

BUILDING THE CCF

Defeating Social Credit,
1936 to 1938

T he crisis was serious. Williams admitted privately that "the organization is in a precarious position."[1] Membership had peaked at
4,900 in 1935 and collapsed to 2,200 in 1936. The FLP had won
103,000 votes in 1934, while federal CCF candidates won only 69,000 in
1935, with most of this loss going to Social Credit. Indeed, after examining the results, Williams concluded the CCF would have won at least
ten of seventeen rural seats had Social Credit not nominated candidates. Word was filtering in to central office that many CCF members
were slipping away to Social Credit. The loss of rank-and-file UFC(SS)
members to Social Credit and the division in their ranks between CCF
and Social Credit adherents were serious, not just organizationally but
ideologically. Williams was concerned that many among the current
leaders of the Wheat Pool and the UFC(SS) were pulling back from political engagement due to the split among farmers. A prominent UFC(SS)
leader reported to a political supporter of Williams, "Politics was taboo
with the pool, and also with the UFC."[2] The CCF organization was still
in some disarray with various affiliated and semi-autonomous forms of

membership: CCF clubs, ILP locals, some UFC(SS) locals, and some union locals. This problem was acute in urban centres, where members spent too much time on internal ideological squabbles. In the 1934 and 1935 elections, the party did reasonably well among middle-class farmers and employed unionized workers in the cities, but failed to reach relief recipients, non-union low-paid workers, the unemployed, poor farmers, and the middle and professional classes. The party had, first, to survive by retaining and expanding its existing base and, second, to grow by making inroads among those voters yet untouched by the CCF message.

Williams concluded that the years leading to the 1938 election were decisive and would require a major tactical shift in order to meet the Social Credit challenge. During the 1935 election campaign Social Credit candidates had made much of the CCF's socialism and freely applied the communist smear, pointing to the use-lease program of land "collectivization." The Social Credit alternative of an easier road to abundance, security, and prosperity through simply socializing the money and credit system, which would not tamper with free enterprise and private property in all other spheres of economic activity, had considerable allure for farmers. Williams decided the 1938 election could not be the clear choice he had hoped for—between the capitalist Liberal Party and the socialist CCF. The CCF had to make a tactical retreat and focus on exposing Social Credit doctrine, while presenting a platform that put voters' minds at ease. The goal was to convince voters "to accept the CCF program by putting a new spring frock on it," as Williams said privately.[3] The party's commitment to socialism would remain in its core program, but would not be emphasized in its election platform. Williams declared, "The progress of the Socialist Movement in Canada depends upon the ability of the Movement to adjust itself to conditions from time to time."[4]

Williams reorganized the CCF into a unitary, centralized political party, composed of individual members in constituency associations, a provincial council with power to act between conventions, a provincial executive, and a president who also served as political leader. Fuelled by a sense of urgency, Williams could be abrasive in dealing with resistance to the reorganization. Many, especially his old foes on the right, were comfortable with the way things were, happy with the congenial atmosphere of the CCF clubs. Though they could not defeat his proposals, they complained about his highhandedness in imposing convention decisions. All members were members of constituency associations, the locale of their involvement in the party's affairs. All forms of affiliated membership were eliminated. Williams also insisted the party needed its own newspaper to offset the influence of the capitalist press. A party newspaper would bind members and supporters together in a common fight and provide a forum for education. Despite opposition from many on the right in the leadership, from 1933 to 1936 Williams personally engineered relationships with four left-leaning weekly newspapers, all of which proved unsatisfactory because they lacked clear party control. In April 1938 he finally secured sufficient funding to establish the *Saskatchewan Commonwealth* as the party's newspaper. It survived and flourished. He organized fundraising drives and membership campaigns through the constituency associations, slowly rebuilding the membership and the depleted coffers. He set up election schools for candidates, campaign managers, and party activists. He designed a series of educational programs to solidify the membership's ideological commitment and understanding. He proposed that CCF constituency associations, much like the locals of the organized farm movement, should become centres of a many-sided and rich ongoing community life. Slowly the party was resurrected.

In addition to approving Williams's proposed constitution and reorganization plan, the 1936 convention embraced his tactical shift in the election platform. Gone were use-lease land nationalization and ringing declarations about socialism and the eradication of capitalism. In fact, the word "socialism" did not appear in the platform. Its preamble called for the cooperative commonwealth and contained attacks on trusts, monopolies, and "big business." There were no elaborately complex policy proposals, unlike the 1934 campaign; instead, there was a simple, direct, moderate, and pragmatic nine-point platform: "security for farmers on their farm and to urban dwellers in their home," "drastic reduction of debt," "socialized Health Services," "useful public works with wages at trade union rates," "standardized adequate relief," "equal education opportunity," "increased social services," support for "the national issue and control of currency and credit," support for "a Growers' Marketing Board," and a goal of "Peace" and the "retention and extension of the Democratic rights of the people."[5] Opponents of the CCF, whether on a political platform or in the editorial pages of the press, would be hard pressed to find anything in the platform that could be interpreted as inspired by communism.

Another issue tested Williams's tactical ingenuity. The membership, frustrated by the 1935 split in the "progressive, reform" vote, called for political cooperation in the next election. In fact, the rank and file of the party demanded cooperation. At the 1936 convention, a resolution calling for "an alliance of all groups opposed to the present social order" and "a united front against the forces of reaction" passed by a vote of 306 to 8.[6] Williams was aware the CP was influential in this grassroots call for cooperation. With the rise of Hitler, the Communist International had abandoned the line that the CP's primary opponent was the "social fascism" of democratic socialist and social democratic parties, instead embracing a policy of a united front against fascism. The CP dissolved the Workers' Unity League and the Farmers' Unity League, directing its members and supporters to rejoin popular organizations and trade unions to work to bring progressive parties and organizations into united fronts wherever possible. Many joined the CCF, keeping silent about their CP membership.

Williams had no choice but to agree to the demand from below for cooperation. Long an opponent of cooperation with other parties, believing that the CCF's organizational and policy integrity would be compromised, Williams recognized an opportunity to deal with the present crisis. The motion raised the ire of the Ottawa office and became the subject of contention at the national convention. In response, at the 1937 provincial convention, support for cooperation was even stronger (346 to 7 when put to a vote), despite personal appeals from Coldwell and Woodsworth not to embrace cooperation. Woodsworth expressed his opposition at the convention, insisting, "I am not going to enter into a political alliance with those who uphold capitalism."[7] Despite strong opposition from Coldwell, Woodsworth, the national office, and Ontario, where cooperation was seen as a CP manoeuvre, Williams was able to prevail, thanks to the constitution he had drafted protecting provincial autonomy. The national convention reluctantly agreed it was up to provincial parties to decide the issue, as long as the CCF's organizational integrity was protected. Williams defended his position by allowing that he was "not so hot after co-operation" but was "trying to be careful not to consolidate the Social Credit party in Saskatchewan."[8] To resist this grassroots demand for cooperation would have risked internal splits and perhaps a loss of members to Social Credit. Williams insisted that if the demand for cooperation was "wisely used it may well become the vehicle on which the CCF rides to power."[9] Hence, Williams embraced cooperation subject to certain conditions: no fusion party, no joint candidates (like Douglas in Weyburn), no burying the CCF with other groups behind a "unity" candidate (as the CP wanted). Cooperation must take other forms.

Williams began to explore cooperation with the Social Credit and Communist parties. The CP was eager to join the CCF in supporting unity "people's candidates," but Williams declined. The Tories wanted to discuss it since they had little hope of winning any seats without saw-off arrangements. Douglas strongly supported such arrangements with Tories. He negotiated with a Saskatchewan Tory MP in Ottawa to reach a deal, and he proposed to Williams that a comprehensive arrangement be worked out with the Tories for 1938. Williams, and many others in the leadership, were of the opinion that the grassroots push for unity included only reform or progressive groups, not the Tories, so it was dangerous political territory on which to tread openly. Williams had no intention to give the Tories very much, but as an electoral tactician he knew every vote counted in the effort to stave off Social Credit and defeat the Liberals.

Williams was seriously interested in negotiating saw-off agreements only with Social Credit. The best-case scenario would be to emerge with a number of seats sufficient to win a majority in which the CCF was unopposed by Social Credit. Williams's firm position was that all CCF candidates would run as CCF candidates on the party platform. The issue was which seats each party would contest. Williams found the membership of the Social Credit party, like that of his own party, eager to work out cooperation. Given Aberhart's autocratic control of Social Credit parties in Alberta and Saskatchewan, Williams knew there would be no deal without Aberhart's approval. In 1936, Williams and Macauley travelled to Edmonton to discuss cooperation with Aberhart. Though the meeting was congenial, Aberhart was evasive. No deal was struck, nor was an agreement in principle made.

Throughout 1937 Williams worked hard to persuade the Saskatchewan Social Credit party to cooperate with the CCF. He found strong support among the party's membership and among some of the leadership. He attended the 1937 Social Credit convention to state his case. The debate was heated; a strong faction of the party, encouraged by Aberhart's young protégé Ernest Manning, were convinced they could take the province in a landslide in 1938.[10] Though a motion to approve cooperation narrowly passed, Manning, possessing dictatorial power from Aberhart, declared the motion lost. He ruled that such a motion required a two-thirds majority, signalling that Aberhart's Social Credit movement was out to win the province and had no inclination to cooperate. Williams was disappointed his plan had failed, but he recovered quickly.

In a January 14, 1938, province-wide radio broadcast, Williams declared war on Social Credit. He attacked the party head on, heaping scorn and ridicule on its theories as an "illusion" purveyed by those desperate to save capitalism. To have the kind of society Social Credit promised required the socialization of wealth. It required socialism. Aberhart was failing in Alberta because he had been "bluffing" all along. Williams detailed how the CCF had tried in good faith to achieve cooperation, only to be rebuffed again and again. He reported on Manning's dictatorial rejection of the Social Credit convention's majority decision to cooperate with the CCF: "[It] sounds more like Italy than Canada; more like Fascism than Democracy."[11] It was not the CCF's fault there would be no cooperation, Williams told listeners; it was Aberhart's arrogant ambition to win the province. In that broadcast Williams was appealing directly to the CCF's membership and popular base to stay the course, since he had tried to achieve the cooperation they wanted. But he was also appealing to those members and supporters of Social Credit who strongly favoured cooperation. For the average voter, Williams was subjecting Social Credit to criticism from the left and exposing the authoritarian tendencies of the party's leadership. The text of the broadcast was printed as a pamphlet and distributed throughout the province.

In March 1938, Williams wrote to Aberhart appealing to him to stay out of Saskatchewan for the election, in order to allow the CCF to win. Saw-offs were still possible, he suggested, but there would be "no sacrifice of CCF principles, policy or platform, no fusion party, no fusion candidates."[12] The next month, in a final attempt, Williams sent Macauley to Edmonton to appeal to Aberhart for cooperation in the form of saw-offs. But Aberhart was angry about the radio broadcast. He rejected any form of cooperation and threatened Macauley that one hundred speakers from Alberta would be sent to Saskatchewan to campaign and that he personally would make a series of radio broadcasts appealing for support of Social Credit. Aberhart and Manning took personal control of the Saskatchewan campaign. No candidate could stand for Social Credit without the approval of either Manning or Aberhart. The campaign would be run from Alberta, which angered many among the provincial Social Credit Party membership and leadership. Williams now declared to CCF members and supporters that this was an all-out confrontation with Social Credit.

Aberhart was secure in his Alberta bastion. Following its August provincial sweep, Social Credit won fifteen of Alberta's seventeen federal seats on October 14, with 48 per cent of the vote. But problems began to beset Aberhart's government, providing the Saskatchewan CCF much-needed ammunition in its battle. Social Credit began to look less and less like an attractive political export. Social credit's founder and guru, Major C. H. Douglas, had been appointed Aberhart's chief reconstruction advisor immediately upon victory; Douglas resigned very quickly, disappointed with the Aberhart government's first budget introduced in 1936. He described it as "orthodox retrenchment," with cuts in spending, increases in taxes, and the introduction of a new tax on retail sales.[13] There was nothing Social Credit about it, and Douglas did not want his name associated with it. Aberhart kept the resignation secret, but it was leaked in March 1936 during budget debates. Douglas's resignation wounded the government seriously, provoking much confusion and concern in the movement and the caucus. Where was the promised plan to achieve social credit?

Only one law on social credit was passed. It had no significant content, except to give the cabinet the power to act to implement social credit policies by orders-in-council. Using this power, in the summer of 1936 the cabinet called on all citizens to sign a covenant with the government. Over half the population dutifully signed an elaborate, lengthy document. In exchange for cooperating with the government in implementing social credit, the people would receive just wages and prices, as well as monthly dividends. The promise of dividends had been central in Aberhart's election campaign. The people who signed the document assumed it was to ensure their dividends would shortly be in the mail.

The sums promised were significant in the Depression context: citizens twenty-one and over would receive $25 a month; those twenty, $20; those nineteen, $15; those seventeen and eighteen, $10; and children up to sixteen, $5. These payments were to be universal, paid to all "bona fide" citizens as "stockholders" in Alberta, and to be paid over and above a citizen's other earnings in the marketplace. Douglas had proposed paying national dividends to all citizens when necessary—a sort of floating guaranteed annual income—in order to ensure people's purchasing power with the ups and downs of the economy. Aberhart seized upon the idea, promising unqualified dividends to all citizens, from cradle to grave. While the massive sign-up ceremony—lines were long at each signing locale—kept alive the conviction that things were changing, it also raised expectations that the dividends were coming soon.

Aberhart took other measures by order-in-council in the summer of 1936 to sustain his momentum. In April, the government defaulted on its payment of a 1916 $3.2 million twenty-year bond issue at 6 per cent. The government simply refused to pay, though it continued to pay bond-holders 2.5 per cent in annual interest. In May, the interest rates on all public debt were cut in half with a floor of 2 per cent. In June, $2 million in "prosperity certificates" was printed, backed up by "Alberta's credit." Citizens were asked to accept the certificates in economic transactions in the province whenever possible. The certificates failed to circulate. The University of Alberta, the King's Printer, and Premier Aberhart and his cabinet wanted payment in Canadian dollars, hardly an inspiration to the population. Only about a quarter of a million in certificates was ever issued, but no one used them for economic transactions. Instead, they became collectors' items, and a major embarrassment for the government. The unilateral cut in interest rates on the public debt and the bond default, on the other hand, were immensely popular. They were also eminently practical measures for a government in the midst of the Depression. One-half of the Alberta government's annual revenues went just to pay the interest on the public debt. By this action, Aberhart freed up revenue to enhance relief payments to the hard-pressed population.

Aberhart next convened a special session of the legislature, from August 25 to September 1. The Throne Speech was the shortest in history—six paragraphs. The session was necessary due to the "calamitous drought" and "the grave economic conditions resulting therefrom."[14] A full Social Credit program would be implemented: "further action in regard to the introduction of Social Credit principles, Debt Adjustment legislation, the Reduction of Interest and such other matters as may be deemed necessary for the good and welfare of our people." With this session the Aberhart government embarked on a course of sustained constitutional confrontation with Ottawa and economic confrontation with finance capital that would last two tumultuous years. During this time, Aberhart battled toe to toe with what Major Douglas described as "the Eastern financial interests, acting through the Dominion Cabinet." The premier began to implement a central but risky aspect of the original Douglas strategy, proposed from the beginning and earlier urged on the former UFA government: the deliberate use of provincial powers "to inflict severe penalties upon the financial interests."[15]

The flagship legislation was the Alberta Credit House Act. The credit house would "furnish to persons entitled to Alberta credit facilities for the exchange of goods and services...in order to effect the equation between the purchasing power of such persons within the Province and production within the Province."[16] This credit was available "to any person engaged in agriculture or manufacture or industry in the Province and to any person...to defray the cost of building a home or the establishment of...any business, vocation or calling." There was a 2 per cent administrative charge. This legislation appeared to fulfill a long-cherished dream of farmers: cheap credit. But the law went further, promising a home for every worker, a business or trade for any aspiring entrepreneur, the wherewithal to achieve a measure of economic independence and security, no longer relying on the whims of bankers but on one's own productivity, hard work, and ingenuity. The fact the law was impossible to put into effect did not detract from its immediate political impact.

The credit house law was clearly beyond both the province's constitutional authority and its financial resources. As such, it was not taken seriously, nor was any concerted effort made to act on it. A series of debt adjustment laws passed by the special session was another matter, however. Property and civil rights were unambiguous areas of provincial constitutional authority. The province, therefore, had the right to pass laws affecting the ownership of property in the province. Further, provinces had the right to legislate on matters of debt and its collection. Put simply, Aberhart's laws reduced debt, lowered interest rates, made it impossible for creditors to initiate legal proceedings on defaulted debt without the government's permission, protected the assets of debtors to the point they were beyond seizing for debt, and voided all existing agreements on public debt (lowering interest rates and forbidding court action to challenge the law). Granted, the government was stretching its constitutional power over property and civil rights far beyond reason, but it was an area of provincial legislative constitutional competence.

The laws were all eventually found to be *ultra vires* by the courts, but such decisions were appealed to higher courts by the Aberhart government. As long as the appeals were in process, proceedings for debt could not occur. When a law was struck down, the Aberhart government simply massaged it and passed it again. This cat-and-mouse game went on until the whole edifice of Aberhart's debt protection laws was struck down by the Privy Council in 1941. In the end, effective debt protection was provided to the people of Alberta throughout the worst years of the Depression. In subsequent sessions the Aberhart government passed further laws reducing banks to little more than provincially controlled credit clearing houses and imposing punitive taxes on them. These laws went far beyond the constitutional authority of provinces. By the time the confrontation was over, the federal cabinet had disallowed eleven of Aberhart's laws, and the Ottawa-appointed Lieutenant-Governor had invoked the Crown's power of reservation, refusing to sign three duly passed bills into law. Only the debt protection laws continued to haunt Ottawa and finance capital.

Aberhart's summer offensive shocked the Ottawa government and the establishment press. Up to that point, his regime had not been taken seriously, often being dismissed with ridicule. Suddenly, what was going on in Alberta was taken very seriously. During the fall the *Financial Post* raised the alarm in a series of detailed articles, stating, for example, "Alberta's brand of Social Credit is a thin disguise for Communism" and "an effort at social revolution" with "an unprecedented attack on private capital." More worrisome was the broad support for Aberhart's laws, especially "the laws to cut debts," which were "widely, intensely, dangerously popular." Aberhart himself was "dominated by a handful of radicals." If he could break free of them, the premier "may prove himself to be a socially-minded conservative of deep human sympathies." Millions in oil capital were "poised to enter promising fields if Premier

Aberhart swings away from the left." The alternative was the certain collapse of the province's economy unless the government abandoned its
"religious and economic lunacies."[17] Aberhart responded with a series
of mass rallies across the province, which received detailed coverage
in the *Calgary Albertan*, a paper the Social Credit party had purchased
to ensure that at least one major daily reported the government's program fully. The party membership climbed to thirty-four thousand. At
one rally Aberhart declared, "The mortgage companies, the insurance
companies and other super-financial agencies realize full well that if you
people get free from the clutches of the interest-mongers, you will once
more be free men living in a land flowing with milk and honey."[18] Within
Alberta, Aberhart was at the zenith of his popular support.

Despite his personal popularity, in 1937 Aberhart's government was
in trouble. Ideologically committed Social Crediters were increasingly
unhappy that Alberta was no closer to Social Credit than it had been on
election day. There was no clear plan. The laws passed proved unworkable. Dividends had not been issued. Prosperity certificates were not
circulating. Major Douglas's book assessing Aberhart's performance,
The Alberta Experiment, was released; it included all correspondence
between the two men, resulting in some embarrassment for Aberhart.
It was a devastating review of Aberhart's failures. Douglas characterized the premier as "defective both in theory and practicability."[19] The
1937 Throne Speech was defensive. The proposed budget was another
study in orthodoxy; it was not a Social Credit budget, despite many good
routine expenditure proposals. Aberhart had solemnly promised dividends by March 1937. This was not going to happen. His debt laws were
successfully challenged in the courts. No Alberta credit house had been
established. The government's legislative program to achieve social credit
was a shambles.

Splits began to emerge in the cabinet and caucus as internal acrimony
increased. The split flowered into open rebellion when thirty to thirty-five
backbench MLAs and half of Aberhart's cabinet coalesced and threatened
to refuse to support the budget in the House. The government would fall.
In order to placate the rebels, Aberhart agreed to pass a series of much
more aggressive and radical laws to realize social credit and to punish
the financial interests. The rebellion ended in June 1937 when forty-nine
of fifty-six Social Credit MLAs publicly signed loyalty pledges. The more

radical laws were duly passed. From that point on, the government in Ottawa embarked on a course of almost instant and routine disallowance of social credit laws. This provided Aberhart with a scapegoat—Ottawa, under the sinister direction of the "interest-mongers," was blocking his honest efforts to achieve social credit. While this served to sustain his popularity in Alberta, it made it clear across the country that the whole Social Credit project at a provincial level was fanciful. The Saskatchewan CCF had an abundance of evidence with which to fight Social Credit in the 1938 election.

The 1938 Saskatchewan election was vital for the futures of all major players: Aberhart's Social Credit government, the provincial Liberals, the CCF, and the federal government. It was an event of national significance. Liberal Prime Minister Mackenzie King, elected in October 1935, was eager to see the march of Social Credit stopped. Aberhart, having lost repeatedly in the courts, under attack by the national business lobby, and facing routine use of the superior federal powers of disallowance and reservation, needed to win in Saskatchewan to push Social Credit forward. A victory in Saskatchewan would transform Social Credit from a one-province nuisance to a national political nightmare. With two provinces united in the battle for Social Credit, and a potential bloc of thirty-eight seats in the House of Commons, popular support could grow rapidly across the country. Accordingly, Aberhart and Manning, leading an army of Alberta volunteers, campaigned vigorously in the province. The Alberta legislature took the unprecedented step of approving a $100,000 donation to the Saskatchewan Social Credit League (allegedly for educational purposes). Aberhart's radio broadcasts into Saskatchewan became an effective campaign weapon. If Aberhart failed to win, the Social Credit dream would be locked up firmly in Alberta under relentless siege by powerful forces. Aberhart was out to win; hence, he focused his campaign on attacking the governing Liberals, handmaidens of the federal government. The CCF was largely ignored.

The Liberal Party was terrified. Given Aberhart's growing popularity in Alberta, Social Credit could sweep to power. Gardiner, arguably the most effective Liberal politician in Saskatchewan's history, had gone to Ottawa. There was doubt the new premier, William Patterson, a less than formidable orator, would be a match for Aberhart. There was considerable pressure from King's federal Liberals to stop Social Credit at all costs.

King had been initially reluctant to use the powers of disallowance and reservation to block Aberhart, hoping the losses in the courts would be enough to make the Aberhart government see reason. When this failed, and the laws of 1937 were passed, King, under growing pressure from the business lobby, decided he had no choice but to act decisively by using the powers. But, as he had predicted earlier, the use of overriding federal powers only increased Aberhart's popularity in Alberta. It was in the national interest that a Saskatchewan government not join the legislative fight for Social Credit; otherwise, King risked alienating an entire region. As a result, the Liberal Party's campaign focused on attacking Social Credit and virtually ignored the CCF.

For Williams and the CCF, caught between the governing Liberal machine and a potentially ascendant Social Credit Party, the election was a fight for survival. Williams decided to limit CCF candidates to thirty-one of fifty-two constituencies. With the exceptions of Weyburn, Swift Current, and Yorkton, which contained significant concentrations of urban voters, the constituencies were rural. No CCF candidate ran in three of the four major urban centres: Regina, Saskatoon, and Moose Jaw. In Prince Albert, against the advice of Williams, the local CCF ran a candidate. When it became clear the CCF was to be largely ignored by the Liberal and Social Credit parties, Williams concluded this was a blessing in disguise: the CCF was also largely ignored by the major dailies in the province throughout the campaign, and hence there was no sustained press campaign of communist smears like that of 1934. Williams decided to let the Liberals take the lead in attacking Social Credit, which allowed the CCF to focus on its positive program and record of four years as official opposition. Too many attacks on Social Credit by the CCF would risk alienating the soft Social Credit rural base, which Williams hoped to win over. Given the strong demands for cooperation from the rank and file of both the CCF and Social Credit parties, it was important to present the CCF as a positive alternative that had tried to achieve cooperation only to be rejected by Aberhart.

On May 14, Patterson set the election for June 8, 1938. It was the toughest year of the Depression. The 1937 crop had been devastated by drought as average wheat yields fell to 2.5 bushels an acre. Now in the eighth year of what seemed a disaster without end, the desperation of the people was heartbreaking. Over half the population was on relief,

including two in three farmers. The Liberal Party faced a double challenge: a continuing failure to cope effectively with the Depression and the
Social Credit invasion promising an instant, painless cure. The Liberal
manifesto was billed as coming from the "Government of Saskatchewan."
The longest in the party's history, it detailed the government's accom-
plishments and made the usual extravagant promises about dealing with
the Depression—promises made in 1934 and never fulfilled.

The manifesto was rather restrained stuff, designed for press consumption and to be waved by those speaking on platforms. On the
other hand, the pamphlets issued for mass distribution bordered on
hysteria. One pamphlet, titled *Communism Is the Threat*, warned, "Do
you want Alberta's Stalin regulating your daily life?" Williams doubtless enjoyed the irony that the communist smear at which the Liberal
Party was so adept was now rolled out against Social Credit. Another
pamphlet listed all of Aberhart's broken promises, his "misuse of public
funds," the absence of dividends, his "futile debt legislation," his denial
of civil rights, and his "record of failure." Aberhart was moving toward
a "dictatorship," and "the Social Credit party in Alberta" was "in active
co-operation with the Communist party and other subversive groups in
the province." Saskatchewan would become an "Alberta colony" if Social
Credit won. Aberhart picked all candidates personally—they were his
"henchmen," "only tolerated as long as they did his bidding." According
to this pamphlet, "If Aberhart controls the Saskatchewan government,...Saskatchewan's industrial development will be sacrificed to pay
Social Credit dividends in Alberta."[20]

The Social Credit Party recycled the pamphlets that had proven successful in Alberta in 1935. The problem with this was that a lot had
happened since 1935, much of it discrediting the possibility of achieving social credit at the provincial level. Opponents made much of these
failures, forcing the Social Credit campaign to respond with new pamphlets detailing Aberhart's courageous efforts to achieve social credit
in Alberta and the fact that Ottawa, in league with the financial interests, had blocked every effort. Aberhart made this theme a centrepiece
of his speeches at rallies, where he presented himself as the underdog
champion of the people, under attack by powerful sinister forces. His
denunciations of the federal government and the interest-mongers for
subverting the democratic will of the Alberta people received standing

ovations. The Social Credit platform asked, "How long must we be the dupes of the Old Line Parties in alliance with the Money Monopolists?" It stated, "People should demand results; then stick together until they get what they want." What people wanted was a real economic and political democracy, where the domination of the "Money Barons" was broken and there were "equal rights for all—special privileges to none."[21] It appeared the Social Credit campaign was based on the party riding to power on the charisma of Aberhart. And judging from the desperate tone of the Liberal campaign, the Liberals feared this just might be true.

The Social Credit invasion overshadowed all other issues in the campaign. National attention was riveted on Aberhart's attempted conquest of Saskatchewan. The national press corps poured into the province. As far as they were concerned, the battle was between two major protagonists: the beleaguered Liberal government and the invasion forces led by Aberhart. The Liberal government's sorry record during the Depression was forgotten in the headlines and stories detailing the skirmishes. The Social Credit campaign relied on large public rallies featuring the party's main asset: Aberhart. He drew impressive crowds: three thousand in Wilkie; five thousand in Saskatoon's arena, with over twenty-five hundred outside listening on loudspeakers; four thousand in Prince Albert; five thousand in Melville. Aberhart's efforts were supplemented by lesser lights, like Manning and other members of the Alberta cabinet, speaking at well-attended regional rallies. The Liberals responded with rallies featuring former premier Gardiner, most of which were flops compared to Aberhart's crowds. The press, unapologetically pro-Liberal, stopped reporting on attendance at Liberal rallies, instead devoting detailed coverage to the speeches of Gardiner and Patterson. In the battle of the rallies Aberhart was winning—and creating the impression of impending victory. But the Liberals had the home advantage: a powerful and well-organized election machine to get the vote out. In contrast, the Social Credit campaign was thin on the ground, poorly organized, and shaken by internal divisions over Aberhart's dictatorial control of the campaign. As Williams had observed in his criticism of the 1934 Coldwell campaign's emphasis on rallies, they were often a case of preaching to the converted. In the case of Aberhart, the rallies also attracted the curious and those out for an evening's entertainment. In this era, political rallies were a spectator sport. Furthermore, a denunciation of banks in the Depression era got a standing ovation no matter who was speaking. Would this success in drawing crowds translate into votes on election day?

Caught in the squeeze between the Liberals and Social Credit, and largely ignored by both parties and the press, Williams fought the election on the ground by focusing on constituency and detailed poll organization. He would have done so in any case, but it was even more essential in this battle. The party's printed and radio propaganda detailed the CCF's positive program and criticized the record of the Liberal government. In his January radio broadcast, Williams criticized the Social Credit record in Alberta aggressively and in some detail, but not in a hysterical, fear-mongering manner. The text, released as a pamphlet early in the campaign, was the only substantial attack on Social Credit issued by the CCF. In late May, Williams broadcast a final pre-election appeal that included a final attack on Social Credit—it was responsible for "the split in the reform vote"; it was "the last illusion of capitalism"; it would lead the people astray and fail to solve the problems of the Depression—but also some praise for the movement. Though he conceded that Aberhart had done some good things, like his improved relief payments and efforts at debt protection, Williams noted, "Social Credit has failed to give the things it promised in Alberta" and "those few things it has done were CCF platform, not Social Credit platform."[22] Hoping to win farm voters away from the Social Credit party, Williams vetoed repetitive all-out attacks, which the national office persistently suggested. Though criticisms of Socal Credit were made by CCF candidates in speeches on the hustings, often in response to planted questions, the CCF largely refrained from lambasting Social Credit. The Liberals were doing a good job of that.

In addition to the brief nine-point platform adopted by the 1936 convention, largely composed of emergency measures for immediate implementation, and printed texts of some of Williams's many radio broadcasts (he did fifteen-minute broadcasts every Friday evening at 7:30 throughout the campaign), the CCF produced two lengthy policy documents, clearly authored by Williams. *Are They to Be Trusted?* presented a detailed indictment of the Liberal government's failures to relieve the people's suffering by responding effectively to the Depression, as well as a full explanation of the alternative offered by the CCF. Although the word "socialism" was not used, the proposed alternative was clearly socialism. The blame for the Depression lay with "the capitalist system." This profit-driven system had created a "New Slavery," debt and foreclosure for farmers and unemployment for workers. The solution was "public owner- ship," and "that is what the CCF means by nationalization." The CCF called for "the social use and ownership of all essential means of production and distribution—including banks." It was time "to elect a Government com- posed of those who toil on farms, or in the mines, or on the railways and in the offices, shops, mills and factories—and the unemployed."[23]

The CCF Debt Adjustment and Land Policy was a lengthy, often tech- nical, essay on debt protection. Williams, an acknowledged expert in the area, wrote directly to his fellow farmers as an equal. Like so many other documents he had written as president of the UFC(SS), this was a farmer's document. The pamphlet was delivered to every farm home in the seats contested by the CCF. Williams knew farmers would read the document carefully and critically and discuss it with their neighbours. A heavy debt load and threatened foreclosure were together the key issue facing farmers in the Depression. Williams dissected the historical development of the farm debt problem and the failures of successive governments to address it effectively. The biggest problem was that the current law on mortgage and land sales agreements, drafted by capitalist governments, "gives an undue advantage to invested capital, and works a hardship on the strug- gling home-owner." What was needed was a policy to stop the growth of debt during hard times, while keeping the farmer producing on the land. There had to be fair mechanisms for negotiating debt settlements that included reducing debts from boom times of the past when interest rates were high. Farmers should not bear the total risk of crop failures and poor markets—the risk should be shared by lenders. A detailed CCF debt adjustment and protection plan was presented. This plan, unlike that of Social Credit, would stay within the constitution and therefore—again, unlike the laws of Social Credit—provide certainty and security to farm- ers on their farms and workers in their homes. The document concluded, "The CCF is determined that Humanity will come first" and will use all the powers of government to ensure that "entrenched finance gives a square deal to the Farmers and Home Owners of this province."[24]

Williams was a driven man during the campaign, which began for him with his New Year's radio broadcast as leader of the opposition. He was both party leader and provincial campaign organizer. He put ten thousand miles on his car driving between central office and the thirty-one contested seats. Insisting CCF candidates be nominated early and begin campaigning immediately, Williams was keynote speaker at twenty-three of thirty nominating conventions between March and May. He ran a series of regional schools for candidates, campaign managers, and key volunteers, explaining the details of poll-by-poll organization and repetitive canvassing. He emphasized the necessity of developing a comprehensive election-day plan to ensure every "committed" and "leaning" CCF voter got to the polls. He noted the importance of organizing an intelligence network within the constituency and establishing flying squads of volunteer troubleshooters to go to districts and communities to counter damaging lies and slanders spread by CCF opponents. He welcomed the offers of Coldwell, Douglas, and Woodsworth to help in the campaign, but primarily used them as speakers at locales within the contested seats, avoiding mass rallies. He issued daily bulletins, often by telegram, to candidates and campaign managers with updated intelligence, instructions, and advice. Teams of volunteers under the direction of central office were dispatched where and when needed to shore up faltering local campaigns. Near the end of the campaign, Williams was alerted by his campaign manager that the Liberals planned to send two hundred volunteers into Wadena during the last week of campaigning, hoping to unseat him. Williams set aside a few days during the last week to campaign in Wadena to make sure that did not happen.

The Social Credit invasion was defeated handily. The Liberal fear campaign was more successful than expected. Of equal if not greater significance, the split in the anti-government, reform vote between the CCF and Social Credit helped immeasurably. The Liberals, contesting all fifty-two seats, won thirty-eight with 45 per cent of the vote. Social Credit, contesting forty-one seats, won two with 16 per cent. Ironically, the successful Social Credit candidate in Melville, John Herman, had been the 1934–35 UFC(SS) president. He snatched an eleven-vote win in a two-way fight with a Liberal. The other elected Social Credit candidate successfully split the vote in Cut Knife, taking the seat from the CCF's Andrew Macauley, Williams's close friend and confidant. The Tories, ever hopeful, ran in twenty-five seats, winning none but drawing 12 per cent of the vote. The CCF, running in thirty-one seats, won ten with 19 percent. Two Unity candidates who had pledged to support the CCF won in rural seats.

In the end, the CCF did not compete with Tories in eleven seats, including the six seats in Moose Jaw, Regina, and Saskatoon. Social Credit ran candidates in twenty-six of the thirty-one seats contested by the CCF. The Tories did not compete with CCF candidates in seventeen rural seats. The grassroots demand for fusion Unity candidates proved irresistible in three seats: Yorkton, Maple Creek, and Bengough. The CCF local organizations joined in supporting the Unity candidates, who pledged support for the CCF program. The CP's Labour Progressive Party (LPP) benefited inadvertently. It ran two candidates unopposed by the CCF in Regina, the only seats the LPP contested, and made a respectable showing. The LPP did not throw up any spoiler candidates in the rural seats contested by the CCF, even where the CP had strong local organizations. There is no evidence on the record of how much this had to do with actual agreements reached behind the scenes. The talks likely had some impact on the parties' nomination decisions, but those decisions had little impact on the results. The Tories failed to elect a single member. Unopposed by Social Credit, two of the Unity candidates won. The third Unity candidate lost in a three-way race including Social Credit. In five of the ten seats won by the CCF, a Tory was nominated; in eight, a Social Credit candidate was nominated. CCF candidates in three close races may have benefited. On the other hand, it is dubious that solid Tory supporters voted CCF to stop Social Credit. They more likely went Liberal.

The results were both gratifying and bitter for Williams and the CCF. Williams won in Wadena with 59 per cent of the vote, despite the Liberals' best effort. He concluded the cooperation tactic was of decisive importance: "Had we not tried this co-operation thing out, there would have been continuous and dangerous agitation and a weakening of our strength."[25] Social Credit's confident expectation that it would steal the CCF's rural base was effectively thwarted. The CCF, running in thirty-one seats, won ten with 19 per cent. Since the party had stayed out of twenty-one seats, this popular vote was not an accurate measure of the CCF's support among the general voting population. Williams was quick to point out that the total vote for CCF, Social Credit, and Unity candidates was 43 per cent. He also noted that many voters had held their noses and voted Liberal to prevent a Social Credit victory. In a clear two-way fight between the CCF and the Liberals in all fifty-two seats, fought on the Liberal government's record during the Depression, the CCF probably would have won. In effect, Social Credit had served as a spoiler, assuring a Liberal victory. But the CCF had survived. Not only that, but the party had doubled its seats, from five to ten—becoming eleven when the CCF won the Humboldt by-election on August 4, 1938. In June the CCF had narrowly lost the seat to the Liberals by 190 votes, thanks to Social Credit pulling 385 votes. In August the CCF won a two-way fight with the Liberals, with 51 per cent of votes and a margin of victory of 138 votes. With Social Credit out of the equation, the next general election looked to be a CCF victory.

The pattern of support of 1934 was repeated. All elected CCF MLAS were successful middle-level farmers, prominent and active in their communities. All were active in either Wheat Pool or UFC(SS) locals, typically both. Williams noted, "The fact that the CCF candidates were elected in that portion of the province where crops were harvested is not without significance." This was especially so since 1938 was the darkest year of the Depression, following the 1937 drought that was both severe and widespread. According to Williams, these farmers could not be intimidated by the Liberals' ugly propaganda claiming "that relief would be cut off if the Liberals were not elected."[26] The pattern of the CCF doing best among the more prosperous farmers continued. It remained a farmers' party, most notably a middle-class farmers' party, failing to sway either poor or rich farmers. The CCF still had to win the working class. It ran in Prince Albert and did very badly (9 per cent). The left-leaning vote in the two largest urban centres, Regina and Saskatoon, was split between Independent Labour and the LPP. This vote was respectable, but nowhere near victory. In Moose Jaw, Social Credit made a decent showing, but was far outdistanced by the successful Liberals. The CCF's plan to move beyond its rural base among left-leaning farmers, put on hold to deal with Social Credit, was now revisited. The working class and at least a significant share of the urban middle class must be won to ensure a future victory. Asked to explain the reasons for the CCF's unexpected success in rolling back the Social Credit invasion, Williams repeated his refrain from 1934: "constituency and poll organization wins the day, an active country poll organization cannot be defeated, and where enough work is done by the local men and women it is impossible for even an army of Liberal organizers to undo it." The same went for Social Credit: "all their outside workers could not destroy a loyal local organization."[27]

Provincial CCF parties, and the national office, had feared Aberhart might steal much of the CCF's rural base in Saskatchewan. Some feared the worst—an Aberhart victory. Congratulations from CCF notables across the country poured in, giving Williams full personal credit for the outcome. Both Coldwell and Douglas praised his success. Coldwell made a point of asserting that Williams had "made an excellent job of organizing the province."[28] The national CCF organizer, who had often clashed with Williams, expressed admiration for Williams's campaign, which "was well-organized and efficiently conducted," adding that "the literature was good, the best we have yet had in an election."[29] CCF leaders in Alberta were delighted, having been crushed by Aberhart in 1935. One, referring to Williams's refusal to allow joint or fusion candidates, stated, "There was no confusion in anyone's mind about what the CCF was."[30] The Alberta CCF was particularly relieved that the election had closed the door on any more talk of cooperation with Social Credit. Williams was the man of the hour in the CCF across Canada. He had not only sustained the party, but advanced it, giving the CCF considerable national credibility. Williams agreed with the Alberta CCF: cooperation with Social Credit was over. But Williams went further, re-embracing his earlier firm conviction that the CCF must never cooperate with other political parties, movements, or groups. The CCF must present itself as the singular option for progressive, socialist change, and maintain its ideological and organizational integrity. As a pragmatist, he would consider informal saw-offs useful in advancing the CCF, but no arrangement that compromised the CCF's political independence and integrity.

This hard line against cooperation, and Williams's increasing unease with the national CCF's foreign policy of neutrality in future wars, quickly embroiled Williams in further battles with national office and his opponents in the provincial party. His honeymoon with the national office and his detractors in Saskatchewan was very brief. But in the autumn of 1938, Williams felt proud of what he had accomplished. He was content and enjoyed the long-delayed recognition. He decided to leave farming and devote himself full-time to politics. He auctioned off his farm machinery and leased his land. Williams and his family moved to Regina.

George Hara Williams, 1929, official portrait upon election as President of the United Farmers of Canada (Saskatchewan Section). PAS S-B 476.

Margery and George Williams on their farm, 1924. PAS S-B 477.

George Hara Williams speaking from the back of a truck, Saskatchewan Wheat Pool Picnic, St. Walburg, 1930. Andrew Macauley, a key political figure in Williams' circle, is seated on the truck. PAS S-B 482.

The Douglas Cabinet of 1944. PAS S-B 1203.

CCF Members of the Official Opposition after the 1934 election. PAS R-B 4031.

The Williams farm home, Semans, 1938. PAS S-B 479.

CCF Members of the Official Opposition after the 1938 election. PAS R-B 1395.

the **LAND OF** the **SOVIETS**

A WESTERN FARMER
SEES THE RUSSIAN BEAR
CHANGE HIS COAT
BY G·H· WILLIAMS
PAST PRESIDENT UNITED FARMERS OF CANADA

The Land of the Soviets, Williams's controversial booklet about his 1931 tour of the Soviet Union, was published by the United Farmers of Canada (Saskatchewan Section) in 1931. The booklet was sold during Williams's 1931–32 lecture tour, complete with slides, reporting on what he saw in the Soviet Union. The 66-community tour covered the entire province. Sales of the booklet were brisk, raising considerable funds for the organization. This tour was used as evidence of his alleged communist sympathies by his detractors both inside and outside of the party.

Part III

THE FALL OF WILLIAMS

Chapter 6

FIGHTING THE WAR IN THE CCF AND IN EUROPE

1937 to 1944

The CCF was a deeply committed antiwar political party. This was inevitable for a socialist party founded in the political aftermath of World War I. Canadian public opinion on the war gradually became more negative after 1918. This was certainly true at the centre and on the left of the political spectrum. A widely shared view was that the war had been a catastrophic imperialist adventure in which Canada was obliged to squander blood and treasure for questionable purposes defined by Great Britain's imperial interests. After the war there was a drive to establish Canadian constitutional independence, to ensure the nation was not again dragged into a war just because it was a dominion of the British Commonwealth. The 1931 Statute of Westminster granted Canada full independence, including decisions on war and peace: if Canada went to war again it would only be upon a decision by the House of Commons. Many of the labour and socialist parties at the founding of the CCF had resisted the war, battled conscription, and supported wartime strikes in defiance of the government. Doubtless many of the individuals who founded the CCF were involved in varieties of

war resistance, including aiding draft evaders. Woodsworth, a principled and absolute pacifist, did not shrink from trying to convert party
members and the general public to his views. Coldwell, clearly sympathetic to pacifism, expressed pride during a press interview that his son
had told him of his intention to resist any future wartime draft even if
it meant going to jail. Therefore, not only was the official position of the
party strongly antiwar, but many prominent party members were also
committed to pacifism as a principle.

The *Regina Manifesto* was clear: "We stand resolutely against all imperialist wars" and "Canada must refuse to be entangled in any more wars
fought to make the world safe for capitalism."[1] The CCF position was that
Canada must stay out of future wars, no matter which countries were
involved. There was no commitment to support Britain. Canada would
remain neutral and would limit its military forces to a size necessary
to defend Canadian territory from aggression. The CCF ambivalently
supported the principle of international collective security through the
League of Nations, whose task it was to prevent war between member nations. The manifesto criticized the league as "mainly a League
of Capitalist Great Powers." Nevertheless, the CCF was committed "to
advance the idea of international co-operation as represented" by the
league. Woodsworth argued tirelessly that the CCF should reject "the
whole idea of safety through military strength."[2] The party's foreign policy
was therefore unapologetically one of neutrality in future wars, isolation
from future inter-nation conflicts, and world peace guaranteed through
international collective security overseen by the League of Nations. This
position went unchallenged until the 1936 national convention, when a
group of delegates, Williams among them, unsuccessfully attempted to
delete the section of the policy committing the CCF to neutrality.

Many CCF members, like Williams, opposed imperialist wars—
indeed, war in general—but embraced what they argued was a more
realistic position: that war was sometimes unavoidable. Many among
this group were veterans of World War I. When faced with naked aggression and the imposition of dictatorial regimes by force, the only option
was to fight. In an exchange of letters with an MLA who was considering enlisting to fight in World War II, Williams said, "War is one of the
most horrible activities of the human race, and at the same time one of
the most practical. And when the enemy is at your door, there's a very

practical question you've got to decide. Will I give in, or will I fight?"[3] In 1932, Williams expressed concern about the rise of fascism, fearing an inevitable confrontation between fascism and democracy. Mussolini's National Fascist Party had marched on Rome in 1922, obtained power through constitutional means, and, by 1927, imposed a fascist police state. In Germany, Hitler came to power legally in 1933 when the Nazi Party won the largest bloc of seats in the Reichstag. He was appointed chancellor. The next year the Nazi Party and its parliamentary allies won a majority and imposed a legal dictatorship under Hitler's leadership. In both cases, the first victims of legal state repression, including executions and imprisonment in concentration camps, were communists, socialists, social democrats, trade union leaders, and constitutional liberals. Italian Fascism and German Nazism were founded, in the first instance, on dismantling democracy and constitutional law. The hope for international security through the League of Nations had already been tested and found wanting in 1931, when the Japanese army, directed by a *de facto* military dictatorship, invaded Manchuria and the league did nothing but express its disapproval. Japan, Italy, and Germany withdrew from the league.

The aggressive intentions of the Italian Fascists, German Nazis, and Japan's military dictatorship were clearly stated from the outset. Mussolini claimed as Italy's "vital space" the entire Mediterranean region, the Balkans, and North Africa, proclaiming the goal of establishing a New Roman Empire. In 1935, Italy invaded Abyssinia. Hitler claimed the whole of Eastern Europe as German *Lebensraum* (living space). He foresaw the conquest of Eastern Europe and its gradual occupation by German settlers through first enslaving and then liquidating the existing subhuman population. Japan's military dictatorship foresaw a future where European and American imperialists and colonizers were driven from China, Southeast Asia, and the islands of the South Pacific and replaced by the Southeast Asia Co-Prosperity Sphere under Japanese hegemony. The dividing line between democracy and fascism was brutally clarified when Italy and Germany sent troops, tanks, and warplanes to Spain, intervening in the Spanish Civil War to support the military uprising against the democratically elected Republican government. At the 1937 provincial CCF convention, Williams described what was happening in Spain and urged delegates to support the Republican side with donations. This was a battle between democracy and fascism, he argued, and all socialists must take a stand. He declared that the party's policy should be to "keep us out of war if possible, but fight if necessary."[4] The Republicans were defeated in 1939 and replaced by a military dictatorship under General Franco.

World War II was an imperialist war, but of a different kind than World War I. Angry and frustrated, the new rulers of Germany, Italy, and Japan were determined to achieve the world standing as major imperialist powers that Britain, France, and the United States denied them. They were prepared to engage in wars of aggression to win the territories they claimed. The war was also about the draconian imperialist peace imposed on Germany by the Allies in the Treaty of Versailles. Germany was forced to accept full, unqualified blame for starting and continuing the war and required to pay reparations to the victors as compensation for the costs of the war, which shackled the German economy with unsustainable obligations. The German Empire was dismantled. The Austro-Hungarian Empire, which had allied with Germany, was broken up.

Hungary and Austria became independent. Large chunks of the territory of Germany—some regions under historical dispute and others clearly German—were hacked off and distributed among Belgium, Poland, Czechoslovakia, and France. Danzig, and its hinterland, was declared a free city under the control of the League of Nations. The Saar coalfields were put under league control and their output granted to France. Germany's colonial possessions in Africa, in Asia, and among the Pacific Islands were distributed as just so much war booty to Belgium, Britain, France, Portugal, Japan, and members of the British Commonwealth (Australia, New Zealand, and South Africa). In Germany, the humiliations imposed by the treaty became a festering wound on the national psyche. Hitler rode to power on the combined promises to defy the treaty and to reverse Germany's economic woes in the Great Depression. He argued the two were inextricably linked.

World War II was also a capitalist war. Leading, powerful elements of the capitalist classes of both Germany and Italy supported and facilitated the rise to power of Hitler and Mussolini. Believing they could live with the regimes and effectively influence them, they looked forward to firm "law and order" governments willing and able to take the measures necessary to defeat and contain the rising, militant working class and its powerful institutions, trade unions, and communist and socialist parties. The regimes could be counted on to impose class peace by defeating the working class. A firm, right-wing government could also adopt the harsh economic policies necessary to deal with the Depression. As Williams observed, fascism was an effort to save capitalism from political and economic crisis "using the power of the state to control the 'Common Man' in the interests of 'Big Business.'" The inevitable consequence was that "democracy and dictatorship are coming close to open warfare."[5]

Williams was determined to change the national CCF's war policy. But if that proved impossible, he was willing to break publicly with the national party on the issue, with the Saskatchewan CCF adopting its own war policy. As the largest provincial section in the party, Saskatchewan's influence in the national apparatus was significant. Williams's reasons for taking this hard line were both principled and pragmatic. For him, the principle was self-evident: "We believe in Democracy. We believe in Socialism. We are prepared to defend our country against Fascist Dictatorship."[6] In 1937, in one of many letters to Woodsworth on the war issue, Williams wrote, "Both you and Mr. Coldwell seem to have taken the attitude that the CCF is a pacifist organization and will on no account take part in any war, offensive or defensive. It is quite conceivable that this war will be fought to determine whether Fascism on the one hand or Social Democracy on the other shall be the order of the 20th century."[7] Williams, ever the tactical pragmatist, was genuinely convinced that the CCF's foreign policy of neutrality, and the fact that many of its prominent leaders were self-declared pacifists, would hurt the party at the polls in the 1938 provincial and 1940 federal elections. His reading of the mood of the people was that they were not as enthusiastic at the prospect of war as had been the case in 1914, but a war to defend democracy from fascism would inevitably enjoy determined if reluctant popular support. As the war talk grew, and international events accelerated, Williams's sense of urgency increased. He believed it essential that the national CCF abandon its position on neutrality prior to the 1938 and 1940 elections.

The split between Williams and the national party became public in February 1937 at a Regina public meeting where King Gordon, a prominent national CCF intellectual, spoke on neutrality. Williams declined to appear on the platform as advertised. The chair of the meeting mentioned the reason for Williams's absence: his opposition to pacifism and neutrality as a foreign policy. The conflict was reported on the front page of the Regina *Leader-Post* and picked up by newspapers across Canada. In response, Williams issued a press release clarifying his position as leader of the Saskatchewan CCF: The party did not have a policy supporting pacifism. Its neutrality stand was being debated and was therefore "not a settled platform." "Personally," he went on, "although intensely opposed to war, I am neither an isolationist nor, in the abject sense of the term, a pacifist. The Saskatchewan CCF's policy on pacifism and neutrality will be determined by the provincial executive and provincial council, and, if necessary, by a convention."[8] The battle was now public.

Williams had defied the national party's authority over foreign policy by asserting a provincial section's right to adopt a different position. The Saskatoon CCF, which contained a concentration of pacifist supporters, denounced Williams and demanded his censure. The national CCF executive acted quickly, issuing a reprimand against Williams in March reminding him that the neutrality policy remained binding until it was changed at a national convention. In a letter to Williams, the executive described his stand as "unacceptable" and called it "deplorable" that he had made it a public issue.[9] Williams replied that as far as he was concerned, the neutrality resolution was just that—a resolution, not a confirmed plank in the national platform. It was being debated and would likely change in view of world events. Williams complained of the double standard of the national CCF: namely, it was acceptable for Woodsworth and many prominent CCFers to speak publicly in favour of pacifism, which was not a CCF policy, yet it was not acceptable for Williams to speak publicly against pacifism and in favour of abandoning neutrality.[10]

Williams was relentless and zealous in his opposition to the neutrality policy, unapologetically using all his powers as leader, provincial organizer, and office manager of the party apparatus. He issued an edict to national CCF speakers: "Leave complete neutrality and pacifism alone when speaking from provincial platforms."[11] Woodsworth responded by cancelling a three-week speaking tour in Saskatchewan (it later went ahead after negotiations between the two men). Williams refused to allow offending articles or advertisements to appear in the party newspaper. He declined to cooperate in the national CCF's 1937 "take the profit out of war" campaign on the grounds it was generically antiwar with pacifist overtones—and "a great many of us in the CCF are not pacifists."

He refused to distribute national pamphlets on the neutrality policy, and he declined to distribute copies of Woodsworth's speeches in the House of Commons if they were overly antiwar or advocated pacifism. Williams was not alone in this campaign. He enjoyed the full support of the elected MLAs and overwhelming majority support on the executive and provincial council. After a discussion in caucus with the MLAs, Williams stated the caucus position: that it was a "fundamental duty of Socialists and Democrats to fight for the right of self-government....If we have reached the place where we who believe in democracy and socialism are unwilling to fight for it, and are willing to allow [ourselves] and kindred nations to be trampled on and despoiled by Fascist Dictatorships," we have entered "another one of the Dark Ages."[12]

The war arrived more quickly than expected. In 1935, Hitler began a massive expansion of Germany's armed forces coupled with a crash rearmament program. In 1936, Germany marched into the Rhineland, demilitarized by the Treaty of Versailles, and Germany and Italy formed a military alliance, the Rome-Berlin Axis. In 1938, Germany entered into an alliance with Japan. Also in 1938, Hitler forced the unification of Austria with Germany. He then turned his attention to Czechoslovakia, demanding the annexation of Sudetenland, which contained over three million people of German descent. Sudetenland had been assigned to Czechoslovakia upon the post–World War I dismantling of the Austro-Hungarian Empire. In 1938, Hitler demanded it be annexed to Germany. He promised Britain and France this was his final territorial claim. This created problems for the governments of Britain and France, who were determined to avoid war at all costs. Britain and France had signed treaties with Czechoslovakia promising to protect it from aggression and to guarantee its territorial integrity. Meeting in Munich in September 1938, in the absence of representatives of the Czech government, Britain and France agreed to allow Germany to annex Sudetenland. The Czech government was informed that if it resisted the annexation, Britain and France would provide no military assistance. As an added touch to reassure those in Britain eager to guarantee peace, Hitler also signed a peace treaty with Britain. In March 1939, Germany invaded the rest of Czechoslovakia.

Disturbed by the cavalier abandonment of Czechoslovakia in the face of Hitler's bellicose territorial claims, the Soviet Union feared that Britain and France were hoping Hitler would quickly turn his aggressive territorial claims eastward toward the Soviet Union. Aware of Hitler's claim to the whole of Eastern Europe as Germany's *Lebensraum*, the planned fate that awaited the current inhabitants, and Hitler's repeated commitment to crush the Bolshevik menace to the east, the Soviet Union knew a German invasion was inevitable. The Soviet Union expected no help from governments of the major capitalist powers; indeed, prominent members of the capitalist class and conservative politicians in many capitalist democracies openly expressed the hope that Hitler would crush the Soviet Union. Therefore, the Soviet government sought an arrangement with Germany to postpone the inevitable. The temporary strategic objectives of Germany and the Soviet Union came together. Hitler feared, above all, a war on two fronts at the same time, as Germany had faced in World War I. Further, anticipating inevitable wartime trade embargoes, Germany needed guaranteed access to strategic materials in order to wage war—most importantly, foodstuffs (mainly wheat) and oil. The Soviet Union had ample supplies of both.

The Soviet Union, for its part, needed time to prepare for the coming invasion. As much of its strategic industrial infrastructure as possible must be moved further east. Soviet armed forces must be rapidly expanded. The production of munitions and armaments must be ramped up. In a completely unexpected diplomatic coup, Germany and the Soviet Union entered into a non-aggression pact in August 1939. The two nations agreed not to engage in acts of war against each other, nor to come to the aid of each other's enemies. The Soviet Union agreed to sell wheat and oil, and other needed goods, to Germany. Further, in a secret addendum, the two parties agreed to establish spheres of influence for each nation in Poland and, for the Soviet Union, in Finland, the Baltic States, and parts of Romania. Thus the Soviet Union was able to buy time to prepare for the future invasion and to establish, through annexation and invasion, deep territorial buffers on its northern and western flanks to slow down the inevitable German attack. Hitler got his temporary guarantee of no war on his eastern flank and all the wheat and oil Germany needed as long as the agreement was in force.

The Nazi-Soviet Pact caught the governments of Britain and France completely off guard. Up to that point, it had been universally viewed as inconceivable that Nazis and Bolsheviks, mortal political enemies, could reach any diplomatic agreement. The pact was signed on August 23.

Appeasement had failed to stop Hitler's aggressive territorial ambitions, which now turned to Poland. In response, on August 25, France and Britain agreed to guarantee Poland's sovereignty and territorial integrity. On September 1, Germany invaded Poland. Hitler was convinced Britain and France would back down, as they had before. He miscalculated. On September 3, France and Britain declared war on Germany. Canada followed suit on September 10. World War II began.

The CCF's national council convened an emergency session in Ottawa on September 6, 7, and 8, 1939, to formulate the party's position on the war. It was urgent to do so in time for the House of Commons session on September 9, when it was expected the Liberal King government would declare war on Germany. Woodsworth was in total opposition to any support for the war. Williams challenged him, insisting that the CCF support the war up to and including sending troops into combat if necessary. Williams insisted this war was a different kind of war than those of the past. This war was about the survival of democracy. He asked, "Would the failure of the Allies and the victory of Germany destroy democracy? I think it would. We recognize that war is the outcome of capitalism, but what we're fighting to support is the right to change the economic system."[13] This was a serious crisis for the national party. The divisions were deep and apparently irreconcilable. The Manitoba section supported Woodsworth. The Saskatchewan and Alberta sections supported Williams. The BC section demanded the war be declared an imperialist war and the CCF refuse to support any participation. The Nova Scotia section wanted full support for the war. The Ontario section was deeply divided. Clearly, if the national CCF adopted either Woodsworth's or Williams's postion it could shatter the party. A middle ground was therefore worked out over the three-day meeting, leaving no one fully satisfied but keeping the party together.

The *CCF Statement on Canada and the Present Crisis* recognized the war was a struggle involving "the survival of our democratic institutions" and that "the people of Britain and France" were "waging a war against aggression." Canada's "assistance overseas should be limited to economic aid and must not include conscription of manpower or the sending of an expeditionary force."[14] Economic aid in the form of war material should be organized under public ownership to prevent war profiteering. Canada's war readiness should be limited to the defence of its territory.

The civil liberties of Canadians must be respected, not subjected to "encroachments" under the guise of wartime necessity. Initially, Williams opposed the statement, but after further debate he was won over, and the document passed 15 to 7. Williams was persuaded by the assurance that members were allowed to continue to publicly state differing positions on the war, as long as it was made clear they were not voicing the national CCF's official position. The war debate within the party and in public could therefore continue. Back in Saskatchewan, Williams issued a public statement clarifying where he and the Saskatchewan CCF stood, insisting the national council's statement merely "reflects our present position." He emphasized, "Should the time arrive when military aid in the form of an expeditionary force is necessary, comparable to that given at the time of the last war, then undoubtedly the policy of the CCF will again be considered."[15]

Williams therefore continued to take an aggressive stance in support of the war, including support for committing troops to the struggle. To flesh out the CCF's initial brief statement on the war, the national CCF issued a document, *Canada and the War: The CCF Position.* Williams was outraged at some of its content and threatened to publicly oppose the document. Two statements concerned him most: first, "The CCF believes that the measure of Canada's direct and vital concern in this struggle does not justify the shedding of Canadian blood on European soil"; and second,

> No Canadian who realizes the implications of an expeditionary force can view military intervention in Europe with anything but the gravest misgiving. The militarization of our national life, the slaughter of our youth, the distortion of our economy, the destruction of civil liberties, the rousing of racial animosity and sectional strife, will leave Canada impoverished and embittered and will make the building of a united, free and prosperous Canadian nation even more difficult if not impossible.[16]

How, Williams asked, after making such blunt statements as the CCF position, will it be possible for the CCF to shift to support for sending troops at a later date and maintain any public credibility? Williams, with the support of the provincial council, refused to distribute the document in

Saskatchewan. He continued to make the case for involvement in the war. The moral issue was clear, and the fact this was a world historical crisis was clear; therefore, this was no time for equivocation and half measures.

In October 1939, Williams sent a letter about the war to all party members in the province: "What are we going to do about it? What are *you* going to do about it now? There are two things you must and should do. You and I must do our part to help the people of Britain and France to stop the onward march of dictatorship, force and aggression. And you and I must do our part and see to it that war never comes again, by electing men to govern who believe in Social Democracy rather than Profiteering Capitalism."[17] When an MLA's letter, while supporting Williams's position on the war, expressed admiration for Woodsworth's principled stand on complete pacifism, Williams's reply was brutal in his assessment of Woodsworth: "Mr. Woodsworth as always is an idealist who persistently refuses to see the facts. Unfortunately we cannot alter facts by refusing to see them. The fact is we must either fight or accord government by dictatorship a victory."[18]

The CCF's ambivalence about going to war was very much a reflection of the public mood, given the disaster of World War I. Prime Minister King himself was a reluctant war advocate. Initially, like the CCF, he hoped Canada's participation could be limited and was loath to send troops overseas into combat. Even the manner in which the King government declared war reflected a lack of enthusiasm. The prime minister announced that the simple approval of his address on the Speech from the Throne, in which he stated the government's support for France and Britain in the current conflict, would be taken as the House's approval of the government's intention to declare war. The address was approved on September 9 in an unrecorded vote. The next day, the Canadian government declared war on Germany. King was hoping to avoid sending a large expeditionary force, initially dispatching only one army division to Europe. That had to change with the defeat of the Allies and the fall of France in 1940. Both the Liberals and the Tories had previously agreed there would be no conscription, and King had made that a solemn pledge to the Canadian people. In 1942, a national plebiscite was required to release him from that pledge.

In fact, the CCF's war policy, very much like that of the King government, evolved in stages as each new crisis of the war presented itself.

Indeed, throughout the war, even after embracing full support for sending troops into combat, the CCF retained its reputation as the antiwar party. Throughout the war it sustained a critique of the Liberal government in key areas of war policy: the failure to conscript wealth before conscripting men; inexcusable war profiteering; an unclear recognition of the right to conscientious objection and the fair and honourable treatment of those who invoke it; excessive curtailment of the civil liberties of targeted groups suspected of possible sympathy for enemy nations; failure to agree that only conscripts who volunteered should be posted overseas; a failure to plan meaningfully for peace, reconstruction, and the just, orderly reintegration of returning veterans into civil life. The government should remember the lessons of the postwar debacle in Canada after 1918. As the war continued, such a position resonated deeply with an anxious and war-weary public.

In addition to confrontations over war policy, Williams simultaneously became embroiled in controversy with the national CCF leadership—and elements in the Saskatchewan party—over cooperation with other movements, groups, and political parties in the fight against fascism abroad and right-wing reaction at home. Williams believed the 1938 campaign had put the issue of cooperation to final rest. Having toyed with cooperation, he emerged from that experience with the conviction that the CCF should not again engage in cooperation of any sort, other than informal saw-offs. He had held this conviction previously, but had temporarily abandoned it in order to confront the Social Credit invasion. At the time, he had endured sharp criticism from the national leadership. Based on the messages of congratulation he received for his conduct of the 1938 election, Williams believed the national party had also put the issue of cooperation to rest. But the growth of fascism and the march to war revived calls for cooperation as the 1940 federal election approached. Williams's position was firm: no cooperation, no united front, and a stand-alone CCF candidate contesting every constituency in Saskatchewan.

Three groups emerged advocating a united front against fascism and right-wing reaction and calling on the CCF to join in the fight for the 1940 election: the United Progressive Association, the National Reform Party, and the New Democracy Party. All three groups enjoyed a significant presence in Saskatchewan, and Williams had to contend with them daily on the ground. The United Progressive Association, a united front inspired and largely led by the CP, had strong support in three provincial constituencies where the CP base was large and organizationally effective (Meadow Lake, Redberry, and Turtleford). The seats were all located in the North Battleford federal constituency. Those favouring the option enjoyed some following in other constituencies, particularly in Saskatoon, but nowhere near as strong as in the North Battleford seat. The National Reform Party was composed of the two Unity and two Social Credit MLAs elected in 1938. Williams had expected the two Unity MLAs to join the CCF caucus since they had run pledging support for the CCF program. But, in what Williams considered an act of betrayal of those who had voted for them, the two MLAs united with the Social Credit MLAs, achieving third-party status in the legislature in 1939. The New Democracy Party, established and led by ex-Tory W. D. Herridge, advocated social credit monetary reform and government intervention in the economy to alleviate the Depression.[19] Herridge called on the Social Credit and CCF parties to join him in a united front against monopoly and finance capitalism and the old-line parties.

The National Reform Party, with four seats in the provincial legislature, demanded Williams share the role and indemnity of leader of the opposition with their leader and divide up the provincial constituencies between the two parties for the next election. Williams rejected their demands and denounced them as divisive, engaging in a running battle with the four members in the legislature. The National Reform Party declared support for Herridge's party, assisting him in his efforts to win the Kindersley seat in Saskatchewan in 1940.

The United Progressive Association was established with the blessing of CCF party members of the three provincial constituency associations, who agreed to join forces with all progressive people to run a Unity candidate in North Battleford. Williams and the provincial council demanded the federal CCF constituency association nominate a candidate. The association refused, largely because a long-time, popular, charismatic, and militantly left-wing CCFer, Dorise Nielsen, a local teacher, had been nominated as the Unity candidate.[20] Repeated efforts by Williams to get a CCF candidate nominated failed, effectively blocked by the strong support for Nielsen among local CCF party members. Williams and the provincial council finally relented, agreeing not to run a CCF candidate and publicly advising CCF supporters to vote for Nielsen.

Herridge's New Democracy movement caused Williams the greatest concern, because it was taken very seriously by the national CCF leadership and Herridge had targeted Saskatchewan for his most determined effort to obtain cooperation. The National Reform Party, the CP through the Unity movement, and the Social Credit Party in Saskatchewan were all pushing for Herridge's proposal to unite behind one candidate representing the reform forces in each constituency. Williams was also aware of great spontaneous support for unity among the party's base. The national CCF leadership equivocated, asking local provincial sections not to attack Herridge but to wait to see how things evolved. Some among them, including Coldwell, believed the Herridge movement just might take off. They worried that open attacks on Herridge would offend his mass following, should it emerge. Coldwell initially proposed a conference in Saskatchewan between the CCF and Herridge supporters to see if a plan could be worked out. Williams flatly rejected the idea, with the unanimous support of the provincial council. The council adopted a policy of no cooperation.

Williams, in the midst of having to contend with these forces in Saskatchewan, was angry at the lack of national direction. The daily pressure on him was enormous, given the local strength of the Unity movement, the National Reform Party, and supporters of Herridge's proposal, some of whom were prominent CCF members. Without clear direction and leadership, the CCF's popular base was vulnerable to the Herridge appeal, particularly given the extensive national press coverage his movement was enjoying. Williams's advice to the national office was the same as he gave in correspondence with concerned party members: "We must be loyal and steadfast and not be wobbly people who will wobble from one quack reform to another quack reform."[21] If left too long, it might be too late to keep that base together behind the CCF.

Williams again felt the party's "intelligentsia" were overthinking the issue at a theoretical level, with little understanding of the practicalities of tactical and strategic political leadership. He warned the national leadership that delaying clear direction on the issue was dangerous because the rank and file believed "unity" was a good idea and could "go off the deep end and try to form a fusionist organization."[22] This would be fatal to the CCF at the polls. Williams scoffed at the idea that Herridge's party had, or could get, a mass following, rejecting Coldwell's fear that if Herridge were ignored the CCF might become "an ineffective rump outside the great mass movement of progressive people."[23] That would only happen, Williams argued, if the CCF failed to provide clear political leadership in order to keep its base intact. As Williams had learned in 1938, the CCF's base needed careful tending in the maelstrom of "progressive" and "reform" political options. He urged the national leadership to recognize "the impracticability of attempting to link up incompatible elements in a united front." For his part, Williams intended "to take the action which is necessary in the interests of the Province."[24]

After consulting other provincial leaders of the CCF about the Herridge movement, all of whom expressed concerns, Williams decided to go public with the Saskatchewan CCF's opposition to cooperation. In an April 26, 1939, radio broadcast, he slammed the door on coopera-tion as far as the Saskatchewan CCF was concerned, declaring, "I have always been very dubious of this suggestion that the CCF discard its Socialism and co-operate with such capitalist reform parties. The truth is capitalism cannot be reformed, it must be replaced. Surely we do not want another Progressive party fiasco."[25] Combining sarcasm and analy-sis, he dismantled the three reform groups seeking to form a united front with the CCF: the Unity movement was inspired and largely led by the CP, a party with its own agenda set by the Communist International; the other two groups were capitalist reformers seeking to save the sys-tem by tinkering with it. Herridge was a bitter ex-Tory whose party had rejected his program, and he now presented himself as a "capitalist reformer" who believed capitalism, in order to survive, must be made "less burdensome and less obnoxious." Williams's attack on Herridge was particularly caustic—and deliberately so since Herridge was taken far too seriously by many prominent CCF party members. Williams noted Herridge fancied himself "a Reform Conservative, whatever that is." Herridge still believed "any individual should have the right to own and control natural resources and industries from which he can profit at the expense of others. Mr. Herridge says it should not extend to the point where you make the babies cry." No, he was not a hard Tory who believed in "survival of the fittest and to the Devil with the weak. Mr. Herridge is sorry for the weak, just how sorry, I cannot say." Williams's broadcast was a public declaration that the pressure from these groups on the Saskatchewan CCF would be futile. The CCF would run its own candidates in Saskatchewan in 1940.

At a national council meeting, Coldwell moved a successful motion of censure against Williams for his attack on Herridge. Yet a month later, Coldwell sounded remarkably like Williams when he characterized Herridge's movement as "just another vague movement which may cause the same disillusionment as did the old Progressive Party."[26] The July 1939 Saskatchewan provincial convention overwhelmingly rejected cooperation. Party conventions in British Columbia and Manitoba did likewise. The national CCF finally acquiesced, issuing a statement late in July that, wherever possible, CCF candidates should contest federal constituencies and not participate in cooperation with other groups. The matter was under the authority of the provincial sections.

Contrary to Williams's fears, the national CCF's policy on neutrality and the personal pacifist convictions of its national leader did not become issues in the 1938 provincial election. The Social Credit invasion was the focus of all attention. And, as Williams noted, the people had not yet fully engaged with the rise of fascism and the looming clouds of war. The 1940 federal election was another matter. After the success of 1938, Coldwell and Douglas begged Williams to organize the 1940 campaign in the province. Williams was reluctant, first suggesting it would be better if it were "distinctly a Federal Campaign" spearheaded by Coldwell and Douglas as federal MPs.[27] Behind his reluctance were his fears about being pressured to defend the national CCF's neutrality policy and the pacifism of its leader. After much pleading, and despite Williams's continuing battle with the national party over war policy, he finally agreed. But he made it clear he would not associate the provincial party with the national CCF's war policy.

In his Christmas 1939 radio broadcast as leader of the opposition, Williams essentially declared full support of the provincial CCF for participation in the war.[28] He argued that the final judgment on the use of military force must be made based on its aims and purposes. The real pacifist, he declared, fights when it is necessary to save lives and "cherished freedoms." According to Williams, "The CCF recognizes force and aggression must be stopped." At the same time, he presented a vigorous defence of the right of freedom of conscience for conscientious objectors. He told the audience there had not yet been a national CCF convention to decide the party's war policy given the events of September 1939. He therefore made it clear he was speaking only on behalf of the Saskatchewan CCF. His broadcast angered the national leadership and those in the Saskatchewan party who supported neutrality and pacifism. Many expressed support for Woodworth's position on the war. Williams faced a barrage of criticism within the Saskatchewan party over his stand, but the attacks clearly failed to gain traction among the rank and file: a petition criticizing Williams for his war stand, circulated by the Saskatoon CCF, failed to gain significant support. He declared that in the coming election, war policy would be a "vital issue" and "very little quarter will be given" by the party's opponents.[29]

Provoking Coldwell's vigorous objections, Williams proposed a meeting of all federal candidates and campaign managers to discuss how to handle the war policy issue during the election. The meeting was not convened. However, in January 1940 such a meeting did occur, convened by Tommy Douglas, who now supported full participation in the war. Though stopping short of advocating support for Canada's active military involvement, the meeting declared that now that Canada was fully involved in the war, it was "necessary to prosecute it successfully and efficiently."[30] The meeting favoured conscription if necessary, as long as it included the conscription of wealth as well as men. The majority of candidates had no intention of defending the national CCF's war policy during the coming campaign. Though Woodsworth was the only CCF MP to vote against the war in the House of Commons on September 9, the party's official policy nevertheless remained unchanged.

The March 26, 1940, federal election results vindicated Williams. He received no congratulations, not even from the re-elected Coldwell and Douglas, who had benefited from his strong stand supporting complete participation in the war. As Williams had predicted, the national CCF's war policy was used aggressively by the Liberals and Tories, who accused the CCF of disloyalty to Britain, pacifism, and a lack of patriotism. Efforts were made to equate the CCF's "socialism" with Hitler's "national socialism."[31] The usual communist smears were trotted out.

In 1935 the CCF had won seven seats with 9 per cent of the vote: three in BC, with 33 per cent; two in Saskatchewan, with 21 per cent; and two in

Manitoba, with 19 per cent. In 1940 the CCF won eight seats with 8 per cent: five in Saskatchewan, with 28 per cent; one in BC, with 28 per cent; one in Manitoba, with 20 per cent; and one in Nova Scotia, with 6 per cent. Saskatchewan was the only province in which the CCF vote went up significantly (by 7 per cent), and this increase in popular vote netted five seats, instead of the two won in 1935. In contrast, in BC the vote fell 4 per cent, and two seats were lost. The result was particularly bad in Ontario, where the CCF vote fell from 8 to 4 per cent. By publicly rejecting the national CCF's war policy and adopting a policy of support for full participation in the war, Williams had arguably salvaged the party, not only in Saskatchewan, but as a national force.

The detailed results were gratifying for Williams and the Saskatchewan party. Dorise Nielsen, the North Battleford Unity candidate endorsed by the CCF, crushed her Liberal opponent (10,500 votes to 7,868). In Saskatoon City, Rev. W. G. Brown, a second Unity candidate endorsed by the CCF, enjoyed a similar victory (13,868 votes to 8,346). Herridge, the leader of the New Democracy Party, ran a close third behind the CCF in Kindersley, delivering the seat to the Liberals. The New Democracy Party failed spectacularly across the country. These three seats would probably have gone CCF had there been no effort at cooperation. The general pattern of results augured well for the CCF's political future. Social Credit was dead, winning just over 3 per cent of the vote, injured by its alliance with Herridge. Four of the five CCF seats were won with majorities of over 50 per cent, including Melfort, where Social Credit pulled 8 per cent. In the seven rural seats where the CCF was not elected, and no Unity candidate stood, the CCF ran a strong second. The federal results suggested that provincial power had only to await the next provincial election. Nevertheless, Williams believed he had failed on the big issue of changing the national CCF's war policy. Indeed, the change in policy did not occur until Woodsworth's death in March 1942. In April 1942, the national CCF urged a "yes" vote in the national plebiscite on conscription (66 per cent voted in favour); in July, Coldwell succeeded Woodsworth as leader and the CCF's official war policy was changed to one of full support for Canada's participation in the war. Confirming Williams's insistence that the war policy suppressed the party's popular support, the CCF's national popularity jumped dramatically, to 21 per cent in September 1942 and then to 29 per cent in 1943.

By 1940, Williams had led the CCF to the threshold of victory. Party membership had reached and was fluctuating around six thousand, finances were in good order, and the party newspaper was widely read. The party's election machinery, based on an active membership and detailed poll organization, was in good form and experienced in fighting elections. Organizing in the major cities was going well as the CCF began to overcome working-class resistance to supporting what was still widely viewed as a farmers' party. The CCF's provincial caucus had grown to eleven MLAS and the party boasted five Saskatchewan MPs. Williams established a government in waiting, naming a shadow cabinet. He insisted the caucus prepare a full legislative program for its first term in power. It was crucial, he argued, that upon winning power a CCF government move quickly to implement its core program. Anticipating the job as premier of the first CCF government, Williams was determined to begin implementing the party's program in a special session of the legislature convened quickly after victory. But, especially as the war intensified and casualties grew, he remained fearful that the national CCF's war policy—still two years away from being changed—could derail the march to victory.

Ironically, Williams's success set the stage for the successful culmination of the organized effort to oust him from the leadership. Over the years he had acquired a long list of dedicated opponents who rankled under his apparently unassailable leadership, given his strong support among the party membership. His defeated opponents in the old Progressive Party, in the SGGA, and on the right of the UFC(SS) had largely ended up in the CCF carrying historical grudges. The Coldwell group was still bitter over Williams's replacement of Coldwell as leader after the 1934 election disaster. Williams's very public battle with the national CCF leadership over war policy offended committed pacifists, including a considerable number of his former ideological supporters, who expressed deep disappointment in his position on the war. The battle over cooperation had humiliated and embarrassed leading members of the Saskatchewan party, including Coldwell. Some on the left of the party, especially those under the influence of the CP, were angry at Williams for successfully blocking the Unity strategy. All those who supported cooperation had suffered Williams's public ridicule and sarcasm as he successfully fought any form of cooperation for the 1940 election.

Many were offended by Williams's often harsh and condescending public attacks on pacifism, which were seen as reflecting badly on the CCF's
revered national leader, J. S. Woodsworth. Galvanized and united by the
battle over war policy, these groups finally coalesced into an opposition
bloc committed to pushing Williams from office. The effort began in earnest in 1940.

Williams was aware of the opposition to his leadership. He had dealt
with systematic antagonism from his opponents from the beginning. He
felt no personal animosity, having weathered many battles in the farm
movement and the party, which typically resolved into a willingness to
work together for a common cause. His frustrated opponents accused
him of being dictatorial and controlling, given his firm grasp on the
levers of power in the party. One referred to him privately as "a tin pot
dictator."[32] But the criticisms had gone nowhere among the party membership, who continued to elect and re-elect Williams. His opponents
accepted the futility of opposing his leadership openly on the convention
floor. Until the 1940 convention, the executive and provincial council
had consistently given Williams overwhelming support. Even after certain control of the executive began to slip from Williams's grasp after the
1940 convention, he was often able to sway opponents to his position.
This annoyed Carlyle King, a leading opponent of Williams.[33] Williams's
persuasive skills often frustrated King's planned opposition to Williams
on key issues. In a letter, King complained, "I don't know how he does
it, but he has a way with him, there's no doubt about it." Earlier, King
had confided to a friend that Williams was "an able politician, an excellent organizer, and a reasonably good speaker" who "remains leader
only because we can't find anyone either able or willing to replace him."[34]
Williams recognized such open opposition as an inevitable reality of the
political terrain. This was dramatically true in the war debate. King, a
strong pacifist, was moved to fierce opposition over the issue. So were
many others.

Williams was not, however, initially aware of the long-standing subterranean campaign to unseat him as leader. Nor was he aware of the
personal treachery of Coldwell and Douglas. Williams clashed with
Coldwell repeatedly, but in face-to-face meetings they agreed to resolve
their differences and work together. Each time Williams made peace with
Coldwell, he accepted at face value Coldwell's assurances of support. He

also believed Douglas's frequent assurances of friendship and support. But while Coldwell and Douglas were publicly congratulating Williams on the outcome of the 1938 election, begging him to organize the 1940 federal campaign, and assuring him of their support, they were privately systematically undermining him.

Nuggets of evidence for this are contained in scattered private correspondence between Coldwell and prominent members of the Saskatchewan party. In 1937, for example, Coldwell stated, "I have little confidence in his [Williams's] judgment or political sense."[35] In 1938, a prominent member wrote to a Coldwell supporter suggesting Coldwell replace Williams, noting, "A leader must have confidence and support of all in order to make a success. G.H. does not command that confidence and the situation is getting worse."[36] Just after the 1938 election, while congratulating Williams on his success to his face, Coldwell wrote to a prominent party member, "I have made up my mind that I will be no party to placing George H. Williams in the premier's chair."[37] In a 1939 exchange between members of the Coldwell faction, the following appears: "George Williams must be eliminated, a leader, unfortunately, whom no one trusts. Tommy Douglas and Coldwell are going to call on you to discuss this."[38] In 1940, Coldwell wrote, "I am sorry to say I have no confidence in George. His actions over the past 6 months have disgusted me completely. With another leader we could carry the province next time."[39] Up until March 1940 it was assumed Coldwell would replace an ousted Williams, but that changed when Coldwell became CCF House leader in Ottawa, replacing an ailing Woodsworth. Coldwell decided then that Douglas was the ideal replacement for Williams. Meanwhile, a Saskatoon CCF executive member resigned in protest over "the constant and unwarranted attacks" on Williams.[40] Later, an MLA reported to Williams he had attended a house party with Douglas present where the chief topic of conversation was how to get rid of Williams. Williams also learned later that Douglas had attended many meetings in private homes discussing the need to replace him.

The campaign to replace Williams became public in 1940. The first move was an effort to limit Williams's complete control of the party apparatus, in the hope this would begin to undermine his authority and uncontested influence among the membership. In June the Saskatoon CCF constituency association approved resolutions proposing two amendments to the party's constitution and submitted them for the July convention: one proposed limiting the president and vice-president to two successive one-year terms in office; the other proposed the offices of party leader and president could not be occupied by the same person simultaneously. The Saskatoon *Star-Phoenix* reported this as a direct attack on Williams's leadership.[41] President of the Saskatoon association, Carlyle King, denied this, insisting the division of leadership responsibilities between two people was intended "to create democratic control of the organization." Williams saw it otherwise. This was the first direct and open challenge to his leadership since becoming leader. The resolution came from the Saskatoon CCF, on record as strongly endorsing Woodsworth's position on the war. The Saskatoon CCF spearheaded an unsuccessful petition campaign among the membership protesting Williams's war policy and his failure to follow the policy of the national CCF. There was no doubt in Williams's mind that these proposed amendments were an attack on his leadership. The issue was the extent of support for this challenge among party members.

At the July 22 meeting of the provincial council, the day before the convention convened, there was considerable discussion about the implications of the resolutions and whether wider support for the proposals existed among the membership. It was reported that one other constituency association had proposed a general review of the constitution, but the issue had never come to a vote. Williams was therefore confident that the resolution reflected the isolated opposition to him in Saskatoon over the war issue. This sense of confidence was shattered when A. M. Nicholson, the MP for Mackenzie and secretary of CCF MPs in Ottawa, revealed he had been asked to present a brief from the Saskatchewan MPs on just this issue.[42] His directions were to present the brief directly to the convention, circumventing Williams, the MLAs, and the provincial council. (Douglas later admitted he was the author of the brief.) Given the discussion over the Saskatoon resolutions, Nicholson realized the serious implications of doing this and therefore shared the brief's contents and his instructions with council members.

The Brief from the Saskatchewan CCF Members of Parliament, most importantly, proposed a division between the offices of president and political leader.[43] The immediate rationale provided for this was if the CCF were elected and Williams became premier, the party would lack organizational leadership. In turn, this could "destroy the basis of our movement by failing to have an active organization…to help formulate Government policies and to bring the needs of the people constantly before its elected members." The proposed solution was to establish the positions of president and provincial secretary, separate from political leader, "who are not elected members." This should be done now to ensure the organization was not "decapitated…nor left weak and leaderless." Further, the brief suggested a constitutional mechanism "to provide the necessary controls and collaboration between the CCF organization…and the CCF Government." This would safeguard the continuing democratic influence of the party membership over an elected government. The party organization should have a constitutionally protected consultative role in cabinet appointments and government policy, including examining drafts of planned legislation. The brief concluded by suggesting the convention set up a special committee to draft constitutional amendments "embodying the purposes outlined."

Williams was angry at the proposals in the brief coming in the midst of the battles over war policy and cooperation with the Herridge movement. He later described the brief as "the final straw that broke the camel's back."[44] He interpreted it as the culmination of a campaign against his leadership. The proposals were an effort to strip him of much of his power and influence and to reduce the role of the elected caucus that solidly supported him. Two of his three key functions—provincial secretary and president—would be taken away, leaving him as political leader. The justification was an obviously manufactured, hypothetically inevitable crisis of leadership after winning power. This was just plain silly. In fact, as Williams knew, it would take no time at all, upon victory, for the party to fill the organizational gaps left by his becoming premier. He saw it as no accident the presentation of the brief was planned to blindside him at the convention in tandem with the Saskatoon resolutions. Quite frankly, he believed it was a cowardly and sneaky move. He was most angry at the attempted subterfuge in not first openly consulting him, the executive, the caucus, and the council before the brief went to a convention. The council agreed not to present the brief to the next day's convention, referring it instead to the new council for action.

The next day, Williams was clearly aroused and angry during his presidential address to the convention:

> I plead for both frankness and toleration. I do not suggest
> that you mince words or refrain from saying anything you
> believe should be said, but I do suggest that personalities and
> backbiting be avoided as would be the plague. I particularly
> plead for tolerance in discussion of the war issue. In asking
> you for tolerance I am trying to remind myself to be toler-
> ant, for as you know I am a man of decided opinions and
> convictions.[45]

He dismissed the false rumours that had been circulating since he enlisted as an officer in the Non-Permanent Active Militia. No, he was not getting rich on his officer's pay for his days of training at Dundurn. In fact, his per diems did not cover the cost of uniforms and kit. Nor was it true, as had been broadcast, that his duties with the NPAM interfered with his ability to do the job of leader of the opposition and president of the party. He informed delegates that his commanding officer had assured him, in writing, he was completely free to fulfill all his political duties as both president and leader of the opposition "until such time as I should be called to Overseas Service." He made it clear to delegates he intended to serve overseas if he had the opportunity. In the meantime, after all training exercises he would "return to civil life." Even during training exercises he was free to leave to attend to his political obligations, as he was doing today, having obtained leave to attend council and conven-tion meetings. He reminded delegates he was not alone in doing his part: "Many of our best workers have answered the call to the colors....For those of our associates who are taking their place in the front lines of the battle for democracy we extend our appreciation and pray for their safe and victorious return."

Williams issued a blunt challenge to his detractors to have the courage of their convictions:

> It may be that there are delegates who are opposed to my con-
> tinued leadership of the CCF because of my whole-hearted
> support of Canada's war efforts. If that be the case, I would
> suggest that these delegates arrange to place someone in
> nomination against me for President, who will frankly appeal
> for support on the grounds that Canada's interest in this war

does not justify the placing of Canada's resources and manpower behind the prosecution of the war and I will take the
other side of the case.

Carlyle King was nominated. After the candidates' remarks, Williams
handily defeated King. Uncharacteristically, the vote was not recorded
in the minutes, but in Williams's correspondence after the convention
he reported that his victory had been decisive. King noted in his correspondence that he had won 35 per cent of delegates.[46] The Saskatoon
resolutions were defeated. The convention passed an overwhelming vote
of confidence in Williams's leadership, accompanied by the usual ovation. Williams remained in firm control of the party, though now he was
clearly under open siege. After the convention, he faced a split executive
and a significant united minority opposition on the provincial council.
His position on King in particular, and pacifists in general, hardened as
Hitler marched from victory to victory. The May 1940 Dunkirk evac-
uation of the British Expeditionary Force from France, and the fall of
France in June, signalled the war was to be long and bloody. In a letter to
a friend after the convention, Williams remarked harshly, "I have no personal quarrel with Dr. King but his mental outlook in the present crisis
is repugnant not only to myself but to every man who believes that each
and every one of us has an equal responsibility in the defense of democracy and the maintenance of progress."[47]

There is little doubt Williams could have prevailed as leader had he
decided to stay in Saskatchewan and fight to retain his position. Now that
his opposition was out in the open, the contest could go forward with
clarity. He could have embraced the MPS' brief, established a favourable
party committee to review it, and massaged the document to remove its
most objectionable parts. He could have embraced the idea of dividing
the offices of president and party leader, mobilized for the next convention to elect a supportive president, and run for political leader. The
brief made some valid points about the movement's democratic right to
have significant oversight over an elected government. The populist in
Williams could easily have embraced this and turned it to his advantage.
He could have proposed a similar mechanism of membership assessment
and oversight of the speeches and votes of MPs in Ottawa. He could have
devoted himself to speaking tours of constituencies, as he had so often in

the past when the party was in crisis. This would have revitalized his personal grassroots support and gained the party new members. In fact, he could have turned the tour into a blunt and rousing defence of his views on the war and the need to change the national CCF's war policy. In the context of Hitler's triumphs in Europe, the mood of the people was ripe for such a pro-war mobilization.

He did none of these things. Williams, in fact, made no serious effort to fight to keep the leadership, essentially leaving a clear field to his adversaries. In May 1940, he made a firm decision to enlist in the army and "to pull strings" to get posted overseas.[48] Having taken a principled stand on fighting the war against fascism, he believed he had to set an example and do his part. He realized he could not fight a war on two fronts. By deciding to enlist, Williams recognized he might never fulfill his dream to be the premier of a CCF government.

Williams's former regiment, now the Canadian Light Horse, was called to active duty in August. Williams immediately volunteered, but was rejected due to his wound from World War I. He appealed, noting that his 1918 wound was not classified as disabling at the time. If it was so judged now, then considerable back pension was owed him. He exercised to get into better physical shape for the appeal medical, and he was judged fit for active duty. In November he attended the training school for infantry officers at Dundurn, where he also took a quartermaster's course. In December he wrote a long letter to a friend explaining his reasons for enlisting. First, he was concerned about the negative impact the national CCF's war policy would have on the coming provincial election. That policy remained unchanged, and Williams had reconciled himself to the fact it would never be changed as long as Woodsworth remained national leader. Therefore, the only way to meet the inevitable charges of disloyalty and pacifism during the election campaign was "to have someone who is recognized as a leader of the CCF in the fighting forces." Williams went on to admit that the constant intrigue against him had played a role in his decision: "circumstances [in the party] being what they are have increased my natural desire to join the army," and "by doing so I am rendering the CCF the greatest service." After publicly advocating the need to fight the war, Williams felt obliged to demonstrate it at a personal level. He admitted the MPs' brief had also contributed to his decision because it revealed "an organized attempt to take control of the

CCF out of the hands of the MLAs and place it in the hands of others, who at this moment happen to be pacifists and isolationists, and to render the future leadership impotent and thus destroy the possibility of success."[49]

In January 1941, Williams was informed of his posting overseas to Great Britain. In February he resigned as party president. He continued officially to be leader of the opposition in the legislature; with the consent of caucus, he appointed J. H. Brockelbank, MLA for Tisdale, as acting leader.[50] Williams remained the sitting member for Wadena. In February, the *Saskatchewan Commonwealth* published Williams's farewell message:

> I believe the most important of all human possessions is freedom. I believe that if our free democratic rights are destroyed, social democracy is impossible of attainment, therefore to me the winning of the war in order to preserve the right of democratic government is the most vital thing in the world. Without democratic freedom all the things we have worked for crumble to dust. If the CCF is to be any use to us we must have a democracy to use it in.
>
> In order to do what I could to influence the future policy of the CCF, I deliberately embarked upon an active campaign of advocating complete military support of the Allies in the present conflict, within the ranks of the CCF. Having done what I could do to influence CCF policy toward complete participation, and because I am completely sincere in it; when urging others to serve, I gave myself for the same service.
>
> Who has greater responsibility to fight for democracy than I who as Leader of the Opposition in government represent the essence of the difference between Democracy and Dictatorship? Someday I hope to return and again join you in your struggle to obtain a Social Democratic Government.[51]

If Williams's opponents believed his farewell message and posting overseas marked the end of the confrontation, they were mistaken. On March 6, 1941, Williams sent a letter to members of the provincial council laying out the details of the campaign to drive him from office.[52] If withdrawing from the leadership in favour of Coldwell in 1932 was Williams's first major tactical error, this letter was the second. He possessed an uncanny ability to make the correct tactical and strategic decisions when it came to building and then guiding the party through crisis after crisis, but when it came to making tactical and strategic decisions to protect and advance his career as leader, he clearly made major errors. This reflected his political principles. He had contempt for office seekers and personal opportunists. He prided himself on putting the interests of the movement and the party before his own career ambitions—hence his decision to step aside for Coldwell because he believed it was in the best interests of the party. This last hurrah with the provincial council was a principled presentation of the facts and events as he knew them. Williams believed it was in the interests of the party for the facts to be known. He believed it was up to the council to take steps to remedy the situation if they wished.

The letter represented remarkably poor political judgment from a career perspective. It did, however, reflect Williams's emotional pain at the humiliations he had endured. And it certainly reflected his anger and contempt for those responsible. The letter was not dealt with until the May council meeting, giving his opponents ample time to prepare for the showdown. But it was a showdown with a letter, not with an aroused and angry Williams in person. Williams expressed confidence that "those of the Council who are not personally implicated in this internal struggle for power will be able to look at the situation objectively." He charged Douglas, Coldwell, and others with orchestrating a secret campaign to "remove me from the leadership of the CCF." He traced the origins of the campaign back to his fight with Coldwell and his supporters over the leadership after the 1934 election. He provided details of the "double-crossing and intrigue" and the "indignities and injustices" he had suffered; the "running fire of petty criticism" he had endured from the beginning; the many efforts to "ruin my reputation by attacks on my personal integrity;" and the systematic broadcasting of "lies and slander." If something was not done to rectify the situation, Williams warned, he would distribute the letter to all delegates at the next convention. He also threatened to take legal action. He did neither.

Williams was overseas, and therefore could not be present to defend his allegations. Douglas and Coldwell, and the others mentioned, were present and able to deny the charges, pleading it was all a series of unfortunate misunderstandings. Though they had had their differences with

Williams, they admired and supported him. Those prepared to take Williams's side had no ammunition, no evidence, no smoking gun. All they had was Williams's bitter and impassioned letter, which laid out circumstantial and hearsay evidence. The debate lasted from 10:30 a.m. until near midnight. In the end, a motion that Williams's charges against Coldwell, Douglas, and others were "without foundation in fact" passed.[53] There was one dissenting vote. Williams's letter inflicted damage on his political reputation within the party, and most importantly among the middle leadership core. It provided *sub rosa* ammunition for his opponents as they moved to the final coup.

At the July 1941 convention, Douglas was nominated for party president. Williams's supporters nominated Williams *in absentia*. Douglas won. The MLAS insisted that Williams, as leader of the opposition, remained the political leader and would therefore lead the party in the coming election. That rearguard action was foreclosed at the July 1942 convention. A constitutional amendment separating the offices of president and political leader was passed. Douglas resigned as president and ran for political leader. Again, Williams was nominated *in absentia* by his supporters. Again, Douglas won. Upon receiving the news in a letter from Brockelbank, Williams replied,

> T.C. Douglas has been elected....Perhaps I should have stuck it out [but] no organization can withstand internal intrigues for power and position. I shall never give any one the opportunity of accusing me of the actions and attitudes adopted by M. J. Coldwell and friends. Despite the methods used, Douglas has been elected and I shall not be guilty of sabotage.[54]

The MLAS promised Williams they would protect Wadena for him by blocking any effort to take the nomination away from him. Williams was duly nominated *in absentia*. In his regular correspondence with Brockelbank, Williams commented, "What will happen to the CCF I do not know. Some felt I should not have gone and that I let them down. I know no matter what happens, social democracy will triumph."[55] Williams went on to note that his problems in the CCF often paled into insignificance when one was trying to survive the daily German bombing blitz.

Despite everything, Williams still clung to the fading hope that the CCF would reconsider and ask him to come home to lead the party into the election. As he informed the provincial executive, his commanding officer confirmed that upon receiving a telegram from the executive requesting that Williams return to fight an election, he would be released and could be in Regina in fourteen days. Even as late as June 1943, Williams wrote to the provincial council offering to lead the party in the coming election. However, the letter was not revealed to delegates at the July 1943 convention. Brockelbank was assigned the duty to gently break the news to Williams: Douglas, not Williams, would lead the party in the election. Brockelbank declared his support for Williams's leadership, but within limits: "never again civil war."[56] Williams realized that to regain the leadership he would have to challenge Douglas at a convention. It would be an ugly and divisive battle, doing irreparable harm to the party on the eve of an election that all now conceded was the CCF's to lose. Williams surrendered his final illusion.

There is little on the record detailing Williams's role in the war effort. His extensive correspondence with Brockelbank contains few details on his war work, instead focusing mainly on political events in Saskatchewan. Williams obviously had to exercise care in commenting on the war, given the imposition of strict censorship. In fact, much of Williams's work was considered top secret. We know that his regiment of enlistment, the Canadian Light Horse, was first assigned to the Canadian Amoured Corps Holding Unit. From there, he was assigned as quartermaster of the 8th Reconnaissance Regiment (14th Canadian Hussars), an armoured unit of the 2nd Canadian Infantry Division. (The quartermaster of a regiment is responsible for securing all necessary supplies.) From there, Williams was transferred to the Royal Canadian Ordnance Corps, serving in the Canadian Ordnance Reinforcement Unit (Administrative Wing). The corps was responsible for securing and supplying combat troops with all that is needed to fight, from rations to tanks. Williams told Brockelbank he enjoyed his work and felt it was important—but that was all he said.

Williams was evidently successful, as he enjoyed rapid promotion: second lieutenant upon enlistment in 1940; lieutenant in 1941; captain in 1942; major in 1943. Upon promotion to major he was appointed commanding officer of the Canadian Ordnance Reinforcement Unit (Administrative Wing). In that role he was involved in planning for the D-Day invasion. Along with hundreds of other officers and enlisted ranks, his area of responsibility was to plan for, secure, and arrange transport for all supplies necessary for invasion, securing beachheads and supplying combat troops as they advanced against the enemy. Not only did quartermaster units serve a key function in planning and organizing supplies, but selected units would follow the invasion force onto the beaches to establish supply depots and transport supplies forward to the front lines. Though not in a direct combat role, quartermaster units suffered heavy casualties. Supply depots and supply lines were high-priority targets for enemy aircraft and counterattacking enemy ground troops. Hence, quartermaster units often found themselves in direct combat defending depots and supply lines. As the front line ebbed and flowed, quartermaster units often fought side by side with the infantry. Williams hoped to get across the Channel and join more directly in the war effort.

As invasion fever increased and excitement grew that the final stage of the war was about to commence, Williams began to think he might like to stay overseas. Given he no longer had a vital role to play in a CCF victory, he expressed a desire to see the war through to the end. In a January 1944 letter to Brockelbank, Williams noted that if he stayed he would "come out of this thing a full Colonel or at least a Lieut. Colonel, but I recognize the right of Wadena constituency to ask for my return." But frankly, he would rather stay: "Personally I would rather like to stay here and see this job done, but as I say I will do whatever they wish me to."[57] There is little doubt Williams was moving toward a decision to stay. And there is little doubt his supporters in Wadena would have given him permission to do so if he had asked for it.

An army doctor closed the door on that option. Williams knew he was ill; he suffered what he suspected was a mild heart attack, but told no one, and he experienced spells of dizziness. The only hint of illness in his correspondence with Brockelbank was, uncharacteristically, frequent complaints of exhaustion due to the demands of his work. Yet Williams evaded the annual medical examinations required of all officers, successfully pleading conflicts with work. In preparation for D-Day, the high command ordered medical examinations for all officers. The exam was compulsory and high priority—no exceptions were allowed. In March 1944, Williams presented himself for the medical examination. The doctor told him he had dangerously high blood pressure—so high that he could face death at any moment due to a stroke or heart attack. The doctor immediately relieved Williams of all duties and sent him to hospital, ordering complete rest. Williams would be going home with a medical discharge. In late April, the required message from the CCF provincial executive was sent to the army requesting Williams's immediate return to Saskatchewan to fight the June 1944 election.

The army arranged for Williams's expedited return to Regina.

Chapter 7

ENDGAME

The 1944 Election

U pon returning to Saskatchewan, Williams was inevitably pulled into the election campaign. His return received considerable positive press coverage, with interviews and photo-ops with Williams in full uniform standing with party notables beside an emblazoned CCF campaign car. Some party officials approached Williams to undertake a campaign tour of rural seats. He declined, citing doctor's orders. He did, however, do a speaking tour of Wadena, addressing enthusiastic crowds at fourteen town hall meetings. Due to health concerns, he limited his speeches to a half-hour, which was perhaps difficult for an orator who, in his heyday, could mesmerize large crowds during speeches lasting two or three hours. The party asked him to do a province-wide radio broadcast on May 30, 1944, two weeks before the June 15 vote. Williams saw it as his last chance to address the people of the province more or less on his own terms. He made the most of it. He laid out his socialist political credo and embraced a final vindication of his principled stand on war policy:

> This short address will be my only contribution in the provincial
> election campaign, outside a few meetings in my constituency.

> I have been advised by my doctors to take a complete rest for
> six months, but somehow that does not seem quite possible,
> so perforce I must compromise by doing about one quarter of
> what I would like to do.[1]

Williams commented on the importance of planning the effective
reintegration of returning soldiers to civil life as the end of the war
neared. He reported on the left-wing ideas held widely among troops
overseas:

> The average soldier is a forthright sort of fellow and cannot
> see how profits can be maintained without some of them
> being made out of him. He remembers the miserable failure
> of attempted capitalistic rehabilitation schemes following the
> last war: the depression, the box cars, relief instead of work
> and wages, and no longer has much faith in promises. In a
> war for democracy it has often shocked me to hear soldiers
> express an utter lack of faith in all political parties.
>
> Immediately after this war we will face the parting of the
> ways—profits or production for use. Canada must become a
> country in which we produce things solely so our people may
> possess, use and enjoy them, even if such and such a corpo-
> ration makes no profits. Canada must become a country in
> which everyone will find that the harder he or she works the
> higher their standard of living will be. A country in which
> there is safety and security for all.
>
> It is because I have always believed that ccf policies, put
> into full and complete effect, will give us that security that I
> now support ccf candidates, and urge you to do likewise.
>
> I dare to prophesy that when the soldiers return at least 80
> per cent will support socialistic measures and policies. Today
> they talk that way. Tomorrow when they come home they
> will act that way; for at long last the average lad in the Army
> has come to realize that socialism just means the co-operative
> principle of "each for all" carried into the greatest business,
> the business of government.

He then reminded his audience of the reasons for the sacrifices of this war to defeat fascism and defend democracy:

> For what? Not just to defeat Germany and Japan, but also to have the right to build a new world, not a patched up old world, but a new one. So the man who is now called the little man and the failure may become a man without fear, proud and independent, because he is secure. So the so-called big man may become real big by helping to make the world secure not just for himself and his friends, but for all.
>
> There are some who will be mourning for dear ones, lost in this battle for freedom. Let us each and every day realize what this feedom is that they bought with their lives and their broken bodies. You see, my friends, "Liberty" is all the small liberties as well as all the great freedoms of life, only to be found in a democracy. In times past we have almost lost democracy and became ripe for dictatorship by carelessness by not exercising full and complete citizenship, by letting little wrongs slide past and condoning big ones, because we got something out of it personally.
>
> Paths like these lead to a lost democracy, no matter what party is in power, for it is true no nation is greater than the public conscience.
>
> Let us all see to it that the price is not paid in vain, and in all our public and civic duties, be it a vote, at the coming provincial election or at municipal meetings, or in a legislature, or whatever it may be, having heard both sides, vote fearlessly for a new deal and a square deal, without trying to corner a small personal advantage, which in the end will destroy us all.
>
> Fear not to try the new when the old has failed.

One CCF organizer later offered the opinion that this broadcast delivered three or four extra seats to the CCF.

Williams discussed the leadership coup only with his closest friends. Though admitting he had been deeply hurt by the events, especially the failure of many of his close political colleagues to stand by him, he was now fully reconciled with what had happened. His decision to enlist and go overseas had been the best decision both for him personally and for the party. He had contributed significantly to the war effort and had lived through exciting times in Britain. It had become clear to him that fighting his ouster could have been a political disaster for the party on the threshold of victory. To fight it out was not worth the risk, even if he had prevailed. Williams was generous in his praise of Douglas. He had always recognized Douglas was an excellent "platform socialist," as he put it. Douglas had remained committed to the CCF's socialist program and the governing plans made by caucus since 1938. Give Douglas a solid policy and he could put it across very effectively; put a good organization behind him and he could win elections. Williams had nothing but praise for Douglas's performance in the campaign. Above all, Williams wanted to avoid appearing bitter. It would do the party no good to have rumours of strife among the top leadership gain public traction. In public and in private, therefore, Williams remained a team player.

In what he would later describe as his biggest mistake, Liberal Premier Patterson postponed the election, citing the war crisis. Traditionally in Saskatchewan the election should have occurred in 1942; constitutionally, it was required no later than 1943. But legislatures and parliaments can postpone elections in times of great crisis. By delaying the election until 1944, Patterson provided the CCF additional time to build an irresistible political movement. By 1944 the CCF had just under twenty-six thousand members; the party coffers were full; the foundational policies of 1934 and 1938 had been refined and extended, and glaring policy gaps filled; constituency organizations, following the Wadena template, were in fighting form; an army of volunteers had attended campaign schools; candidates were nominated and already fighting the election; and the public mood for radical change had grown dramatically.

In a barrage of propaganda, the CCF carried its message to the electorate. Hysterical Liberal pamphlets smeared the CCF as communists and claimed a CCF government would expropriate farms and that the lives of citizens would be regimented by a socialist bureaucracy. They equated the CCF's socialism with Hitler's national socialism and accused the CCF of disloyalty in the war effort. These outlandish attacks hurt the Liberals more than the CCF, however, clearly reflecting equal parts panic and desperation. Some of the CCF propaganda proudly outlined the party's record as the legislative opposition. Some of the propaganda was defensive, explaining the unfairness of attacks on the CCF. But most of the propaganda was aggressive, positive, and forward-looking.

The CCF Program for Saskatchewan, the most detailed manifesto yet presented by the party, represented remarkable continuity with the 1934 and 1938 programs. A CCF government's first priority was "the provision of security": both "farm security" and "urban security." A CCF government would "stop foreclosures on and eviction from the farm home," "protect from seizure that portion of a farmer's crop that is needed to provide for his family," "use the power of debt moratorium to force the loan and mortgage companies to reduce debts and mortgages to a figure at which they can reasonably be paid," "prevent accumulation of new debt," "encourage the development of the co-operative movement to replace capitalism and the profit system by community ownership for the common good," and "press for closure of the Winnipeg Grain Exchange and the setting of parity prices for agricultural products."[2] The CCF would modernize rural Saskatchewan, bringing to farm families the amenities of urban life: electricity, telephones, modern plumbing, adequate housing, and access to modern educational and health facilities.

The CCF's "urban security" package contrasted sharply with its simple "work and wages" labour programs of 1934 and 1938. Between 1938 and 1944, the CCF had made great strides organizing the province's working class, and the party now presented a comprehensive program to win that class. "Security for the worker in town and city means regular employment, adequate wages, and a voice in determining the conditions under which he works." A separate pamphlet, *Labour and Urban Security*, presented a comprehensive program appealing not only to the working class but to other urban classes. To the urban working class the CCF promised compulsory union recognition by employers when a majority of workers signed union cards; a higher minimum wage and better labour standards, with sufficient staff to enforce the law on employers; no waiting period and higher payments in workers' compensation; appointments of labour members to boards and commissions dealing with labour issues after consultation with trade unions; and the establishment of a department of labour and appointment of a minister of labour. Farm wage labour, however, was denied these gains. Beyond such measures of direct interest to the urban working class, the party promised to establish "a complete system of socialized health services"; to raise old-age pensions and press

Ottawa to lower the eligibility age to sixty-five; to press Ottawa to establish a national housing program, to provide "low-cost and low rental homes"; to guarantee "workers' security of tenure in their homes"; and to impose the "adjustment of debts for urban dwellers."[3] The final plank of the package appealed to public anxiety about what was to come after the war:

> *Unemployment and Post-War Reconstruction*: Mass unemployment in wartime is not tolerated. In peace-time it should be equally intolerable.
>
> The CCF demands that our natural resources, now used to bring about Victory, shall be used in peace-time to bring about security and a higher standard of living. The CCF is determined that we shall not drift back to the chaos of unemployment and depression which preceded the war; and therefore will formulate definite, practical plans for post-war reconstruction and adjustment of our social and economic life.

The most controversial section of the program was its core proposals for building a socialist economy: "planning, public ownership and finance." In response to a common Liberal question—Where is the money to come from for this elaborate set of promises?—the answer was provocatively simple: more of the wealth produced in the province would be retained in the province:

> The lion's share of the wealth of the province has been stolen from the people who produced it. This must cease. No program of reform is worth the paper it is written on unless it provides for keeping this wealth within the province. The CCF maintains that our natural resources must henceforth be developed in the public interest and for public benefit. They cannot continue to be exploited in a hit-and-miss manner for the benefit of promoters, investors, and absentee capitalists. The CCF stands for the planned development of the economic life of the province and the social ownership of natural resources.
>
> We must proceed to the public development and public ownership of our natural resources.

More specifically, a CCF government would increase revenues by elim-
inating graft, corruption and patronage in the public service; refuse to
pay the existing high interest rates to force the refunding of the public
debt which consumed 48 per cent of annual government revenues; establish public marketing agencies for fuel and petroleum products, as well
as for staples like food and machinery; establish small publicly owned
industries to process the province's natural products into finished goods;
and expand the electrical system through a program of rural electrification. The government would introduce progressive income taxes and
heavier taxes on corporations, particularly those active in developing the
province's resources.

In a final touch, the CCF distributed a pamphlet listing all CCF candidates and their occupations. The list emphasized the nature of the CCF, its
core leadership, and the class constituencies to which it appealed. Of the
fifty-two candidates listed, twenty-nine were farmers, eight teachers, seven
workers, three professionals, three merchants, and two housewives. The
professionals included a doctor, a lawyer, and a preacher (Douglas). Six of
the seven workers were railway workers, the aristocracy of labour in those
days in Saskatchewan. If one goes by the candidates nominated—a crucial
indicator of the vital middle leadership—the party remained a farmers'
party that had successfully established alliances with key non-agricultural
classes: workers, teachers, small merchants, and middle-class professionals.

The CCF triumphed on June 15. Running in all fifty-two seats, the CCF
took forty-seven with 53 per cent of the vote. The Liberals won five seats,
with 35 per cent. All other parties and independents were shut out. The
CCF swept city, town, and country. It won thirty-seven rural seats, while
the Liberals won five. The CCF won all urban seats, and all rural seats
with a strong urban presence. It won 58 per cent of the rural vote and 39
per cent of the small-town vote. Victories in the large urban seats were
decisive: in Moose Jaw, the margin of victory for CCF candidates was two
to one; the pattern was similar in Prince Albert, Regina, and Saskatoon.
The working class voted solidly for the CCF: in Regina, for example, the
CCF won 61 per cent among skilled workers and 62 per cent among
unskilled workers, while taking 32 per cent of the middle-class vote.[4]

Nevertheless, in 1944, elections in Saskatchewan were still won or lost
in rural areas. The CCF won its majority in rural Saskatchewan: thirty-
seven of forty-seven seats. The urban victories finally realized the old

1932 FLP dream of Williams and the UFC(SS), and of Coldwell and the ILP, to unite farmer and worker in the fight for socialism. The farmers and workers of Saskatchewan had joined together to give the CCF a clear mandate to implement a socialist program.

Upon his return, Williams was not invited into the inner circle of the top leadership of the party, nor had he expected to be. Relations between Williams and his old foes remained distant and tense. Douglas did not reach out to him to meet or to seek his advice. Some among the Douglas/ Coldwell faction worried about Williams's intentions, fearing renewed conflict. There was speculation in the press about Douglas's likely cabinet appointments, including what position might be offered Williams. Some speculated he might receive minister without portfolio, an insulting position Williams probably would decline. Finally, on July 3—the day before the first meeting of the full CCF caucus, at which the cabinet would be introduced—Douglas went to Williams's home. The meeting was formal and cordial. Douglas asked Williams what cabinet position he wanted; Williams requested agriculture, and Douglas immediately agreed. Douglas had obviously considered this move carefully, and his best political instincts won out over personal animosity. This was a significant first step in the reconciliation of the two men. The minister of agriculture was second only to the premier in political importance in the Saskatchewan of 1944. Williams was the obvious choice, given his background as the most well-known and widely admired farm leader in the province. He was being welcomed back into the leadership fold. Later, Douglas admitted that Williams's advice in cabinet meetings had been of key importance in his first days as premier.

Williams enthusiastically plunged into his ministerial duties. The immediate problem he faced was a projected serious shortage of labour to bring in the fall harvest. He and his staff worked on the extent of the projected crisis and possible scenarios for acquiring the necessary labour. He approached his contacts in the army in Ottawa to see if the province could obtain cooperation in offering the work to demobilizing soldiers returning after completing their tours of duty. He invited the leaders of all farm organizations to a July 13 meeting in his office to discuss the problem and possible remedies.

July 13 was a long and exhausting day for Williams, who continued to ignore the warnings and advice of his doctors and family. In the morning he attended a cabinet meeting. All afternoon he met with farm leaders to discuss remedies for the harvest labour shortage. Then he felt obliged to at least make an appearance at the party's victory banquet that evening at a downtown hotel. He had not been invited to sit at the head table, nor was he included on the speakers' list. This was to be expected—it was Douglas's night. Nevertheless, Williams felt he had to show up. His absence would be noted. After Williams and Madge were seated at a table in the back of the hall, the emcee rushed up to beg him to take a seat at the head table and be prepared to make a few remarks. Williams reluctantly agreed. Before he could be introduced, a spontaneous chant of "We want Williams" spread through the crowd. Williams rose to applause and cheers. As promised, he kept his speech brief, telling the crowd he was "a happy and fortunate man" to have been instrumental in two great successes in his lifetime: the successful founding of the provincial cooperative dairy pool and the victory of the CCF. After commenting on all the good things the CCF could accomplish now that the party had won power, he ended his speech. The crowd gave him a standing ovation and began chanting his name, demanding more. The emcee gave him five minutes more. Williams talked about his war experiences and his concern for the returning soldiers, especially those who had been wounded.

As Williams was leaving the banquet he was informed that he was expected to be the kick-off speaker at the public victory rally that evening at city hall. This was news to him. Obviously the initial plans for these major events had not included him, but a decision was made at the last minute to include him—clearly another effort by the new leadership to seek reconciliation with Williams. He was exhausted, and Madge, clearly worried about him, begged him not to go. He needed to come home and rest. She recalls his reply:

> Yes Madge, I know. I should go home and go to bed. But it'll look like sour grapes if I don't show up and give Tommy my blessing. I have to do it. I don't want anyone in the press given any excuse to start rumours about any falling-out amongst the leadership. Not now, when we have a chance to finally do something worthwhile. I might as well go back to the Buildings,

then, and get some work done before the meeting. I'll drop you
off at home, and you can meet me at the meeting.[5]

Williams arrived at the city hall meeting just as it was convening. His
intention was to give his brief introductory speech and then slip away
home. Again he was greeted with enthusiastic applause. Again he talked
about the war, which was on everyone's mind since D-Day had just happened the previous month. Williams began to stumble on his words. He
quickly ended his speech with thanks and began to walk unsteadily off
the platform. He collapsed into the arms of a close friend who had rushed
up, knowing something was terribly wrong. Williams lost consciousness.
He was taken to hospital, where he suffered a stroke. Williams had been
ordered to take complete rest when the army doctor first diagnosed his
condition in Britain. His doctors in Regina had given him the same
advice. He ignored them. His family and his doctors concluded that the
only way to get Williams to cooperate in taking a rest from all work and
stress was to get him out of Regina.

Williams and Madge and their two youngest daughters left for British
Columbia, committed to ensuring Williams had the complete rest he
needed. After a time in Nanaimo's military hospital, Williams joined his
family in a cottage near the seaside. His condition did not improve. On
February 10, 1945, he resigned from cabinet, writing to Douglas, "It is
with the deepest regret that I find this course necessary, it is, however,
quite apparent I cannot carry on."[6] After a further relapse he was transferred to a Vancouver hospital, where his decline continued. In May his
doctors said there was nothing more that could be done, and Williams
wished to return home to his family.

His new home was in Capilano with a view of Lion's Gate Bridge.
Williams died during the night of September 12, 1945, with Madge at his
bedside. He was fifty years old.

Williams was kept informed of events in Saskatchewan throughout his
illness. Before his death he applauded the great strides made by the CCF
government in implementing its socialist program. To his great disappointment, he missed the first legislative session of the new government,
a three-week special session from October 19 to November 10, 1944.

The session, as declared in the Throne Speech, "must enact legislation that will bring to fulfillment the pledges upon which this Government was elected."[7] The Farm Security Act, 1944 delivered all promises made to farmers. A special government department was set up to encourage the development of cooperative enterprises. The promises to the urban working class were delivered in the Trade Union Act, 1944, the most pro-labour trade union legislation in North America. The necessary amendments were made to the Department of Natural Resources Act to empower the government to acquire "any land or works or land and works by purchase, lease, or otherwise, or by expropriation." The government was authorized to engage directly in resource development and to "do all such things necessary to develop and utilize the resources of the province."[8] A law allowing the government to go into the insurance business was passed. In order to encourage development and prevent speculation, the government imposed heavy taxes on owners of mineral rights and on the assessed value of all minerals on which rights were held. Failure to pay led to automatic forfeiture to the government. A law was passed allowing the government to impose final and binding debt adjustments for school districts and municipalities unable to manage the debt load accumulated during the Depression. The government began to construct a coherent system of universal social welfare and to embark on modernization of the education system.

Needless to say, the business lobby was angry and shocked, caught off guard by the speed with which these major changes were introduced. The national business lobby, led by the CPR and the Dominion Loan and Mortgage Association, petitioned the federal cabinet to disallow the laws on farm security, mineral taxation, and mandatory binding debt adjustment. Despite great pressure from the business lobby to rein in this socialist government, Prime Minister King refused the requests for disallowance. The laws were challenged in the courts. (Only the crop failure clause of the Farm Security Act was finally declared *ultra vires* by the Privy Council, in 1948.)

In the 1945 legislative session, the CCF government embarked on an ambitious program of economic development through public ownership. The Crown Corporations Act, 1945 gave the government carte blanche to establish "any designated industrial or commercial enterprise or undertaking, the operation of which is deemed advisable for the public good," enabled by sweeping powers of expropriation.[9] Major Crown corporations were quickly established in insurance, electrical power, and bus transportation. In order to help diversify the economy, modest publicly owned industries were set up to process the province's natural resources: clay into bricks, leather into boots, pulp into cardboard boxes, timber into lumber, fish into fillets, and wool into blankets. The government expanded the Department of Agriculture and added programs and services to enable farmers to diversify out of the heavy reliance on wheat. The social welfare system was reorganized to provide social security "as a right, not measured out as a matter of charity."[10] More and more health services for designated groups were included in a revamped publicly funded health system. Farm debt owed the government from loans granted to maintain production during the Depression was forgiven. Legislation supporting the development of provincial marketing boards for all agricultural products, based on the pooling principle, was enacted; the same was done for marketing northern furs. A rural housing improvement program was set up. Complete rural electrification through the new Power Commission was begun. The government was on course to deliver its core promises of social and economic security for all and economic development through public ownership as quickly as the province's fiscal reality allowed.

Williams was pleased with the progress and direction of the government. He was still somewhat free with his advice. In a letter to Brockelbank in October 1944, he wrote:

> I think we will have no trouble maintaining our popular support. The Liberals are of course trying to drive a wedge between the farmer and labour. We must see to it that the farm security legislation and public health legislation is really good so that cannot be done.[11]

He was also full of praise. He wrote to another political colleague, "I think the boys are doing very well. Particularly Tommy Douglas, Tom Johnston, and Joe Phelps. Each for a different reason. But then all the Cabinet are doing a good job. And it is hard to single any out for special praise."[12] Williams lived to witness the results of the June 11, 1945, federal election. The CCF won eighteen of Saskatchewan's twenty-one seats with 44 per cent. Federal candidates campaigned on the record of the new CCF government.

Williams died "a happy and fortunate man." Before his death he witnessed the victory of socialist agrarian populism in Saskatchewan, the culmination of his life's work since joining the farm movement in 1922. And he witnessed the defeat of fascism in Europe on May 6, 1945, and in Japan on August 15. The struggle to defeat fascism had dominated the final years of his life.

Part IV

WILLIAMS IN CANADIAN HISTORY

Chapter 8

THE SHAME OF THE INTELLECTUALS

No public building in Saskatchewan is named to honour Williams for his definitive role in founding and building the CCF and bringing it to the threshold of power. The Saskatchewan Government Insurance head office is located in the C. M. Fines Building, so named to honour Clarence Fines, provincial treasurer in the 1944 government, a protégé of Coldwell, a key member of the faction that ousted Williams, and party president elected in 1942.[1] It was Fines who suppressed Williams's 1943 letter offering to lead the party in the coming election, thereby ensuring delegates at the 1943 convention knew nothing of his offer. The T. C. Douglas Building houses the province's health ministry. Douglas's birthday, October 20, was designated "Tommy Douglas Day" by the Saskatchewan New Democratic Party (NDP), which called on party members "to build together on the work Tommy Douglas started."[2] Only minor, obligatory attention is paid to Williams in the historical reminiscences of the leaders instrumental in his ouster. All accounts mention that the organized farmers went socialist and this ultimately led to the CCF victory in 1944; of course, Williams is mentioned as the farm leader who led them into socialist political action. But no detailed explanation is offered for this rather unprecedented event. We are left in the dark.

Nowhere else in Canada did the farmers go socialist. How did this happen in Saskatchewan? Typically, Williams's role is downplayed in its importance, while those of Coldwell and Douglas are exaggerated. The facts often appear to be massaged to paint a picture favourable to Coldwell and Douglas and unfavourable to Williams, and other facts seem invented. Facts that don't lend themselves to easy massaging or cannot safely be reworked tend, it seems, to simply be overlooked. This is not necessarily unusual or surprising in politics. The victors in inter-necine power struggles in political parties rarely want the full story on the historical record. One can understand why Douglas would want to downplay, or reinterpret, the ouster of Williams while the latter was overseas. One can readily see this as a rather dishonourable way to defeat a political adversary. Taking the leadership away at a convention where Williams stood *in absentia*, and where only Douglas ran a leadership campaign, might be seen as less than admirable—especially when the defeated incumbent is overseas fighting fascism.

Douglas and Coldwell went on to live long lives, enjoying distinguished careers as successful CCF politicians. Douglas served as Saskatchewan's premier from 1944 until 1961, when he became national leader of the newly founded NDP, holding that post until 1971. He served in the House of Commons from 1935 to 1944 and from 1962 to 1979. He died in 1986 at eighty-one. In 2004, Douglas was named the Greatest Canadian in a CBC online poll. At least six biographies of Douglas have been published, three of which deal extensively with the early years,[3] as well as a book of his detailed recollections.[4] Coldwell served in the House of Commons from 1935 to 1958 and was national CCF leader from 1942 to 1960. He died in 1974 at eighty-five. The one biography of Coldwell is composed largely of much of the text of his unfinished autobiography.[5] Douglas's and Coldwell's versions of events in Saskatchewan have therefore been entered into the record. Of even more significance, the CCF phenomenon in Saskatchewan arguably became one of the most studied political events in English Canadian political history. Hence, journalists, graduate students, and scholars lined up to get first-hand accounts of events from the two men, thus ensuring their versions dominated both popular and scholarly records. No biography of Williams was published. Nor could he write his memoirs and recollections. As a result, the versions provided by Coldwell and Douglas became, over time, the accepted, established historical record.

Discrepancies between the versions presented by Coldwell and Douglas and the events as they actually unfolded are revealed by an examination of four pivotal events in the conflict between Williams and the Coldwell/Douglas faction: the battle between Williams and Coldwell over the leadership after the 1934 election; the controversy over Douglas's acceptance of the endorsement of the Social Credit Party in the 1935 federal election; the controversy over cooperation with other parties in the 1938 election; and the events leading to Williams's loss of the leadership at the 1941 and 1942 conventions.

The 1934 Leadership Battle

In their memoirs, neither Douglas nor Coldwell pay much attention to the 1934 election. Indeed, both men downplay its significance, which seems odd since the FLP elected five members and became the official opposition. From then on, the FLP/CCF was the clear alternative to the Liberal Party. Coldwell recalls he was asked to stand for party leader because he had "wider electoral appeal" than Williams. He was approached by top party officials, including a number from the UFC(SS), who thought it "unwise to elect Williams as leader" because, in Coldwell's words, "he had been to Russia, returned and held meetings across the province, and while he was critical of some of the things he had seen, he had not been really unenthusiastic about what they were doing in Russia."[6] Coldwell's biographer, Walter Stewart, notes that the FLP "returned five members. M. J. was not one of them; more *ominously* George Williams was" (emphasis added).[7] Coldwell blames the party's poor showing on the use-lease policy, open opposition from the Catholic Church, and the communist smear. Coldwell ran in Regina, but was on the speaking circuit as leader during much of the campaign. Regarding his personal defeat in 1934, Coldwell said, "In Regina, Booze, Boodle, and Bigotry account for our defeat....I shall never seek election in Regina again."[8] Coldwell recounts he was exhausted and ill after the election, taking a rest cure in Alberta under doctor's orders.

Douglas ran as the FLP candidate in Weyburn. He admitted, "We all thought we were going to win. Coldwell spoke to tremendous crowds, six and seven thousand."[9] After his defeat, Douglas considered leaving the province to accept an offer of a large Baptist church in Chicago, where he could also continue his PhD studies. He changed his mind when he was approached by a group of local party members asking him to contest the Weyburn federal seat in 1935. The federal seat included a large rural area around the city, where the CCF's prospects were good. The provincial seat just included the city, which was hostile territory for the left-wing, populist FLP/CCF. In the 1934 election Douglas did badly, running third in a field of four. In Regina, Coldwell ran fifth in a field of seven (Regina was a two-member riding). Both therefore suffered devastating personal defeats, given the optimistic expectation of victory. According to their memoirs, Douglas, a younger man and a political novice, took the defeat in his stride and reflected on the mistakes made, whereas Coldwell was clearly bitter about his personal defeat in Regina. As leader, Coldwell also suffered a larger humiliation, having devised a campaign strategy that led the party to an unexpected electoral disaster.

Both men say very little in their memoirs about the struggle over the leadership between Williams and Coldwell in the aftermath of the election. Coldwell's recollections of the battle over the House leader issue were recounted by his biographer: "George Williams, despite an undertaking he had given M. J., not to fill the post of house leader in the legislature until M. J. got back from his recovery period, had taken the job himself. There was no place for M. J. in the provincial party, it seemed, even if he wanted it.... If he ran federally, he could simply bypass the problem of the provincial leadership, which George Williams had successfully *usurped*" (emphasis added).[10] Douglas recalls Coldwell suggesting to Williams that one of the five elected MLAs resign so he could contest a by-election. Douglas notes to his biographer that Williams rejected the idea because "he wanted to be party leader himself."[11]

Accounts by both Coldwell and Douglas are highly selective and consistently put Williams in a negative light while presenting Coldwell as a man of principle. What is absent from the recollections of the two men is any mention of Williams's impressive accomplishment. He won Wadena with 51 per cent of votes. And he and four other leading activists of the UFC(SS) won five seats, giving the FLP the status of official opposition. Coldwell's account leaves out all the key post-election events, including Williams's rationale for convening an urgent meeting of the caucus to name a House leader and prepare for the special session of the legislature initially slated for July. Coldwell does not mention Williams's repeated efforts to communicate with him by phone and telegram prior to Coldwell's departure for Alberta. In their confrontation on the street in Saskatoon, Williams had made no promise not to act, but rather had made it clear to Coldwell that as president Williams intended to act in the interests of the party. Stewart fails to mention Williams was ratified as House leader by the July 1934 party convention. Nor does he mention that Coldwell continued as party leader with an income guaranteed by the party. Coldwell neglects to mention the meeting he convened the day before the July convention at which he launched a personal attack on Williams, deeply polarizing the party and setting in motion the division that haunted Williams's leadership to the end.

Stewart's choice of words appears to be designed to besmirch Williams's reputation and present him as personally ambitious, power hungry, and soft on communism. Williams's election, given Coldwell's defeat, was "ominous" (meaning "of doubtful or menacing aspect") and Williams "usurped" the leadership ("to appropriate wrongfully to one-self"). Yet it appears that Williams was not personally ambitious, having stepped aside to give the leadership to Coldwell. Williams's election may have been personally ominous for Coldwell; Williams was his obvious replacement, given Coldwell's failure. Yet it is hard to see it as ominous for the party. Nor had Williams usurped the leadership. He was ratified as House leader at the 1934 convention and, after Coldwell's 1935 resignation, elected as party leader at the 1936 convention. Nor do Coldwell or Douglas revisit the "wider electoral appeal" Coldwell was supposed to bring to the movement. On any test of electoral appeal, Williams had won. Williams was indeed openly opposed to vacating a seat to make way for Coldwell in a by-election. But he was not alone in this—all elected members agreed this would be a mistake. The reason presented frankly to Coldwell and the political directive board was that Coldwell would lose, since he did not have the confidence of farmers. Understandably, Coldwell did not appreciate this rationale. Coldwell repeats the allegation that Williams was perhaps a communist sympathizer given that he was "not really unenthusiastic about what they were doing in Russia."

Coldwell and Woodsworth, both very hard-line anti-communists, were consistently uncomfortable with Williams's tactical approach to the "CP problem." The two men believed the CCF should have nothing whatsoever to do with the CP and those influenced by it.

Douglas's Endorsement by Social Credit in 1935

On the controversy surrounding Douglas's acceptance of the endorsement of Weyburn's Social Credit Party in 1935, the versions presented by Coldwell and Douglas in their biographies and memoirs appear both evasive and contradictory. Read alongside each other, they appear not to be in accord with the facts. The details are important, since this confrontation played a major role in committing Douglas and Coldwell firmly to Williams's ouster. Coldwell's biographer provides this account:

> The rivalry between Socreds and CCFers both before and during the [1935] election led to calls for sanctions against anyone suspected of co-operation, and George Williams reacted savagely when he found that Tommy Douglas was charged with this crime. Douglas had been endorsed by Social Credit at a meeting called in his riding without his approval or attendance, and no Social Credit candidate was nominated to run against him. As soon as he found out about it, he repudiated the endorsement—which he was required to do by the party by laws. Nevertheless, Williams wanted to eject him and kept hounding the provincial leader on the subject; Coldwell refused; and then buried the issue in benign neglect.[12]

In his own words, Coldwell provides this version:

> George Williams and some members of the organization wanted me to issue a statement repudiating Tommy Douglas and this I refused to do. We had quite a warm executive meeting about this, and it ended in a rather unpleasant sort of atmosphere. I had to go on to Moose Jaw...and when I got there, waiting for me was a telegram from George Williams

saying that he had received a lot of criticisms from various people in the province, and that he would turn these over to me, since I had been instrumental in keeping Douglas as a candidate.[13]

In his recollections Douglas provides the following version:

> They [the Weyburn Social Credit Party] called on any Social Crediters...to support me. This was published and played up by the press that I was running as the CCF-Social Credit candidate. But at no time was I ever associated with the Social Credit party, except that I did accept their endorsement and support....They didn't nominate me, they simply endorsed my nomination....Mr. George Williams, who at the time was leader of the opposition...became very much perturbed about these reports that I was running as a CCF-Social Credit candidate, and at one time wanted the executive to expel me. Mr. Coldwell, who was still provincial president and provincial leader of the CCF, would have no part of it until he heard my side of the story. When the election was over, and I laid all the facts before them...the whole matter was dropped.[14]

Douglas's biographer provides a different, more detailed, less erroneous, and less flattering account:

> On October 9, five days before the vote, Douglas was haled before the provincial executive...to explain why he should not be repudiated as a candidate for collaborating with Social Credit, against the express directions of J. S. Woodsworth. The precedent was discouraging. Jacob Benson, the CCF candidate in Yorkton, had been denounced by the party in September and stripped of his status as an official candidate....Benson's crimes were that when he had been asked, "Will you agree to support Social Credit members in the House?" he answered, "Yes," and that he had presented a signed resignation to the Social Credit executive....Tommy had not signed any papers allowing the Socreds to recall him,

but he had certainly collaborated, and George Williams, the provincial president and house leader, wanted his head on a platter. He nearly succeeded.

It is hard to escape the feeling that Williams was more concerned with getting back at his enemy, M. J. Coldwell, through Douglas, Coldwell's protégé, than he was with the niceties of electoral politics, but Williams did have a pretty good case. Tommy had not only accepted Socred support, he had sought it, and his backers had strung up at least one poster that read: "VOTE DOUGLAS: Weyburn CCF-Social Credit Association."

Four of the five executive members were ready to vote to renounce Tommy; his only ally was Dr. John MacLean [*sic*, Dr. Hugh MacLean], a party stalwart and a close friend of M. J. Coldwell's. Coldwell, although a member of the executive, was not at the meeting; he was at a party rally in Moose Jaw. MacLean persuaded the others not to take a vote in his absence. He warned them that if they did move against Douglas, Coldwell would resign. (Coldwell had said so, and had meant it.)

The meeting petered out....[I]t was apparent both that the cocky young candidate was not going to be fazed by the executive, whatever it did, and that M. J. Coldwell was not going to allow Tommy to be repudiated, nor—perhaps just as importantly—Williams to triumph.[15]

Douglas made a rather astonishing admission to one of his biographers, bragging that "he had, in effect, cobbled together a mock political party to attract Social Credit as well as CCF voters, and he made no apology for it." Douglas claimed he had privately shared his plan with Coldwell, who had not disapproved. In Douglas's words: "Here was a mob of people, farmers, small businessmen, railway workers, who knew that something was wrong and wanted to support something. And they didn't give a tinker's damn about all the fine points."[16] This biography of Douglas, published in 1987, contains the most detailed and accurate account of the episode.

The facts contradict the versions given by both Douglas and Coldwell. Benson was indeed repudiated as a CCF candidate for accepting the endorsement of the Social Credit Party in Yorkton and for signing a recall pledge. The national CCF, including Woodsworth personally, took a hard line against allying with Social Credit in the 1935 federal election. Coldwell voted with the executive to repudiate Benson. Coldwell was in fact at the October 9 meeting of the provincial executive held to consider the case against Douglas, though he left before the final adjournment to attend a meeting in Moose Jaw. Woodsworth had earlier written that Douglas should be repudiated if he did not renounce the endorsement of Social Credit. Only Coldwell and MacLean voted against the executive motion to repudiate Douglas, and Coldwell did threaten public resignation if Douglas were repudiated. After a day's delay and a further canvass of executive members, a majority of the executive nevertheless instructed Williams as president to issue a press release stripping Douglas of his status as an official CCF candidate.

For tactical reasons Williams did not issue the press release, convinced that Coldwell's public resignation would seriously injure the party just days before the election. Douglas was elected. On October 21, the provincial executive met and passed a motion, 5 to 2, that Douglas be repudiated as a CCF candidate. This would have forced Douglas to decide to sit as either an independent or a Social Credit MP. Again, Williams did not issue a press release making the repudiation public. It was agreed to delay action until the matter could be discussed by the political directive board. Douglas promised to sit as a CCF MP. A November 30 meeting of the CCF's national council upheld the actions of Williams and the provincial executive, as they were in line with the policy of the national party. The matter was finally resolved at a December 21 meeting of the Saskatchewan CCF's political directive board. A motion of censure was passed against Douglas for accepting the endorsement of Social Credit. This fact and the reasons for the censure were released to the press. However, the board also accepted Douglas's promise of allegiance to the CCF and its program; this fact was also released to the press. The matter was settled. Douglas had his knuckles rapped in public and was welcomed back into the fold. The same meeting welcomed back Jacob Benson as well.

In light of all this, the versions presented by Coldwell and Douglas appear to be largely fabrications, involving a reconstruction of events leading to a postmortem character assassination of Williams. Douglas had not only accepted Social Credit support, but, as demonstrated, aggressively sought it. And the election materials put out by the Douglas campaign did indeed present him as a joint CCF–Social Credit candidate. Much later, Douglas admitted this had been a conscious election strategy, done to organize "a mock political party to attract Social Credit as well as CCF voters." This strategy was a violation of the national CCF's policy of no collaboration with Social Credit in the 1935 election. CCF candidates across Canada, most especially in Alberta and Saskatchewan, were in a bitter struggle to defeat Social Credit in its effort to replace the CCF as the party of choice among the disaffected. There is no doubt the CCF's national council would have supported stripping Douglas of his CCF candidacy, had Williams acted on the executive's motion. But Williams did not. In fact, for tactical reasons, Williams rescued Douglas from the full consequences of his political manoeuvring. Others on the provincial executive were much more firm than Williams in their desire to repudiate Douglas despite Coldwell's threat to resign.

Nevertheless, both Coldwell and Douglas choose to present this event as a somewhat irrational personal vendetta by Williams against Douglas because the latter was Coldwell's protégé. Again the choice of words by biographers is worth noting: Williams "reacted savagely," "wanted [Douglas's] head on a platter," and "kept hounding" Coldwell to repudiate Douglas. Coldwell is the hero of the piece because he stood firm against an unreasonable Williams and buried "the issue in benign neglect." Williams, in fact, was the one who exercised benign neglect to rescue Douglas. Coldwell claims, "Williams and some members of the organization wanted me to issue a statement repudiating Tommy Douglas and this I refused to do." This is untrue. It was a majority of the provincial executive that wanted to repudiate Douglas and it was Williams, as president, who did not act on the repudiation. Douglas's 1982 recollection of the event therefore appears to be a complete fabrication. Both Douglas's and Coldwell's versions paint Douglas as the proxy victim in Williams's determination to attack Coldwell; that is, Williams was on a personal vendetta against Coldwell, and Douglas was collateral damage. It was all personal—no mention of national CCF policy, the two meetings of the provincial executive, the national council meeting, or the meeting of the provincial political directive board.

As a result of this experience, Williams concluded that Douglas and Coldwell were primarily careerist office seekers and political opportunists. Douglas violated party policy by what appears to be his collaborating with Social Credit in order to achieve personal victory, thus damaging the CCF in its overall battle with Social Credit. And Coldwell seems to have been willing to hurt the movement in Saskatchewan, and across Canada, by publicly resigning as leader on the eve of the election if Douglas were repudiated. Williams only shared this assessment in confidence with his closest associates in the party, commenting sarcastically and with some prescience, "If Douglas says he was just double-crossing Social Credit, it is just possible that we would be on the receiving end of the cross next time."[17]

The Controversy Over Cooperation in the 1938 Election

Williams's plan to defeat the Social Credit invasion was controversial. Both J. S. Woodsworth and M. J. Coldwell spoke at provincial conventions strongly opposing any kind of cooperation, including saw-offs. They failed to persuade the delegates. Party conventions in 1936 and 1937 voted overwhelmingly in favour of political cooperation among progressive, reform groups. The motions originated from the floor and reflected a growing consensus among the rank and file of the party. Williams read the mood carefully. If the CCF failed to embrace some form of cooperation, the party could lose large numbers of members and supporters to an independent fusion movement. The CCF was already bleeding members and supporters to the new provincial Social Credit Party. The UFC(SS) and the Wheat Pool had backed off from political engagement, due to the split among farmers between Social Credit and the CCF. Aberhart had swept Alberta in 1935, and many feared he could do the same in Saskatchewan in 1938. Hence, Williams agreed with the rank and file that the CCF should work toward some form of cooperation with other reform forces. But he insisted on—and won the support of the membership for—firm limits on this cooperation: no fusion candidates; no joint candidates; and all CCF candidates running as clear CCF candidates on the CCF platform. However, the party would work to arrange saw-offs with Social Credit. Both parties would agree not to oppose each other and work out an arrangement on which seats each would contest.

Williams's plan was to ensure the CCF ran in a sufficient number of seats to win a majority. As the established official opposition, the CCF could negotiate from a position of strength. Aberhart, in the event, rejected the saw-off proposal, forcing Williams and the CCF into a clear fight with Social Credit. But the CCF retained its popular base because the party had tried in good faith to gain Social Credit's cooperation. The blame for splitting the reform vote therefore lay with Aberhart and Social Credit. Williams was successful, winning ten seats and thwarting Social Credit's ambition to sweep the province.

Williams was congratulated in 1938 by Douglas, Coldwell, leaders of CCF provincial parties, and the top national CCF leadership. He had blocked the Social Credit invasion and doubled the CCF's seats. But much later, in his recollections and in interviews with biographers, Douglas reversed his position on the 1938 election, and there appears to be a misrepresentation of the key role he played at the time. A retrospective revision of events is thus presented, which charges Williams with making a major tactical error and thereby deeply wounding the party's credibility. One of Williams's major triumphs was transformed into a political catastrophe for which Williams was personally responsible. This version became widely accepted as the correct version of the events of 1938.

Douglas's 1982 recollection of the 1938 policy of cooperation reads as a personal indictment of Williams. Douglas fails to mention his own active role in arranging saw-offs. In fact, his account suggests he had nothing to do with it:

> Then there was a provincial election in 1938. That was a terrible schermozzle from our standpoint. George Williams got the idea that the government would be almost impossible to defeat, and to prevent the CCF from being annihilated, he should enter into an arrangement with the Conservatives and the Social Crediters to saw-off seats. The result was that we only ran thirty-one candidates.
>
> Consequently our total vote fell from about 105,000 in 1934 to about 83,000 in 1938. We went up from five seats in 1934 to ten seats in 1938, but our popular vote had dropped. To some extent, I think our prestige dropped because of these deals. I know there were constituencies where people who

had fought hard in the CCF were being asked by the CCF to vote for a Tory or a Social Credit candidate. This went against the grain, so some of them voted Liberal because they had voted Liberal before.[18]

When prompted—"That was Mr. Williams' idea?"—Douglas replied:

Maybe I shouldn't put the blame on him. It was the provincial executive's idea; I assume that as provincial leader, he probably was the main instigator.

It was a disastrous move, because you remember that the Liberals came out with great big posters saying, "Are you going to vote for a mulligan stew?" and had pictures of these three or four parties all trying. People are always suspicious of a government made up of bits and pieces.

When asked if he had been involved in the discussions, Douglas replied, "No." When pressed, he admitted the policy had had the support of the provincial CCF: "It caused a bit of friction between the federal men in Ottawa and the provincial people here in Saskatchewan. But Mr. Williams had the provincial people behind him in this policy. Certainly the members of the legislature executive supported him."[19]

Douglas's 2003 biographer paints an even more unflattering portrait of Williams, riddled with inaccuracies:

During the 1938 provincial election Williams, who ran the party almost single-handedly and seldom consulted anyone else, had decided that the Liberal government could not be defeated, so the CCF ran candidates in only thirty-one ridings.

Moreover, he made a deal with both the Conservatives and the Socreds to "saw-off" a number of seats. That is, the CCF would not run candidates in certain ridings, so as not to divide the vote, and the other parties would return the favour. The result was that the CCF won 10 provincial seats in 1938 but its share of the popular vote dropped from 24 per cent to 19 per cent. This did not bode well for the future. Moreover, many loyal CCFers were upset and disillusioned that Williams, who had tried to drive Tommy from the party for flirting with the Socreds, was himself, if not exactly flirting with other parties, standing by to hold the door for them in selected ridings.[20]

Only McLeod and McLeod in their 1987 biography get the basic facts straight, indicating that they did considerable independent archival research rather than relying on Douglas's recollections. They note, "Douglas was a strong supporter of the saw-off idea, and helped to arrange a deal with Social Credit that was intended to benefit the CCF in the long run."[21] Douglas and Coldwell travelled to Edmonton to convince the CCF not to oppose Social Credit in a 1938 by-election in Edmonton East. Douglas, misreading the entire situation, reported to Williams, "We incurred some criticism from our own people, but it has changed the entire attitude of the Social Credit forces here in Ottawa, and we are told it has inclined Aberhart very favourably toward giving us almost a free hand in Saskatchewan."[22] The biographers recount Douglas's work trying to arrange a deal with the Saskatchewan Tories: "Douglas also tried to arrange saw-offs with the Saskatchewan Conservatives, working with Ernie Perley, the Tory MP for Qu'Appelle. Douglas felt that if the CCF stayed out of the way for a few prominent Tories, such as party leader John Diefenbaker, then the Tories would agree to support some CCF candidates....A month before the election, Douglas urged Williams to make a comprehensive deal with Diefenbaker's people."[23] Douglas persisted in his personal use of saw-offs even after the 1938 provincial convention adopted a policy of no more deals with other parties. In the 1940 federal election, Douglas made a private deal with Qu'Appelle Tory MP Perley: Douglas would ensure no CCF candidate opposed Perley in Qu'Appelle, in exchange for the Tories not running a candidate against Douglas in Weyburn. The deal was struck and both Douglas and Perley were re-elected. (Both men had won by narrow margins in 1935: Douglas by 301 votes, Perley by 190. In 1940, Perley won by over 1,400 votes, Douglas by 900.)

The most striking feature of these accounts, aside from the uniformly negative misrepresentation of Williams's role and the many inaccuracies, is a failure to analyze the larger dynamics of the political context. The CCF was at risk and did indeed face the possibility of annihilation if the party failed to effectively counter the Social Credit invasion. The efforts to arrange saw-offs were desperate measures in a menacing crisis. The CCF was losing members and supporters to Social Credit. The CCF's popular base demanded unity of all reform forces, and if Williams had not captured that mood and harnessed it, CCF members and supporters might have been swept up into the Unity movement. Instead of three Unity candidates, there could have been ten or twenty. Survival was the goal, despite Williams's occasional fantasy that the CCF just might slip into power if they played their cooperation cards wisely. The decision to run in thirty-one seats did not achieve any saw-off benefits, in the final analysis, but it did allow the CCF to concentrate its forces and resources on rural seats, where the party was strongest. This was a wise move.

There were no saw-offs with Social Credit. Aberhart flatly refused. In twenty-six of the thirty-one seats contested, the CCF faced a Social Credit candidate. In eight of the ten seats won, the CCF faced a Social Credit candidate. In five of the ten seats won, the CCF faced a Tory candidate. So perhaps Douglas's efforts paid off. It appears he delivered to John Diefenbaker— no CCF candidate opposed Diefenbaker in Arm River, but he lost. And it should be noted that saw-offs do not necessarily involve instructing members and supporters to vote for the other party. Typically, the term simply means a party does not nominate a candidate, leaving the other party a less cluttered field.

Douglas and his biographers attach a great deal of significance to the fall in the CCF's popular vote between 1934 and 1938, insisting Williams led the party to a serious decline in popular support. The fall in popular vote when the CCF ran only thirty-one candidates rather than a full slate was to be expected. This in no way reflected a true comparison in province-wide popular support for the CCF between the two elections. In 1934, the FLP ran fifty-three candidates and won 24 per cent. In 1938, the CCF ran only thirty-one candidates and won 19 per cent. The 1938 figure is not a reliable measure of the CCF's popular support across the province. In fact, 19 per cent on only thirty-one candidates suggests a significant rise in popular support for the CCF between 1934 and 1938. A look at the actual numbers of CCF voters demonstrates that Williams turned the party around after the 1935 and 1938 battles with Social Credit: 103,000 votes in the 1934 provincial election; 73,505 in the 1935 federal election; 82,527 in the 1938 provincial election; and 106,257 in the 1940 federal election. It is not unreasonable to surmise that, absent the Social Credit invasion and in a clear fight with the Liberal government on its Depression record, Williams might well have led the CCF to victory in 1938.

Williams's Loss of the Leadership, 1941 and 1942

Douglas's recollections of his role in the provincial party are rather inconsistent and at times unreliable. When asked when he "entered the provincial scene," Douglas replied:

> Not until 1940 or 1941, when I was literally dragged into it because the organization was failing so badly. We dropped to the lowest membership we'd had in years, and after Mr. Williams went overseas the whole organization seemed to go dormant. There was a general feeling, with the Saskatchewan leader absent, that it was necessary to take fairly aggressive measures to pick up the party's fortunes. In 1941 at the leadership convention, we had to decide whether or not Mr. Williams was going to continue to lead the party in the event of an election *in absentia*, or whether someone else would lead the party. I was selected both as provincial president and provincial leader. Mr. Williams was overseas.[24]

Douglas denies any "bad blood" between himself and Williams, stating, "He and I had no personal animosity toward each other." He claims he was reluctant about taking the leadership:

> When I agreed to accept the leadership in the province, it was with a good deal of hesitancy....I wasn't keen about it....I came back because of a good deal of pressure mostly from farmers and people whom I knew very well, who said, "It's going to be a long time before we can ever form a federal government, but there are things you could do here provincially to give us a certain amount of protection, particularly to farmers who were losing their farms, and also in the area of basic health and welfare, and educational reform. You owe

it to the movement to come back into the provincial field and try to pull things together." It would be honest, looking back on it now, to say I didn't think there was any prospect of forming a government at the next election when I accepted the leadership. But I thought it might be possible to give the movement a shot in the arm to see it through the next election.[25]

Stewart's biography relies heavily on Douglas's recollections and on the two more thorough biographies published earlier: Doris Shackleton's *Tommy Douglas* (1975) and Thomas McLeod and Ian McLeod's *Tommy Douglas: The Road to Jerusalem* (1987). These previous biographies provide more detail and their bibliographies indicate more research done and hence greater accuracy. Their versions of events contradict much in Douglas's own narrative. Nor do these two biographies suffer from the seemingly sarcastic and too often dismissive animus against Williams that runs throughout Stewart's 2003 biography. Frankly, Stewart's biographies of Douglas and of Coldwell (2000) could be deemed hagiographies—Douglas and Coldwell could do no wrong, it seems, while Williams was the *bête noire* of the party; the party was well rid of him. Whatever the Coldwell/Douglas faction did to bring off Williams's fall is presented favourably. Williams's actions are consistently presented in a negative light. Even when Stewart is compelled to confront facts about less-than-admirable activities of Coldwell or Douglas that are well documented in the other two versions, he justifies these actions in terms of Williams's destructive and dictatorial behaviour.

At the same time, the biographies by Shackleton and by McLeod and McLeod also present a negative portrait of Williams. However, they are less inclined to present Douglas as the reluctant saviour of the party, "dragged" into the leadership to save the movement from impending disaster. This reflects the historical fact that the Coldwell/Douglas faction won, took over the party, and, when interviewed by researchers, presented a version of Williams reflecting the victorious faction's narrative. Only researchers prepared to do some digging among the documents and archives, to search out members of the Williams faction for interviews, and to examine Williams's papers could come close to a more balanced characterization of the three men.

As the faction fight reached a crescendo from 1940 to 1942, the party suffered organizationally. Energy was diverted to the infighting and the two factions had difficulty working together. As Williams became preoccupied with his decision to go overseas and devoted time to his preparatory military training, he had less time and energy to devote to organizing and building the party. And, of key importance, by 1941 Williams had decided not to fight aggressively to retain the leadership. Nevertheless, under Williams's leadership the party had rebuilt its membership base, which had reached 4,900 in 1935 and then fallen to 2,300 in 1936. Much of this loss went temporarily to Social Credit, though some was no doubt due to disappointment over the 1934 and 1935 election results. But Williams recouped and surpassed these losses. By 1940 the membership had reached 6,000. But in 1941, during the defining moments of the faction fight, Williams's enlistment in the army effectively removed him from the scene. In January 1941, Williams was informed of his posting overseas. In February he resigned as president, and by April he was in England. He did, however, continue officially to occupy the office of leader of the opposition in the legislature, with Brockelbank serving as acting leader. He also remained the sitting MLA for Wadena. In the legislature, therefore, Williams officially remained political leader of the party. He had the agreement of the army that, in the event of an election call, he would be released and could be back in Regina within a fortnight; hence, he would not need to fight an election as leader *in absentia*. The executive and council were informed of this arrangement.

Douglas's recollections contain no reference to his activities in the faction committed to replacing Williams. Yet he was very active from the outset, beginning in earnest in the wake of his embarrassment over the Social Credit endorsement. He attended private meetings of party members to discuss how to oust Williams. By 1940 the anti-Williams faction had decided, under Coldwell's guidance, that Douglas rather than Coldwell was the candidate most suitable to defeat Williams. The war debate, during which Williams had offended both pacifists and those committed to the neutrality policy, crystallized and increased the opposition forces against the leader. Douglas and Coldwell conceived the MPs' brief that set in motion the final denouement. After the 1940 convention, the new provincial council appointed Douglas to the committee assigned to draft constitutional amendments based on the brief. Douglas agreed to stand for president against Williams at the 1941 convention and actively sought election. After the fight with the caucus over who was now political leader, and provincial council's ruling that the position of political leader remain unresolved until the 1942 convention, Douglas aggressively pursued the leadership. Given the view of the caucus that Williams remained political leader, Douglas embarked on a one-candidate leadership campaign to ensure his election in 1942. Stewart notes that after the 1941 convention, "Tommy ranged across the province, beating the bushes and raising the hopes...of party stalwarts. By the 1942 convention, he was the unquestioned leader of the provincial party in everything but formal title."[26] Douglas actively sought and fought for the leadership. He was not, as in his words, "literally dragged into it." Nor did his behaviour, as in his words, seem to suggest he accepted the leadership "with a good deal of hesitancy" and that he "wasn't keen about it."

Douglas's claim he had "entered the provincial scene" in "1940 or 1941" is also inaccurate. He was very active in the provincial party from the time he joined the FLP. He served as an ILP representative on the joint UFC(SS)/ILP political directive board of the FLP. After election as an MP in 1935, he was a speaker in great demand at party meetings across the province. He was a superb orator, and Williams often expressed appreciation to Douglas for his tireless efforts. Douglas regularly attended provincial conventions and was active on the provincial council and provincial executive. In 1936 he ran for council and was defeated, perhaps due to fallout over his encounter with Social Credit. In 1937 he was elected to both the council and the executive. In 1938 he was elected to council, but defeated for the executive. In 1939 he was nominated for council but declined to stand. In 1940 he ran for neither. At the 1937, 1938, 1939, and 1940 conventions, Williams's supporters dominated and the most contentious issues were war policy and cooperation with other groups. The faction fight came out into the open over these two issues at the 1940 convention. Williams remained in command, but the faction fight was heating up. In 1941, Douglas was appointed to the provincial council and executive to represent Saskatchewan's CCF MPs. In July of that year, he was elected president.

Finally, Douglas says, "I didn't think there was any prospect of forming a government at the next election when I accepted the leadership." He only "thought it possible to give the movement a shot in the arm to

see it through the next election." While it is a truism there are no guarantees in electoral politics, the prevailing view of the leadership of the
Saskatchewan CCF at the time was that the party would win the coming
election. Williams certainly believed this, based on a detailed analysis
of the election results from the 1938 provincial and 1940 federal elections. His one gnawing doubt was the possibility that the Liberals might
effectively use the CCF's war policy to attack the party. The Liberal Party
certainly assessed the political situation and foresaw a looming CCF victory, hence the postponement of the election in the hope that Liberal
fortunes would turn around. The Liberal organization was strong and
deeply rooted across the province, providing a solid basis for such an
assessment. The Liberal defeat in 1944 may not have been as crushing
had they gone in 1942 or 1943, but defeat was likely. The CCF's faction
fight was just coming to an end in 1942 and the official war policy was
still unchanged, though CCF MPs in Ottawa gave consistently strong support to the war effort. In 1942 the CCF's official war policy was changed
to one of complete and full support for the war, including conscription.

Coming out of the faction fight and the war policy debate, the party
was certainly vulnerable, but still on track to victory. By 1943 the faction
fight had come to a decisive end. Even the strongly pro-Williams legislative caucus rallied behind Douglas and the party got back to the business
of recruiting members, raising funds, organizing a government in waiting, and preparing the party's election machine. When Douglas won the
leadership, it was a foregone conclusion he would be the next premier,
barring an unforeseen catastrophe. Given the considerable time and
energy Douglas had put into taking the leadership from Williams, it is
difficult to believe his purpose was simply "to give the movement a shot
in the arm to see it through the next election." The final stage of the faction fight was so intense and bitter precisely because it was understood
that whoever prevailed, Williams or Douglas, would become premier
after the election. In Douglas's narrative, he paints himself as selflessly
and reluctantly serving the movement, not seeking personal power. The
Coldwell/Douglas faction's attacks on Williams had already made it
clear that it was Williams who was personally ambitious and hungry for
power. These versions of the roles of Douglas and Williams are reflected
in virtually every account of the events leading up to Douglas's election
as leader.

As effective and successful politicians, it is not surprising that, in their personal memoirs and recollections, Douglas and Coldwell would tend to present—even, it appears at times, to completely reconstruct—events so as to place themselves and their actions in a favourable light. It is also understandable that they would wish to present a negative picture of Williams in order to justify seizing the leadership from him while he was serving overseas. Particularly after his election as premier, Douglas would rather not have to admit what appears as his personal opportunism in engaging in questionable actions, in flagrant violation of party policy, in order to ensure his election as MP for Weyburn in 1935 and 1940. The optics of taking the leadership away from Williams while he was serving overseas was a serious problem, hence the careful reconstruction not only of actual events, but of Williams's behaviour and character as leader. A compelling case had to be made for Williams's ouster. Douglas and Coldwell avoid acknowledging the historically significant role of Williams in leading the organized farmers into socialist political action and his decision to ally the farmers with the then tiny and largely politically irrelevant ILP. The defining importance of the victory of Williams and four other UFC(SS) activists in the 1934 election is virtually overlooked. Arguably, Williams's most important tactical triumph occurred in 1938, when he successfully blocked the Social Credit invasion. My reading of this suggests it is totally reconstructed by Douglas and presented as a tactical error of monumental proportions, doing almost irreparable harm to the party.

A systematic assault on Williams's leadership style colours all accounts of his time as leader. Williams is painted as an astute and effective organizer, but a leader obsessed with personally controlling all aspects of the party. Frequent charges emanated from the Coldwell/Douglas faction accusing him of being dictatorial, impatient, and abrasive in his dealings with party members. Coldwell describes Williams as "the most cunning individual with whom it has ever been my misfortune to be associated." He notes Williams was "a prickly leader."[27] Douglas characterizes Williams's time as leader as "a one-man show." Williams "aroused resentment...because of his complete control of the party apparatus"; that is, he kept "all the different jobs in his own hands:...provincial leader, provincial organizer, and in charge of publicity."[28] Douglas also remembers Williams as "humourless and uncompromising." Based on interviews with Douglas, Shackleton describes Williams as an "irascible man, sometimes abrasive," and "impatient."[29] This character portrayal helps to justify the leadership coup.

Again, what is missing from these assessments of Williams is the context. Supporters and detractors agree Williams was certainly formidable in debate, using sarcasm and wit freely to defeat opponents. He was relentless and uncompromising in arguments over what he considered vital issues, both in the convention hall and in meetings of the council and executive. He was blunt and brutally honest in his assessments of the positions taken by his opponents. Even Brockelbank, one of Williams's staunchest supporters to the end, noted he "wasn't the most diplomatic man in the world."[30] Douglas once slipped off his narrative on Williams when talking to Shackleton: "I understood him—his abrasiveness, his impatience—because I've a good dose of it myself; I could conceal it better than George did."[31]

Williams took on all the key jobs, a plan initially proposed by Coldwell, for some very practical reasons. The party was broke and in organizational tatters after the 1934 election. There were no funds to hire staff beyond an office manager/secretary-treasurer, who was often not paid on time due to lack of funds. Coldwell's $4,000 leader's salary was a financial albatross around the party's neck until he resigned as party leader in 1935, when he won a federal seat and hence an MP's indemnity. Williams, as a farmer, enjoyed more economic independence than those holding waged or salaried jobs. He devoted himself virtually full-time to the party from its founding in 1932. He received no salary, just expenses, and he often did not bother to claim expenses because there was no money to repay him. As a farmer he was relatively free to work full time for the party after spring seeding and fall harvest. A goodly portion of the proceeds from the farm went to hiring farm labour to help out. Things improved after Williams's election, since he could work full-time for the party, relying on his indemnity as MLA and leader of the opposition. Therefore, after 1934 he could depend more heavily on hired help on the farm, giving him even more time to devote to the party's work. As Williams reorganized and rebuilt the party, things improved, allowing him to hire party organizers as needed and as funds allowed, rather than on a full-time basis. In the expenditure of funds, he gave political priority not to hiring full-time staff, but to making radio broadcasts and establishing a newspaper and hiring an editor. Building a full-time party bureaucracy, something Williams had enjoyed as president of the UFC(SS), was just not possible given the shortage of funds.

As the newly elected leader in 1935, Williams embarked on welding together an organizationally incoherent and disparate party, composed of constituency associations, CCF clubs, and affiliated labour and farm groups, into a centralized, unitary political party. This task was urgent in order to prepare for the 1938 election. The new constitution eliminated the separate offices of president and party leader, uniting these roles in the office of president. The party was restructured into constituency associations, a provincial council, and an executive. In order to be a member of the CCF, one had to be in a constituency association (though individual at-large memberships continued in unorganized constituencies). In imposing the new structure, Williams faced opposition and resistance—the source of many of the charges of him being abrasive and dictatorial. Williams was firm: this was the new structure and CCF members were obliged to comply with the constitution. He ran unopposed for president, a position that now included the role of political leader, each year until 1940. Hence, by all accepted standards of democracy, he was the overwhelming democratic choice for leader at each and every convention, including that of 1940 when he faced an opponent for the first time and won handily.

Though it provides no justification for sloppy and inaccurate research, biographers are often favourably disposed to their subjects. This might tend to make them less capable of providing critical, disinterested accounts of their subjects' actions. Biographers favourably disposed to their subjects might more readily accept as accurate a subject's self-interested account of events. Even when partisan biographers do delve into independent and conflicting accounts of events, they might tend to cast events unfavourable to the subject in a more positive light. Scholars, however, presenting accounts of the larger historical picture—such as the record of events in the formation and victory of the CCF in Saskatchewan—are obliged to be wary of versions presented by the interested actors directly involved in the events under examination. There is no guarantee such versions are either complete or accurate. There is no excuse for scholars uncritically accepting as factual and complete the accounts of Douglas and Coldwell regarding the crucial events in the emergence and success of the CCF.

Scholarly works on the Saskatchewan CCF tend to echo the version of events presented by Coldwell and Douglas in characterizing the 1938 election as a disaster rather than a triumph, as well as their accounts of Douglas's defeat of Williams as leader. On Douglas's endorsement by Social Credit in 1935, some accounts are more accurate than others, but all scholars share in casting a sympathetic light on Douglas's behaviour and a negative light on that of Williams. Accounts of the conflict between Coldwell and Williams after the 1934 election, again, tend to side with Coldwell while presenting Williams as the source of the conflict. Perhaps this has to do with looking back on events through the prism of the later successes Coldwell and Douglas went on to achieve. Douglas's victory in 1944 and his record as premier became a set or rose-coloured glasses through which the past was examined. Williams suffered from this; his role is variously diminished, dismissed, or overlooked, and depictions of his behaviour as leader largely echo Coldwell and Douglas, as faithfully recorded in their biographies.

There are two major published scholarly works on the rise to power of the CCF in Saskatchewan, as distinct from biographies of Coldwell and Douglas. Seymour Martin Lipset's *Agrarian Socialism: The Cooperative Commonwealth Federation in Saskatchewan*, first published in 1950 and revised in 1968, remains the most cited and widely accepted. Lipset's account gives Williams credit for leading the organized farmers into socialist politics, but reproduces the version of the 1938 election as a disaster that represented a turn away from socialism.

However, Lipset's work suffers from considerable confusion about the details and dynamics of the political struggles between left and right in the UFC(SS) in the years immediately preceding the founding of the FLP. The only detailed text devoted to Williams in the book concerns the change in leadership in 1941–42. The Coldwell/Douglas narrative is faithfully reproduced, while Lipset manifests a considerable lack of knowledge about the party's constitution and the realities of the structure over which Williams presided. Lipset seems to imply that Williams was in command of a huge party apparatus instead of a full-time office staff of one, irregular part-time organizers, and a newspaper editor:

Increasing resentment had developed within the party against George Williams, who had been leader since 1935. Williams had antagonized many in the party by his attempts to extend his control over all facets of party activity. He had assumed the position of party legislative leader, president of the provincial organization, director of the party newspaper, and head of the party's organizational and office staff. Many felt that Williams was ambitious for power, and that he had deliberately attempted to eliminate prospective rivals from influence in the party.[32]

As a reference, Lipset cites "interviews with CCF leaders." These were no doubt those who had successfully ousted Williams.

Evelyn Eager's *Saskatchewan Government: Politics and Pragmatism*, published in 1980, provides a history of governing in Saskatchewan and therefore includes a large section on the rise of the CCF to power and its record as government. It includes two references to Williams, both echoing the narrative of the Coldwell/Douglas faction:

G. H. Williams, president of the party, then [after Coldwell's 1935 resignation] assumed the duties of leader, but he aroused considerable resentment through aggressive control of party activities. In 1941 and 1942 the party moved to forestall future concentration of power with one person. The move was a direct result of concern which developed when the energetic and aggressive George Williams, in addition to the duties of an MLA, the House leader, and the president of the party, also took on the role of provincial leader.[33]

Eager provides no specific references for these depictions. In the section titled "Bibliographical Outline," interviews with Douglas and Lipset's book are mentioned.

A notable exception to the tendency to uncritically adopt the Coldwell/Douglas negative narrative on Williams is A. W. Johnson's *Dream No Little Dreams: A Biography of the Douglas Government of Saskatchewan, 1944–1962* (2004).[34] The book's focus is on the record of the Douglas government; hence, there is little material on events leading up to the

1944 victory. Johnson shares the common error that Williams and the UFC(SS) supported the Progressives in the 1929 and 1930 election campaigns. He does not appear aware of the complex struggle between the left and the right as Williams manoeuvred to lead the UFC(SS) into politics on a socialist platform. He mentions Williams's "capacity to ruffle feathers," but does not repeat the usual negative descriptors applied to Williams. He fails to make clear why none of the five elected MLAs in 1934 agreed to resign to allow the defeated Coldwell to run in a by-election. He gets much wrong on Douglas's flirtation with Social Credit in 1935. He overlooks the conspiracy to oust Williams leading up to the events of 1941 and 1942. On the other hand, Johnson recognizes Williams as a key leader in the CCF's rise to victory, giving him equal standing with Woodsworth and Coldwell. He also reports on Williams's role in policy development during his tenure as leader of the opposition, particularly in the development of an ambitious program of public ownership and central economic planning. These policies were central to the Douglas government's innovations during its first term in office.

Academic historians and *The Encyclopedia of Saskatchewan* accord Williams more balance, resisting the pull of the Coldwell/Douglas faction's narrative. John Archer, in his 1980 *Saskatchewan: A History*, puts it simply and directly: "George Williams was a dynamic leader—with a seeming facility to ruffle feathers. As a result he was often at odds with other party members and certainly differed at times with Coldwell [and] T.C. Douglas."[35] Gerald Friesen, in his 1984 *The Canadian Prairies: A History*, provides a crisp account of the ideological differences between Coldwell and Williams that lay at the roots of their ongoing disagreements:

> He [Coldwell] was not a socialist, or even a labour party Representative in the mid-1920s....Coldwell espoused the usual western Canadian critique of eastern-dominated party caucuses; his was a "people's party," aiming to "hasten the day when the forces of special privilege will be decisively defeated." By the late 1920s, when Progressivism faltered, he moved easily into an alliance with the Saskatchewan labour movement...and thence into a coalition with representatives of the farm movement. For Coldwell...sympathy with working people and a commitment to "loyalty, fair play and

honesty" rather than to socialist ideology were the underpin-nings of his public career.

Saskatchewan farmers, not urban radicals, injected a strain of socialism into prairie provincial politics in the 1920s....George Williams was probably the most influen-tial spokesman in the long run....Williams belonged to a left-wing caucus in the farmers' movement, spoke of the "exploitation of the mass of the people, agricultural and industrial alike, by the capitalistic class," and wished to create a co-operative commonwealth distinguished by "producer control of industry and powers of government."[36]

The Encyclopedia of Saskatchewan provides a straightforward factual account of Williams's career, without the usual negative embellishments. The entry on Williams is based on the only major scholarly effort to tell his story—Friedrich Steininger's unpublished MA thesis. This careful appraisal is somewhat offset by this nugget that somehow slipped into the encyclopedia's entry on Douglas:

> In 1940 many Saskatchewan CCF activists called for Douglas to return to provincial politics and lead the provincial CCF. The local party was embroiled in internal strife as party leader George Williams' style alienated him from a large sec-tion of the party. Douglas challenged Williams for the party presidency in 1941 and won.[37]

The entry then recommends two of the Douglas biographies for further reading, with no further comment.

But for rare exceptions, Canadian historiography fails to provide a fair and balanced account of Williams's vital role in the formation and rise to power of the CCF in Saskatchewan. The most shameful feature of this failure is the willingness, inadvertent or deliberate, of many intellectuals to give relatively uncritical credence to versions of events as presented by Coldwell and Douglas. The incontestable facts on the record—that Williams led the organized farmers into socialist political action, served as party leader and leader of the opposition in the legislature from 1935 to 1942, and was ousted from the leadership while he was serving overseas—should have alerted any reasonably competent intellectual that there is much more to the story than the versions presented by Coldwell and Douglas. It is frankly astonishing that this, for the most part, has not been the case.

Chapter 9

CONCLUSION

Williams in Canadian History

Given his role in founding and building the CCF in Saskatchewan, and bringing it to the cusp of power, Williams deserves a prominent place in Canadian history. He made a significant contribution to shaping the history of the province, indeed of Canada, given the impact of the CCF victory on Canadian politics and the resulting accelerated construction of the Canadian welfare state. It is not possible to prove with certainty that the victory would not have happened in the absence of Williams's contribution. Nevertheless, given the complex and indeterminate struggle to lead Saskatchewan's organized farmers into politics on a socialist program, it is difficult to imagine the rise and success of the CCF in 1944 without Williams's contribution. The evidence is clear. Had the organized farmers not gone into politics on a socialist program and initiated the founding of the CCF in Saskatchewan, the 1944 victory would have been less likely. The farmers of Saskatchewan elected the CCF. Elections were won or lost in rural Saskatchewan in 1944. The contribution of the working class, through its trade unions and small affiliated labour party, transformed a solid victory into a landslide. No doubt a Saskatchewan section of the CCF would have been founded without the leadership of Williams and the organized farmers, but it would have been much smaller and more moderate, and unlikely to have enjoyed the mass support of farmers so instrumental in the 1944 victory.

Organized farmers taking political action was an established feature of Canadian electoral politics in the postwar period. In the early 1920s the agrarian populist offensive achieved many successes, attesting to their advanced class consciousness and their organizational effectiveness in contesting for political power. But there was no precedent for successfully persuading the organized farmers to seek power on a socialist platform. Efforts to unite with the working class had failed. But for a limited commitment to public ownership of selected industries, and a detailed reform program, the Progressive Party rejected socialism—indeed, had trouble accepting the right of the working class to organize and to strike. The party, and the various farmer provincial governments, embraced no coherent vision of what it would do with power once it was won. The party's core economic program was free trade. Its core political program was to cleanse politics of the corruption caused by the tariff system. Its core sociological program was to stop and reverse rural depopulation. The party had no alternative modernization program. The rapid disintegration of the agrarian populist political offensive seemed to confirm the view that farmers, as small, self-interested capitalists, were unpredictable in their political orientation, swinging from right to left and back again. Leaders of organized farmers won eager support from their members and popular base when farmers had sharp grievances. But the rank and file was willing to quickly abandon the political project when times were good. The idea that the organized farmers could be persuaded to adopt a clear socialist program as the basis for seeking power, while retaining support of their popular base among farmers, seemed fanciful.

Williams's main contribution to shaping Canadian history rests on his success in leading Saskatchewan's organized farmers into politics on a socialist platform. No one denies the defining importance of this event. But few bother to analyze and explain how Williams was able to lead and shape this turn to socialism. The left turn of the farmers was not merely a brief episode in the province's political history. The work of the UFC(SS) and the FLP/CCF, under the leadership of Williams, transformed the essence of rural politics in the province, establishing the basis for a relatively hegemonic left-wing or "socialist" agrarian populist political culture that persisted for over two generations. This loyal rural base was of key importance to the CCF's becoming "the natural governing party" of the province from 1944 to the 1970s. This astonished observers at the time. The Saskatchewan Liberal Party was unable to understand this opponent, especially throughout the 1940s and 1950s. In the Liberal experience, farmers did not vote socialist. And if they did, it was an isolated anomaly—farmers did not keep voting socialist in election after election. Even the intelligentsia and core leadership of the national CCF could not comfortably come to theoretical grips with the phenomenon. The national party elite intended to build a party of labour, with a focus on the working class and its trade unions. Based on the experiences of the Progressive Party, and the implosion of the Ontario farmer government, they did not have confidence in the political reliability of farmers. This might help explain some of the clashes with Williams and the uneasiness he provoked among the national leadership. He was too populist. He was too left-wing. He was a farmer. He was therefore ideologically unreliable. Williams was treated as an outsider from the beginning. Hence, when forming the national core of CCF organizers, the elite picked Coldwell to organize Saskatchewan rather than Williams, the more obvious choice given his established political base. Coldwell's tiny Independent Labour Party had a few hundred members. Williams's UFC(SS) had twenty-seven thousand. But Coldwell was judged a reliable, moderate labour man.

Williams's biography intersects with what historian Eric Hobsbawm describes as "an Age of Catastrophe" on a world scale:

> The decades from the outbreak of the First World War to the aftermath of the Second, was an Age of Catastrophe [for world capitalism]....For forty years it stumbled from one calamity to another. There were times when even intelligent conservatives would not take bets on its survival.
>
> It was shaken by two world wars....[A] world economic crisis of unprecedented depth brought even the strongest capitalist economies to their knees...While the economy tottered, the institutions of liberal democracy virtually disappeared between 1917 and 1942 from all but a fringe of Europe and parts of North America and Australasia...as fascism and its satellite authoritarian movements and regimes advanced.[1]

It was, in the words of Hans Gerth and C. Wright Mills, "an epoch of transition."[2] More and more people lost faith in the existing institutions and their false promises of security and prosperity. Insecurity and fear of the future grew as many began to believe "the old way is unworkable."[3] Spontaneous collective movements demanding help and change emerged. All the old values and assurances were in doubt. Criticism and angry complaints became commonplace. People lost confidence in their established leaders. They yearned for a better life, for basic security, becoming open to alternatives to the existing order of things. In such a context, new leaders can rise to the fore, capturing the collective mood, providing a vision of change to satisfy people's yearnings and rekindle their hope, becoming "the pivot" of transition. In such a historical context of crisis and transition, Plekhanov's "great man" can rise to prominence: "He possesses qualities which make him most capable of serving the great social needs of his time;...he sees *farther* than others do and his desires are *stronger* than in others;...he indicates the new social needs created by the previous development of social relations; he assumes the initiative in meeting those needs."[4]

Williams became a working farmer in 1921. His first years involved the hard labour of breaking virgin prairie with horse and plow and the disappointment of facing a market weighed against a farmer seeking a fair price. As a war veteran, Williams had had his courage tested in the trenches and, more dramatically, in a final cavalry charge against machine guns, repeating rifles, and a Howitzer. Perhaps later depictions of him as a fearless man with steely determination had their roots in his war experience; after all, there is not much in the world to fear after surviving a horseback charge against machine guns. Williams was a voracious and eclectic reader—a habit he acquired during a long recovery from rheumatic fever in his teens. During his convalescence from his war wound in a military hospital in Britain, he took courses from the Khaki University and studied a program of mental discipline. He read widely in history, economics, and socialism. Though he had no experience in politics at that time, except perhaps as a critical observer, he developed a core ideological commitment to socialism that stayed with him until his death. After bringing in his 1922 harvest, Williams, at the age of twenty-eight, decided to go into agrarian politics.

His choice of the FUC rather than the established, much larger SGGA reflected his left-wing orientation. The FUC advocated "class struggle" by "the Great Agricultural Class," seeking economic power in the marketplace

while rejecting electoral political action. At this point, Williams's view was
that the only way to achieve significant positive change for farmers was to
tie agrarian populism to socialism. From his early years in the FUC he was
committed to the strategy of leading the farmers into politics on a socialist platform. Contrary to the anti-electoral doctrines of the existing FUC
leadership, Williams believed political power must eventually be sought
and won in order to achieve real, meaningful, and lasting change. And
real, meaningful, and lasting change meant socialism, not the reformism
of the Progressives. He also concluded that alliances with other popular
classes, most importantly the working class, were necessary to win political power. Everything he did in the FUC and its successor, the UFC(SS),
worked toward that final objective.

The FUC, with its few hundred members, engaged in radical agitation
and direct action to picket and disrupt land sales of foreclosed farms.
The organization distinguished itself from the rival SGGA by its radical,
left-wing orientation to the agrarian populist struggle. And Williams, as
an advocate of electoral political action, was in a distinct minority in the
organization. In 1925 the FUC board fired Williams as an organizer and
censured him when he and a group of like-minded militants set up an
electoral political organization, the Farmers' Political Association, outside the FUC. The FPA combined the core agrarian populist program of
the FUC with a few fundamentals of socialism. Williams quietly buried
the FPA, regaining the good graces of the board.

Both the FUC and Williams would have remained on the cranky
fringes of the larger organized farmers' movement had history not intervened, catapulting the FUC and Williams into prominence. In a small
organization like the FUC, Williams, though young and a political neo-
phyte, could rise quickly to a leadership position. He was energetic,
committed, and, as it turned out, talented. As he worked for the organization, Williams discovered and developed talents and qualities he had
not initially known he possessed. He wrote well, thus becoming a leading
author of FUC propaganda. He found he was an effective public speaker
and quickly became a compelling orator on the public platform. He was
hired as an organizer and discovered he had a talent for detailed organizational work and a knack for persuading farmers to join the FUC.

Two events immediately thrust the fledgling FUC and Williams into
prominence among farmers: the problem of farm debt in the postwar

depression and the collapse in wheat prices. The debt problem was so serious that foreclosures and evictions became epidemic, resulting in FUC-sponsored protest meetings throughout rural areas. Across the province, the organization disrupted land sales of the farms of evicted farmers. Under Williams's guidance, the FUC prepared and distributed a widely popular, complex debt-adjustment plan, which was ultimately supported by the SGGA and became the model for such plans among other farm organizations. The proposed plan kept the farmer producing on the land and provided mechanisms for adjusting boom-time debts downward, extending repayment periods, and lowering interest rates. It exempted enough of a farmer-debtor's crop from seizure to ensure he could provide for his family and continue to plant and harvest crops. It was an aggressive anti-capitalist document, designed to use the law to protect farmers from private financial institutions. The business lobby complained that there was not much left for a creditor to seize through foreclosure if the plan were implemented. That, of course, was the political objective of the plan—to strike a blow against capitalist financial predators.

The farm debt crisis was brought to a head by the collapse in wheat prices with the suspension of the orderly marketing imposed by Ottawa during the war. Farmers enjoyed high prices during the war, allowing them to manage a growing debt load as wartime demand and high prices led to an expansion of seeded acreage and an investment in mechanization to offset labour shortages. With the return of the free market, prices collapsed. The SGGA failed to provide leadership in the establishment of a farmer-controlled voluntary wheat-marketing cooperative. Wheat pools were common in the U.S. Midwest, and in 1923 the UFA led in setting up a pool in Alberta. The FUC seized the initiative and began to organize a pool in Saskatchewan. Williams was selected as the FUC's lead organizer in the province-wide campaign to persuade farmers to commit to pooling their wheat for marketing. Williams and Aaron Sapiro, a populist New York lawyer who had assisted both U.S. and Alberta farmers, embarked on a province-wide series of rallies to sign up farmers, and the farmers flocked to join. In response, the SGGA offered to join the campaign. By 1926 the joint campaign had signed up forty-five thousand farmers, representing over 73 per cent of seeded acreage. The FUC saw this as just the first step in building a system of compulsory pooling—if two-thirds of farmers signed up, the system should become legally compulsory for all. The private grain trade would then be completely shut out as farmers achieved full democratic control of the marketing of their wheat. Neither the leadership of the SGGA, nor that of the newly founded Wheat Pool, agreed with this ultimate objective, characterizing it as "socialistic" and "dictatorial." In 1924, at the height of the wheat pool campaign, the FUC's few hundred members had grown to over ten thousand, and it was on track to replacing the SGGA as the largest organized farmers' movement in the province. Williams's association with the debt adjustment plan and his lead role in the wheat pool campaign greatly enhanced his reputation among farmers as one of the province's most effective farm leaders.

At the end of the successful wheat pool campaign the SGGA proposed the two organizations unite into a single powerful voice for the province's farmers. The FUC agreed, but was determined the new organization would retain the FUC's democratic structure and commitment to militancy. In July 1926 the UFC(SS) was founded. The first full convention with delegates from both organizations was set for February 1927. With Williams as public spokesman, the leaders of the FUC openly organized a left caucus within the organization to prepare for the convention. The core leadership of the SGGA was confident they would emerge in control of the new organization, given their experience and public profile as farm leaders.

Williams and delegates from the FUC were just as determined to gain control, openly campaigning among the rank and file of both the FUC and the SGGA. A struggle for power between what became publicly known as "the left wing" and "the right wing" dominated conventions in 1927, 1928, and 1929. The left caucus out-organized and out-debated the right wing, electing Williams as president in 1929. Skirmishes between left and right continued until Williams prevailed after the right, charging that the organization had been taken over by a left-wing conspiracy, made an unsuccessful attempt to force his resignation. The rank and file at district meetings overwhelmingly supported Williams; right-wing board members resigned and were replaced by Williams's supporters. At the 1930 convention, Williams was in complete control of the organization, with solid support among the membership, as well as on the executive and board of directors.

History again intervened with the 1929 crash followed by the Depression. Williams recognized an unprecedented opportunity to lead the UFC(SS) into politics on a socialist platform, as well as to achieve a political alliance with the working class. But he was cautious. There was instant pressure from both the far left and the right wing to go immediately into politics in response to the onset of the Depression. The far left, under the influence of the CP, argued the time was ripe to enter politics on a radical socialist program in the 1930 federal election. A small minority, they had little chance of persuading the organization. The much larger right wing agreed to an immediate entry into politics, but wanted the organization to throw its considerable weight and resources behind the remnants of the Progressive Party. Protected by a constitution forbidding political action, Williams carefully manoeuvred between the two factions, resisting pleas to move quickly. The organization had not yet adopted a socialist program as a basis for political action. Williams believed that to act prematurely would lead the UFC(SS) into supporting the discredited, irrelevant reformism of the remaining rump of the Progressives, which in turn would lead to disappointment and disillusionment. Williams was successful. The organization did not enter politics for the 1930 election, nor did it provide wholehearted endorsement for the Progressives. For this Williams earned the bitter hostility of both the right wing of the UFC(SS) and the leadership of the Progressives.

At the 1931 convention Williams was ready to lead the organization into politics and into an alliance with the working class. The constitutional amendment allowing political action was passed without dissent. A draft platform, circulated among the membership in the weeks preceding the convention, was presented. Spontaneous amendments from the floor toughened up the socialist measures proposed. The membership was clearly ready. The platform contained the usual socialist economic measures. The cornerstone was the public ownership and control of all natural resources and their development. To this was added public ownership of utilities, insurance, banks, and transportation. These socialist measures were supplemented by a commitment to foster and support the development of cooperatives in all areas of economic activity. Province-wide orderly marketing based on the pooling principle would be provided for all agricultural commodities. Publicly funded social, education, and health programs were proposed. This was the essence of "the co-operative commonwealth" to be established as the new social order, where production was based on need, not profit, and all enjoyed guaranteed social and economic security.

But the platform went further, proposing a form of social owner-ship of farms. It proposed the voluntary "nationalization" of farmland through a "use-lease" system of land tenure. Under this system, the farmer continued to be an independent commodity producer, and the lease to his land was held in perpetuity, including the right to pass it on to the farmer's heir. The farmer enjoyed guaranteed security of ten-ure, fully protected from foreclosure and eviction. This was the hybrid socialism Williams proposed in order to win farmers to the platform. The family farm, with full security of tenure, was fundamental to this socialism, which Williams described as "a socialism that will work." The farmer remains a small capitalist, producing for profit in the market and enjoying full entrepreneurial control of his operation. It was not really a program of nationalization, in the usual sense of the term; it was more a program of securing farm tenure to the farmer through a public land bank, inoculated from speculators and finance capitalists. It was all about security of tenure. In the context of the Depression, this platform was strongly supported by the UFC(SS)'s membership, and it was on this basis that the newly founded Farmer-Labour Party won five rural seats in the 1934 provincial election. Even when the "use-lease" plank was abandoned in 1936, government guarantees of "security of tenure" on the farm remained the leading plank in all iterations of the FLP/CCF plat-form up to and including 1944.

In 1935, when Williams replaced Coldwell as leader after the 1934 election debacle, he inherited a party in organizational incoherence, in financial crisis, and with a declining membership. The Alberta Social Credit invasion had begun with the 1935 federal election and continued as Social Credit prepared to win the province in 1938. Many CCF mem-bers were attracted to Social Credit. In three years, Williams turned the Saskatchewan CCF around. He reorganized the party into a centralized, tightly organized fighting machine. He established schools to train can-didates, campaign managers, and party militants. He documented and shared the techniques he had used to win Wadena in 1934, which became a template for the CCF across Canada: poll-by-poll organization, repeti-tive door-to-door canvassing, and an efficient election-day organization to get the vote out. He established a newspaper and hired an editor. He oversaw constituency-based membership and fundraising drives, insisting these were central to a never-ending election campaign. By 1938, the CCF was prepared to fight the Social Credit invasion on the ground.

On the political level, Williams engaged in a series of effective tactical moves to navigate the party through the turbulent waters of reform politics during the Depression. He resisted efforts to bury the CCF in united fronts, insisting that above all the CCF retain its organizational and political integrity. He forcefully argued that the CCF must present itself as the best option among all competing reform tendencies to achieve a better world. His tactical shifts, especially the effort to negotiate saw-offs with Social Credit in 1938, were strongly opposed by Woodsworth, Coldwell, and the right of the party. Yet Williams prevailed, arguably saving the CCF from disaster in 1938. In that election the CCF not only survived, but doubled its seats in the legislature, making the party even more clearly the only viable alternative to the governing Liberals.

In the 1940 federal election, Williams's public opposition to the national CCF's war policy of neutrality and his relentless advocacy of full support for the war against fascism led to an increase in the CCF's popular vote and seats won in the province. In all other provinces the CCF vote went down in 1940 compared to 1935—a failure that, Williams argued, was largely due to the national party's war policy. But his position on the war was not primarily motivated by electoral opportunism. From the mid-1930s he recognized the fight against fascism as the defining moment of the twentieth century. All principled supporters of socialism and democracy must join the fight. Such a war would inevitably win broad and deep popular support. In 1940 he decided to enlist in the army and go overseas. Later, his analysis of the politics of the war would be completely vindicated. The CCF's share of the national vote in the 1940 election was 8 per cent; a 1942 poll put it at 10 per cent. In March 1942, Woodsworth died and was replaced by Coldwell. In July the party's policy changed to full support for the war, including conscription, and in September, CCF support jumped to 21 per cent, and then to 29 per cent in 1943.

Williams was a complex man of many contradictions. He was a radical agrarian populist and a socialist. Yet he was also a member of the United Empire Loyalist Association, proud of his ancestral family's resistance to the American Revolution. He was an enthusiastic supporter of the monarchy. He held an unassailable belief in British parliamentary democracy. His visit to the Soviet Union deepened his commitment to socialism, because it was now clear that building a socialist economy in the real world was possible. But that visit also deepened his commitment to the democratic road to socialism. He was appalled at the human costs of the Russian Revolution. His conviction never wavered that it was possible to win and implement socialism through parliamentary democracy. Yet he strongly supported extraparliamentary, militant direct action, including working alongside CP members, in the day-to-day struggle to build momentum for the socialist movement.

Williams was a driven man, accused by his detractors of excessive personal ambition. But his ambition was always for the success of the movement, not for his personal career as a politician. When persuaded it was in the best interests of the movement, he stepped aside to give Coldwell the FLP leadership that had been his own for the asking. After 1934, persuaded by Coldwell's failure and the unlikelihood of his success, Williams decided Coldwell had to go—in the interests of the movement.

Williams was an old-fashioned man of honour—his word was his bond. When he discovered the subterranean campaign to oust him as leader, he was both deeply wounded and outraged at the dishonesty and hypocrisy of men like Coldwell and Douglas. Though he could have prevailed as leader had he stayed to fight, he remained committed to going overseas to fight fascism. But first, in writing, he revealed the facts of the conspiracy against him, as he knew them at the time, to the provincial council for action. He was willing to lead the party into the election and arranged release from service to return in order to do so, but the campaign against him must cease. Williams realized an open fight would split the party and do irreparable public damage to its chances of victory. He therefore neither openly campaigned to hold onto the leadership, nor revealed his complaints to the convention as he had initially threatened. In the event, the conspirators denied any effort to oust Williams, and the provincial council, having discussed the issue in Williams's absence, declared there was no evidence to support Williams's allegations. The conspirators proceeded to deliver the final coup in 1941 and 1942.

When Williams, seriously ill, returned in 1944 he did all he could to ensure an election victory. It was for the movement, regardless of his personal disappointment and the risk to his health. To the end Williams gave everything he had to build the movement and bring it to power. He deserves recognition on the historical record for his contributions—recognition that neither the party nor the intellectuals have seen fit to grant him.

AFTERWORD

Almost a century ago, a miracle occurred in the heart of Canada. In little town and village groups, prairie farmers thought and planned together, solving real problems in real time, creating vision out of despair. Those aspirations, as George Williams himself noted, became the platform of the CCF. Williams' genius was to "make it happen." Since the death of the CCF, democracy has become a limp and fading thing in the land, captured by a fetish for "the leader." And since George himself despised such leader-worship, perhaps he wouldn't have minded being invisible to historians...as are all those prairie people who breathed life into social justice.

—Muriel Wiens

In 1938, a worthy tribute was paid to George Williams by Alberta CCF leader Elmer Roper: "capable, astute and fully self-possessed...the best organizer in the CCF, an idealist who is a complete realist—a combination that is as rare as it is useful."

Let no man speak ill of George Hara Williams; he was a man of conscience.

—Friedrich Steininger

CHRONOLOGY

1894	George Hara Williams is born in Binscarth, Manitoba.
1896–1913	The "wheat boom" dominates the Canadian economy; there is massive settlement of the Prairies.
1900	The Williams family moves briefly to Sintaluta, Saskatchewan, then settles in Winnipeg.
1909	The Canadian Council of Agriculture is formed, uniting Prairie farm organizations and the Ontario Grange.
1910 Summer	Prime Minister Wilfrid Laurier tours the Prairies, the first prime minister to do so.
1910	"Siege on Ottawa": over eight hundred farmers present *The Farmers' Platform of 1910* to the government.
1911 Sep 21	Robert Borden and the Tories win the federal election, defeating Laurier's Liberals.
1913 Summer	Farmers organize a "Second Siege on Ottawa."
1914 Aug 4	Britain declares war on Germany.
1914 Aug 5	Canada declares war on Germany.
1914	The War Measures Act categorizes Canadians with roots in enemy nations—Ukrainians, Germans, Austrians and Hungarians—as "enemy aliens."
1916	The federal election is postponed due to war.
1917	The Soldier Settlement Act grants homesteading veterans quarter sections of land and interest-free loans.
1917	The Wartime Elections Act (denying the vote to all war objectors) and the Military Voters Act are passed.

1917 Feb 10	Williams enlists for service.
1917 Aug	Williams is posted overseas.
1917 Dec 17	Borden's Union government wins the federal election.
1918 March	Williams is wounded in battle.
1918 Dec 6	Williams is discharged from service.
1919	The Canadian Council of Agriculture issues a new platform for discussion among its members: the New National Policy.
1919 May/June	The Winnipeg General Strike is one response to postwar unemployment, inflation, and low wages.
1919	Williams accepts a position with the Soldier Settlement Board.
1919 Fall	The Canadian Wheat Board is created for the 1919 crop.
1919 Oct 20	The Ontario Conservatives are defeated in the provincial election, and the United Farmers of Ontario form a coalition government with the support of Labour and Independents.
1920	The Canadian Wheat Board is cancelled.
1920–23	Wheat prices collapse.
1921 July 18	The United Farmers of Alberta win the provincial election with a majority.
1921	Williams leaves the Soldier Settlement Board to go into farming.
1921 Dec 6	The Progressive Party wins enough seats in the federal election to form the Official Opposition, but declines to do so.
1922	Williams marries Margery Cass.
1922 July 18	The United Farmers of Manitoba win the provincial election with a narrow majority, with the support of Independent Labour candidates.
1922 July	The Farmers' Union of Canada (FUC) holds its founding convention in Saskatoon.
1923	Williams is named secretary of the FUC's Debt Adjustment Committee and writes his popular *Debt Adjustment Plan*.
1923	The Canadian Council of Agriculture withdraws support for national political action.

1924	At convention, the Saskatchewan Grain Growers Association officially withdraws from politics.
1924 Dec 17	The founding convention of the Farmers' Political Association is held. (The FPA is defunct in 1925.)
1926 July 15	The founding convention of the United Farmers of Canada (Saskatchewan Section) is held, amalgamating the FUC and SGGA.
1926 July	The Farmers' Educational League (left-wing activists of the FUC) begins meeting.
1927	Benito Mussolini imposes a fascist police state in Italy.
1929	Williams becomes president and chair of the board of directors of the UFC(SS) at its convention.
1929 June 6	The Saskatchewan Liberal government is defeated and replaced by "the Co-operative Government," a coalition of Tories, Progressives, and Independents.
1929 Sep 9	J.T.M. Anderson and the Co-operative Government take office in Saskatchewan.
1929 Oct 29	The stock market crashes.
1930 Feb	At convention, the UFC(SS) passes a resolution in favour of compulsory pooling and Williams is re-elected as president unanimously.
1930 Dec	Founding conventions of the Farmers' Unity League are held in five Western cities.
1931	The convention of the UFC(SS) creates the United Farmers' Political Association and elects Williams as leader of the Association.
1931 Feb 19	Fifteen thousand farmers demonstrate at the Saskatchewan Legislature in favor of compulsory pooling.
1931 Spring	Premier J.T.M. Anderson government passes the Grain Marketing Act, 1931, and the Referendum Act, 1931, and establishes the Saskatchewan Relief Commission.
1931 Mar/Apr	Williams attends an international wheat conference in Rome as the UFC(SS) representative, then travels to the Soviet Union.
1931 June	UFC(SS) delegates and Independent Labour Party (ILP) delegates vote to build a new political party with the goal of a cooperative commonwealth.

1931 Fall	The UFC(SS) sponsors Williams on a lecture tour across Saskatchewan, speaking about his visit to the Soviet Union.
1932 July 27	The UFC(SS) and the ILP come together to found a new provincial farmers' party—the Farmer-Labour Party (FLP)—with M. J. Coldwell as leader.
1932 Aug 1	A group of MPs, the League for Social Reconstruction, and various farm and labour organizations come together in Calgary to found a new national party— the Co-operative Commonwealth Federation of Canada (Farmer, Labour, Socialist)—with J. S. Woodsworth as leader.
1932 Nov 19	Williams is nominated for the FLP in the Wadena constituency.
1933 March	Adolf Hitler comes to power in Germany.
1933 July 19	The first national CCF convention is held in Regina. The *Regina Manifesto* is adopted.
1933 October	The Liberals defeat the CCF in a federal by-election in Saskatchewan.
1933	Shirley-Anne Williams, 18 months old, dies of meningitis.
1934 August	The Nazi Party in Germany imposes a legal dictatorship under Hitler.
1934 June 19	The Liberals win 50 of 55 seats, the FLP win 5 seats, in the Saskatchewan provincial election. Williams wins his Wadena seat. The FLP becomes the Official Opposition with Williams as House leader.
1934 July	The FLP adopts the name Co-operative Commonwealth Federation (Saskatchewan Section)—CCF(SS).
1935	Italy invades Abyssinia. Hitler claims the whole of Eastern Europe as German "living space." Both Germany and Italy intervene in the Spanish Civil War.
1935 April	Relief camps in British Columbia go on strike to protest living conditions, trekking first to Vancouver, and then heading east for Ottawa.
1935 June 14	The On to Ottawa Trekkers arrive in Regina.

1935 July 1	The Regina Riot ends the Trek. Two men die.
1935 Aug 22	William Aberhart's Social Credit Party sweeps the Alberta provincial election.
1935 Oct 14	The Liberals under William Lyon Mackenzie King win the federal election. In Saskatchewan, Social Credit and the CCF each win 2 rural seats. Social Credit wins 15 of 17 federal seats in Alberta.
1935 Dec 13	Coldwell, elected as MP for Rosetown-Biggar, resigns as CCF(SS) leader. Williams is appointed acting leader.
1936 Oct	Germany and Italy form a military alliance, the Rome-Berlin Axis.
1936 Jul 17	At the party convention, Williams is elected political leader and president of the CCF(SS).
1937	Williams works toward cooperation with Social Credit in Saskatchewan, but is unsuccessful.
1937 July 9	At the provincial CCF convention, Williams urges delegates to support the Republican side in the Spanish Civil War.
1938	Germany and Japan form an alliance.
1938 Jan	In a province-wide radio broadcast, Williams attacks Social Credit.
1938 April	The CCF(SS)'s newspaper—*Saskatchewan Commonwealth*—is established.
1938 June 8	The Liberals win 38 of 52 seats in the provincial election in Saskatchewan; the CCF wins 10 seats, and Social Credit, 2. Williams wins his Wadena seat, and continues as leader of the Official Opposition.
1938 Sept	Britain and France allow Germany to annex Sudetenland, part of Czechoslovakia.
1938 Fall	Williams leases out his farmland and moves his family to Regina.
1939	The Republicans in Spain are defeated, replaced by a military dictatorship under General Franco.
1939 March	Germany invades the rest of Czechoslovakia.
1939 Aug 23	Germany and the Soviet Union sign a non-aggression pact.
1939 Sept 1	Germany invades Poland.

1939 Sept 3   France and Britain declare war on Germany.

1939 Sept 6–8   The CCF national council convenes an emergency
                session to formulate their position on the war.
                Woodsworth is a pacifist and opposes any involvement.
                Williams believes that full support is necessary in the
                face of fascism. The council decides to support the
                Allies economically, but declines to send troops.

1939 Sept 10   Canada declares war on Germany.

1940 Mar 26   Mackenzie King's Liberals are re-elected. The CCF
                wins 5 seats in Saskatchewan, and one each in British
                Columbia, Manitoba, and Nova Scotia.

1940 May   Williams decides to enlist and try to get posted
                overseas.

1941 Jan   Williams is informed of his overseas posting.

1941 Feb   Williams resigns as party president, but continues as
                official leader of the Opposition, with Brockelbank as
                acting leader.

1941 July   At the CCF(SS) party convention, T.C. Douglas is
                nominated for president; Williams is nominated *in
                absentia.* Douglas wins.

1942 March   Woodsworth dies.

1942 April   The CCF urges a "yes" vote in the national plebiscite on
                conscription, embracing full support for the war effort.

1942 July   At the CCF(SS) party convention, Douglas runs for
                leader. Williams is nominated *in absentia.* Douglas wins.

1942 July   Coldwell succeeds Woodsworth as leader of the
                national CCF.

1943   Williams is promoted to major and as commanding
                officer of the Canadian Ordnance Reinforcement Unit
                is involved in planning for the D-Day invasion of
                Europe.

1944 March   Williams undergoes a medical examination, is
                diagnosed with high blood pressure, and is ordered to
                go on complete rest.

1944 April   The CCF provincial executive requests Williams's
                immediate return to fight the provincial election.
                Williams is sent home with a medical discharge.

1944 June 15	In the provincial election in Saskatchewan the CCF is elected with 47 of 52 seats. T.C. Douglas is the first CCF premier of the province. Williams wins his seat in Wadena.
1944 July 3	Premier Douglas offers Williams his choice of cabinet positions. Williams opts for Agriculture.
1944 July 13	At the end of a long day of meetings and speeches, Williams collapses and later suffers a stroke. The family journeys to British Columbia so that Williams can have complete rest.
1944 Oct 19	The first legislative session of the new government begins. The Farm Security Act and the Trade Union Act are passed.
1945 Feb 10	Williams resigns from cabinet, unable to resume his duties.
1945	The Crown Corporations Act is passed.
1945 Jun 11	The CCF wins 18 of 21 federal seats in Saskatchewan.
1945 May 6	The Allies declare victory in Europe.
1945 Aug 15	The Allies declare victory over Japan.
1945 Sept 12	George Hara Williams dies in Capilano, British Columbia.

ABBREVIATIONS

BNA Act	British North America Act
CCA	Canadian Council of Agriculture
CCF(SS)	Co-operative Commonwealth Federation (Saskatchewan Section)
CCYM	Co-operative Commonwealth Youth Movement
CMA	Canadian Manufacturers' Association
CP	Communist Party
CPR	Canadian Pacific Railway
FEL	Farmers' Educational League
FLP	Farmer-Labour Party
FPA	Farmers' Political Association
FUC	Farmers' Union of Canada
FUL	Farmers' Unity League
ILP	Independent Labour Party
IWW	Industrial Workers of the World
KKK	Ku Klux Klan
LPP	Labour Progressive Party
LSR	League for Social Reconstruction
MGGA	Manitoba Grain Growers' Association
MLA	Member of the Legislative Assembly
MP	Member of Parliament
NPAM	Non-Permanent Active Militia
OBU	One Big Union

PAS	Provincial Archives of Saskatchewan
RCMP	Royal Canadian Mounted Police
SFPA	Saskatchewan Farmers' Political Association
SGGA	Saskatchewan Grain Growers' Association
TLC	Trades and Labour Congress
UFA	United Farmers of Alberta
UFC(SS)	United Farmers of Canada (Saskatchewan Section)
UFM	United Farmers of Manitoba
UFO	United Farmers of Ontario
UFPA	United Farmers' Political Association
USSR	Union of Soviet Socialist Republics
WUL	Workers' Unity League

Note: Most of these abbreviations are straightforward, with the exception of the FPA, the SFPA, and the UFPA. These have proven to be the bane of many scholars, creating considerable confusion. There was no continuity among the three organizations. The FPA was established by Williams in 1924 as a farmers' party to contest rural seats in the 1925 provincial election. Williams was censured by the FUC board and fired as an organizer for violating the FUC's opposition to electoral politics. The FPA was disbanded and did not contest the election. The SFPA was the resurrected Progressive Party, formed to contest the 1930 federal election. Williams did not throw the support of the UFC(SS) behind the SFPA; indeed, the UFC(SS) made it clear it did not support the organization. The UFPA was a political organization within the UFC(SS) established in 1931 under Williams's leadership to begin establishing constituency associations in rural areas for the new party, the FLP.

NOTES

Author's Note

1   In an effort to counter the received wisdom that points to the alleged moderation of the early CCF and its domination by a cautious middle-class leadership, James Naylor argues that the early CCF contained a large bloc of committed socialists dedicated to the abolition of capitalism and committed to "labour socialism." In his words, "Labour socialists, then, were revolutionaries, in the sense that they believed capitalism had to be supplanted by a working-class, socialist society." He points out that for those "who responded to the new opportunities presented by the Great Depression, the operative principle of political activity was class. It was a shared concept of class and class politics that informed their behavior." Naylor, *The Fate of Labour Socialism* (Toronto: University of Toronto Press, 2016), 10, 14. In the case of Williams, this commitment to class and class politics in the reality of Saskatchewan, according to his left agrarian populism, must include small and medium-sized farmers. His project was to persuade the organized farmers of Saskatchewan not only to embrace socialism, but also to form an alliance with the working class to achieve that goal.

2   *Are They To Be Trusted?*, CCF pamphlet, 1938 Election, CCF Pamphlet Collection, Provincial Archives of Saskatchewan (formerly called the Saskatchewan Archives Board), Regina (hereafter PAS). Copy in possession of the author.

Prologue. George Hara Williams: A Word Portrait

1   Section 98 was added to the Criminal Code in the aftermath of the Winnipeg General Strike. The existing sedition law, which was used against eleven

of the strike's leaders, was not considered robust enough to effectively and lawfully suppress and contain the growing left-wing sentiments and activities of militant trade unions and various labour and socialist parties. Only seven were convicted and the sentences imposed were light, ranging from six months to two years. Section 98 was particularly draconian, making it a criminal offence punishable by up to twenty years in prison to be a member of "an unlawful association." "An unlawful association" was defined as one that advocates the use of force to achieve "governmental, industrial or economic change," or one that "teaches, advocates, advises or defends" force to make such changes. Attending a meeting of "an unlawful association" was considered *prima facie* proof of membership, with the onus on the accused to prove he or she was not a member. Section 98 was used primarily to suppress the Communist Party, but was also selectively applied to socialist parties and militant trade unions throughout the 1920s and, most zealously, in the 1930s. The most infamous use of Section 98 was the 1931 effort to crush the CP by arresting and convicting eight major party leaders and imprisoning them for five years. Public opinion, aroused by a coalition of civil rights groups, turned against the abuse of Section 98. Nevertheless, the law continued to be used to harass leaders and organizers of demonstrations, hunger marches, sit-ins, and strikes in a cat-and-mouse game. Leaders and organizers were arrested under Section 98, held briefly until the strike or sit-in had been suppressed, and then released without charge. This political abuse of the law by the government aroused great public opposition. The newly elected Liberal government of Mackenzie King repealed Section 98 in 1936.

Chapter 1. George Hara Williams: Roots to 1921

1   Williams's discharge certificate from the army listed his occupation as "Book-Keeper." Copy in possession of the author.

2   The sources for the material on Canada in the First World War are provided in the bibliographic note for chapter 1.

3   Canadian casualties in the early battles were as follows: Ypres, in 1915 (2,000 dead; 4,000 wounded); the Somme, 1916 (8,000 dead; 16,000 wounded); Vimy Ridge, 1917 (3,500 dead; 7,000 wounded); and Passchendaele, 1917 (4,000 dead; 15,000 wounded). By war's end, Canada's tally was 66,600 dead and 172,000 wounded. Casualty figures were obtained from the Canadian Great War Project (http://www.canadiangreatwarproject.com/). The final figures on Canadian casualties were announced at the centenary memorial of World War I in Ottawa in 2014.

4   "The organized farmers" refers to the large organizations of farmers built between the turn of the century and the 1920s. These included the United Farmers of Ontario (originally the Ontario Grange), the United Farmers of Manitoba (originally the Manitoba Grain Growers' Association), the

Saskatchewan Grain Growers' Association (SGGA), the Farmers' Union of Canada (FUC), the United Farmers of Canada (Saskatchewan Section) [UFC(SS)], and the United Farmers of Alberta (UFA). The UFC(SS) was created by the fusion of the FUC and the SGGA. These organizations united in a national organization, the Canadian Council of Agriculture (CCA), which organized the Progressive Party's populist challenge to "the old-line parties," as they were called, in the 1921 federal election.

5   There is no record of the books on socialism Williams read during his convalescence. We have a pretty good idea of the probable list from Ian McKay's *Reasoning Otherwise* (Toronto: Between the Lines, 2008), esp. chap. 1 ("Socialism: The Revolutionary Science of Social Evolution") and chap. 3 ("The Class Question"). Whatever Williams read, his writings, speeches, and tactical manoeuvres reveal the essential, core socialism he embraced until his death. He was also persuaded that a scientific approach to the study of the economy and society, including an evolutionary perspective, was fundamental to understanding the trajectory of history. This ideological foundation informed his approach to work within the agrarian populist movement. It was the firm goal, often unspoken, of his political work from the beginning. He left us a record of his socialist vision in a booklet published in 1939, *Social Democracy in Canada*. Williams embraced the central ideological commitments of the left wing of the socialist movement of his era: class struggle as the engine of historical progress; public ownership of the commanding heights of the economy, natural resources , transportation systems, and utilities; the working class, and the other large popular class, small and medium farmers, uniting to win socialism through democratic means; laws to encourage trade unions and to protect workers from excessive exploitation; a universal cradle-to-grave system of social programs to give all economic security and the means for a decent life. The ultimate objective was the abolition of capitalism and the achievement of a socialist society.

6   Muriel Wiens, *Finding George Williams: A Tale of the Grass Roots* (unpublished manuscript, 2007) (hereafter, Wiens ms.), 4, Williams papers, PAS.

7   Wiens ms., 2006 version, 5.

Chapter 2. The Political and Economic Context: The Rise of the United Farmers of Canada (Saskatchewan Section), 1922 to 1926

1   The more militant elements of the working class embarked on a sustained class offensive in the later war years, involving battles against conscription and an illegal strike movement with considerable support. When the postwar depression hit, labour began to fight for union recognition and collective bargaining rights, resisting employers' demands for pay cuts and layoffs. In Western Canada, moderate trade union leaders, centred in the old craft

unions, began to be replaced by a new generation of union leaders proposing
syndicalism, industrial unionism, and militant strike tactics, including general
and sympathetic strikes. These leaders also took strong political positions,
often openly declaring support for radical socialism and communism. This
class mobilization culminated in the March 1919 Western Canada Labour
Conference in Calgary. Almost every Western Canadian trade union was
represented. A decision to secede from the moderate national Trades and
Labour Congress (TLC) and to form a western labour central, the One Big
Union (OBU), was passed overwhelmingly. The conference endorsed industrial
unionism, the tactics of general and sympathetic strikes, as well as making a
series of immediate demands under the threat of a June 1, 1919, general strike.
The conference endorsed socialism, calling for the abolition of capitalism, and
applauded the Bolsheviks in Russia and the Spartacists in Germany. The stage
was set for a serious confrontation between capital and labour, particularly
in the West. In early May 1919, the metal and building trades in Winnipeg
went on strike for union recognition, the eight-hour day, and improved wages.
The employers refused to bargain. The striking workers asked the Winnipeg
Labour Council for support, whereupon the council held a general strike vote
among all Winnipeg trade unions, demanding a living wage, the eight-hour
day, and union recognition backed up by signed collective agreements. A
strong majority vote to strike. The walkout started on May 15, when twenty-
four thousand trade unionists went on strike. Soon thousands of Winnipeg's
non-union workers joined them. It became a general strike. Across the country
tens of thousands of workers joined in sympathetic strikes, involving eighty
strikes and over eighty-eight thousand workers, mostly in Western Canada.
Soon thousands of veterans went on the march in support of the strike, over
ten thousand on one occasion in Winnipeg. This active and growing support
among veterans, who were, as a group, deeply divided by the strike, boosted
the morale among strikers. Among government officials it created dread. If
the veterans were to go over to the strike actively and en masse, many officials
believed, the situation could get seriously out of control, with ominous and
unforeseen results. The Bennett Ottawa government was convinced it faced
a revolutionary situation and acted accordingly. RCMP, regular military, and
militia reinforcements were dispatched to Winnipeg, including an armoured
car and an estimated twenty machine-gun squads. The entire Winnipeg police
force, with the exception of the officers and two constables, was dismissed
because of sympathy for the strike. They were replaced by special constables
largely recruited from among Winnipeg's middle and upper classes, anti-strike
veterans, and farmers. Their inexperience, excessive zeal, and unnecessary
brutality created confusion and violence. Firings of strikers spread, especially
among the civil service. In Ottawa a series of legal measures was put in place to
aid authorities in breaking the strike on the grounds the strike was seditious,
including an amendment to the Criminal Code allowing the deportation of
foreign-born agitators, passed in less than twenty minutes. Section 133 of

the code was repealed, erasing the guarantee of freedom of speech. On June 17, six of the most prominent strike leaders were arrested, as well as five other militants from various unions and socialist parties, and charged with sedition. The expected collapse of the strike did not occur. Protest and support increased in the West and began to grow across the country. Demands now included the release of those arrested. Violent police baton attacks on peaceful demonstrations had the effect of redoubling support for the strike. On June 21 a silent parade to protest the arrests and the police violence was called. The Riot Act was read and the parade of men, women, and children was attacked by RCMP officers and special constables on horseback swinging baseball bats. When this failed to disperse the crowd, the police drew their guns and began firing indiscriminately into the crowd—two were killed, thirty injured, and one hundred arrested. Military rule was imposed on the city, as armed military units patrolled the streets and machine-gun nests became common on the streets. The strike was broken, and as the defeated, but still defiant, workers went back to work they faced severe economic reprisals: firings, pay cuts, demotions. This suppression of the strike was buttressed by a series of nighttime raids of offices of trade unions, ethnic associations, and socialist parties and the homes of trade union and socialist leaders. This occurred not only in Winnipeg but all across Canada, breaking in doors, searching homes, seizing records, files, books, papers, membership lists, and correspondence. These actions were justified by the authorities as necessary to collect evidence for the sedition trials. Eight strike leaders were charged with seditious conspiracy. Seven of the eight were found guilty: one was sentenced to two years, five to one year, and one to six months. The message was clear: determined industrial action by trade unions, especially if it became generalized, would be repressed by all means necessary. Agitations for a living wage, an eight-hour day, and collective bargaining rights were declared seditious. The OBU reached its peak in membership during and immediately following the strike, with 50,000 members (there were about 380,000 trade union members in all of Canada in 1919 out of a workforce of two million). Thereafter, the OBU declined and was replaced by more moderate trade unions. Advocates of moderate socialist politics made great gains in elections immediately following the strike. In 1920 in Manitoba, Labour elected eleven MLAs, including three imprisoned strike leaders, and in 1922, six Labour MLAs were re-elected. In Winnipeg, Labour candidates won three seats on the school board and three on city council. Federally, two strike leaders were elected as MPs in Winnipeg, one in 1921, joined by a colleague in 1925. In the aftermath of the strike, trade unions began to gain general recognition across Canada. See J. F. Conway, *The Rise of the New West* (Toronto: Lorimer, 2014), chap. 5 ("Socialism and Syndicalism: The Rise of the Working Class, 1870–1919," pp. 85–90).

2   These figures were derived from 1911 and 1921 census reports; George V. Haythorne, *Labour in Canadian Agriculture* (Cambridge, MA: Harvard University Press, 1965), 9; and M. C. Urquhart and K. A. H. Buckley, eds.,

Historical Statistics of Canada (Toronto: Macmillan, 1965), 351, 354–55, 364. The 49,000 farm wage labour figure is from 1911.

3 The platform is reproduced in W. L. Morton, *The Progressive Party in Canada* (Toronto: University of Toronto Press, 1957), 298.

4 Quoted in Robert Craig Brown and Ramsay Cook, *Canada, 1896–1921* (Toronto: McClelland & Stewart, 1974), 159.

5 J. A. Flavelle, a Toronto meatpacker, wrote the letter; quoted in ibid., 160.

6 Quoted in ibid., 161.

7 Quoted in Paul Stevens, ed., *The 1911 General Election* (Toronto: Copp Clark, 1970), 2.

8 Hopkins Moorhouse, *Deep Furrows* (Toronto: G. J. McLeod, [c.1918]), 244–47, 281–86, 289–92. Moorhouse was a leading agrarian populist scholar and propagandist.

9 Paul F. Sharp, *The Agrarian Revolt in Western Canada* (Minneapolis: University of Minnesota, 1948), 138.

10 Moorhouse, *Deep Furrows*, 289–92.

11 The text of the New National Policy is provided in Morton, *Progressive Party*, 302–6.

12 W. L. Morton, *Manitoba: A History* (Toronto: University of Toronto Press, 1967), 397.

13 Quoted in Duff Spafford, "The Origins of the Farmers' Union of Canada," *Saskatchewan History* 18, no. 3 (1965): 89.

14 *Constitution and By-laws*, Farmers' Union of Canada, 1925, Farmers' Union of Canada Papers, PAS.

15 The texts of the two platforms are compared and discussed in Spafford, "Origins of the Farmers Union."

16 Sifton is quoted in David E. Smith, *Prairie Liberalism* (Toronto: University of Toronto Press, 1975), 99.

17 *Debt Adjustment Plan, Farmers' Union of Canada*, 1923 FUC Convention, FUC papers, PAS.

18 G. H. Williams, "Provincial Politics," *Western Producer*, March 26, 1925.

19 The complete FPA platform was published in the *Western Producer*, December 18, 1924. The core position is taken from a submission by Williams to the *Western Producer*, February 16, 1925.

20 George Williams, undated letter, quoted in Wiens ms., 8.

Chapter 3. Leading the Farmers into Politics: 1926 to 1931

1 Farmers' Educational League manifesto, UFC Pamphlet Collection, PAS.

2 George Edwards to M. N. Campbell, March 5, 1928, quoted in Friedrich Steininger, "George H. Williams: Agrarian Socialist" (MA thesis, University of Regina, 1976) (hereafter, Steininger thesis), 37.

3   UFC(SS), *Constitution and Bylaws*, 1927, UFC(SS) papers, PAS.

4   UFC(SS), *Report of Proceedings of the Third Annual Convention of the United Farmers of Canada*, February 12–15, 1929, and *Summary of Resolutions Passed at the 1929 Convention of the U.F.C.*, both at UFC(SS) papers, PAS.

5   UFC(SS), *Summary of Resolutions Passed*.

6   UFC(SS), *Report of Proceedings*.

7   Saskatoon *Star-Phoenix*, March 12, 1929.

8   Minutes, UFC(SS) executive meetings, 1926 to 1949, UFC(SS) papers, PAS. The decision to issue the statement was reported at the board meeting following the confrontation (June 19 to 24, 1929).

9   George Edwards to John Wellbelove, April 6, 1929, in Steininger thesis, 39.

10   The text of the radio broadcast was printed in the *Western Producer*, August 21, 1930.

11   UFC(SS), *Applications for Reductions in the Tariff*, 1927, and Research Department, UFC(SS), *Facts, Information and Arguments Regarding the Tariff*, 1929, both in UFC(SS) papers, PAS.

12   *Western Producer*, September 28, 1930.

13   *Western Producer*, October 30, 1930.

14   Leo D. E. Courville, "The Saskatchewan Progressives" (MA thesis, University of Regina, 1971), 34, 105.

15   Smith, *Prairie Liberalism*, chap. 5 ("The Beleaguered Machine: Liberal Politics, 1918–1929").

16   For questions about, and evidence of, patronage and corruption, see *Journals*, Saskatchewan Legislature, 1923–29, vols. 20–27.

17   The material on the Klan is based on William Calderwood, "The Rise and Fall of the Ku Klux Klan in Saskatchewan" (MA thesis, University of Regina, 1968).

18   The data on the Depression's devastating impact are from the *Submission of the Province of Saskatchewan to the Royal Commission on Dominion-Provincial Relations* (Regina: King's Printer, 1937), 107, 139, 145, 148, 169, 172–73, 177–79, 194.

19   James Shaver (J. S.) Woodsworth (1874–1942), a Methodist preacher and proponent of the social gospel, worked to help poor and immigrant workers and their families in north Winnipeg beginning in the early 1900s. His political convictions turned leftward, and by World War I he was a militant, democratic socialist and a strong supporter of the right of the working class to organize trade unions. An absolute and principled pacifist, he opposed conscription in 1917, resigning his post as a clergyman when his church supported the war. He remained a principled pacifist until his death in 1942, including opposing Canada's involvement in World War II. He was among those arrested during the 1919 Winnipeg General Strike. He was charged with sedition, but the Crown quickly dropped the charges. In 1921 he was elected to the House of Commons on the Independent Labour Party ticket, representing a working-class district in Winnipeg's North End. He joined with other left-leaning MPs to form the Ginger Group. A firm anti-communist,

Woodsworth became the leading and most respected advocate of democratic socialism, attaining leadership of the national CCF in 1932.

20 Minutes of the Annual UFC Convention of 1930, UFC(SS) papers, PAS.

21 The "far left" refers to members of the Communist Party (CP) and those influenced by the party in the Farmers' Educational League (FEL), a left caucus in the United Farmers of Canada (Saskatchewan Section) (UFC[SS]), and the Farmers' Unity League (FUL), a CP front committed to organizing farmers. The FEL dissolved itself and joined in founding the FUL in 1930. The FUL enjoyed growing support among desperate farmers as the Depression worsened. It held large public educational meetings and protest rallies throughout rural areas; it also led numerous direct action protests to break up sheriff sales of foreclosed farmers' land and machinery. Minutes of UFC(SS) conventions attest to the far left's influence. Their interventions in debates were often successful in swaying a meeting to adopt strong left-wing positions. There was a great overlap between the left, led by Williams, and the far left, since both political tendencies supported strong socialist measures. Williams had an uneasy relationship with the far left because his strongest supporters had been active in the FEL. Indeed, Williams was a central figure in organizing the left caucus, and the FEL was instrumental in electing Williams as president of the UFC(SS) in 1929. Relations between Williams and the far left deteriorated when they joined the right to push (unsuccessfully) the UFC(SS) into what Williams considered premature political action. They deteriorated further when FEL dissolved and established a Saskatchewan branch of the FUL. Williams viewed this as a serious split on the broad left that jeopardized the emergence of a large and popular socialist party. The CP remained a small but influential force in farm politics. The rural areas encompassed by Nottakew-Willowbunch, in the south of the Palliser Triangle, and Meadow Lake, on the fringe of parkland in the north, were among the hardest hit during the Depression, and the constituencies of Nottakew-Willowbunch and Meadow Lake represented two large concentrations of CP members and supporters active in the CCF. For more on the relationship between the CP and the CCF in the 1930s, see Peter R. Sinclair, "The Saskatchewan CCF and the Communist Party in the 1930s," *Saskatchewan History* 26, no. 1 (1973): 1–10.

22 Minutes, UFC 1930 convention, pp. 234, 271–72, UFC(SS) papers, PAS.

23 Minutes, UFC(SS) executive meeting, March 8–10, 1930, UFC(SS) papers, PAS.

24 *Western Producer*, October 30, 1930.

25 The article and the letter defending Williams are in the Williams family private papers.

26 "Preamble of the Aims of the Farmers' Unity League," in Ivor J. Mills, *Stout Hearts Stand Tall* (Vancouver: Evergreen, 1971), 194.

27 "In Reply to George Williams," *The Furrow*, January 3, 1931.

28 "Open Letter to the Editor, *The Furrow*," *Western Producer*, December 18, 1930.

29 Williams, Memorandum to the Executive, n.d., UFC(SS) papers, PAS.

30 *Western Producer*, October 2, 1930.
31 G. Bickerton, a prominent member supporting the Wilkie Charter, in Steininger thesis, 70. For more on the charter, see F. W. Anderson, "Farmers in Politics, 1915–1935" (MA thesis, University of Saskatchewan, 1949), 149.
32 Williams, "What of Tomorrow?," *Western Producer*, February 12, 1931.
33 Williams, presidential address; this and what follows are from Minutes of the Annual UFC Convention of 1931, UFC(SS) papers, PAS. The approved political platform was published in the *Western Producer* as "The New Economic Policy," March 19, 1931.
34 UFC(SS), *Economic Policy (Saskatchewan): as formulated by the Delegates Assembled in Annual Convention, 1932; Economic Policy and Convention Resolutions*, Seventh Annual Convention, 1932; *The Evolution of a Policy*, 1932; *Land Nationalization Program of the UFC*, 1933, all in UFC(SS) papers, PAS.
35 Joseph Lee ("Joe") Phelps (1899–1983) was born to a farm family near Belleville, Ontario, that moved to Saskatchewan in 1908 to homestead in the Wilkie area. When his older brother went overseas in World War I and his father fell ill, Phelps, still in his teens, took over running the family farm. Besides working as a farmer, Phelps trained in telephone repair and worked for the Narrow Lake Telephone Company, using this off-farm income to help sustain the family farm. He embraced radical agrarian populism and quickly rose to leadership positions in his district, first in the SGGA and then in the FUC. He became a prominent leader and activist in the FUC and then in the UFC(SS). He was a strong supporter of Williams, despite a brief falling-out over Williams's opposition to the secessionist clause of the Wilkie Charter. In 1938, Phelps ran for the CCF in Saltcoats and won. He played a key role in the caucus under Williams's leadership, particularly in preparing an aggressive public ownership program, most importantly of natural resources and their development. He was re-elected in the 1944 CCF sweep, becoming minister of natural resources and industrial development. From 1944 to 1948, Phelps spearheaded the CCF's ambitious public ownership plans, creating many Crown corporations and pushing forward on public ownership of natural resource development and rural electrification. Key members of the right of the party, including provincial treasurer Clarence Fines, advocated the abandonment of public ownership of resources. In the 1948 election, the party fell from the 53 per cent won in 1944 to 48 percent, losing sixteen seats including Phelps's Saltcoats seat. The party leadership saw this as clear evidence that a moderation of the party's program was essential. The party abandoned public ownership of natural resource development as the anchor of its economic policy. The party establishment blocked efforts to find Phelps another seat, and he was thus frozen out of the caucus and hence the cabinet. He returned to his roots as a radical agrarian leader, convincing the UFC(SS) to reorganize as the Saskatchewan Farmers' Union. Phelps became president and revitalized the organization, with a membership exceeding fifty

thousand in the early 1950s. From this position, Phelps continued to agitate for progressive social and economic change. See Kathleen Carlisle, *Fiery Joe* (Regina: University of Regina Press, 2017). The quotation is from the minutes of the 1931 UFC(SS) convention.

36 "Williams Likely to Marshall New Party," *Western Producer*, March 5, 1931.

37 "The Convention," *Western Producer*, March 12, 1931.

38 Canadian Press, March 1, 1931.

39 Williams, *The Land of the Soviets* (Saskatoon: United Farmers of Canada, Saskatchewan Section, 1931), 7, 64.

40 *Mercury* (Estevan), October 8, 1931.

41 "Many Hear Lecture on Soviet Land," *Mercury* (Estevan), October 22, 1931.

Chapter 4. Building the CCF: Leadership Lost and Regained, 1931 to 1936

1 Major James ("M. J.") Coldwell (1888–1974), an immigrant from England, was a leader and founder of the urban wing of the Progressive Party in Saskatchewan. He was a high school teacher and principal in Regina; elected alderman on a reform platform, he served on city council from 1922 to 1932. He was a leading organizer of teachers' associations from 1924 to 1934, championing the right of teachers to negotiate their pay and working conditions. Although prepared to work together for the movement, Williams and Coldwell neither respected nor liked each other due to some basic and long-standing political differences. Coldwell, as a prominent member and leader of the Progressive Party, shared the view widely held among his political colleagues that Williams's refusal to throw the UFC(SS)'s political support behind Progressive candidates in the 1929 provincial and 1930 federal elections was the major cause of their humiliating failure at the polls. Williams was too uncomfortably left wing and agrarian populist for Coldwell. Williams saw Coldwell as typical of the overly moderate element in the movement, who sought opportunities for electoral success above all else. Though Williams admired Coldwell's ability as what he called "a platform socialist," able to give rousing speeches, he considered Coldwell inept as a fundraiser and organizer. The relationship between Coldwell and Williams worsened after the founding of the FLP, most notably after the 1934 election.

2 "United Farmers Hold Successful Convention," *Western Producer*, March 3, 1932; UFC(SS), *Economic Policy, 1932*, UFC(SS) papers, PAS; "UFC Political Policy," *Western Producer*, May 3, 1932.

3 The Ginger Group initially broke with the Progressive Party in 1924 over the party's support for the budget of King's Liberal government. The group initially included six UFA MPs from Alberta and one UFO MP from Ontario; it was later joined by four Labour MPs, including Woodsworth. The group formed the parliamentary nexus around which the CCF was formed. Walter

Young, in *The Anatomy of a Party* (Toronto: University of Toronto Press, 1969), reports, "On May 26, 1932, the members of the group met in William Irvine's office, which served as the group's caucus room, and agreed to extend their parliamentary organization into the country at large [members of the LSR were also present]. They decided to set up a federation of groups to promote cooperation between the constituent organizations in the provinces. The new organization was to be called the 'Commonwealth Party'" (p. 30). Organizational duties were assigned in the provinces across the country. Coldwell was assigned to organize Saskatchewan.

4   The League for Social Reconstruction (LSR) was a group of left-leaning academics centred at the University of Toronto and McGill University in Montreal. Providing the intellectual foundation for Canada's emerging democratic socialist movement, they advised the CCF on policy issues. Though the group had long worked together informally, in 1932 they established the organization. The group's analyses and policy proposals, essentially advocating the construction of a welfare state and a Keynesian approach to economic planning, also began to influence the federal Liberal Party. The league's most influential publication was *Social Planning for Canada* (Toronto: Thomas Nelson and Sons, 1935). The LSR also published *Canadian Forum*, the leading democratic socialist magazine in Canada. The LSR continued as a left-leaning think tank until 1942.

5   *Western Producer*, May 3, 1932.

6   UFC(SS), Minutes of the Annual Convention of July 25-26, 1932, and Minutes of the First Annual Joint Political Convention, July 27, 1932, both in UFC(SS) papers, PAS. For a summary of the meetings, see "UFC and ILP Launch a Farmer-Labour Alliance," *Western Producer*, August 4, 1932; and "Highlights of the Convention," *Western Producer*, August 11, 1932.

7   Louise Lucas (1885–1945) was a leading feminist who prided herself on working the farm as an equal partner with her husband, Henry. They immigrated from Germany in 1911, finally settling at Mazenod, Saskatchewan, in 1920. She became active in the UFC(SS) and was elected to the board of directors in 1930 and then was president of the women's section from 1931 to1933. She was a strong opponent of Williams, particularly of him becoming leader of the party. After the effort to oust Williams became open in 1940, however, Lucas switched to supporting Williams against what she called "the Ottawa boys." She was an outstanding orator, touring the province on behalf of the UFC(SS) and then the FLP/CCF. She unsuccessfully ran in the federal elections of 1935 and 1940. Her illness and death in 1945 prevented her from winning the Melville seat in 1945. John Evans (1867–1958) was a farmer, an activist in the UFC(SS), and a successful Progressive politician. He was elected on the Progressive ticket for Saskatoon in 1921 and then for Rosetown in 1925 and 1926; he was defeated in 1930, and unsuccessfully ran for the CCF in Saskatoon in 1935. Like most leaders of the Progressives in Saskatchewan, he was an opponent of Williams. Andrew Macauley (1887–

1939) moved to Saskatchewan from Ontario in 1905. He worked as a farm labourer before becoming a farmer and rancher. He was an activist and leader of the UFC(SS) and a friend, collaborator, and close confidante of Williams—a member of Williams's leadership circle from the outset. In 1931, Macauley succeeded Williams as president of the UFC(SS). In 1934 he was one of the five FLP candidates elected to the legislature. In 1938 he lost his bid for re-election. He died suddenly of a brain tumour the next year.

8　Archibald Key, "Creating a National Federation," *Canadian Forum*, September 1932, 451–52.

9　Dorothy Steeves, *The Compassionate Rebel* (Vancouver: Evergreen, 1960).

10　Frank Underhill (1889–1971) and Eugene Forsey (1904–1991) were prominent members of the LSR. Underhill, a historian, was educated at the University of Toronto and Oxford University before teaching history first at the University of Saskatchewan and then at the University of Toronto. His flirtation with left-wing politics was brief, fuelled by the Depression crisis. He was the founding president of the LSR, but returned permanently to the Liberal Party in the 1940s. Forsey studied at McGill and Oxford. He went to Oxford a Tory and returned to Canada a democratic socialist. He remained committed to social democracy for the rest of his life, remaining active in the CCF and the NDP. He broke with the NDP in 1961 over its support of the "two nations" doctrine on the status of Quebec in Confederation. He became a Liberal supporter for a time, initially attracted by Trudeau's constitutional initiatives, but left the party over its constitutional policies in the early 1980s. McGill fired Forsey for his political radicalism in 1941. After a brief stint studying at Harvard, Forsey became the research director of the newly formed Canadian Congress of Labour, the forerunner of the Canadian Labour Congress. His PhD dissertation—which addressed the constitutional crisis provoked in 1926 when Governor General Lord Byng refused Prime Minister Mackenzie King's request for the dissolution of Parliament and the calling of a general election—was published by Oxford University, establishing Forsey's credentials as a constitutional expert. He remained one of the most prolific commentators on Canadian politics, publishing many books and articles—a perfect example of the "public intellectual," providing guidance to civil society on the pressing issues of the day. Forsey retired from the CLC in 1969, and Trudeau appointed him to the Senate in 1970.

11　We will probably never solve the mystery of who wrote the phrase. All members of the LSR were involved in the drafting and redrafting of the manifesto. Williams never claimed authorship, though the economic policy he wrote for the UFC and FLP clearly had a big impact on the manifesto. Many believed he was likely the author. No one among the LSR intellectuals claimed authorship. In the days just prior to the convention, members of the National Council of the CCF, which included Williams, met for hours with LSR members to fine-tune the draft. It is quite likely the phrase got included during these meetings. In 1979, J. King Gordon, a prominent LSR member who had attended the founding convention, reported a vague recollection of perhaps drafting the phrase with Frank Scott over lunch at a Regina restaurant on the eve of the convention; he recalled that their desire was to give the manifesto a "ringing challenge at the end." Eileen R. Jantzen, *Growing to One World* (Montreal/Kingston: McGill-Queen's University Press, 2013), 94.

12   UFC(SS), *Economic Policy and Convention Resolutions, Seventh Annual Convention 1932*, UFC(SS) papers, PAS.

13   Quoted in G. J. Hoffman, "The Saskatchewan Provincial Election of 1934" (MA thesis, University of Regina, 1973), 50.

14   Quoted in George Hoffman, "The Saskatchewan Farmer-Labour Party, 1932–1934," *Saskatchewan History* 28, no. 2 (1974): 57.

15   Anderson is quoted in Peter A. Russell, "The Co-operative Government in Saskatchewan, 1929–1934" (MA thesis, University of Saskatchewan, 1970), 48.

16   Data on the impact of the Depression are from the *Saskatchewan Submission to the Royal Commission on Dominion Provincial Relations*, 1937, see chap. 3, n18. The data on the numbers on relief, the province's expenditures on relief, and the farm debt problem are from the following: Blair Neatby, "The Saskatchewan Relief Commission, 1931–1943," *Saskatchewan History* 3, no. 2 (1950): 41–56; Alma Lawton, "Urban Relief in Saskatchewan during the Years of the Depression, 1930–1937" (MA thesis, University of Saskatchewan, 1969); W. Allen and C. C. Hope, *The Farm Outlook in Saskatchewan* (Saskatoon: University of Saskatchewan, 1933); and *The Census of Agriculture, 1931* (1932). All figures on the price of wheat are from the province's 1937 submission to the Royal Commission, noted above, p. 177. Evidence on the occurrence of starvation is provided in Hoffman, "Saskatchewan Provincial Election," 22–24. The Depression remedies of the Anderson government are outlined in Russell, "Co-operative Government."

17   *Journals*, Saskatchewan Legislature, 1934, vol. 32, 7–8.

18   This and quotations in the following paragraph are from pamphlets titled *Relief; A Merciless Mess of Mismanagement and the Way Out*; and *Supplementary Platform Resolutions of the Saskatchewan Liberal Party, 1934 Election*. Liberal Party Pamphlet Collection, 1934 Election, PAS.

19   Quotations are from the pamphlets *Is Your Home Safe?* and *Declaration of Policy, Official Manifesto of the Saskatchewan Farmer-Labour Group, 1934 Election*. Farmer-Labour Party pamphlet collection, 1934 Election, PAS.

20   Williams to Sophie Dixon, October 28, 1933, in Wiens ms., 58.

21   W. D. Summers (provincial organizer) to F. Eliasan (campaign manager), in Steininger thesis, 134.

22   Agnes Macphail (1890–1954), a rural schoolteacher, was a member of the United Farmers of Ontario (becoming a prominent leader of its women's section), a member of the United Farm Women of Ontario, and a columnist for the UFO's newspaper, *The Farmers' Sun*. In 1921 she won election as a Progressive MP for the Ontario rural seat Grey Southeast, making history as the first woman elected to the House of Commons. She won re-election in

1925, 1926, and 1930. She joined the Ginger Group and became a founding member of the national CCF as well as the founding president of its Ontario section in 1932. She left the CCF in 1934 when the UFO withdrew, citing the excessive influence of the Communist Party in the Ontario CCF. Macphail remained active in the Ginger Group and the CCF caucus, continuing to attend meetings. She was treated as a *de facto* CCF member despite having run on a UFO-Labour ticket. The CCF did not field candidates against her. She formally rejoined the Ontario CCF in 1942, after her defeat as a federal MP in 1940. In 1943 she was elected as a CCF MPP in the Ontario legislature. She was defeated in 1945, re-elected in 1948, and defeated in 1951.

23 Hoffman, "Saskatchewan Provincial Election," 278, 284.

24 Farmer-Labour Party, Minutes of the Third Annual Convention of the Saskatchewan Farmer-Labour Party, July 27 and 28, 1934, FLP papers, PAS. The Coldwell quotes are from Hoffman, "Saskatchewan Provincial Election," 253; and Steininger thesis, 134.

25 F. Eliason (campaign manager in 1934 election) to Williams, March 9, 1932, in Steininger thesis, 133.

26 Thomas Clement (Tommy or T. C.) Douglas (1904–86), an immigrant from Scotland and a Baptist preacher and advocate of the social gospel, worked at a variety of trades in Winnipeg before enrolling in the Baptist-affiliated Brandon College, where he studied theology and sociology. After six years at the college he graduated with a BA in theology and an MA in sociology. He was radicalized by what he witnessed first as a teenager during the Winnipeg General Strike and later during the Depression. After graduating from Brandon College in 1930, now ordained, Douglas moved to Weyburn to serve the Calvary Baptist Church. He was twenty-six years old. He became active in the FLP/CCF; he ran unsuccessfully in the 1934 provincial election, but he was elected in 1935 to the House of Commons for Weyburn, a sprawling rural riding that included Weyburn, serving until 1944. In 1942 he successfully challenged George Williams for the leadership of the CCF while Williams, the incumbent leader, was serving overseas in the Canadian Army. In 1944, Douglas led the CCF to victory in Saskatchewan, where he served as premier until 1961. At that time, he became the first national leader of the New Democratic Party, formed when the Canadian Labour Congress affiliated with the CCF. He retired as leader in 1971, but continued to sit as an MP until 1979, when he retired from politics.

27 *Conference of Elected Members and Political Directive Board*, July 1934, in Steininger thesis, 145. Copy also in possession of the author.

28 Ibid.

29 Lewis H. Thomas, ed. *The Making of a Socialist: The Recollections of T. C. Douglas* (Edmonton: University of Alberta Press, 1982) (hereafter, Douglas, *Recollections*), 144.

30 Williams was speaking at an organization meeting in Wynyard (within the Wadena constituency) in July when he issued the warning, adding, "Do not

pick a candidate who doesn't know your platform, or who can be bought and sold." *Western Producer*, July 23, 1931, cited in Steininger thesis, 130.

31   Williams, "Address in Reply to the Speech from the Throne," *Journals*, Saskatchewan Legislature, 1935, vol. 33; see also Saskatchewan's *Scrapbook Hansard*, 1934–40, PAS.

32   Williams, *Social Democracy in Canada*, 55. Williams also published an earlier booklet, *What Is This Socialism?*, in 1933. Much of it was concerned with defending the CCF from accusations of being un-Christian; it also presented Williams's socialist credo. Both booklets were widely distributed among the membership. A copy of *Social Democracy in Canada* is in the possession of the author. The 1933 booklet can be found in the CCF papers, PAS.

33   Williams to Macauley, October 22, 1934, in Wiens ms., 71.

34   "CCF and Communists Unite on Three Fronts," Regina *Leader-Post*, March 15, 1935; "CCF Leader Warns against Yorkton Riots," Regina *Leader-Post*, March 19, 1935; Steininger thesis, 154.

35   Williams, memorandum to CCF campaign managers and candidates, March 19, 1935, in Steininger thesis, 154.

36   Williams to E. Dyer, March 27, 1935, in Steininger thesis, 156.

37   Memorandum from the Board, Central Office, to CCF campaign managers, candidates, and board members, June 11, 1935, in Steininger thesis, 160.

38   The incidents outlined in the following paragraphs are described by Lorne Brown, in *When Freedom Was Lost* (Montreal: Black Rose, 1986) and *On to Ottawa* (Toronto: Lorimer, 1987).

39   Williams, on reasons for supporting the trekkers, in Wiens ms., 77.

40   "Williams Defies Bennet Edict on Aiding Strikers," undated *Western Producer* clipping in Johnson papers, in possession of Williams family; there is also an undated press clipping, clearly from either the *Leader-Post* or the *Star-Phoenix*, in the Williams family private papers (copies in possession of the author).

41   Williams to Macauley, August 28, 1934, in Wiens ms., 70.

42   William Aberhart (1878–1943), born and raised in Ontario, was a schoolteacher and later earned a BA at Queen's University. In 1910, after teaching for a decade in Brantford, he accepted a post as principal of a school in Calgary, where he became active in the evangelical Christian movement. An effective lay preacher, Aberhart soon had his own church and congregation. In 1925 his Sunday sermons began to be broadcast by radio across Western Canada, also reaching audiences in the northern United States. He participated in founding the Calgary Prophetic Bible Institute and quickly became its leading figure. In response to the suffering he witnessed during the Depression, he was attracted to social credit theories, and in 1932 he began to preach social credit doctrine as well as evangelical Christianity. The public response to his talks on social credit was overwhelmingly positive, and Aberhart therefore focused more and more on social credit. He became active in provincial politics, demanding the provincial government implement social credit. In 1935 his Social Credit Party swept to power in Alberta; Aberhart did not seek personal election, though he

campaigned as leader. After victory, his supporters clamoured for his leadership in the legislature. The Social Credit MLA for Okotoks–High River resigned to make way for Aberhart. Since no other candidate was nominated, Aberhart was acclaimed. As premier, Aberhart fought the banks, the press, the courts, and Ottawa in his efforts to achieve social credit. Eleven of his laws were disallowed by the federal cabinet, while the Alberta Lieutenant-Governor exercised the power of reservation, refusing to sign three laws passed by the legislature. Although his debt protection laws, which made foreclosures on farms, businesses, and homes virtually impossible, were finally struck down by the Privy Council in 1941, Aberhart provided farmers and workers debt protection through the worst years of the Depression. Due to the attention focused on this battle, Aberhart is rarely recognized as the first pioneer of the welfare state in Canada: during his tenure, relief was made more generous and easier to get; aspects of health became publicly funded; a modernization and reform of the educational system was begun; and the most progressive trade union law in Canada was enacted. Aberhart believed it was the duty of the state to provide for those who, through no fault of their own, fell into economic difficulty. Further, he believed it was a right of citizenship to receive such support from the state. Though he failed to implement social credit, Aberhart won a second majority government in 1940. He died in office in 1943.

43 Major C. H. Douglas (1879–1952), the British founder of social credit economic doctrine, argued that the economic system was organized to maximize profits, not to achieve a balance between available goods and the ability of the people to purchase the goods. To achieve a balanced economy, the credit and currency system must be taken into public ownership and run on the basis of credit at cost, rather than allowing interest rates set by private interests to dominate the availability of credit. "Poverty in the midst of abundance" (a common refrain among critics of capitalism) resulted from a lack of purchasing power among the masses. To remedy this, in addition to socializing the credit and currency systems, national dividends—over and above wages, salaries, and investment earnings—would be distributed universally. In order to prevent inflation, just prices would be imposed. This would ensure a true economic democracy. Douglas was hired by Aberhart in 1935 to serve as his chief reconstruction advisor. Douglas resigned in disgust during the preparation of Aberhart's first budget, dismissing it as "orthodox retrenchment." Aberhart did not reveal Douglas's departure until the news leaked out the following year. Douglas outlined his disagreements with Aberhart after resigning as his advisor (C. H. Douglas. *The Alberta Experiment* [London: Eyre and Spottiswood, 1937]). Douglas's first book, *Social Credit*, published in 1924 and revised in 1933, became a veritable bible among the agrarian populist movement. Douglas briefly served as advisor to the UFA government in 1927. In addition to believing Aberhart had a poor grasp of social credit theory, Douglas advised him that provinces in Canada did not possess the required constitutional powers for its implementation.

44   *The Douglas System of Social Credit, Evidence Taken by the Agricultural Committee of the Alberta Legislature,* Session 1934, no. 38 (Edmonton: King's Printer, 1934); *Journals,* Alberta Legislature, 1934, vol. 31.

45   *Calgary Albertan,* January 14, 1935.

46   *Calgary Albertan,* March 29, 1935.

47   Aberhart, *Social Credit Manual* (Calgary: Western Printers and Litho, 1935), 5–17.

48   Coldwell and Williams, joint memorandum to campaign managers, candidates, and speakers, September 3, 1935, in Steininger thesis, 163.

49   Jacob Benson (1892–1987) was the son of English immigrants who homesteaded in the Last Mountain Lake region in 1903. As an adult, Benson became a farmer in the Semans area and a neighbour of Williams. Active in the SGGA and the Progressive Party, Benson served as Last Mountain's MLA from 1929 to 1934. After the founding of the UFC(SS), he became one of Williams's harshest critics—a role he continued to play in the FLP and the CCF. Williams saw Benson as an office-seeking opportunist. In 1934 Benson lost as the FLP candidate. In 1935, running in the federal seat of Yorkton, he lost after being stripped of the CCF nomination. He ran for Last Mountain in the 1938 provincial election and sat as MLA from 1938 to 1952. In 1950, uncomfortable with the CCF's continuing left-leaning tendencies, he quit the caucus to sit as an independent. In 1952 he was defeated by CCF candidate Russ Brown.

50   Woodsworth to an executive member, in Wiens ms., 90; Steininger thesis, 174.

Chapter 5. Building the CCF: Defeating Social Credit, 1936 to 1938

1   Williams to Macauley, January 28, 1936, Williams family private collection.

2   Eliason to M. Freely, January 21, 1937, in Steininger thesis, 227. This was reported to Williams by Freely.

3   Williams to Mrs. Barker, March 5, 1937, in Steininger thesis, 247.

4   Williams to national CCF organizer, December 23, 1936, in Steininger thesis, 242–43.

5   Saskatchewan CCF, *Provincial Platform 1936,* CCF papers, PAS.

6   Minutes of First Annual CCF Convention, 1936, CCF papers, PAS; Steininger thesis, 244.

7   Speech at 1937 CCF Convention, Saskatoon. This speech did not appear in the minutes but was covered by the Saskatoon *Star-Phoenix,* July 18, 1937.

8   Williams to William Irvine, December 23, 1936, in Steininger thesis, 263.

9   Williams to Coldwell, November 10, 1936, in Steininger thesis, 260.

10   Ernest Manning (1908–96) was born, raised, and educated in Carnduff, Saskatchewan, the son of English immigrants who homesteaded in the area. He was so attracted to the religious messages in Aberhart's radio broadcasts

that he enrolled in the Calgary Prophetic Bible Institute and was its first
graduate. He became Aberhart's protégé and was eventually allowed to share
the radio broadcasts with him. When Aberhart began to preach social credit,
Manning was his first and most loyal convert. When Aberhart took the
social credit movement into politics, Manning became his first lieutenant
and chief political hatchet man. Manning was elected in Calgary in 1935.
He was appointed provincial secretary and minister of trade and industry at
the age of twenty-seven. Upon Aberhart's death in 1943, Manning became
premier. In his first election as leader, in 1944, Manning abandoned social
credit and turned the party sharply to the right. He settled with the bond
holders Aberhart had refused to pay and opened Alberta to the oil industry,
something Aberhart had resisted. In the 1944 campaign, Manning did not
run against the banks and the Fifty Big Shots, as Aberhart had in 1935 and
1940; rather, he ran against the only threat to re-election, the CCF, in a vicious,
red-baiting smear campaign. From 1944 on, Manning was a loyal servant of
corporate Canada; he was repeatedly re-elected, serving as premier until 1968.
Alberta returned to the fold as a safe place to invest, and under Manning's
leadership, became a solid foundation of the right in Canadian politics.

11 Radio broadcast slamming Social Credit, January 14, 1938. Text in Williams
family private collection.
12 *Statement on Co-operation by the Leader of the Saskatchewan CCF and
Endorsed by the Central Executive*, March 19, 1938, and Minutes of the
Executive Meeting, March 19 and 20, 1938, CCF papers, PAS (in Steininger
thesis, 273).
13 Douglas, *Alberta Experiment*, 61.
14 *Journals*, Alberta Legislature, 1936, vol. 34 (Special Session—August 25, 1936,
to September 1, 1936), 7.
15 Douglas, *Alberta Experiment*, 91, 95.
16 Alberta Credit House Act, *Statutes of Alberta,* 1936 (Second Session), ch. 1.
17 *Financial Post*, September 19 and 26, October 17, November 12 and 14, 1936.
18 *Calgary Albertan*, January 25, 1937.
19 Douglas, *Alberta Experiment*, 21–22.
20 Liberal Party Pamphlet Collection, 1938 Election, PAS.
21 *Social Credit Manifesto for Saskatchewan*, 1938, Social Credit Pamphlet
Collection, 1938 Election, PAS.
22 Text of final pre-election radio broadcast, including a careful rebuke of Social
Credit, May 28, 1938, Williams family private collecton.
23 *Are They To Be Trusted?*, CCF Pamphlet Collection, 1938 Election, PAS.
24 *The CCF Debt Adjustment and Land Policy*, CCF Pamphlet Collection, 1938
Election, PAS.
25 Williams to Coldwell, June 30, 1938, in Smith, *Prairie Liberalism*, 236.
26 Williams quoted in the *Western Producer*, June 16, 1938.
27 Williams to M. Rankin, June 11, 1936, in Steininger thesis, 303.
28 Coldwell to Williams, June 24, 1938, in Steininger thesis, 306.

29 E. J. Garland to D. Lewis, June 14, 1938, in Steininger thesis, 304.

30 E. Roper to D. Lewis, June 14, 1938, in Steininger thesis, 304.

Chapter 6. Fighting the War in the CCF and in Europe: 1937 to 1944

1 Co-operative Commonwealth Federation, *Regina Manifesto*, 1933. Copy in possession of the author.

2 Woodsworth to Earl Orchard, March 22, 1939, in Young, *Anatomy of a Party*, 92.

3 Brockelbank, taped recollections, in Wiens ms., 146.

4 Minutes of the Second Annual CCF Convention, July 15–17, 1937, Saskatchewan CCF papers, PAS.

5 Presidential address, Saskatchewan CCF Convention, July 12–14, 1939, CCF papers, PAS (in Steininger thesis, 368).

6 Williams to W. Irvine, January 11, 1937, in Steininger thesis, 358.

7 Williams to Woodsworth, January 14, 1937, in Steininger thesis, 355–57. Both quotations are in the same letter.

8 Regina *Leader-Post*, February 25, 1937.

9 Minutes of the National Executive Meeting, March 3, 1937, CCF papers, PAS (in Steininger thesis, 360-61).

10 Williams to D. Lewis, April 5, 1937, in Steininger thesis, 362.

11 Ibid.

12 Williams to Irvine, in Steininger thesis, 358.

13 Quoted in Thomas H. McLeod and Ian McLeod, *Tommy Douglas* (Edmonton: Hurtig, 1987), 83.

14 *CCF Statement on Canada and the Present Crisis*, adopted by the national council, September 6–8, 1939. Copy in possession of the author.

15 Saskatoon *Star-Phoenix*, December 16, 1939.

16 *Canada and the War: The CCF Position*, issued in 1939. Copy in possession of the author.

17 The letter was reported in the *Western Producer*, October 26, 1939, and appeared in the CCF's *Saskatchewan Commonwealth*, October 14, 1939.

18 Williams to Brockelbank, October 23, 1939, in Steininger thesis, 377.

19 W. D. Herridge (1887–1961), a diplomat and politician, served Prime Minister R. B. Bennett as a policy advisor and speech writer during the 1930 election. As a reward, Bennett appointed him ambassador to the United States, a post he held until 1935, when the Bennett government was defeated by King's Liberals. Herridge played a prominent role in the 1938 Conservative convention, unsuccessfully advocating a version of the New Deal that combined social credit monetary doctrines with support for an activist, interventionist government in the economy. His ideas were rejected overwhelmingly by the Tories. In response, Herridge founded the New Democracy Party, which advocated social credit doctrines and a bigger role

for government in the economy. He urged the Social Credit and CCF parties to unite with him under the New Democracy banner to provide a credible progressive alternative to the old-line parties. The national Social Credit Party agreed and adopted the New Democracy name. Many prominent CCFers, including Coldwell, seriously considered joining in a united front with Herridge. Williams played the key role in torpedoing that possibility by mobilizing leaders of other provincial sections to oppose the idea and successfully urging his own Saskatchewan CCF convention to reject the idea. The national CCF finally agreed, formally rejecting Herridge's proposal. Herridge targeted Saskatchewan as the focus of his united front effort, personally running in Kindersley. His failure to persuade the CCF to join him and the Social Credit Party in the united front ensured his party's failure. In the 1940 federal election, the New Democracy Party elected three MPs, all former Social Credit MPs. Herridge ran third behind the CCF in Kindersley, allowing the Liberal candidate to win. Had Herridge not run, the seat would have gone to the CCF. The New Democracy Party died a quiet death, and in 1944, the national Social Credit Party reverted to its old name.

20 Dorise Nielsen (1892–1980), a schoolteacher in rural Saskatchewan, was an FLP/CCF activist since the party's founding. In 1937 she joined the CP, but kept her membership secret while working successfully as a local CCF organizer and activist. In 1940, after Nielsen won a stunning victory in North Battleford under the United Progressive banner, Williams unsuccessfully attempted to persuade her to join the CCF caucus in Ottawa. Throughout her time in the House of Commons, her speeches echoed the policy positions advocated by the CP. The CP had again been declared illegal in 1940 for opposing the war in support of the political line of the Comintern. In 1943, the CP re-established the Labour Progressive Party (LPP) as its legal electoral front. Nielsen declared her support for the LPP. In her bid for re-election in North Battleford in the 1945 election, Nielsen ran third behind the successful CCF candidate and the Liberal. She moved to Ontario and ran again, unsuccessfully, in 1953. In 1957, impressed by events in the People's Republic of China under Mao's new revolutionary regime, she went to Beijing. She remained in China until her death, working as an editor for the regime's foreign-language press.

21 Williams to a party member, March 24 or 25, 1939, in Wiens ms., 132.

22 Williams to Coldwell, March 13, 1939, in Steininger thesis, 337.

23 Coldwell to Williams, March 26, 1939, in Wiens ms., 130.

24 Williams to D. Lewis, May 23, 1939, in Steininger thesis, 340.

25 "Co-operation or Disunity," radio broadcast, April 26, 1939, reported in the *Western Producer*, May 4, 1939. Copy of the text of the broadcast in possession of the author.

26 Coldwell to Markaroff, May 9, 1939, in Wiens ms., 134.

27 Williams to Coldwell, June 30, 1938, in Steininger thesis, 312.

28 Williams, Christmas radio broadcast, December 10, 1939. Copy in possession of the author.

29   Williams to I. C. Nollett, November 10, 1939, in Steininger thesis, 390.

30   Minutes of a meeting of federal candidates and campaign managers, January 20, 1940, CCF papers, PAS (in Steininger thesis, 394).

31   Liberal Party Pamphlet Collection, 1940 Federal Election, PAS.

32   Accusations of Williams's dictatorial role in party affairs began with his reorganization of the party when he became leader in 1935. His opponents in the Coldwell faction regularly hurled this accusation against him.

33   Carlyle King (1907–88) came to Saskatchewan with his parents from Ontario. His father was a CPR station agent. King gained his BA in English at the University of Saskatchewan in 1926 and his MA (1927) and PhD (1931) from the University of Toronto. He was appointed to the faculty of the University of Saskatchewan's English department in 1929, a post he held until 1977. King was a democratic socialist and a principled pacifist. He admired J. S. Woodsworth and consistently supported his position on World War II. King was active in the FLP/CCF from the beginning. He was also a fierce public opponent of Williams's stand on the war. In an early unsuccessful campaign against Williams, he circulated a petition among party members demanding Williams support the national CCF's war policy. He became a leading member of the campaign to oust Williams. In 1939 he won a position on the provincial executive, and in 1940 he unsuccessfully challenged Williams for the leadership. At the 1940 convention King was elected vice-president of the party, a position he used to continue his opposition against Williams. In 1945 he was elected party president, a post he held until 1960.

34   King to a party member, undated letter, in Wiens ms., 147; and King to Jack Douglas, undated letter, in Wiens ms., 162.

35   Coldwell to Dr. McLean, March 28, 1937, in Steininger thesis, 400.

36   Benson to Dr. McLean, July 3, 1938, in Steininger thesis, 401.

37   Quoted in Clarence Fines, "The Impossible Dream," (unpublished memoir, 1981), in McLeod and McLeod, *Tommy Douglas*, 101.

38   Jim Wright to P. Makaroff, May 17, 1939, in Wiens ms., 135.

39   Coldwell to Dr. McLean, April 7, 1940, in Steininger thesis, 402.

40   Gordon to Williams, October 13, 1939, in Wiens ms., 148.

41   Saskatoon *Star-Phoenix*, June 5 and 7, 1940, in Steininger thesis, 402.

42   Alexander M. ("Sandy") Nicholson (1900–91) was a United Church preacher and a farmer in the Sturgis area who was active in the UFC(SS) and the FLP/CCF. Williams hired him as a CCF organizer in 1935. In 1940 he was elected to the House of Commons for Mackenzie, and he was re-elected in 1945, 1953, and 1957. He was defeated in the Diefenbaker sweep of 1958. He then served as a CCF MLA for Saskatoon from 1960 to 1967, serving in the cabinet from 1960 to 1964. Nicholson was defeated in 1967.

43   *Brief from Saskatchewan Members of Parliament*, July 22, 1940. Copy in possession of the author.

44   Williams to B. Johnson, December 7, 1940, in Steininger thesis, 407.

45   The speech was published in the *Saskatchewan Commonwealth*, July 24, 1940.

46   Cited in Naylor, *Fate of Labour Socialism*, 280.

47   Williams to D. C. Kyle, August 13, 1940, in Steininger thesis, 407.

48   Williams to W. McInnis, May 15, 1940, in Steininger thesis, 396.

49   Williams to B. Johnson, December 7, 1940, in Steininger thesis, 407.

50   John H. ("Brock") Brockelbank (1897–1977) came to Saskatchewan with his homesteading parents in 1911. After serving in World War I, he went into farming in the Bjorkdale region. He was a militant in the UFC(SS) and active in the Wheat Pool campaign. He became a protégé of Williams, with whom he established a close friendship; he was among Williams's most loyal supporters to the end. In 1938, Brockelbank was elected CCF MLA for Tisdale. In 1941, on Williams's recommendation, the caucus selected him as acting leader of the opposition. In 1942 he stood against Douglas for the leadership in order to voice his support for Williams, including reading a telegram from Williams to the convention. Williams was nominated from the floor. Brockelbank remained acting leader of the opposition until the 1944 victory, since Douglas remained an MP in Ottawa. After Williams's clear defeat in 1942, Brockelbank and other caucus members closed ranks behind Douglas. In 1944, Douglas appointed him minister of municipal affairs; in 1948, Brockelbank was awarded the key post of minister of natural resources, a position he held until 1962. That year, Woodrow Lloyd, Douglas's successor as premier, named Brockelbank deputy premier and provincial treasurer. He retired in 1967.

51   *Saskatchewan Commonwealth*, February 12, 1941.

52   *G. H. Williams to Members of the Provincial Council*, March 6, 1941, CCF papers, PAS (in Steininger thesis, 412). Copy also in possession of the author.

53   Minutes of Provincial Council Meeting, Saskatchewan CCF, May 31 to June 1, 1941, CCF papers, PAS (in Steininger thesis, 416).

54   Williams to Brockelbank, July 31, 1941, in Wiens ms., 172.

55   Williams to Dr. McLean, October 4, 1941, in Wiens ms., 173.

56   Brockelbank to Williams, June 5, June 27, and July 8, 1943, in Wiens ms., 177.

57   Williams to Brockelbank, January 25, 1944, in Wiens ms., 181.

Chapter 7. Endgame: The 1944 Election

1   Election radio broadcast, 6 May 1944, in Wiens ms., 182. Copy also in possession of the author.

2   *The CCF Program for Saskatchewan*, 1944, CCF Pamphlet Collection, 1944 Election, PAS. Copy in possession of the author.

3   *Labour and Urban Security*, CCF Pamphlet Collection, 1944 Election, PAS.

4   Seymour Martin Lipset, *Agrarian Socialism* (Berkeley: University of California, 1971), 192–206.

5   Wiens ms., 189.

6   Williams to Douglas, February 10, 1945, in Wiens ms., 192

7   *Journals*, Saskatchewan Legislature, 1944 (Second Session), vol. 43, October 19 to November 10, 1944, pp. 10–15.

8   The Department of Natural Resources Act, ss 1944, c. 8.

9   The Crown Corporations Act, ss 1945, c. 17.

10   These words were used in the 1944 Throne Speech.

11   Williams to Brockelbank, October [no day], 1944, in Wiens ms., 191.

12   Williams to Dr. McLean, November 9, 1944, in Wiens ms., 191.

Chapter 8. The Shame of the Intellectuals

1   Clarence M. Fines (1905–93), a teacher and vice-principal at the school where Coldwell was principal, became a protégé of Coldwell. Like Coldwell, Fines was active in organizing teachers. Under Coldwell's mentorship, Fines was active in the Independent Labour Party and the FLP/CCF from the beginning. And like Coldwell, he was active in Regina's municipal politics, sitting on city council from 1934 to 1939 and from 1942 to 1944. Fines was an effective behind-the-scenes organizer in the campaign to oust Williams from the leadership. When Douglas won the presidency of the CCF from an absent Williams in 1941, Fines was elected vice-president. In 1942, when Douglas resigned as president and ran for political leader against an absent Williams, Fines was elected president. In 1944, Fines was elected MLA from a Regina seat, and Douglas appointed him provincial treasurer. Fines was an important leader of the right wing of the party, successfully imposing fiscal conservatism on the budgeting process and spearheading the successful campaign within the party to drop the commitment to public ownership of natural resources and their development. This was the foundational economic policy of the UFC(SS)'s economic program upon entering politics in 1931 and had remained foundational in the economic platforms of the FLP/CCF, including that of 1944. Fines served as provincial treasurer until 1960, when he retired and joined the corporate sector.

2   Saskatchewan New Democratic Party, *Notice to Party members and supporters*, sent out electronically on October 20, 2016. Copy in possession of the author.

3   Doris F. Shackleton, *Tommy Douglas* (Toronto: McClelland & Stewart, 1975); McLeod and McLeod, *Tommy Douglas*; Walter Stewart, *The Life and Political Times of Tommy Douglas* (Toronto: McArthur, 2003).

4   Douglas, *Recollections*.

5   Walter Stewart, *M. J.: The Life and Times of M. J. Coldwell* (Toronto: Stoddart, 2000).

6   Coldwell in ibid., 97.

7   Stewart, *M. J.*, 104.

8   Coldwell in ibid., 106.

9   Douglas, *Recollections*, 79.

10   Stewart, *M. J.*, 110, 113.

11 Stewart, *Life and Political Times*, 107–8.
12 Stewart, *M. J.*, 120–21.
13 Coldwell in ibid., 121.
14 Douglas, *Recollections*, 88–89.
15 Stewart, *Life and Political Times*, 121–23.
16 Douglas in McLeod and McLeod, *Tommy Douglas*, 67.
17 Williams to Mrs. Kavemer, undated letter, in McLeod and McLeod, *Tommy Douglas*, 67.
18 Douglas, *Recollections*, 139–41.
19 Ibid.
20 Stewart, *Life and Political Times*, 144–45.
21 McLeod and McLeod, *Tommy Douglas*, 98.
22 Douglas to Williams, undated letter, in ibid., 98.
23 Douglas in McLeod and McLeod, *Tommy Douglas*, 99, 100.
24 Douglas, *Recollections*, 141–43.
25 Ibid.
26 Stewart, *Life and Political Times*, 156.
27 Quoted in Fines, "The Impossible Dream," in McLeod and McLeod, *Tommy Douglas*, 101.
28 Douglas, *Recollections*, 144.
29 Shackleton, *Tommy Douglas*, 65.
30 Brockelbank, interview with Steininger, November 25, 1971, Steininger thesis, 205.
31 Douglas in Shackleton, *Tommy Douglas*, 120.
32 Lipset, *Agrarian Socialism*, 150.
33 Evelyn Eager, *Saskatchewan Government* (Saskatoon: Western Producer Prairie Books, 1980), 55, 170.
34 A. W. Johnson, *Dream No Little Dreams* (Toronto: University of Toronto Press, 2004), 13, 23, 25, 33, 46, 56.
35 John H. Archer, *Saskatchewan: A History* (Saskatoon: Western Producer Prairie Books, 1980), 254.
36 Gerald Friesen, *The Canadian Prairies* (Toronto: University of Toronto Press, 1984), 377.
37 *Encyclopedia of Saskatchewan* (2005), s.v. "Douglas, Thomas Clement."

Chapter 9. Conclusion: Williams in Canadian History

1 Eric Hobsbawm, *The Age of Extremes* (1995), 6–7.
2 Hans Gerth and C. Wright Mills, *Character and Social Structure* (1953), 405, 429.
3 Ibid.
4 Georgi Plekhanov, "On the Question of the Individual's Role in History," *Selected Philosophical Works*, vol. 2 (Moscow: Progress, 1976[1898]), 314.

BIBLIOGRAPHIC NOTES

The original research on which this essay relies is contained in my PhD dissertation, Friedrich Steininger's biography of Williams (an unpublished master's thesis in history), and Muriel Wiens's unpublished manuscript on her father. All three are based on extensive examinations of archival material—documents, correspondence, and deposited papers of important historical actors. Steininger's thesis additionally uses interviews he conducted during the 1960s and 1970s of surviving participants in the events. I also had the good fortune to have access to the private papers of the Williams family. These sources are listed in the bibliography. I also relied on the usual secondary sources.

Endnotes have been used sparingly, for direct quotations, explanations of roles of key personalities mentioned in the text, details on important historical facts or events with which the average reader might not be familiar, and controversial issues of fact. For biographical information on the individuals mentioned in the text I relied on the *Encyclopedia of Saskatchewan*, the *Dictionary of Canadian Biography*, and the *Canadian Parliamentary Guide* (1921 to 1945), as well as my own research. The economic data quoted are taken largely from the 1940 *Report of the Royal Commission on Dominion-Provincial Relations, Book I* and Urquhart and Buckley's 1965 *Historical Statistics of Canada*. Various census reports were also consulted. The federal election results cited are taken from Scarrow's

1962 *Canada Votes: A Handbook of Federal and Provincial Election Data,* while those for Saskatchewan elections are taken from the provincial Chief Electoral Office's 1987 *Provincial Elections in Saskatchewan 1905–1986.*
Bibliographic notes are provided for each chapter.

Preface

The book relies heavily on the following: J. F. Conway, "To Seek a Goodly Heritage: The Prairie Populist Resistance to the National Policy in Canada" (PhD diss., Simon Fraser University, 1979); Friedrich Steininger, "George H. Williams: Agrarian Socialist" (MA thesis, University of Regina, 1976); and Muriel Wiens, *Finding George Williams: A Tale of the Grass Roots* (unpublished manuscript, 2007). Copies of these are in the possession of the author. The Conway dissertation and Steininger thesis are available from the libraries of the respective universities. The Wiens manuscript is deposited in the Williams papers at the Provincial Archives of Saskatchewan.

Prologue. George Hara Williams: A Word Portrait

This word portrait is based on the following materials from the Williams family private papers: Williams's "Open Letter to the People of Saskatchewan," January 21, 1933, written while Williams was grieving the death of one of his daughters; the typed manuscript of an interview with Margery Williams by Lloyd Rothwell, January 27, 1970; daughter Ruth's "Reminiscences about her father," undated; daughter Muriel's "Treasured memories of her father," undated; a clipping from the *Commonwealth,* November 14, 1945, recording the memories of an organizer who travelled rural areas with Williams; an incomplete photocopy of a press clipping titled "Personalities in the CCF: George Hara Williams," undated, no publication given. Copies of these are in the possession of the author. The author also wrote down fragmentary impressions of Williams from a variety of sources while examining the various papers and files.

Williams won Wadena with 68.74 per cent of the popular vote—the top victory among the fifty southern seats. There were two northern seats, Athabasca and Cumberland, with very few votes spread over sprawling ridings: in the former, 784 votes were cast; in the latter, 622. The Liberal candidate won Athabasca with 80.77 per cent, having garnered 626 of the 784 votes cast.

Chapter 1. George Hara Williams: Roots to 1921

The characterization of Williams's early life, his recovery from his war wound, and his return to Canada is based on Wiens manuscript, chapter 1 ("Hard Scrabble and New Wine") and Steininger thesis, chapter 1 ("Introduction") and chapter 2 ("The Making of the Agrarian Radical").

When war was declared, Canada was swept away by patriotism and jingoism. The sentiment of the overwhelming majority was decidedly pro-war. Critics and opponents of the war were either initially, and carefully, silent, or they spoke out—and were shouted down. After the war the official line was that it was a major event in Canada's maturation as a nation. The official narrative created a series of myths to sustain the widely accepted version of the benefits of the war: Canada as a united nation was born in this test of fire and steel; Canada asserted and acquired a respected place on the world stage; the war had been necessary to stop German expansionism and to defend democracy and our cherished values. This consensus dominated the discourse in scholarly works, popular accounts, and school textbooks. Vance's *Death So Noble* (1997) provides an excellent account of the construction of these myths. But minority opposition to the war had existed from the beginning; the story of that opposition was rarely told, and when it was, it was dismissed. It was not fully recorded in scholarly works and certainly never mentioned in textbooks. That began to change in the 1960s and 1970s, when scholars began documenting the resistance to the war in Quebec (already fully documented in French-language scholarly works) and among militant trade unions, farmer organizations, certain ethnic groups, and the various small socialist and labour parties in English Canada. As the war seemed to go on without end and the number of casualties was shocking, the opposition became more vocal, particularly during the debate on conscription. The size of the opposition was reflected in the 1917 conscription election, when Laurier's anti-conscription rump of the Liberal Party won 39 per cent of the vote and eighty-two seats, with the largest bloc in Quebec, but a significant number also in English Canada. Only one hundred thousand civilian votes separated

Borden's Union government and Laurier's anti-conscription opposition. But two hundred thousand military votes went to Borden, giving him a decisive victory. World War I had a defining impact on Williams. Given what he did after he returned from the war, it clearly marked a sharp left turn in how he saw the world.

The discussion on Canada and World War I benefited from many published works: Brown and Cook's *Canada: 1896–1921: A Nation Transformed* (1978); Cook's *Shock Troops: Canadians Fighting the Great War, 1914–1918* (2008); Heron's *The Workers' Revolt in Canada, 1917–1925* (1998); Jamieson's *Times of Trouble: Labour Unrest and Industrial Conflict in Canada, 1900–1966* (1968); Kordan's *Enemy Aliens, Prisoners of War: Internment in Canada during the Great War* (2002); Robin's *Radical Politics and Canadian Labour: 1896–1930* (1968); McCormack's *Reformers, Rebels and Revolutionaries: The Western Canadian Radical Movement, 1899–1919* (1977); Thompson's *The Harvests of War: The Prairie West, 1914–1918* (1978); and Vance's *Death So Noble: Memory, Meaning and the First World War* (1997).

The resistance to conscription and the 1917 conscription election are well documented in Canadian historiography: Armstrong's *The Crisis of Quebec, 1914–1918* (1974 [1932]); Auger's "On the Brink of Civil War: The Canadian Government and the Suppression of the 1918 Quebec Easter Riots," *Canadian Historical Review* (2008); Dafoe's *Laurier* (1963); Granatstein and Hitsman's *Broken Promises: A History of Conscription in Canada* (1977); and Williams's *Conscription, 1917* (1969).

The life and death of Albert Goodwin was recorded in Mayse's *Ginger: The Life and Death of Albert Goodwin* (1990).

Williams participated in the last cavalry charge of World War I. His brother Samuel documented the event in *Stand to Your Horses; Through the First World War with the Lord Strathcona's Horse (Royal Canadians)* (1961).

Chapter 2. The Political and Economic Context: The Rise of the United Farmers of Canada (Saskatchewan Section), 1922 to 1926

The wheat boom dominated the Canadian economy from 1896 to 1913. Saskatchewan grew rapidly as settlers poured into the province. The resulting boom saw Saskatchewan become the third-largest province in the Dominion. The wheat boom is well documented in the published scholarship and in the report of a Royal Commission. This chapter's discussion of the wheat boom of 1896–1913 is based on the *Report of the Royal Commission on Dominion-Provincial Relations, Book I, Canada 1867–1939* (1940), chapter 3 ("The Wheat Boom, 1896–1913"). Most of the economic data are taken from this source. Also of great use were Britnell's *The Wheat Economy* (1939) and Fowke's *The National Policy and the Wheat Economy* (1957). The 1913 figures on the number of farmers and workers on the Prairies are derived from 1911 and 1921 census reports, Haythorne's *Labour in Canadian Agriculture* (1965), and Urquhart and Buckley's *Historical Statistics of Canada* (1965). The 49,000 farm wage labour figure is a 1911 figure.

The CPR contract remained a festering grievance for westerners for generations. The terms of incorporation of Saskatchewan into the Dominion, which denied the province control of its natural resources, angered westerners. They complained that the province was a colony of Ottawa and of the industrial, financial, and commercial interests that controlled the government. Details on the development of the CPR, in particular the agreement between Ottawa and the CPR, are reported in Innis's *The History of the Canadian Pacific Railway* (1923). The details of the agreement with the Hudson's Bay Company, whereby Ottawa simply purchased the Prairies and the North, are outlined in Morton's *The West in Confederation, 1857–1871* (1958). The federal land policies that angered westerners are documented in Martin's *"Dominion" Lands Policy* (1938).

The agrarian populist movements in Canada have been thoroughly researched. The best scholarship, forming the basis for the narrative of this book, includes McGibbon's *The Canadian Grain Trade* (1932), Moorhouse's *Deep Furrows: which tells of Pioneer Trails along which the Farmers of Western Canada fought their way to great achievements in Co-operation* (1918), A. S. Morton's *History of Prairie Settlement* (1938), W. L. Morton's *Manitoba: A History* (1957), Patton's *Grain Growers' Co-operation in Western Canada* (1928), the Porritts' *Sixty Years of Protection in Canada, 1846–1912: Where Industry Leans on the Politicians* (1913), Sharp's *The Agrarian Revolt in Western Canada* (1948), Stanley's *The Birth of Western Canada* (1948),Thomas's *The Struggle for Responsible Government in the North-West Territories* (1956), and Wood's *A History of Farmers' Movements in Canada* (1924).

The books by Moorhouse and the Porritts are especially useful since they were leading agrarian populist intellectuals and exercised a great deal of influence on the ideological development of the movement. Every thinking farmer of the era owned copies of their books. Also, Hann's *Some Historical Perspectives on the Canadian Agrarian Political Movements: The Ontario Origins of the Agrarian Criticism of Canadian Industrial Society* (1973) provides a thoughtful overview of early agrarian populist ideology in Canada, in particular, its critique of capitalist industrialization. The early agrarian populist view of the perfectly ordered and just society is discussed in MacDougall's *Rural Life in Canada: Its Trends and Tasks* (1913).

With the turn of the century the agrarian populist movement became a significant political power in Canada, mounting a challenge to the hegemony of the National Policy of industrialization behind a tariff wall. Liberal and Tory parties supported the policy. The rapid growth in farm organizations and the initial battle over the unfair marketing system facing farmers are documented in McGibbon's *The Canadian Grain Trade* (chap. 3, "Organization of the Grain Growers"), the Porritts' *Sixty Years of Protection* (chap. 16, "The Farmers' Organizations of Ontario and the Prairie Provinces"), Moorhouse's *Deep Furrows* (chap. 2, "A Call to Arms"; chap. 3, "The First Shot is Fired"; and chap. 4, "That Man Partridge"), and Wood's *A History of Farmers' Movements in Canada* (part 3, "The Rise of the Grain Growers' Movements in the Prairie Provinces—1892–1912").

By 1910 the organized farmers on the Prairies had grown to over 23,000 members: the Manitoba Grain Growers' Association (MGGA) had 9,000; the SGGA, 6,000; and the UFA, 8,500. In 1909 all three united with the Dominion Grange of Ontario's 9,000 members in the CCA. The Ontario Grange later became the United Farmers of Ontario (UFO) and the MGGA became the United Farmers of Manitoba (UFM). By 1921, the year of the agrarian populist political challenge to the National Policy of tariff-forced industrialization, the number of organized farmers had increased dramatically, to over 140,000: the UFO had 60,000 members; the UFM, 16,000; the SGGA, 29,000; and the UFA, 38,000.

The 1911 election was decisive in turning the organized farmers toward independent political action. Any hope the Liberal Party could be persuaded to return to its former free-trade principles was finally abandoned. The material on the election is based on Dutil and

McKenzie's *Canada 1911: The Decisive Election that Shaped the Country* (2011), Ellis's *Reciprocity, 1911* (1939), Masters's *Reciprocity: 1846–1911* (1961), and Stevens's edited *The 1911 General Election: A Study in Canadian Politics* (1970). The population figures noted are found in the *Census of Canada 1911*, vol. 1, *Area and Population* (p. 530), Urquhart and Buckley's *Historical Statistics of Canada* (pp. 59, 351), and Fowke's *National Policy and the Wheat Economy* (p. 72). The political options debated by the organized farmers in the *Grain Growers' Guide* are canvassed in Morton's *The Progressive Party in Canada*.

The wheat boom's faltering in 1911, 1912, and 1913 threatened a national depression. That was forestalled by the war boom beginning in 1914. The price of a bushel of No. 1 Northern wheat at Fort William provides a good barometer of this cycle of bust and boom in the wheat economy: in 1911, $1.00; in 1912 and 1913, 89 cents; in 1914, $1.32; in 1916, $2.08; and in 1918, $2.24. The war boom had a dramatic impact on the Prairies. The population grew from 1.3 million in 1911 to over 1.9 million in 1921. The number of farms grew from 199,000 to 255,000 in the same period. Wheat and flour exports grew from just under 87 million bushels in 1915 to 269 million bushels in 1916. In Saskatchewan, the average size of a farm grew from 297 acres in 1911 to 369 acres in 1921. Mechanization took off; for example, by 1921 there were over 38,000 tractors on Prairie farms. Details on the war boom are provided in *The Royal Commission on Dominion-Provincial Relations, Book I*, chapter 4 ("The War Period, 1914–21"). The figures on the average size of a Saskatchewan farm are from *The Encyclopedia of Saskatchewan* (pp. 40–41), while the figures on farm tractors, the price of wheat, and wheat and flour exports are from Urquhart and Buckley's *Historical Statistics of Canada* (pp. 359, 363, 381).

The final, united, and coherent agrarian populist assault on the National Policy is discussed and analyzed in Irvine's *The Farmers in Politics* (1920) and Morton's *The Progressive Party in Canada* (1950). It is also discussed, in less detail, in many of the sources cited above.

The New National Policy platform is reproduced in Morton's *The Progressive Party in Canada*. For further empirical, theoretical, and comparative analyses of the phenomenon, the reader can refer to the following by the author: "Populism in the United States, Canada, and Russia: Explaining the Roots of Canada's Third Parties" (*Canadian*

Journal of Political Science [1978]); "The Prairie Populist Resistance to the National Policy: Some Reconsiderations" (*Journal of Canadian Studies* [1979]), and "Agrarian Petite-Bourgeois Responses to Capitalist Industrialization: The Case of Canada" (in Bechhofer and Elliott's *The Petite Bourgeoisie: Comparative Studies of the Uneasy Stratum* [1981]).

The general postwar economic downturn and a return to the free market for marketing wheat brought economic calamity to Prairie farmers. In September 1920, a bushel of No. 1 Northern wheat sold for $2.85. In December it fell to $2.00. By 1923 the price had fallen to 93 cents. Thus, between October 1920 and December 1923, the price declined 67 per cent. Due to the importance of wheat to the national economy, the depression in agriculture very quickly became a general depression.

The implosion of the Progressive Party after the 1921 election, the defeat of the UFO government in Ontario, the gradual reabsorption of the UFM government by the Liberals, and the shift to the right of the UFA government in Alberta are outlined in Morton's *The Progressive Party in Canada*, Drury's *Farmer Premier* (1966), and Conway's dissertation (chap. 4, "Defeat from the Jaws of Victory: The United Farmers of Alberta Regime, 1921 to 1935").

The rise of the FUC, the decline of the SGGA, and the amalgamation of the two organizations into the United Farmers of Canada (Saskatchewan Section) [UFC(SS)] after the success of the wheat pool campaign have not received a great deal of scholarly attention. The author studied the archival papers of the FUC, the SGGA, and the UFC(SS) for his dissertation. The available research on these events includes Spafford's "The Origins of the Farmers' Union of Canada" (*Saskatchewan History* [1965]), Spafford's "The 'Left Wing:' 1921–1931" (in Ward and Spafford's *Politics in Saskatchewan*, (1965), Anderson's *Farmers in Politics, 1915–1935: Some Political Aspects of the Grain Growers' Movement (1915–1935) with particular reference to Saskatchewan* (MA thesis, 1949), Courville's *The Saskatchewan Progressives* (MA thesis, 1971), Conway's dissertation (chap. 7, "Prelude to Victory: The Saskatchewan Organized Agrarian Petite Bourgeoisie Goes into Politics"), Steininger's thesis (chap. 2, "The Making of an Agrarian Radical"), and Wiens's manuscript (chap. 1, "Hard Scrabble and New Wine").

Spafford's articles are particularly useful. He provides the texts of the constitutions of the FUC and the One Big Union (OBU), noting their similarities. He also reviews the pamphlets distributed by the FUC. The FUC membership estimate of ten thousand after the wheat pool campaign was calculated by Spafford based on a careful examination of the FUC's financial records, specifically, computing the number of members required for the declared revenues from membership dues. The FUC was a very secretive organization. It did not welcome press coverage and left only a small paper trail. Williams's debt adjustment plan was dropped from the priority list in the mid-1920s due to a return of good times and a preoccupation with the wheat pool campaign. It was revived unchanged by the UFC(SS) when the Depression hit the province in 1929–30.

The closeness of the relationship between the Liberal Party and the SGGA is reflected in comments on the Liberal government by SGGA secretary F. W. Green. While reporting to a convention on the organization's successes in lobbying the government, he said, "We also keep the different departments of our government machinery alert, watchful, careful, active, running down the path of duty, trying to forestall us in our demands. They are anxious in many cases to do for us the thing they see we are about to ask. They fear us more than they do the opposition. They respect us well and court us tenderly" (Minutes, Eleventh Annual Convention, SGGA, 1912, PAS). Smith's *Prairie Liberalism: The Liberal Party in Saskatchewan, 1905–1971* (1975) provides a full account of the relationship between the Liberal Party and the SGGA and its eventual souring when the SGGA supported the Progressive Party in the 1921 federal election. The Liberal Party was defeated across the province by Progressive candidates.

Chapter 3. Leading the Farmers into Politics: 1926 to 1931

A discussion of the FEL manifesto is provided in Anderson's *Farmers in Politics, 1915–1935*, and in Steininger's thesis. The battles between the left wing and the right wing in the UFC(SS) are carefully recorded in the minutes of the organization's conventions from 1927 to 1930. A detailed account of the decisive UFC(SS) board meeting in March 1929, right after Williams's election as president, at which the right wing tried to force his resignation, is contained in Steininger's thesis (chap. 2, "The Making of an Agrarian Radical") and Wiens's manuscript (chap. 2, "The Old Guard and the Young Whippersnapper."). The article in the Saskatoon *Star-Phoenix*, when the right wing made the battle public, appeared on March 12, 1929. Just after the convention, George Edwards, the former SGGA president and leader of the right wing of the UFC(SS), circulated a document among the membership ("Some Observations on the Convention"). Edwards declared, "At the next convention, there should be a showdown and a thorough understanding arrived at as to whether the left wing are going to retain their membership in the organization, unless they cease their disruptive methods." The call to expel the FEL was repeated often by the right wing, but most members shrugged it off as sour grapes. When it became clear Williams enjoyed the overwhelming support of the rank and file of the membership, the right gave up efforts to oust him. Edwards was seen more and more as suffering from thwarted ambition rather than acting to defend basic democratic principles.

The private trade controlled 213 million bushels of the 1928–29 wheat crop, while the Wheat Pool, with 60 per cent of farmers signed up, controlled 230 million bushels. As far as Williams was concerned, the battle would end only when the pool controlled all 443 million bushels (G. H. Williams, "100 P. C. Control by Legislation," *Western Producer*, August 21, 1930). Details of the debate on compulsory pooling at the 1928 convention are available in UFC(SS), *Report of the Second Annual U.F.C. Convention of 1928*, UFC(SS) papers, PAS. The following resolution was passed narrowly: "Resolved that we go on record as being in favour of having the Provincial Legislature enact a law which will make it compulsory for every wheat grower and farmer to market his or her wheat through the Wheat Pool when 75 per cent of the farmers in Saskatchewan sign the Wheat Pool contract."

For details on the campaign for compulsory pooling, see the following: *Report of the Second Annual UFC Convention of 1928* and *Minutes of the Annual UFC Convention of 1929*, UFC(SS) papers, PAS; "Williams Opposes Two Pool Plan," *Western Producer*, October 24, 1929; UFC(SS), *Facts About 100% Control*, n.d. [1930?], UFC(SS) Pamphlet Collection, PAS; "To All Contract Signers," *Western Producer*, August 14, 1930; "One Hundred Per Cent Control of Market by Growers," *Western Producer*, October 9, 1930; "The Pool and the U.F.C.," *Western Producer*, January 9, 1930; and G. H. Williams, "100 P.C. Control by Legislation." A detailed summary of the campaign is provided in the Steininger thesis.

All figures on the average price of wheat in Saskatchewan are taken from the *Submission of the Province of Saskatchewan to the Royal Commission on Dominion-Provincial Relations* (1937, p. 177).

The *Journals*, Saskatchewan Legislature, 1923–29, vols. 20–27, abound with questions about, and evidence of, patronage and corruption. The going became particularly heavy for the Liberal government in the 1928 and 1928–29 sessions (vols. 25 and 26), as scandal after scandal was exposed. Smith provides a summary of the corruption controversies in his *Prairie Liberalism* (chap. 5, "The Beleaguered Machine, Liberal Politics, 1918–1929").

The material on the Klan is based on Calderwood's *The Rise and Fall of the Ku Klux Klan in Saskatchewan* (MA thesis,1968) and Kyba's "Ballots and Burning Crosses: The Election of 1929," in Ward and Spafford's *Politics in Saskatchewan* (1968). The extent of the direct relationship between the Klan and the Tories is impossible to know with certainty, nor can we know if the Klan and the Tories were deliberately working together. The important fact is the Klan publicly attacked the Liberal government and personally attacked Premier Gardiner. This benefited the opposing parties. Whether the Liberals would have faced defeat in the absence of the Klan agitation can never be known. It is certainly true that the Klan publicly stated in inflammatory fashion the private bigotries generally held in that period by white Anglo-Saxon Protestants, including many members and supporters of the Liberal Party. At least one Liberal MLA joined the Klan and Premier Gardiner often defended his government against Klan attacks by showing that his government was most definitely not pro-immigrant or pro-Catholic. He pointed out that Catholics and those not of British origin were significantly underrepresented in both the civil service and the teaching profession. The message conveyed was that his government was responsibly and judiciously discriminatory; hence, the Klan allegations were wrong and therefore undeserved.

Russell's "The Co-operative Government in Saskatchewan, 1929–1934" (MA thesis, 1970) outlines the responses of the Anderson government to the depression. The figures on the early economic collapse in Saskatchewan are from the *Report of the Royal Commission on Dominion-Provincial Relations, Book 1* (chap. 6, "The Depression"), Alberta's *The Case for Alberta: Alberta's Problems and Dominion-Provincial*

Relations, Part I (1938), and Saskatchewan's *Report of the Saskatchewan Reconstruction Council* (1944).

The discussion of debt in Saskatchewan is based on Allen and Hope's *The Farm Outlook in Saskatchewan* (1936); the *Census of Agriculture, 1931, Total Number of Farms, Farm Tenure, Farm Acreage, Farm Values, Mortgage Debt, Farm Expenses by Province* (1932); the provincial treasurer's February 10, 1931, budget speech (*Journals*, Saskatchewan Legislature, 1931, vol. 29) and the *Report of the Saskatchewan Reconstruction Council*.

The policies of the Farmers' Unity League are detailed by Mills in "Preamble of the Aims of the Farmers' Unity League," a chapter of his book *Stout Hearts Stand Tall: A Biographical Sketch of a Militant Saskatchewan Farmer, Hopkins Evan Mills* (1971).

The characterization of Williams's presidential address and the following discussion are based on the Minutes of the Annual UFC Convention of 1931, UFC(SS) papers, PAS. The approved political platform was published in the *Western Producer* as "The New Economic Policy," March 19, 1931. A complete version is contained in a series of published pamphlets: *Economic Policy (Saskatchewan): as formulated by the Delegates Assembled in Annual Convention, 1932*; *Economic Policy and Convention Resolutions* (Seventh Annual Convention, 1932); *The Evolution of a Policy* (1932); and *Land Nationalization Program of the UFC, 1933* (all in UFC(SS) papers, PAS).

For more details on the Rome conference and Williams's tour of the Soviet Union, including his role at the Rome conference, see "Williams Will Attend World Wheat Meeting," *Western Producer*, March 12, 1931; "Williams at Rome," *Western Producer*, April 30, 1931; "Mr. Williams' Report on His Tour to Europe," UFC(SS) papers, PAS; and Williams's booklet, *The Land of the Soviets* (1931).

Chapter 4. Building the CCF: Leadership Lost and Regained, 1931 to 1936

Williams urged Coldwell to move quickly to establish a provincial Independent Labour Party in preparation for the founding convention. Details are provided in Minutes of the Joint Conference of UFC and ILP Delegates in Regina, June 26–27, 1931, UFC(SS) papers, PAS; "Fusion of the Farmer-Labour Forces Urgent," *Western Producer*, October 15, 1931;

and "Independent Labour Party of Saskatchewan Formed," *Western Producer*, October 29, 1931. Details on thwarting Williams's efforts to convene a national conference of radical organizations, and the informal meeting of the political directive board to persuade Williams to forego the leadership, are contained in the Williams family private papers. The Wiens manuscript also provides an account in chapter 4 ("The Getting Together Movement") and chapter 5 ("The Co-operative Commonwealth Federation").

The minutes of the founding convention of the FLP are particularly detailed, and the event was extensively reported in the *Western Producer*; *Minutes of the Annual Convention of July 25–26, 1932*; Minutes of the First Annual Joint Political Convention, July 27, 1932, UFC(SS) papers, PAS; "UFC and ILP Launch a Farmer-Labor Party," *Western Producer*, August 11, 1932. Details on these meetings, as well as on the founding of the national CCF in Calgary in 1932, are contained in the Wiens manuscript, chapter 4 ("The Co-operative Commonwealth Federation") and in the Steininger thesis, chapter 4 ("The New Party").

The 1934 election is thoroughly documented in Hoffman's "The Saskatchewan Election of 1934: The Political, Social and Economic Background" (MA thesis, 1973). Chapters 4 and 5 provide an extensive account of the relentless ideological smear campaign the new party endured. Despite these attacks the FLP refused to back away from its "use-lease" proposal, defiantly reissuing the detailed policy during the election campaign: *Land Nationalization Programme of the UFC, 1933* (FLP papers, PAS). The pamphlets mentioned in the text can be found in the FLP and Liberal Party Pamphlet Collections, 1934 Election, PAS. The following pamphlets were centrepieces of the Liberal campaign: *Relief, A Merciless Mess of Mismanagement and the Way Out* and *Supplementary Platform Resolutions of the Saskatchewan Liberal Party (adopted January 9 to 11, 1934)*. The quotes from FLP campaign pamphlets are from *Is Your Home Safe?* and *Declaration of Policy, Official Manifesto of the Saskatchewan Farmer-Labour Group,1934 Election*.

The data on the devastating impact of the Depression are from the province's *Submission of the Province of Saskatchewan to the Royal Commission on Dominion-Provincial Relations* (1937, pp. 39, 107, 139, 145, 148, 169, 172–73, 177–79, 194). The depression remedies of the Anderson government are described and assessed in Russell's "The Co-operative Government in Saskatchewan, 1929–1934" (MA thesis, 1970). The depression measures proposed by the Ottawa government are characterized in Riddell's "The Bennett New Deal: An Essay" (MA thesis, 1967). Documented evidence on starvation in the province under the Anderson government is contained in the Hoffman thesis, "The Saskatchewan Election of 1934," pp. 22–24. The data on the numbers on relief in the province are presented in Neatby's "The Saskatchewan Relief Commission, 1931–1943" (*Saskatchewan History* [1950]), Lawton's "Urban Relief in Saskatchewan during the Years of the Depression, 1930–1937" (MA thesis, 1969), Russell's "The Co-operative Government in Saskatchewan, 1929-1934," the province's *Submission of the Province of Saskatchewan to the Royal Commission on Dominion-Provincial Relations* (1937), and the *Report of the Royal Commission on Dominion-Provincial Relations, Book I* (1940).

The narrative on events after the 1934 election and the power struggle between Williams and Coldwell is based on the Williams family private papers, the Wiens manuscript (chap. 5, "The Co-operative Commonwealth," and chap. 6, "Leader of the Opposition"), and the Steininger thesis (chap. 4, "The New Party"; chap. 5, "The Struggle for Power"; chap. 6, "From Movement to Party"; and chap. 7, "Preparing the Battleground"). The confrontation between Williams and Coldwell the day before the 1934 convention is recorded extensively in Minutes of a Conference of Elected Members, Defeated Candidates, Campaign Managers, and Members of the Political Directive Board, 26 July 1934, FLP/CCF papers, PAS.

The characterization of Williams in debates in the legislature is based on his replies as leader of the opposition to Speeches from the Throne (*Journals*, Saskatchewan Legislature, 1934–40), pamphlet reprints of many of his speeches in the assembly, and a number of his radio broadcasts published as pamphlets. Some of these can be found in the CCF Pamphlet Collection in the archives, while others are in the Williams family private papers. In 1939, Williams presented his critique of capitalism and vision of his socialist alternative in *Social Democracy in Canada*, published as a booklet. A complete published record of proceedings in the legislature did not begin until 1946, a reform introduced by the CCF government. I reviewed the compilation of press clippings of legislative debates in Saskatchewan's *Scrapbook Hansard*, 1934–40, PAS. Comments on Williams's excellence in the legislature, typically from those who

listened from the public gallery, occur throughout the papers and documents and in correspondence to Williams. Chapter 6 of Steininger's thesis
("From Movement to Party") provides further evidence of Williams's
effectiveness in debate, as well as detailing Williams's successful reconstruction of a party in debt and disarray after the 1934 election.

Both the Wiens manuscript and the Steininger thesis provide a great
deal of detail on the party debate between Williams and the right wing
over the day-to-day struggle, including the criticism Williams faced for his
support of the Trek upon its arrival in Regina. In addition, Brown's *When
Freedom Was Lost: The Unemployed, the Agitator, and the State* (1986),
Waiser's *All Hell Can't Stop Us: The On-to-Ottawa Trek and the Regina Riot*
(2003), and Brown's *On to Ottawa: The Rise and Fall of the Relief Camp
Workers' Union* (1987) were also consulted. The description of Williams's
role in the Trek and the riot is partly based on his recollections as recorded
by family members. These are in the Williams family private papers.

Many in the CCF national office and the Ontario CCF engaged in an
anti-communist crusade in this period to purge communists and those
seen to have excessive communist sympathies from the party. The battle
over purges rendered the Ontario CCF particularly politically ineffective
throughout the height of the Depression—precisely the time when great
strides could have been made. J. S. Woodsworth was a particularly strong
supporter of this purging process. Williams consistently resisted this
pressure, and no doubt much of the hostility toward him from the right
of the Saskatchewan CCF resulted from this resistance. There had been
a whispering campaign in the party regarding his alleged communist
sympathies since his lecture tour on his Soviet visit. Despite enormous
pressure, Williams's position remained firm and, given his strong support
among party members, effective, thus avoiding fratricidal purge battles.
On April 5, 1935, Williams made the Saskatchewan CCF's position clear:
"The CCF in Saskatchewan is prepared to fight shoulder to shoulder with
any group opposing this system of greed and graft" (quoted in Naylor,
The Fate of Labour Socialism [2016], p. 233). Many on the right saw this
as confirmation of Williams's alleged communist leanings. Naylor's book
provides details on this purging process and its political fallout (chap. 3,
"Class War in the CCF").

The narrative on the rise of Aberhart's Social Credit movement in
Alberta relies on Conway's dissertation (chap. 5, "Defeat from the Jaws of

Victory: The United Farmers of Alberta Regime, 1921–1935," and chap.
6, "Victory Again in Alberta: The Social Credit Regime, 1935–1944");
Irving's *The Social Credit Movement in Alberta* (1959); Macpherson's
Democracy in Alberta: Social Credit and the Party System (1962);
Mallory's *Social Credit and the Federal Power in Canada* (1954); Barr's
The Dynasty: The Rise and Fall of Social Credit in Alberta (1974); and
Finkel's *The Social Credit Phenomenon in Alberta* (1989). Useful PhD
dissertations include Schultz's "William Aberhart and the Social Credit
Party: A Political Biography" (1959) and Anderson's "The Alberta Social
Credit Party: An Analysis of Membership Characteristics, Participation,
and Opinions" (1972). Aberhart's *Social Credit Manual: Social Credit as
Applied to the Province of Alberta; Puzzling Questions and Their Answers*
(1935) was also examined. Aberhart's and Douglas's testimony on the
applicability of Social Credit to Alberta's economic crisis was reviewed
(*The Douglas System of Social Credit: Evidence taken by the Agricultural
Committee of the Alberta Legislature* [1934]).

The discussion of Social Credit's 1935 political invasion of
Saskatchewan is based on the following: Steininger thesis, chapter 5
("The Struggle for Power"); Wiens manuscript, chapter 7 ("Spite and
Expediency") and chapter 8 ("Adventures in Funny Money Land"); and
Conway dissertation, chapter 8 ("Victory in Saskatchewan: The Struggle
for Power and the CCF Regime, 1944–1952"). Details on T. C. Douglas's
hearing before the CCF executive regarding evidence he had agreed
to stand as a joint CCF–Social Credit candidate in Weyburn are con-
tained in the Steininger thesis. The full transcript is in the CCF papers
(*Transcript of Discussion between T. C. Douglas and CCF Executive
Members, October 9, 1935*, PAS). The report on Douglas's censure was
published in the Saskatoon *Star-Phoenix*, December 21, 1935.

Chapter 5. Building the CCF:
Defeating Social Credit, 1936 to 1938

A more detailed summary of Aberhart's efforts to implement Social
Credit in Alberta, and of the CCF's evolving tactical approach to the
challenge of Social Credit, is provided in Conway's dissertation (chap. 6,
"Victory Again in Alberta: The Social Credit Regime, 1935–1944," and
chap. 8, "Victory in Saskatchewan: The Struggle for Power and the CCF

Regime, 1944–1952"). The 1937 rebellion of the Social Credit caucus is examined in Macpherson's *Democracy in Alberta: Social Credit and the Party System* (1969) and in Schultz's PhD dissertation, "William Aberhart and the Social Credit Party: A Political Biography" (1959). Schultz's "The Social Credit Back-Benchers' Revolt" (*Canadian Historical Review* [1960]) presents a good summary of causes, events, and outcomes. Mallory's *Social Credit and the Federal Power in Canada* (1954) presents a comprehensive analysis of the use of the overriding federal powers of disallowance and reservation to block Aberhart's efforts.

Claudin documents the Communist International's shift, after Hitler's rise to power in 1933, from viewing social democratic and democratic socialist parties as social fascist enemies to calling for a united front of progressive forces against reaction and fascism, in *The Communist International: From Comintern to Cominform* (1975), chapter 4 ("The Crisis of Policy"). The impact of this shift in political line on the CP in Canada is discussed in Angus's *Canadian Bolsheviks: The Early Years of the Communist Party in Canada* (1981), especially chapter 14 ("The Third Period in Canada: United Front From Below"), and in Avakumovic's *The Communist Party in Canada: A History* (1975). The CP was initially eager to see the CCF in Saskatchewan fuse with Social Credit, or run joint candidates. Later, the party more closely conformed to the International's line, proposing joining CCF, Social Credit, Liberal, and Tory progressive voters behind united front candidates.

The crisis the CCF faced after the 1935 federal election, leading up to the Social Credit challenge in the 1938 provincial election; the battles over cooperation and saw-offs; and Williams's reorganization of the party are documented in the Steininger thesis (chap. 5, "The Struggle for Power"; chap. 6, "From Movement to Party"; chap. 7, "Preparing the Battleground"; chap. 8, "The 1938 Election"; and chap. 9, "The Triumph of the New Co-operators") and the Wiens manuscript (chap. 9, "A Certain Amount of Worldly Wisdom," and chap. 10, "Herding Cats").

Chapter 6. Fighting the War in the CCF and in Europe: 1937 to 1944

To refresh my memory on the details of the outbreak of World War II, I consulted the best single-volume history of the war, Max Hasting's *All*

Hell Let Loose: The World at War 1939–1945 (2011), and Eric Hobsbawm's *The Age of Catastrophe: The Short Twentieth Century, 1914–1991* (1995).

The narrative detailing Williams's struggles over the war issue is based most importantly on the Steininger thesis (chap. 10, "The War: A Crisis of Conscience," and chap. 11, "I Will Decide My Course . . .") and the Wiens manuscript (chap. 12, "The Pacifist Pamphlet Guerilla War"; chap. 13, "Encirclement"; and chap. 14, "The Rotten Mess"). The Williams family private papers were also consulted. More background on the details of the debate over the war in the provincial and national CCF are provided in Groome's "M. J. Coldwell and CCF Foreign Policy, 1932–59" (MA thesis, 1967) and Young's *Anatomy of a Party* (1969).

Chapter 7. Endgame: The 1944 Election

The depiction of Williams's role in the 1944 election and the events leading to his death is based on the private papers of the Williams family and the Wiens manuscript, chapter 15 ("A Happy and Fortunate Man").

Chapter 8. The Shame of the Intellectuals
Chapter 9. Conclusion: Williams in Canadian History

These two chapters do not require bibliographic notes since the text and supporting endnotes cover the sources on which the narrative is based.

BIBLIOGRAPHY

Personal Papers

Public Collections—Provincial Archives of Saskatchewan—Regina and Saskatoon: J. H. Brockelbank; T. C. Douglas; George F. Edwards; Carlyle King; Hugh MacLean; G. Makaroff; Violet McNaughton; J. and G. Telford; George H. Williams.

Private Collections: Williams Family; Barney Johnson (held in the Williams family private collection).

Pamphlet Collections—Provincial Archives of Saskatchewan—Regina and Saskatoon

Political Parties: Co-operative Commonwealth Federation; Conservative; Farmer-Labour; Liberal; Social Credit.

Others: Saskatchewan Grain Growers' Association; Farmers' Union of Canada; United Farmers of Canada (Saskatchewan Section).

Documents, Minutes, Convention Proceedings—Provincial Archives of Saskatchewan

Co-operative Commonwealth Federation (Saskatchewan Section); Farmer-Labour Party; Farmers' Union of Canada; United Farmers of Canada (Saskatchewan Section); Saskatchewan Grain Growers' Association.

Newspapers and Periodicals

Calgary Albertan, 1935–43; *Canadian Forum*, 1932–44; *Financial Post*, 1935–43;
  The Furrow, 1927, 1929–31; Regina *Leader-Post*, 1930–41; Estevan *Mercury*,
  October 1931; *Saskatchewan Commonwealth*, 1938–44; Saskatoon *Star-Phoenix*,
  1935–39; *Western Producer*, 1921–40.

Booklets by George Hara Williams

The Land of the Soviets. Saskatoon: United Farmers of Canada (Saskatchewan
  Section), 1931.
Social Democracy in Canada. Regina: Office of the Leader of the Opposition, 1939.

Government Publications and Documents

Alberta
Alberta Gazette, 1936.
Budget Speech, 1935–40.
*The Case for Alberta, Alberta's Problems and Dominion-Provincial Relations:
  Addressed to* THE SOVEREIGN PEOPLE *of Canada and Their Governments*.
  Edmonton: King's Printer, 1938.
*The Douglas System of Social Credit: Evidence Taken by the Agricultural Committee
  of the Alberta Legislature*. Edmonton: King's Printer, 1934.
Journals, Alberta Legislature, 1920–45.
Statutes of Alberta, 1935–46.

Canada
Dominion Bureau of Statistics. *Census Reports*, 1911–41.
Public Assistance and Social Insurance, a study prepared by A. E. Grauer for the
  Royal Commission on Dominion-Provincial Relations. Ottawa: King's Printer,
  1939.
Report of the Royal Commission on Banking and Currency in Canada. Ottawa:
  King's Printer, 1939.
Report of the Royal Commission on Dominion-Provincial Relations. Ottawa: King's
  Printer, 1940.
Report of the Royal Commission to Enquire into Trading in Grain Futures. Ottawa,
  King's Printer, 1931.
Report of the Royal Commission on Price Spreads. Ottawa: King's Printer, 1935.

Saskatchewan
*A Submission by the Government of Saskatchewan to the Royal Commission on
  Dominion-Provincial Relations (Canada, 1937)*. Regina: King's Printer, 1937.
Journals, Saskatchewan Legislature, 1920–45.

Report of the Royal Commission on Immigration and Settlement. Regina: King's
    Printer, 1930.
Report of the Saskatchewan Reconstruction Council. Regina: King's Printer, 1944.
Scrapbook Hansard, 1934–40.
Statutes of Saskatchewan, 1944, 1945.

Reference Works

Bliss, J. M. *Canadian History in Documents, 1763–1966.* Toronto: Ryerson Press, 1966.
Brown, Robert Craig, and Margaret Prang, eds. *Canadian Historical Documents
    Series.* Scarborough: Prentice-Hall, 1966.
Canadian Annual Review, 1921–45.
Canadian Parliamentary Guide, 1921–45.
Dictionary of Canadian Biography.
Encyclopedia of Saskatchewan.
Public Archives of Canada. *The Canadian Directory of Parliament, 1867–1967.*
    Ottawa: Queen's Printer, 1968.
Reid, J. H. Stewart, Kenneth McNaught, and Harry Crowe. *A Source-Book
    of Canadian History: Selected Documents and Personal Papers.* Toronto:
    Longmans, 1959.
Saskatchewan Archives Board. *Saskatchewan Executive and Legislative Directory,
    1905–1970.* Regina, 1971.
Saskatchewan. *Provincial Elections in Saskatchewan, 1905–1986.* 3rd ed. Regina:
    Chief Electoral Office, Province of Saskatchewan, 1987.
Scarrow, Howard A. *Canada Votes: A Handbook of Federal and Provincial Election
    Data.* New Orleans: Hauser, 1962.
Urquhart, M. C., and K. A. H. Buckley, eds. *Historical Statistics of Canada.* Toronto:
    Macmillan, 1965.

Unpublished Theses, Disserations, and Manuscripts

Anderson, F. W. "Farmers in Politics, 1915–1935: Some Political Aspects of
    the Grain Growers' Movement (1915–1935) with Particular Reference to
    Saskatchewan." MA thesis, University of Saskatchewan, 1949.
Anderson, Owen A. "The Alberta Social Credit Party: An Empirical Analysis of
    Membership Characteristics, Participation and Opinions." PhD diss., University
    of Alberta, 1972.
Betke, Carl Frederick. "The United Farmers of Alberta, 1921–1935: The
    Relationship between the Agricultural Organization and the Government of
    Alberta." MA thesis, University of Alberta, 1971.
Calderwood, William. "The Rise and Fall of the Ku Klux Klan in Saskatchewan."
    MA thesis, University of Regina, 1968.
Conway, J. F. "To Seek A Goodly Heritage: The Prairie Populist Resistance to the
    National Policy in Canada." PhD diss., Simon Fraser University, 1979.

Courville, Leo D. E. "The Saskatchewan Progressives." MA thesis, University of
  Regina, 1971.
Embree, D. G. "The Rise and Fall of the United Farmers of Alberta." MA thesis,
  University of Alberta, 1956.
Godfrey, W. G. "The 1933 Convention of the Co-operative Commonwealth
  Federation." MA thesis, University of Waterloo, 1965.
Groome, A. J. "M. J. Coldwell and CCF Foreign Policy, 1932–1950." MA thesis,
  University of Saskatchewan, 1967.
Hoffman, G. J. "The Saskatchewan Provincial Election of 1934: Its Political,
  Economic, and Social Background." MA thesis, University of Regina, 1973.
Johnson, A. W. "Biography of Government: Policy Formulation in Saskatchewan,
  1944–1961." PhD diss., Harvard University, 1963.
Knuttila, K. Murray. "The Saskatchewan Agrarian Movement, 1900–1930." MA
  thesis, University of Regina, 1975.
Lawton, Alma. "Urban Relief in Saskatchewan during the Years of the Depression,
  1930–1937." MA thesis, University of Saskatchewan, 1969.
Riddell, Norman. "The Bennett New Deal: An Essay." MA thesis, University of
  Saskatchewan, 1967.
Rolph, William Kirby. "Henry Wise Wood and the Agrarian Movement in Western
  Canada." PhD diss., Brown University, 1949.
Russell, Peter A. "The Co-operative Government in Saskatchewan, 1929–1934:
  Response to the Depression." MA thesis, University of Saskatchewan, 1970.
Schultz, Harold John. "William Aberhart and the Social Credit Party: A Political
  Biography." PhD diss., Duke University, 1959.
Silverstein, S. "The Rise, Ascendancy and Decline of the Co-operative Commonwealth
  Federation Party of Saskatchewan." PhD diss., Washington University, 1969.
Steininger, Friedrich. "George Hara Williams: Agrarian Socialist." MA thesis,
  University of Regina, 1976.
Whalen, Hugh J. "The Distinctive Legislation of the Government of Alberta,
  1935–1950." MA thesis, University of Alberta, 1951.
Wiens, Muriel. "Finding George Williams: A Tale of the Grass Roots." Unpublished
  manuscript, 2007.

Articles and Book Chapters

Auger, Martin F. "On the Brink of Civil War: The Canadian Government and the
  Suppression of the 1918 Quebec Easter Riots." *Canadian Historical Review* 89,
  no. 4 (2008): 503–40.
Britnell, G. E. "Saskatchewan, 1930–1935." *Canadian Journal of Economics and
  Political Science* 2, no. 2 (1936): 143–66.
Brown, Lorne A. "Unemployment Relief Camps in Saskatchewan, 1933–1936."
  Saskatchewan History 23, no. 3 (1970): 81–104.

Conway, J. F. "Agrarian Petit-Bourgeois Responses to Capitalist Industrialization: The Case of Canada." In Bechhofer and Elliott, *The Petite Bourgeoisie*, 1–37. London: Macmillan, 1981.

Conway, J. F. "Populism in the United States, Canada, and Russia: Explaining the Roots of Canada's Third Parties." *Canadian Journal of Political Science* 11, no. 1 (1978): 99–124.

Conway, J. F. "The Prairie Populist Resistance to the National Policy: Some Reconsiderations." *Journal of Canadian Studies* 14, no. 3 (1979): 77–91.

Fowke, V. C. "Royal Commissions and Canadian Agricultural Policy." *Canadian Journal of Economics and Political Science* 14, no. 2 (1948): 163–75.

Hoffman, George. "The Entry of the United Farmers of Canada, Saskatchewan Section into Politics: A Reassessment." *Saskatchewan History* 30, no. 3 (1977): 99–109.

Hoffman, George. "The Saskatchewan Farmer-Labour Party, 1932–1934: How Radical Was It at Its Origin?" *Saskatchewan History* 28, no. 2 (1975): 52–64.

Irving, John A. "The Evolution of the Social Credit Movement." *Canadian Journal of Economics and Political Science* 14, no. 3 (1948): 321–41.

Kyba, Patrick. "Ballots and Burning Crosses—The Election of 1929." In Ward and Spafford, *Politics in Saskatchewan*, 105–23. Toronto: Longmans, 1969.

Mallory, J. R. "The Lieutenant-Governor as a Dominion Officer: The Reservation of the Three Alberta Bills in 1937." *Canadian Journal of Economics and Political Science* 14, no. 4 (1948): 502–7.

Morton, W. L. "Direct Legislation and the Origins of the Progressive Movement." *Canadian Historical Review* 25, no. 3 (1944): 279–88.

Morton, W. L. "The Western Progressive Movement and Cabinet Domination." *Canadian Journal of Economics and Political Science* 12, no. 2 (1946): 136–47.

Neatby, Blair. "The Saskatchewan Relief Commission, 1931–1934." *Saskatchewan History* 3, no. 2 (1950): 41–56.

Reid, Escott M. "The Saskatchewan Liberal Machine before 1929." *Canadian Journal of Economics and Political Science* 2, no. 1 (1936): 27–40.

Saywell, John T. "Reservation Revisited: Alberta 1937." *Canadian Journal of Economics and Political Science* 27, no. 3 (1961): 367–72.

Schultz, Harold J. "Aberhart: The Organization Man." *Alberta Historical Review* 7, no. 2 (1959): 19–26.

Schultz, Harold J. "A Second Term: 1940." *Alberta Historical Review* 10, no. 1 (1962): 17–26.

Schultz, Harold J. "The Social Credit Back-Benchers' Revolt." *Canadian Historical Review* 41, no. 1 (1960): 1–18.

Silverstein, Sanford. "Occupational Class and Voting Behaviour: Electoral Support of a Left-Wing Protest Movement in a Period of Prosperity." In Lipset, *Agrarian Socialism*, 435–79. Berkeley: University of California, 1971.

Sinclair, Peter R. "The Saskatchewan CCF and the Communist Party in the 1930s." *Saskatchewan History* 26, no. 1 (1973): 1–10.

Spafford, Duff. "The Elevator Issue, the Organized Farmer and the Government, 1908–1911." *Saskatchewan History* 15, no. 2 (1962): 81–92.

Spafford, Duff. "The 'Left-Wing,' 1921–1931." In Ward and Spafford, *Politics in Saskatchewan*, 44–58. Toronto: Longmans, 1968.

Spafford, Duff. "The Origins of the Farmers' Union of Canada." *Saskatchewan History* 18, no. 3 (1965): 89–98.

Wilbur, J. R. H. "H. H. Stevens and the Reconstruction Party." *Canadian Historical Review* 45, no. 1 (1964): 1–28.

Books

Angus, Ian. *Canadian Bolsheviks: The Early Years of the Communist Party in Canada*. Montreal: Vanguard Publications, 1981.

Archer, John H. *Saskatchewan: A History*. Saskatoon: Western Producer Prairie Books, 1980.

Armstrong, E. *The Crisis of Quebec, 1914–1918*. Toronto: McClelland & Stewart, 1974 (1932).

Avakumovic, Ivan. *The Communist Party in Canada: A History*. Toronto: McClelland & Stewart, 1975.

Avery, Donald. *"Dangerous Foreigners": European Immigrant Workers and Labour Radicalism in Canada, 1896–1932*. Toronto: McClelland & Stewart, 1979.

Barr, John J. *The Dynasty: The Rise and Fall of Social Credit In Alberta*. Toronto: McClelland & Stewart, 1974.

Bechhofer, Frank, and Brian Elliott, eds. *The Petite Bourgeoisie: Comparative Studies of the Uneasy Stratum*. London: Macmillan, 1981.

Bercuson, David J. *Confrontation at Winnipeg: Labour, Industrial Relations, and the General Strike*. Montreal/Kingston: McGill-Queen's University Press, 1974.

Bercuson, David J. *Fools and Wise Men: The Rise and Fall of the One Big Union*. Toronto: McGraw-Hill Ryerson, 1978.

Berger, Thomas R. *Fragile Freedoms: Human Rights and Dissent in Canada*. Toronto: Clarke, Irwin, 1981.

Betcherman, Lita-Rose. *The Swastika and the Maple Leaf: Fascist Movements in Canada in the Thirties*. Toronto: Fitzhenry & Whiteside, 1975.

Black, N. F. *History of Saskatchewan and the Old North West*. Vol. 1. Regina: North West Historical Co. 1913.

Britnell, G. E. *The Wheat Economy*. Toronto: University of Toronto Press, 1939.

Britnell, G. E., and V. C. Fowke. *Canadian Agriculture in War and Peace, 1935–1950*. Stanford, CA: Stanford University Press, 1962.

Brown, Lorne. *On to Ottawa: The Rise and Fall of the Relief Camp Workers' Union*. Toronto: Lorimer, 1987.

Brown, Lorne. *When Freedom Was Lost: The Unemployed, the Agitator, and the State*. Montreal: Black Rose, 1986.

Brown, Robert Craig, and Ramsay Cook. *Canada, 1896–1921: A Nation Transformed*. Toronto: McClelland & Stewart, 1974.

Carlisle, Kathleen. *Fiery Joe: The Maverick Who Lit Up the West*. Regina: University of Regina Press, 2017.

Claudin, Fernando. *The Communist International: From Comintern to Cominform*. Harmondsworth, UK: Penguin, 1975.

Colquette, R. D. *The First Fifty Years: A History of the United Grain Growers Limited*. Winnipeg: The Public Press, 1957.

Conway, J. F. *The Rise of the New West: The History of a Region in Confederation*. 4th ed. Toronto: Lorimer, 2014.

Cook, Tim. *Shock Troops: Canadians Fighting the Great War, 1914–1918*. Toronto: Viking, 2008.

Dafoe, John W. *Clifford Sifton in Relation to His Times*. Toronto: Macmillan, 1931.

Dafoe, J. W. *Laurier: A Study in Canadian Politics*. Toronto: McClelland & Stewart, 1963.

Dawson, C. A. *Group Settlement: Ethnic Communities in Western Canada*. Toronto: Macmillan, 1936.

Dawson, C. A., and Eva R. Younge. *Pioneering in the Prairie Provinces: The Social Side of the Settlement Process*. Toronto: Macmillan, 1940.

Douglas, C. H. *The Alberta Experiment: An Interim Survey*. London: Eyre and Spottiswoode, 1937.

Drury, E. C. *Farmer Premier*. Toronto: McClelland & Stewart, 1966.

Dutil, Patrice, and David McKenzie. *Canada 1911: The Decisive Election that Shaped the Country*. Toronto: Dundurn, 2011.

Eager, Evelyn. *Saskatchewan Government: Politics and Pragmatism*. Saskatoon: Western Producer Prairie Books, 1980.

Ellis, L. Ethan. *Reciprocity, 1911: A Study in Canadian-American Relations*. New Haven: Yale University, 1939.

England, Robert. *The Colonization of Western Canada: A Study of Contemporary Land Settlements (1896–1934)*. London: King & Son, 1936.

Finkel, Alvin. *The Social Credit Phenomenon in Alberta*. Toronto: University of Toronto Press, 1989.

Finlay, John L. *Social Credit: The English Origins*. Montreal/Kingston: McGill-Queen's University Press, 1972.

Fowke, Vernon C. *Canadian Agricultural Policy: The Historical Pattern*. Toronto: University of Toronto Press, 1946.

Fowke, Vernon C. *The National Policy and the Wheat Economy*. Toronto: University of Toronto Press, 1957.

Francis, R. Douglas. *Frank H. Underhill: Intellectual Provocateur*. Toronto: University of Toronto Press, 1986.

Friesen, Gerald. *The Canadian Prairies: A History*. Toronto: University of Toronto Press, 1984.

Gerth, Hans, and C. Wright Mills. *Character and Social Structure: The Psychology of Social Institutions*. New York: Harcourt, Brace, 1953.

Granatstein, J. L., and J. M. Hitsman. *Broken Promises: A History of Conscription in Canada*. Toronto: Oxford University Press, 1977.

Hastings, Max. *All Hell Let Loose: The World at War 1939-1945.* London: HarperPress, 2012.

Haythorne, George V. *Labour in Canadian Agriculture.* Cambridge, MA: Harvard University Press, 1965.

Heron, Craig, ed. *The Workers' Revolt in Canada, 1917-1925.* Toronto: University of Toronto Press, 1998.

Hesketh, Bob. *Major Douglas and Alberta Social Credit.* Toronto: University of Toronto Press, 1997.

Higginbotham, C. H. *Off the Record: The CCF in Saskatchewan.* Toronto: McClelland & Stewart, 1968.

Hobsbawm, Eric. *The Age of Extremes: The Short Twentieth Century, 1914-1991.* London: Abacus [Little, Brown], 1995.

Hooke, Alf. *30 + 5: I Know, I Was There.* Edmonton: Co-op Press, 1971.

Horn, Michael. *The League for Social Reconstruction: Intellectual Origins of the Democratic Left in Canada.* Toronto: University of Toronto Press, 1980.

Innis, Harold A. *A History of the Canadian Pacific Railway.* Toronto: University of Toronto, 1971 (1923).

Innis, Harold A. *The Problems of Staple Production in Canada.* Toronto: Ryerson Press, 1933.

Irvine, William. *The Farmers in Politics.* Toronto: McClelland & Stewart, 1920.

Irving, John A. *The Social Credit Movement in Alberta.* Toronto: University of Toronto Press, 1959.

Jamieson, S. M. *Times of Trouble: Labour Unrest and Industrial Conflict in Canada, 1900-1966.* Ottawa: Privy Council, 1968.

Janzen, Eileen R. *Growing to One World: The Life of J. King Gordon.* Montreal/Kingston: McGill-Queen's University Press, 2013.

Johnson, A. W., with Rosemary Proctor. *Dream No Little Dreams: A Biography of the Douglas Government of Saskatchewan, 1944-1961.* Toronto: University of Toronto Press, 2004.

Johnson, L. P. V., and Ola J. MacNutt. *Aberhart of Alberta.* Edmonton: Institute of Applied Art, 1970.

Johnston, Faith. *A Great Restlessness: The Life and Politics of Dorise Nielsen.* Winnipeg: University of Manitoba Press, 2006.

Kordan, Bohdan S. *Enemy Aliens, Prisoners of War: Internment in Canada during the Great War.* Montreal/Kingston: McGill-Queen's University Press, 2002.

Lerohl, M. L. *Assets, Liabilities and Net Worth of Canadian Farm Operators, 1935-64.* Ottawa: Agricultural Economics Research Council, 1967.

Lewis, David. *The Good Fight: Political Memoirs, 1909-1958.* Toronto: Macmillan, 1981.

Lingard, C. Cecil. *Territorial Government in Canada: The Autonomy Issue in the Old North-West Territories.* Toronto: University of Toronto Press, 1946.

Lipset, Seymour Martin, ed. *Agrarian Socialism: The Cooperative Commonwealth Federation in Saskatchewan—A Study in Political Sociology.* Rev. and expanded ed. Berkeley: University of California, 1971.

MacDougall, John. *Rural Life in Canada: Its Trends and Tasks.* Toronto: Westminster, 1913.

Mackintosh, W. A. *Agricultural Co-operation in Western Canada.* Kingston: Queen's University, 1924.

Mackintosh, W. A. *The Economic Background of Dominion-Provincial Relations.* Toronto: McClelland & Stewart, 1964.

Mackintosh, W. A. *Economic Problems of the Prairie Provinces.* Toronto: Macmillan, 1935.

Mackintosh, W. A. *Prairie Settlement: The Geographic Setting.* Toronto: Macmillan, 1934.

Macpherson, C. B. *Social Credit in Alberta: Social Credit and the Party System.* Toronto: University of Toronto Press, 1962.

Mallory, J. R. *Social Credit and the Federal Power in Canada.* Toronto: University of Toronto Press, 1954.

Martin, Chester. *"Dominion Lands" Policy.* Toronto: Macmillan, 1938.

Martin, Robin. *Radical Politics and Canadian Labour, 1896-1930.* Kingston: Industrial Relations Centre, Queen's University, 1968.

Masters, D. C. *The Winnipeg General Strike.* Toronto: University of Toronto Press, 1950.

Mayse, Susan. *Ginger: The Life and Death of Albert Goodwin.* Vancouver: Harbour, 1990.

McCormack, A. Ross. *Reformers, Rebels and Revolutionaries: The Western Canadian Radical Movement, 1899-1919.* Toronto: University of Toronto Press, 1977.

McHenry, Dean E. *The Third Force in Canada: The Co-operative Commonwealth Federation, 1932-1948.* Toronto: Oxford University Press, 1950.

McGibbon, Duncan Alexander. *The Canadian Grain Trade.* Toronto: Macmillan, 1932.

McGibbon, Duncan Alexander. *The Canadian Grain Trade, 1931-1951.* Toronto: University of Toronto, 1952.

McKay, Ian. *Reasoning Otherwise: Leftists and the People's Enlightenment in Canada 1890-1920.* Toronto: Between the Lines, 2008.

McLeod, Thomas H., and Ian McLeod. *Tommy Douglas: The Road to Jerusalem.* Edmonton: Hurtig, 1987.

McNaught, Kenneth. *A Prophet in Politics: A Biography of J. S. Woodsworth.* Toronto: University of Toronto Press, 1959.

Milligan, Frank. *Eugene A. Forsey: An Intellectual Biography.* Calgary: University of Calgary Press, 2004.

Mills, C. Wright. *The Sociological Imagination.* 40th anniversary ed. New York: Oxford University Press, 2000.

Mills, Ivor J. *Stout Hearts Stand Tall: A Biographical Sketch of a Militant Saskatchewan Farmer, Hopkins Evan Mills.* Vancouver: Evergreen, 1971.

Moorhouse, Hopkins. *Deep Furrows: which tells of Pioneer Trails along which the Farmers of Western Canada fought their way to great achievements in Co-operation.* Toronto: G. J. McLeod, 1918.

Mormon, James B. *Farm Credits in the United States and Canada.* Toronto: Macmillan, 1924.

Morton, Arthur S. *History of Prairie Settlement.* Toronto: Macmillan, 1938.

Morton, W. L. *Manitoba: A History.* Toronto: University of Toronto Press, 1967.

Morton, W. L. *The Progressive Party in Canada.* Toronto: University of Toronto Press, 1957.

Murchie, R. W. *Agricultural Progress on the Prairie Frontier.* Toronto: Macmillan, 1936.

Naylor, James. *The Fate of Labour Socialism: The Co-operative Commonwealth Federation and the Dream of a Working-Class Future.* Toronto: University of Toronto Press, 2016.

Nicholson, G. W. L. *Official History of the Canadian Army in the First World War: Canadian Expeditionary Force, 1914–1919.* Ottawa: Queen's Printer, 1964.

Patton, H. S. *Grain Growers Co-operation in Western Canada.* Cambridge, MA: Harvard University Press, 1928.

Penner, Norman, ed. *Winnipeg, 1919: The Strikers' Own History of the Winnipeg General Strike.* Toronto: James Lewis & Samuel, 1973.

Pennington, Doris. *Agnes Macphail: Reformer.* Toronto: Smith and Pierre, 1989.

Plekhanov, Georgi. *Selected Philosophical Works.* Vol. 2, *On the Question of the Individual's Role in History.* Moscow: Progress, 1976 (1898).

Porritt, Edward. *The Revolt in Canada against the New Feudalism: Tariff History from the Revision of 1907 to the Uprising in the West of 1910.* London: Cassell, 1911.

Porritt, Edward, and Annie G. Porritt. *Sixty Years of Protection in Canada: 1846–1912: Where Industry Leans on the Politician.* Winnipeg: Grain Growers' Guide, 1913.

Robin, Martin. *Radical Politics and Canadian Labour: 1896–1930.* Kingston: Industrial Relations Centre, Queen's University, 1968.

Rolph, William Kirby. *Henry Wise Wood of Alberta.* Toronto: University of Toronto Press, 1950.

Safarian, A. E. *The Canadian Economy in the Great Depression.* Toronto: McClelland & Stewart, 1970.

Shackleton, Doris F. *Tommy Douglas.* Toronto: McClelland & Stewart, 1975.

Sharp, Paul F. *The Agrarian Revolt in Western Canada: A Survey Showing American Parallels.* Minneapolis: University of Minnesota, 1948.

Smith, David E. *Prairie Liberalism: The Liberal Party in Saskatchewan, 1905–1971.* Toronto: University of Toronto Press, 1975.

Stanley, G. F. C. *The Birth of Western Canada: A History of the Riel Rebellions.* 2nd ed. Toronto: University of Toronto Press, 1960.

Steeves, Dorothy. *The Compassionate Rebel: Ernest E. Winch and His Times.* Vancouver: Evergreen, 1960.

Stevens, Paul, ed. *The 1911 General Election: A Study in Canadian Politics.* Toronto: Copp Clark, 1970.

Stewart, Margaret, and Doris French Shackleton. *Ask No Quarter: A Biography of Agnes Macphail.* Toronto: Longmans and Green, 1959.

Stewart, Walter. *The Life and Political Times of Tommy Douglas.* Toronto: McArthur, 2003.

Stewart, Walter. *M. J.: The Life and Times of M. J. Coldwell.* Toronto: Stoddart, 2000.

Swanson, D., ed. *Historical Essays on the Prairie Provinces.* Toronto: McClelland & Stewart, 1970.

Thomas, Lewis H., ed. *The Making of a Socialist: The Recollections of T. C. Douglas.* Edmonton: University of Alberta Press, 1982.

Thomas, Lewis Herbert. *The Struggle for Responsible Government in the North-West Territories, 1870-97.* Toronto: University of Toronto Press, 1956.

Vance, Jonathan F. *Death So Noble: Memory, Meaning, and the First World War.* Vancouver: UBC Press, 1997.

Thomas, L. G. *The Liberal Party of Alberta: A History of Politics in the Province of Alberta, 1905-1921.* Toronto: University of Toronto Press, 1959.

Thompson, J. H. *The Harvests of War: The Prairie West, 1914-18.* Toronto: McClelland & Stewart, 1978.

Waiser, W. A. *All Hell Can't Stop Us: The On-to-Ottawa Trek and the Regina Riot.* Calgary: Fifth House, 2003.

Ward, Norman, and Duff Spafford, eds. *Politics in Saskatchewan.* Toronto: Longmans, 1968.

Williams, A. M. *Conscription, 1917.* Toronto: University of Toronto Press, 1969.

Wood, L. A. *A History of Farmers' Movements in Canada.* Toronto: Ryerson Press, 1924.

Young, Walter D. *The Anatomy of a Party: The National CCF, 1932-1961.* Toronto: University of Toronto Press, 1969.

Zakuta, Leo. *A Protest Movement Becalmed: A Study of Change in the CCF.* Toronto: University of Toronto Press, 1964.

Other Sources

Aberhart, Wm. *Social Credit Manual: Social Credit as Applied to the Province of Alberta: Puzzling Questions and Their Answers.* Rev. ed. Calgary: Western Printers and Litho, 1935.

Allen, W. and C. C. Hope. *The Farm Outlook in Saskatchewan.* Saskatoon: University of Saskatchewan, 1936.

Coldwell, M. J. *Left Turn, Canada.* Toronto: Duell, Sloan and Pearce, 1945.

Hann, Russell. *Some Historical Perspectives on Canadian Agrarian Political Movements: The Ontario Origins of the Agrarian Criticism of Canadian Industrial Society.* Pamphlet. Toronto: New Hogtown Press, 1973.

Kristjanson, Leo F. *Population Trends in the Incorporated Centres of Saskatchewan, 1926-1961.* Saskatoon: Centre for Community Studies, 1963.

Lewis, David, and Scott, Frank. *Make This Your Canada: A Review of CCF History and Policy.* Toronto: Central Canada Publishing, 1943.

Masters, D. C. *Reciprocity, 1846-1911.* Historical booklet no. 12. Ottawa: Canadian Historical Association, 1961.

McCrorie, James Napier. *In Union Is Strength*. Pamphlet. Saskatoon: Centre for Community Studies, 1964.

Morton, W. L. *The West and Confederation, 1857–1871*. Historical booklet no. 9. Ottawa: Canadian Historical Association, 1958.

Research Committee of the League for Social Reconstruction. *Social Planning for Canada*. Toronto: Thomas Nelson and Sons, 1935.

Thomas, Lewis H. *The North-West Territories, 1870–1905*. Historical booklet no. 26. Ottawa: Canadian Historical Association, 1970.

Williams, Samuel H. *Stand to Your Horses: Through the First World War with the Lord Strathcona's Horse (Royal Canadians)*. Altona: Friesen and Son, 1961.

INDEX

A

Aberhart, Premier William: as evangelical Christian, 285n42, 287n47; as founder of Social Credit Party, 285n42; as promoting social credit ideas, 132–33, 146–51, 154, 310–11; as rejecting saw-off proposal, 228, 231; and social credit movement/party, 134, 143–45, 152–53, 230, 309–10; as winning 1935 Alberta election, 159, 227

agitation: by farmers, 26–27, 29–30; by organizations/parties, 52, 56, 63, 68, 249, 305; as political, 24, 28, 157; as populist, 21, 24, 28, 31; by unions, 275n1

agrarian populism, 21, 34, 88, 101, 132, 246, 254, 279n35; as movement, 17–18, 25, 51, 286n43, 299–300; as response to capitalism, 20, 22; and socialist ideas, 18, 45, 64, 86, 97, 103, 113–14, 213, 249

Agrarian Socialism: The Cooperative Commonwealth Federation in Saskatchewan, 240, 292n4

agriculture, 20, 85, 96, 302; as important export, 22, 30, 33, 63

Alberta Co-operative Commonwealth Federation, 159

Alberta Credit House Act, 147

The Alberta Experiment, 149, 286n43

Alberta Federation of Labour, 132

Alberta Social Credit Party, 145, 148–49, 152, 154; invasion into Saskatchewan, 153, 156, 158, 180, 184, 227–28, 231–32, 237, 253–54, 310–11

All-Canadian Labour Congress, 78

Anderson, Premier J. T. M.: association with Ku Klux Klan, 67; cooperative government of, 62, 68–69, 71, 76, 101, 104–6, 115, 121, 308; responses to Depression, 103, 283n16, 305, 307

Angus, Ian, 311

anti-monopoly laws, 29

Archer, John H., 242, 294n34

Are They to Be Trusted?, 154

Association Opposing a Compulsory Pool, 62

B

banks, public ownership of, 39, 108, 155, 252

Bennett, Prime Minister R. B., xxiv, 77,
103, 128–31, 289n19
Benson, Jacob, 136, 223, 225, 287n49
birth control, legalization of, 82–83
The B.N.A. Act and Social Credit, 133
Board of Grain Supervisors (Wheat
Board), 30, 34
Borden, Prime Minister Robert: Union
government of, 8–9, 11, 298
boycotts, of sales of seized land, 42
Bracken, Premier John, 103
Brockelbank, John H., 195, 197–99,
212, 234, 238, 292n50
Brown, Rev. W. G., 186
Brownlee, Premier John E., 134
Buck, Tim, 127

C
Calgary Albertan, 149
Calgary Prophetic Bible Institute, 132,
285n42, 288n10
*Canada and the War: The CCF
Position,* 178
Canadian Broadcasting Company
(CBC), 218
Canadian Council of Agriculture
(CCA), 25, 31–33, 36, 273n4
Canadian Forum, 99
Canadian Great War Project, 272n3
Canadian Labour Congress (formerly
Canadian Congress of Labour),
282n10
Canadian Manufacturers' Association,
27–28
Canadian Pacific Railway (CPR), 19,
23, 129–30, 211, 299
The Canadian Prairies: A History, 242,
294n36
Canadian Press, 84
Canadian Wheat Board, 34, 36–37, 66
capitalism: abolition of, 57, 63, 100,
120, 141, 271n1, 273n5, 274n1;
denunciation of, xxiv, 32, 79, 135;
as economically unsound, 80, 101,

154; and farm land speculation,
89; and financial institutions, 39,
41, 80, 89, 135, 147, 181, 250, 253;
and industry, 19–20, 24, 26, 28, 30,
300; as opposed to socialism, 29,
42, 97, 101, 122–23, 125, 135, 142,
179, 205; and organized farmers,
18, 21, 24, 81; and populism, 29, 45;
reform of, 102, 108, 183; relation
to fascism, 173; relation to social
credit, 39, 144; relation to war, 144,
154, 170, 177, 247; special interests
of, 6, 28–29, 66; victims of, 126,
128. *See also* class struggle
Catholic Church, 82, 102, 219
*The CCF Debt Adjustment and Land
Policy,* 155
The CCF Program for Saskatchewan,
205
*CCF Statement on Canada and the
Present Crisis,* 177
chilled-meat industry, as publicly
owned, 26
class struggle, 32, 38–39, 45–46, 52, 62,
273n5. *See also* capitalism
Coldwell, Major James (M. J.),
95–96, 121, 142, 159; and 1934
Saskatchewan election campaign,
109–15; in historical accounts,
217–22, 224–28, 233–34, 236–38,
240–44, 255, 308; as leader of FLP/
CCF, 93–94, 98, 100, 103, 114–16,
119, 138, 186, 195, 247, 253; as
leader of ILP, 91–92, 208; as a
leader of Progressive Party, 280n1;
and New Democracy supporters,
182–84; and pacifism, 170, 173,
184–85, 187; and rift with G. H.
Williams, 117–18, 120, 123, 127,
132, 184, 188–89, 196–97; and
social credit ideas, 135–37
collective bargaining rights, 17, 125,
127, 273n1, 275n1. *See also* trade
unions

collectivization, in agriculture, 85, 88, 96, 102, 140

communism, xxiv, 86, 95, 97, 102, 142, 148, 221, 274n1. *See also* Communist Party (CP)

Communism Is the Threat, 152

Communist International (Comintern), 142, 183, 290n20, 311

Communist Party (CP), 18, 95, 102, 127, 129, 181, 222, 272n1; and CCF, 124–25, 142–43, 157, 255, 311; as denouncing capitalism, 124, 126; involvement with Saskatchewan parties, 42, 73–75, 85, 152, 182–83, 187, 311; in the Ontario CCF, 284n22, 309; as part of "far left," 71, 252, 278n21

conscientious objection, 180, 184. *See also* draft dodging/resisting; war resistance

conscription, 9, 169, 177, 179, 186, 277n19; CCF support for, 236; debate over, 9–11, 17, 273n1, 297; resistance to, 10, 298; of "wealth over men," 8, 31, 180, 185

Conservative Party, 36, 103, 108, 125; in 1935 Alberta election, 135; in 1938 Saskatchewan election, 143, 156–57, 228–30; and capitalism, 22; on conscription/war, 179, 185; and farmers, 6, 27; and tariff protection, 25, 66

Conservative Party of Saskatchewan, 65–66, 102, 112, 114; and Ku Klux Klan, 67–68

constituency associations, 189–90, 204, 239; for FLP/CCF, 86, 91–92, 95, 110–11, 126–27, 131, 140–41, 181

Co-operative Commonwealth Federation (CCF): and 1933 federal by-election, 109; and 1935 federal election, 135, 137–40, 142–43, 162, 185–86; and 1938 Saskatchewan election, 150–51, 154, 156–59, 164;

building up of, 120, 141, 187, 191, 217, 247, 254; communist smears of, xxiv, 85–86, 94–95, 97, 102–3, 114, 121, 123, 125, 140, 151, 185, 204, 219; conventions of, 99–100, 110–11, 115–16, 119–20, 133, 138, 140–42, 154, 156, 170, 185, 188, 191–93, 196–98, 217–19, 221, 232, 235; as elected government in 1944, xxvi, 114, 207, 209, 211–12, 217, 242, 245; and Herridge movement, 181–84, 191; leadership of, 110, 121, 145, 180, 192, 196, 198; party platform of, 102, 123, 127, 140, 155, 205, 259; political/social principles of, 122, 125–26, 204–6, 208, 210; relation to Communist Party, 124–25, 128, 142, 222; relation to Social Credit, 136–37, 143–45, 223–28, 230–31; urban security package, 205–6; war policy of, 169–70, 173, 177–80, 185–88, 190, 194

Co-operative Commonwealth Federation (Saskatchewan Section) (CCF[SS]): and 1938 Saskatchewan election, 150, 240; and 1944 Saskatchewan election, 200–204, 208, 217; association with other parties, 180, 229, 254; conventions of, xxi, 171, 174, 184, 190, 227, 230, 234; formation/victory of, xv, 119, 145, 147, 218–20, 241; leadership of, 232, 235–36, 242–43, 246; membership requirements of, 239; as natural governing party of Saskatchewan, 247; pacifism and war neutrality of, 174, 178, 185–86; platform of, 253

cooperative commonwealth government, 52, 64–65, 77, 91, 100–101, 133, 141, 205, 243, 253

Co-operative Commonwealth Youth Movement (CCYM), 124–25

Co-operative Creamery, 106

cooperatives, 23, 63, 101, 211, 252;
dairy pool, 209; international
marketing, 85; pool marketing, in
Alberta, 42
credit and currency systems: and
monetary reform, 132; socialization
of, 286n43
credit/credit assistance, 36; for
agriculture, 19
Criminal Code, 82; Section 98, xxiv,
271n1, 272n1
Crown corporations, 212, 279n35
Crown Corporations Act, 211
Crown lands, in Saskatchewan, 80

D
Debt Adjustment Act, 123
debt adjustment plan, 40–43, 52, 55,
76, 79–80, 105–7, 147, 155, 211,
250–51, 303
debt protection laws, 148, 286n42
democracy, 172, 175–77, 193, 195, 203,
239, 247, 254, 259; as direct, 29,
33; and district council system of
decision-making, 54; and socialism,
29, 74, 142, 171, 173, 179, 197, 254,
278n19, 311
Department of National Defence
(Canada), 129
Department of Natural Resources Act,
211
Depression, 61, 89, 172; and
Communist Party organizing, 124;
debt protection for farmers, 148,
155, 211–12; political responses to,
103, 107, 146, 152–54, 157, 173,
181, 232, 252; post–World War I,
32, 34, 40, 112, 250; remedies
for, 133, 137, 303; as result of
capitalism, 122; as worsening, xxiii,
85, 94, 101, 106, 120, 151, 158. *See
also* debt adjustment plan
Diefenbaker, John, 67, 230–31
direct relief, during Depression, 104

Dominion Labour Party, 34
Dominion Loan and Mortgage
Association, 211
Douglas, Major C. H., 145–47, 149,
243, 286n43
Douglas, Thomas Clement (T. C.)
(Tommy), 114, 123, 190, 210, 212,
217, 255; as CCF candidate, 136–37,
143, 204, 207, 224, 231; as CCF
organizer/campaign manager, 156,
185; censure against, 225, 310; and
G. H. Williams, 119, 121, 159, 184,
188–89, 196, 208, 238; in historical
accounts, 218–26, 228–30, 232–34,
236–37, 241, 243–44; as president
of CCF, 197–98, 209, 235–36,
240, 293n1; as Saskatchewan CCF
premier, 162, 284n26; and Social
Credit, 133, 227, 242
draft dodging/resisting, 10–11, 170.
See also conscientious objection;
war resistance
*Dream No Little Dreams: A Biography
of the Douglas Government of
Saskatchewan, 1944–1962*, 241,
294n34
drought, 29, 104, 146, 151, 158

E
Eager, Evelyn, 241
economic development: through
public ownership, 211–12
education system: modernization of,
63, 68, 101, 108, 141, 205, 211, 232,
286n42
Edwards, George, 46, 53, 55–57,
59–60, 304
The Encyclopedia of Saskatchewan,
242–43, 295, 301
Evans, John, 98, 281n7

F
family farms, 108; as cornerstone in
socialist Canada, 88–89, 96, 102,

253; foreclosures on, 42, 70, 76, 79, 88, 101, 104–5, 123, 125, 155, 205, 249–50, 253, 278n21, 286n42; as lacking urban amenities, 205; and mechanization, 69, 88, 250, 301; and mortgage debt, 70, 249–50. *See also* farm/farmers' movement

Farmer-Labour Party (FLP), xxv, 109, 116–17, 128, 208, 255; in 1934 Saskatchewan election, 111–14, 135, 139, 219–20, 231, 235, 240, 253; conventions of, xxi, 113, 115; founding convention of, 96–99, 102; and Liberal Party, 106, 108; as political expression of organized farmers, 112; as separated from UFC(SS), 119; socialist platform of, 96–98, 101, 108, 246, 307

Farmers' Educational League (FEL), 56–57, 70–71, 73–74, 278n21, 304; manifesto of, 51–52, 55, 303

farmers/organized farmers, 36, 46, 52, 101; alienation of, 81; and capitalism, 18, 21–22, 24, 26; as facing bankruptcy, 70, 76, 84, 88–89, 104; as heavily in debt, 15, 20, 37, 39–41, 52, 69, 104, 123, 155; as moving towards socialism, 217, 243, 246, 271n1, 272n4; in political action, 25, 32, 34–35, 84, 237, 240, 243, 245–46, 249, 300; and populism, 20; position on war/war boom, 7–8, 29–31; and wheat marketing, 42. *See also* debt adjustment plan; farm/farmers' movement; wheat marketing

The Farmers' Platform of 1910, 25

Farmers' Political Association (FPA), 45–46, 71, 81, 249

farmers' political party, 25, 37, 45, 65, 72, 86, 114, 187, 207

Farmers' Union of Canada (FUC), 15, 39, 41, 66, 71, 74, 273n4, 279n35,

302; as activist farmer organization, 38; conventions of, 38, 42, 44; Debt Adjustment Committee, 40; G. H. Williams's involvement in, 16, 18, 37, 40, 43–46, 51, 53, 55, 57, 64, 76, 81, 113, 248–49; and merger with SGGA, 46; policies of, 45, 123; as secretive organization, 303; wheat pool campaign of, 43, 54, 250–51, 302

Farmers' Unity League (FUL), 73–77, 95, 102, 124–25, 142, 278n21, 306

farm/farmers' movement, 15, 57, 62, 89, 141, 188, 213, 242–43, 249, 251; and capitalism, 18; and political action, 31–32, 36, 44, 46, 53, 56, 70–73, 81–82, 84, 97; "Second Siege on Ottawa" (1913), 28; "Siege on Ottawa" (1910), 25; socialist left wing of, 33, 38, 64, 66, 237. *See also* family farms; farmers/organized farmers

farm land policy, use lease, 88–89, 96, 99, 102, 119, 140–41, 219, 253, 307

Farm Loan Board, 105

farm machinery, 40; tariffs on, 26, 36. *See also* tariffs, protective

Farm Security Act, 211

fascism, 142, 144, 171–73, 180, 184, 194, 203, 213, 218, 247, 254, 311

Financial Post, 148

Fines, Clarence M., 217, 279n35, 293n1

First Nations reserve lands: as distributed to veterans, 15

Flavelle, J. A., 26

Flowerdew, Lieutenant Gordon, 13

foreclosures, on farms. *See* family farms, foreclosures on

Forsey, Eugene, 100, 282n10

free trade, 19, 24, 29, 31, 33, 35, 63, 246, 300; expansion of, 27; with Great Britain, 77; with United States, 25–26

freight rates, 36, 66, 79; as excessive,
20, 23
Friesen, Gerald, 242, 294n36
The Furrow, 74, 102

G
Gardiner, Premier Jimmy, 68, 115, 121,
131, 150, 153, 305
Gerth, Hans, 248, 294n2
Ginger Group, 93, 99, 277n19, 280n3,
284n22
Goodwin, Albert (Ginger), 10, 298
Gordon, J. King, 173, 282n11
grain elevators, public ownership of, 26
Grain Growers' Grain Company, 24
Grain Growers' Guide, 31–32
Grain Marketing Act, 62
grain trade: as private, 24, 26, 36, 43–
44, 56, 251, 304; regulation of, 23
Great Depression. *See* Depression
Grey, Governor General Earl, 27

H
Hantelman, Louis, 113
health services, socialization of, xxiii,
63, 97, 101, 107–8, 141, 205
Herman, John, 156
Herridge, W. D., 181–84, 186, 191,
289n19
Historical Statistics of Canada, 295, 301
Hitler, Adolf, 82, 142, 171–72, 175–77,
185, 193–94, 204, 311
Hobsbawm, Eric, 247, 294n1, 312
homesteading, 15, 20, 79
Hudson's Bay Company, 19, 299

I
immigration, 7, 62–63, 66–68
Independent Labour Party (ILP), 92–
93, 96, 140, 158, 235, 237, 277n19,
293n1, 306; in 1935 Alberta
election, 135; economic policy of,
99; as labour political party, 91, 98,
114, 208, 247

industrialization, 20, 25; brought on
by World War I, 7. *See also* tariffs,
protective
industrial unionism, 7, 274n1
Industrial Workers of the World
(IWW), 32, 95
International Council of Peasants, 42
International Institute of Agriculture,
84
isolationism, 174, 195

J
jingoism, 5, 297
Johnson, A. W., 241–42, 294n34
Johnson, Barney, xxv
Johnston, Tom, 81, 212

K
Kempler, Herman, 113
Khaki University, 13, 248
King, Carlyle, 188, 190, 193, 291n33
Ku Klux Klan, 66–69, 83, 277n17, 305

L
Labour and Urban Security, 205
Labour Progressive Party (LPP),
157–58, 290n20
land colonization companies, 20
The Land of the Soviets, 86, 165, 306
land seizures. *See* family farms,
foreclosures on
Laurier, Prime Minister Wilfrid, 8–9,
25–28, 36, 298
League for Social Reconstruction
(LSR), 93, 99–100, 281n4, 282n10–
282n11
League of Nations, 84, 170–72
Liberal Party of Canada, xxiv, 6,
8–9, 53, 83, 114–16, 121, 125,
138, 150, 186; in 1934 federal
election, 101–2, 106–9, 112,
152–53; and capitalists, 22, 122,
140; and conscription, 177, 179–
80, 297; corruption of, 66; and

farmers/sGGA, 28, 35–38, 53, 65; and free trade, 25; as running against CCF, 154, 156–58, 185, 219, 229, 232, 236
Liberal-Progressive Party, 36
Lipset, Seymour Martin, 240–41, 292n4
liquor prohibition, 29, 33
Lord Strathcona's Horse, 4, 12
Lucas, Louise, 98, 113, 281n7

M
Macauley, Andrew J., 83, 98, 113, 123, 132, 143–45, 156, 161, 282n7
Mackenzie King, Prime Minister William Lyon, 36, 121, 150–51, 177, 179, 211, 272n1
MacLean, Dr. Hugh, 224–25
Macphail, Agnes, 111, 283n22
Manitoba Agricultural College, 14
Manitoba Grain Growers' Association (MGGA), 300
Manitoba Labour Party, 275n1
Manning, Premier Ernest, 144–45, 150, 288n10
marketing, of agricultural products, 38; as farmer-controlled, cooperative, 23–24, 42, 44, 141; through pools, 252; through provincial boards, 212; as voluntary, 42; in the world, 61–62. *See also* pools/pooling; wheat marketing
Marxism, 39, 96, 99
May Day parades, 128–29
McLeod, Ian, 230, 233, 293n3
McLeod, Thomas, 230, 233, 293n3
McNamee, L. P., 40, 51, 71
The Mercury (Estevan), 86
Military Service Act, 11
Military Voters Act, 9
Mills, C. Wright, 248, 294n2, 306
monopolies, 33, 141, 153, 181
Montreal *Star*, 10

mothers' allowances, 108
Mussolini, Benito, 171–72

N
National Fascist Party, 171
National Policy, 18–20, 24–25, 27, 300
National Reform Party, 180–82
National Unemployment Association, 78
natural resources, 135, 183, 212; public ownership of, 33, 79–80, 101, 206, 252, 273n5, 279n35, 293n1
New Democracy Party, 180–82, 186, 289n19, 290n19
New Democratic Party (NDP), 218, 284n26
New National Policy, 32, 34
New National Policy Association, 37
New National Policy platform, 301
New Saskatchewan Farmers' Party, 72
Nicholson, Alexander M., 190, 291n42
Nielsen, Dorise, 181–82, 186, 290n20
Non-Permanent Active Militia (NPAM), 192
North West Grain Dealers' Association, 23

O
old-age pensions, 29, 36, 205
Old Age Pensions Act, 37
One Big Union (OBU), 15, 32, 39, 274n1, 275n1, 302
Ontario Co-operative Commonwealth Federation (CCF), 309
On to Ottawa Trek, 128–31

P
pacifism, 7, 10, 170, 173–75, 179, 184–85, 188, 194–95
partyism, 7, 29, 31, 35, 65–66, 79
patriotism, 5, 67, 185, 297
patronage, 7–8, 22, 29, 66, 106, 108, 121, 207, 277n16, 305
Patterson, Premier William, 121, 150–51, 153, 204

Pelman Institute of London/
Pelmanism, 13
Perley, Ernie, 230
Phelps, Joseph Lee (Joe), 82, 212,
279n35
Plekhanov, Georgi, 248
pools/pooling, 85, 106, 212, 252. *See
also* marketing, of agricultural
products; wheat pools
populism. *See* agrarian populism
prairie farm organizations, 22–23, 25,
31, 35–36, 41, 52, 93, 99, 119. *See
also* farmers/organized farmers
price controls: on industrial inputs to
farm production, 31
price-fixing, of agricultural products,
23–24
Priestly, Norman, 100
Progressive Party, 121, 184; in 1921
federal election, 17, 33–34, 38,
53, 70; collapse of, 36–37, 302;
encounters with G. H. Williams, 94,
96, 187, 242; and farmers, 35, 45,
56, 71–72, 247; and Ku Klux Klan,
67–68; as opposing wheat pool, 57,
61; populism of, 273n4; reformism
of, 246, 249, 252
Progressive Party of Manitoba, 103
Progressive Party of Saskatchewan, 36,
44, 52–53, 64–65, 72, 287n49
property seizures. *See* family farms,
foreclosures on
proportional representation, 29, 33
prosperity certificates, 146, 149
public ownership program: under CCF,
279n35
public works projects, 104, 124–25

R
radicalism, 7, 42, 75, 102, 121, 129
railways, 18, 22, 28, 95
Referendum Act, 62
Regina Board of Education, 119
Regina *Leader-Post,* 111, 174

Regina Manifesto, 100, 170
relief, during Depression, xxiii, 105–6,
108, 124–25, 128, 141, 151
Relief Camp Workers' Union, 129
resistance, to war. *See* war resistance
Royal Canadian Mounted Police
(RCMP), 128–30
rural depopulation, 24–25, 28, 33, 246
rural electrification, 205, 207, 212,
279n35

S
Sapiro, Aaron, 42–43, 250
Saskatchewan, class politics in, 271n1
Saskatchewan: A History, 242, 294n34
Saskatchewan Association of Rural
Municipalities, 62
Saskatchewan Commonwealth, 141, 195
Saskatchewan Co-operative
Commonwealth Federation. *See*
Co-operative Commonwealth
Federation (Saskatchewan Section)
(CCF[SS])
Saskatchewan Department of
Agriculture, 212
Saskatchewan Farmers' Political
Association (SFPA), 64, 72–73
Saskatchewan Farmers' Union, 279n35
Saskatchewan Government Insurance,
217
*Saskatchewan Government: Politics and
Pragmatism,* 241
Saskatchewan Grain Growers'
Association (SGGA), 47, 53, 55,
57, 65–66, 251, 273n4, 279n35,
287n49, 303–4; amalgamation
with UFC(SS), 58, 62–63; and
cooperative marketing, 42–43,
46; and debt adjustment plan, 40;
decline of, 302; and farmer political
action, 38; and G. H. Williams, 187,
248, 250; membership in, 36–37,
300; as moderate/conservative
organization, 15, 39, 51–52, 71

Saskatchewan Home Protective
Association, 123
Saskatchewan Liberal Party, 68, 121,
135, 137, 143, 150–51, 204, 303, 305
Saskatchewan New Democratic Party
(NDP), 217
Saskatchewan Power Commission, 212
Saskatchewan Relief Commission, 104
Saskatchewan Wheat Pool, 161, 227,
251, 304
Saskatoon *Star-Phoenix*, 59, 111, 190,
304, 310
secession, as part of Wilkie Charter,
77, 81–82
separate schools, for Catholics, 66–68,
82
Shackleton, Doris, 233, 238, 293n3
"sieges" on Ottawa, 25, 28
Sifton, Clifford, 39
Social Credit invasion. *See* Alberta
Social Credit Party
*Social Credit Manual: Social Credit as
Applied to the Province of Alberta;
Puzzling Questions and Their
Answers,* 134, 287n47, 310
social credit movement, 133, 144,
285n42, 288n10, 309; and
dividends, 145–46, 149, 152;
Douglas's system of, 39, 132;
monetary reform of, 181, 289n19;
principles of, 132–36, 140, 145, 147
Social Credit Party of Canada, 290n19
Social Credit Party of Saskatchewan
(formerly Social Credit League),
134, 143, 150–55, 157; and 1935
federal election, 135, 138–39,
219, 222; and 1938 Saskatchewan
election, 158, 181, 184, 232, 237;
CCF challenge to, 140, 143–45, 154,
156, 180, 186, 227–28, 231, 254,
310; and cooperation with other
parties, 136–37, 142–43, 225, 230;
Douglas's endorsement of, 222–27,
234–35, 240, 242

Social Democracy in Canada, 122,
273n5, 285n32, 308
socialism, 13, 102, 121, 140, 202,
248, 255, 274n1; and agrarian
populism, 18, 64, 101, 113, 213,
249; and Catholic beliefs, 82–83;
and CCF, 128, 183, 185, 204, 208,
246; and democracy, 74, 142,
173, 175, 254, 278n19, 311; and
farmers, 21, 52, 74, 240, 243,
253, 271n1; FLP platform of,
108, 114, 120, 246; as opposed to
capitalism, 80, 122–23, 135, 141,
154; as opposed to communism,
xxiv, 97, 140; in Soviet Union,
85, 87–88; through cooperative
commonwealth, 88, 92, 95–96,
100, 144; and trade unions, 7
Socialist Party of British Columbia, 99
social justice, 22–23, 88, 122, 259
social welfare, 211–12
soldiers, returning: as integrated, 202
Soldier Settlement Act, 15
Soldier Settlement Board, 14
Southeast Asia Co-Prosperity Sphere,
171
Soviet Union, 175–76, 255;
agricultural policies in, 85, 88;
socialism in, 85, 87–88; G. H.
Williams's tour of, 84–88, 91, 93,
98, 165, 306, 309
starvation, of unemployed, xxiv, 84,
283n16, 308
Statute of Westminster (1931), 169
Steininger, Friedrich, 243, 259
Stewart, Walter, 219, 221, 233, 235,
293n3, 293n5
stock market crash (1929), 69, 252
Stoneman, John, 46, 55
Stork, Clarence, 113
strikes, 7, 10, 32, 35, 95, 124, 128–29,
246, 274n1
syndicalism, 7, 39, 274n1

T

tariffs, protective, 18, 24, 26–27, 29, 32–33, 36, 66, 85, 246, 300; abolition of, 35, 63

taxation reform, 29, 33

telegraph systems, public ownership of, 33

Thrasher, W. M., 59

Tommy Douglas, 233, 293n3

Tommy Douglas: The Road to Jerusalem, 230, 233

Trades and Labour Congress (TLC), 7, 10, 78, 274n1

Trade Union Act, 211

trade unions, 33, 141, 171–73, 277n19; and CCF, 245, 247; class radicalism of, 7; and CP influence, 142; and draft resistance, 8, 10; and free trade, 27; as militant, 18, 95, 99, 124, 128, 272n1, 297; recognition of, 17, 25, 35, 205, 273n1

transportation systems: public ownership of, 33, 252, 273n5

Treaty of Versailles, 172, 175

Trudeau, Pierre Elliott, 282n10

U

under-grading practices: of private grain elevators, 23

Underhill, Frank, 100, 282n10

under-weighting: by private grain elevators, 23

unemployment, xxiv, 8, 29, 34, 105, 108, 124, 128–29, 134, 140, 155, 206

United Empire Loyalist Association, 4, 254

United Farmers of Alberta (UFA), 34–37, 41–42, 53, 81, 103, 132–34, 147, 250, 273n4, 300

United Farmers of Canada (Saskatchewan Section) (UFC[SS]), xxv, 86, 93, 102, 156, 165, 235, 240, 249, 273n4, 278n21, 279n35,

304; agricultural policy of, 123; and CCF, 135, 139–40, 158, 187, 227; and compulsory pools, 106; conventions of, xxii, 52–57, 61, 70–72, 78–84, 91–94, 96, 251–52; and debt adjustment, 105; educational program of, 56; and farmers, 62, 76, 95, 103, 112, 115, 119, 155, 253; and FEL, 51, 66; formation of, 251, 302; fusion with ILP, 92; and Ku Klux Klan, 67; members in, 75–76; and political action, 72–73, 81, 83, 92; socialist platform of, 53, 61, 63–65, 68, 70–71, 74–77, 79, 81–83, 98–99, 242, 252, 303

United Farmers of Manitoba (UFM) (formerly Manitoba Grain Growers' Association), 34, 36, 272n4, 300, 302

United Farmers of Ontario (UFO) (formerly Ontario Grange), 25, 34–37, 272n4, 283n22, 300

United Farmers' Political Association (UFPA), 84, 92

United Farm Women of Ontario, 283n22

United Progressive Association, 180–81

United States, free trade with, 25–26

Unity movement, 182–83, 231; candidates, 143, 156–57, 181, 186, 231

Urquhart, M. C., 295, 301

utilities, public ownership of, 101, 252, 273n5

W

Wall Street crash, 69, 252

war boom, 31, 69, 301; and agriculture, 40

War Measures Act, 6, 10, 36

war profiteering, 7–8, 30–31, 177, 180

war resistance, 6, 8, 10, 170, 297

Wartime Elections Act, 9

Weekly Sun, 27

Western Canada Labour Conference (Calgary), 274n1

Western Producer, 45, 64, 76, 84, 87, 92, 111

Weyburn CCF-Social Credit Association, 224

wheat, as monoculture, 69

wheat economy, 31, 34, 69, 302; boom-and-bust cycle of, 18, 29–30, 61, 298–99, 301

wheat marketing, 85, 250–51, 302. *See also* marketing, of agricultural products; wheat pools

wheat pools, 139, 158; campaign for, 43, 46, 52, 55, 60–61, 71, 251, 292n50, 302–4; as compulsory, 44, 54–57, 59–62, 70–71, 94, 97, 106, 120, 250–51, 304

wheat prices, 29–32, 34, 37, 40, 46, 56, 61–62, 85, 283n16, 305; as collapsing, 69–70, 104, 250

Wiens, Muriel (nee Williams), xxiv, xxv, 14, 259, 273n6, 295–97, 302–3, 307–8, 310–12

Wilkie Charter, 77, 81, 279n31

Williams, Betty, xxiv

Williams, George Hara: charisma of, xxi; confrontations of, xxii, 96, 116–17, 180, 195; contribution to Canadian history, 246, 249–50, 256; early life of, 3–4, 14, 297; as farmer, xxiii, 4, 15–16, 37, 161, 238, 248; as grassroots organizer, 40, 97, 113, 194, 243, 249, 271n1, 278n21; in historical accounts, 218–35, 237–38, 240–41, 243–44; illness/death of, xxv, 4, 13, 199–200, 210, 213, 255, 312; as Jeffersonian democrat, 88; as Minister of Agriculture, 208–10; as orator/debater, 201, 235, 238, 249, 308–9; public speeches of, xxi, xxiv, 58, 71, 89, 96, 99, 121, 163; socialist convictions of, 123;

as soldier/veteran, 5–6, 11–14, 195–99, 209, 234, 248, 254, 297; as unrecognized, 217, 219

Williams, George Hara, as CCF(SS) leader, 123, 139, 196, 217, 234, 245; during 1938 Saskatchewan election, 140–41, 145, 151–52, 154, 156–59, 181, 189; cooperation with other parties, 142–44, 180; as defeating Social Credit invasion, 144–45, 151–52, 154, 156–59, 180, 184, 227–28, 230–32, 237, 253–54; as losing the leadership, 193–94, 196–99, 218; and New Democracy movement, 182–84, 186, 191; position on war, 170–71, 173–75, 177–79, 185–87, 190–92; reorganization plan of, 140–41

Williams, George Hara, as UFC(SS) leader, xxi, 94, 115, 155, 160, 220, 237; and confrontations/criticism, 59–60, 73–74, 116, 124, 219, 239, 247; democratic vision of, 54; move to political action, 71–72, 74–75, 76, 79, 242, 252, 303; move towards socialism, 113–14, 208, 246, 278n21; as vice-president, 55–56, 58

Williams, Harry, 5

Williams, Margery (nee Cass), xxii, xxiv, xxv, 4, 16, 161, 209–10, 296

Williams, Rosemary, xxiv

Williams, Ruth, xxii, xxiv, 296

Williams, Samuel, 4–5, 12, 14, 298

Williams, Shirley-Anne, xxiv

Winch, Ernest, 99, 124–25

Winnipeg General Strike, 18, 32, 271n1, 274n1, 275n1, 277n19, 284n26

Winnipeg Grain Exchange, 30, 36, 205

women's equality, 29, 33

Woodsworth, James Shaver, 70, 92, 95, 156, 189, 223; and cooperation with other parties, 126, 136–37, 142,

222, 225, 227, 309; as democratic socialist, 96, 277, 278n19; as leader of CCF, 93, 99, 111, 186, 188, 242, 254; as pacifist, 170, 173–75, 177, 179, 185, 190, 194, 277, 291n33
Workers' Unity League (WUL), 74, 124, 142
World War I, 4, 16, 95, 169–70, 172, 175–76, 179, 194, 247; Canadian casualties in, 5, 8, 272n3, 297; economic boom brought by, 30; impact on G. H. Williams, 298; as major event for Canada, 297; postwar depression, 34, 37, 302; support for/resistance to, xxv, 5–7, 297
World War II, 87, 170, 172, 177, 247, 311

Y
Yorkton strike, 125, 127